Horodetz:
History of a Town, 1142 - 1942
(Haradzets, Belarus)

Translation of
Horodets; a geshikhte fun a shtetl, 1142 - 1942
Original Book Edited by: A. Ben-Ezra

Originally published in New York, U.S.A. 1949

A Publication of JewishGen
Edmond J. Safra Plaza, 36 Battery Place, New York, NY 10280
646.494.2972 | info@JewishGen.org | www.jewishgen.org

©JewishGen 2025. All Rights Reserved.
JewishGen is the Genealogical Research Division of the
Museum of Jewish Heritage – A Living Memorial to the Holocaust

Horodetz: History of a Town, 1142 – 1942 (Haradzets, Belarus)
Translation of *Horodets; a geshikhte fun a shtetl, 1142 - 1942*

Copyright © 2025 by JewishGen. All rights reserved.
First Printing: June 2025, Sivan, 5785
Original Yizkor Book Edited By: A. Ben-Ezra
Project Coordinator: Hannah Kadmon
Project Coordinator Emeritus: Gene Sucov
Cover Design: Irv Osterer
Layout, formatting and indexing: Jonathan Wind
Name consolidation: Chaya Friedman

This book may not be reproduced, in whole or in part, including illustrations in any form (beyond that copying permitted by Sections 107 and 108 of the U.S. Copyright Law and except by reviewers for public press), without written permission from the publisher.

JewishGen Press is not responsible for inaccuracies or omissions in the original work and makes no representations regarding the accuracy of this translation. Digital images of the original book's contents can be seen online at the New York Public Library website or the Yiddish Book Center website.

Library of Congress Control Number (LCCN): 2025935606

ISBN: 978-1-962054-27-0 (hard cover: 350 pages, alk. paper)

About JewishGen.org

JewishGen, is a Genealogical Research Division of the Museum of Jewish Heritage - A Living Memorial to the Holocaust, serves as the global home for Jewish genealogy.

Featuring unparalleled access to 30+ million records, it offers unique search tools, along with opportunities for researchers to connect with others who share similar interests. Award winning resources such as the Family Finder, Discussion Groups, and ViewMate, are relied upon by thousands each day.

In addition, JewishGen's extensive informational, educational and historical offerings, such as the Jewish Communities Database, Yizkor Book translations, InfoFiles, Family Tree of the Jewish People, and KehilaLinks, provide critical insights, first-hand accounts, and context about Jewish communal and familial life throughout the world.

Offered as a free resource, JewishGen.org has facilitated thousands of family connections and success stories, and is currently engaged in an intensive expansion effort that will bring many more records, tools, and resources to its collections.

Please visit https://www.jewishgen.org/ to learn more.

Vice President for JewishGen: Avraham Groll

About the JewishGen Yizkor Book Project

Yizkor Books (Memorial Books) were traditionally written to memorialize the names of departed family and martyrs during holiday services in the synagogue (a practice that still exists in many synagogues today).

Over the centuries, as a result of countless persecutions and horrific atrocities committed against the Jews, Yizkor Books (Sefer Zikaron in Hebrew) were expanded to include more historical information, such as biographical sketches of famous personalities and descriptions of daily town life.

Following the Holocaust, the idea of remembrance and learning took on an urgent and crucial importance. Survivors of the Holocaust sought out other surviving residents of their former towns to memorialize and document the names and way of life of those who were ruthlessly murdered by the Nazis. These remembrances were documented in Yizkor Books, hundreds of which were published in the first decades after the Holocaust.

Most of these books were published privately, or through *Landsmanshaftn* (social organizations comprised of members originating from the same European town or region) that still existed, and were often distributed free of charge. The languages used to document these crucial histories and links to our past were mostly Yiddish and Hebrew. JewishGen has undertaken the sacred responsibility of translating these books into English so that the culture and way of life of these communities will be preserved and transmitted to future generations.

In 1986, a group of farsighted JewishGenners started a project to pool their efforts together in groups based upon their ancestors' towns and donate funds to translate the Yizkor books of their ancestral towns into English. As the translated material became available, it was made accessible for free at https://www.JewishGen.org/Yizkor . Hardcover copies can be purchased by visiting https://www.jewishgen.org/Yizkor/ybip.html (see section below).

It is our hope that the translation of these books into English (and other languages) will assist the countless Jewish family researchers who are so desperately seeking to forge a connection with their heritage.

Director of JewishGen Yizkor Book Project: Lance Ackerfeld

About JewishGen Press

JewishGen Press (formerly the Yizkor Books-in-Print Project) is the publishing division of JewishGen.org, and provides a venue for the publication of non-fiction books pertaining to Jewish genealogy, history, culture, and heritage.

In addition to the Yizkor Book category, publications in the Other Non-Fiction category include Shoah memoirs and research, genealogical research, collections of genealogical and historical materials, biographies, diaries and letters, studies of Jewish experience and cultural life in the past, academic theses, and other books of interest to the Jewish community.

Please visit https://www.jewishgen.org/Yizkor/ybip.html to learn more.

Director of JewishGen Press: Joel Alpert
Managing Editor – Peter Harris
Publications Manager - Susan Rosin

Notes to the Reader

The images in the original book were reproduced from photographs from the time of the first edition. These reproductions were already of poor quality, most being pre-war and others at least 60 or more years old. As a result, the images in the book are the best achievable.
A reader can view the original scans of the book on the websites listed below.

The original book can be seen online at the Yiddish Book Center website:

https://www.yiddishbookcenter.org/collections/yizkor-books/yzk-nybc313676/ben-ezra-akiva-zusman-horodets-a-geshikhte-fun-a-shtetl-1142-1942

OR

at the New York Public Library Digital Collections website:

https://digitalcollections.nypl.org/items/5e53f030-0969-0133-0481-58d385a7bbd0#/?uuid=6c781ac0-7518-0133-410c-00505686a51c

To obtain a list of Shoah victims from **Horodetz (Haradzets, Belarus),** the reader should access the Yad Vashem web site listed below; one can also search for specific family names using family name option. These lists are continually updated by Yad Vashem, so it is worthwhile to periodically search them.

There is more valuable information (including the Pages of Testimony, etc.) available on this website: https://yvng.yadvashem.org/

A list of all books available from JewishGen Press along with prices is available at:
https://www.jewishgen.org/Yizkor/ybip.html

Cover Photo Credits

Cover Design: Irv Osterer

Front Cover:

Cover based on line drawing used for the original Yahrzeit book by Irving Sussman (Israel Zussman)

Back Cover:

Text:
Excerpt from "The Shtetl" by Rabbi Dr. Jacob Bosniak; Translated from the Yiddish by Eugene Sucov, July 2000

Top:

Left:
The Cold Synagogue
(Drawn by Israel Zussman, based on guidelines of the old Jews of Horodets) [page 37]

Middle:
R' Israel, the "Stoliner Rabbi"
Under the photo: a facsimile of his signature [Page 47]

Right:
Rabbi Yehoshua Yaakov z"l [Rabinovitz]
(Painted especially for the book of Horodets by Israel Zussman) [Page 29]

Bottom:

Left:
Aharon Itche Leyzer's house (about 200 years old) [since 1949 another 60 years have passed...] (Drawn by Israel Zussman) [Page 9]

Right:
Facsimile of the Rashi section from a sermon by R' Khayim [page 34]

Geopolitical Information

Map of Belalrus showing the location of **Haradzets**

Haradzets

Haradzets, Belarus is located 52°12' N 24°40' E 168 miles SW of Minsk

	Town	District	Province	Country
Before WWI (c. 1900):	Gorodets	Kobrin	Grodno	Russian Empire
Between the wars (c. 1930):	Horodec	Kobryń	Polesie	Poland
After WWII (c. 1950):	Gorodets			Soviet Union
Today (c. 2000):	Haradzets			Belarus

Alternate Names for the Town:

Haradzets [Bel], Gorodets [Rus], Horodec [Pol], Horodets [Yid], Haradziec, Haradzec, Horodetz, Gorodec, Gorodets (Polesie)

Nearby Jewish Communities:

Antopol 5 miles E
Kobryn 13 miles W
Divin 17 miles SSW
Malech 20 miles N
Simonovichi 20 miles ENE
Drahichyn 21 miles E
Linovo 21 miles NNW
Charniany 25 miles SW
Pyershamayskaya 25 miles NNE
Kortelesy, Ukraine 25 miles SSW
Pruzhany 26 miles NNW
Khomsk 26 miles ENE
Byaroza 27 miles NNE
Zhabinka 28 miles W
Syalyets 28 miles NNE
Shchedrohir, Ukraine 28 miles S
Yakovleva 28 miles E

Jewish Poulation: 648 (in 1897), 269 (in 1921)

Horodetz: History of a Town, 1142-1942

Table of Contents

Title	Author	Page
Introduction		3
First Section		

General History

Foreword		6
Map of Horodetz and Surroundings	Israel Zussman	8
Horodetz, an historical overview	A. Ben-Ezra	9
"Once There Was . . . ." (poem)	Israel Zussman	17
The Shtetl	Rabbi Dr. Jacob Bozniak	21
The Social-Economic Structure	A. S.	26

The Rabbis

The Rabbinic Context	Rabbi Mordechai Greenberg	34
The Rabbi Moshe Tzvi	Rabbi Mordechai Greenberg	36
Rabbi Yehoshua Yaakov	Rabbi Mordechai Greenberg	37
The Death of the "Old Rabbi"	Alter Ellman	39
The Old Rabbi (a picture)	Israel Zussman	41
The Wisdom Of The "Old Rabbi"	A. K.	41
The Rabbi Yaakov Khayim, z"l	Rabbi Mordechai Greenberg	45
The Last Rabbi	Rabbi Shalom Podolevsky	50

Synagogues

The Cold Shul (memories)	Rabbi Dr. Jacob Bozniak	53
Comments About the Old Shul	A. Ben-Ezra	58
The Besmedresh	M. Rubinstein	60
The Daveners in the Besmedresh	Rabbi Dr. Yaakov Bosnyak	62
The Besmedresh and its Visitors	M.G.K.	63
The Stoliner Shtiebl	Israel Zussman	67
The Kobriner Shtiebl	Shlomo Podolevsky	74

Institutions

The "Khevre Kadi'she"	A. S. Horodetser	79
The Small Societies	A. Alman	82
Hakhnoses-O'rkhim	I. Yitskhaki	83

The Village Autonomy

a. The "Oprave"	Shlomo Libers	87
b. The "Korovke"	Shlomo Libers	89

Holidays (Memories)

Rosh Hashana	Tzivia Greenglass	92
Yom Kippur	Tzivia Greenglass	93
Sukkot	Tzivia Greenglass	94
Hanukkah	Tzivia Greenglass	95
Fifteen of Shvat (poem)	Tzivia Greenglass	97
Purim	Tzivia Greenglass	97
Passover	David Kaplan	99
Lag B'Omer	Shlomo Gar'in	100
Shavuot	Tzivia Greenglass	102

Episodes

a. The Dispute	A. Kostrometski	105
b. The Ta'are Bret	A. Kostrometski	107
c. A Blut-Bilbl	A. Kostrometski	109

Good Jews

Horodetser Rabbis	K. Rushevsky	112
Pinkhas Mikhael, z"l	A. Ben-Ezra	113
R' Mordkhi'le	M. Mishkin	116
The Kholozshiner	Gedalyahu Kaplan	121

Cultural Awakening

The Revolution	A. S.	125

Zionism

The First Step	A. Tzioni	131

A Political Criminal	Naftali Goldberg	134
The National Revival	Shmuel Hoizman	137

Personalities and Characters

Dr. Israel Mikhl Rabinowitz	A. Ben-Ezra	141
Motye Hillel's	A. M. Tzeitelson	146
Rabbi Isaac Aaron	Rabbi Mordechai Greenberg	148
R' Shalom Kostrinsky	Yaakov Kostrinsky	150
Motye Itsik's	A. Katrosy	153
Berl Rodetser	Itka Podolovsky	155
A Wedding in Horodets of Berl Rodetser's grandson (a picture)		157
Panya Shaf, (Itzikl)	I. Zis	158
A Community Leader	S. Ben Haviv	161
The Town's Joker	David Kaplan	163

Teachers and Students

Sender the Melamed	Ami	167
Shmuel the Cobbler	Ami	169
Chayim Itzik's	Ami	171
Yankel Kodliner	Ami	175
A Melamed-Merchant	Ami	178
R' Shimon Izik	Ami	181
R' Asher	Ami	184
Yudl the Melamed	Ami	187
R' Asher David	Ami	189
An Improved Kheyder	Ami	192
Herschel, the Teacher	Ami	194
Moshe son of Khaya-Dvorah	Ami	198
Kheyders for Girls	Ami	200

Doctors

Naphthali the Doctor	Rabbi Mordechai Greenberg	204
Vitkin	M. Timoner	206

Second Section

A Quarter Century (1914-1939)

In the First World War	B. S. Sussman	209

The Economic Situation	S. Podolevsky	213
The Transition Period	Benjamin M. Israel	215
The Pole	Yudl Greenberg	217
My Visit	Israel Zussman	219
The Pioneer Movement	Bella Feinshtein	224
Under the Polish Regime	Rabbi S. Podolevsky	228
Lament	A. Warsaw (Varsha)	236
My Little Town (poem)	Tzivia Greenglass	239

Third Section

Folklore

Folklore	Rabbi Akiva	242
Sayings – Manners of Speéch	Rabbi Akiva	243
The Yiddish Language	A. Ben-Ezra	245
Customs	A. Ben-Ezra	247
Nicknaming	A. Ben-Ezra	253
Folk Medicine	Dr. Y. Farber	254
Remedies and Medications	Yudel Kaplansky	258
Two Bobbes	A. Kostrinsky	259

Legends

On A Stick	M. Timoner	263
Motl, the Jew	Itchke	264
Ghosts	A. Elman	266

Folk Songs

Dark, Slippery, Late at Night	268
The Song of the Workman	269
From Asia to Europe	270
Children's Songs	272

Fourth Section

The End

The End, (a drawing)	Israel Zussman	273
The End		274
The Letter		275
Abraham Winograd		279
David Volinietz		280

Map (Horodetz in the Final Battle)		282
Yizkor (a drawing)	I. Sussman	283
Remarks		284
Our Martyrs (pictures)		284
Our Martyrs (names)		291
Yizkor (text and drawing)	I. Sussman	297

Fifth Section

Horodetzers in the World

Globus (a drawing)	Israel Zussman	298
In America	Bessi Greblovsky	299
"Society Yeshu'ot Ya'akov Support Union of the people of Horodetz"	Chayim Greblovsky	312
"Young Horodetz"	Benjamin Solomon Sussman	315
Horodetzer "Ladies Auxiliary"	Feigl Greenberg	317
Horodetser in Russia	A. Horodetser	318

In Eretz Israel

Former Years	A. Kastrinsky	322
Present Times	Joseph Montag	323
R' Khayim Mendl, z"l	A. Kast	325

Conclusion

Picture of the Horodetz Book Committee	329
Thanks to the Contributors	330

Name Index for the English Translation — 331

Horodetz:
History of a Town, 1142 - 1942
(Haradzets, Belarus)

52°12' / 24°40'

Translation of
Horodets; a geshikhte fun a shtetl, 1142 – 1942

Edited by: A. Ben-Ezra, 1949

Published in New York, N.Y., U.S.A. 1949

Acknowledgments

Project Coordinators:

Hannah Kadmon

Gene Sucov (emeritus)

This is a translation from: *Horodets; a geshikhte fun a shtetl, 1142-1942* (Horodetz; history of a town, 1142-1942),
Editors: A. Ben-Ezra, "Horodetz" Book Committee, 1949 (Y, 238 pages).

Note: The original book can be seen online at the NY Public Library site: Horodets (1949)

This material is made available by JewishGen, Inc. and the Yizkor Book Project for the purpose of fulfilling our mission of disseminating information about the Holocaust and destroyed Jewish communities. This material may not be copied, sold or bartered without JewishGen, Inc.'s permission. Rights may be reserved by the copyright holder.

JewishGen, Inc. makes no representations regarding the accuracy of the translation. The reader may wish to refer to the original material for verification.
JewishGen is not responsible for inaccuracies or omissions in the original work and cannot rewrite or edit the text to correct inaccuracies and/or omissions.
Our mission is to produce a translation of the original work and we cannot verify the accuracy of statements or alter facts cited.

Introduction

Page 1

A full page drawing containing, in white outline on black background, a weeping yizkor candle, the title of the yizkor book (in Yiddish) "HORODETZ", and the years of its existence as a Jewish community, 1142-1942.

Page 2

HORODETZ YIZKOR BOOK

Copyright by "Horodetz" Book Commiittee, 1949

Except for purposes of literary criticism, no portion of this book may be used or reproduced without permission of HBC, c/o A. Ben-Ezra, 2044 E. 13 St., Brooklyn 29, N.Y.

Printed in the United States of America by

WALDON PRESS, INC.

203 Wooster Street, New York 12, N.Y.

Page 3

H O R O D E T Z: A STORY OF A VILLAGE (1142-1942)

Literary Editor, A. Ben- Ezra

Art Editor, Irving Sussman

Produced by the Book Committee, "Horodetz".

New York, 1949

A Gift from YIVO, N.Y. to Yad Vashem Library

Page 4

A BRIEF THANK YOU

We express our appreciation and thanks to our typist and to the Literary Editor, Akiva Ben-Ezra, to Irving Sussman, the Art Editor, and to Julius Greenberg, the Finance Secretary, for their untiring and willing work in making real the memorial to our home village, Horodetz.

May they be blessed.

THE BOOK COMMITTEE OF "HORODETZ"

(Note at bottom of the page)

For technical reasons, the orthography of the book, "Horodetz", is not unified. Also we have not been able to display all the pictures of the important Horodetzers. Not all whom we asked to send pictures have identified themselves. The reader will pardon us.

The Editors

Page 5

[Page VII]

General History

Foreword

The idea to produce a book about Horodetz had been stirring in the minds of several Horodetz natives for a long time. The enthusiasm for the idea to advertise this small shtetl, in which our cradles had stood, and where we spent our childhood and a part of our youth, would not let them rest. And even while they were getting established in Horodetz they dreamed of such a book, especially when they saw the cultural value which such a book could have for Jewish history.

Horodetz was one of the oldest communities in Russia-Poland. It had survived all types of Jewish martyrology – and still existed!

This small shtetl, Horodetz, was well known as an important community. Thanks to its favorable geographical location she had preserved in herself the caring face of Jewish life. Horodetz had been careful to keep the traditional Jewish spirit in spite of the violent attacks on that spirit. It was saturated with Jewish learning and self-awareness.

All these themes together had awakened in a few Horodetzers the desire to create such a book. But not every idea finds its way into the receptive ears and hearts of those who can make real this idea.

With great regret we came too late, when the Jewish Horodetz no longer existed, when all was destroyed, burned and uprooted by brutal men who were in the world.

May this book, "Horodetz", serve as a literary memorial to the martyrs who were killed to sanctify the name of God (kiddush ha Shem) and who were not able to be buried in the land of Israel. May the articles which find themselves inside this book be the epic eulogy for those brave and heroic Jews in Horodetz who gave up their lives with honor as humans and Jews.

May this book, "Horodetz", be a memorial for those people who, for a period of 100 years spun the golden threads of Jewish identity. They have given us the courage and hope to rearrange our lives in strange lands.

May the names of our father and mothers, grandfathers and grandmothers be inscribed in our own land, the land for which they dreamed for many long years.

This book, "Horodetz", will be the bridge which binds our sweet memories to our present situation, a bridge on which we will stride to a new future for our people and our land, Eretz Israel.

[Page VIII]

To conclude, I want to remind you of a few historical facts about the book, "Horodetz".

In the summer of 1946, when our countryman, Moshe Vinograd, received a query from Buenos Aires, there was already established in the home of a second countryman, Benjamin Shlomo Sussman, a committee to produce such a book. In this committee were the following Horodetzers: Israel Sussman, chairman; Yudl Greenberg, treasurer, Shlomo Podolevsky, recording secretary; Michalah Timoner, corresponding secretary. And in the executive were the following: Moshe Vinograd, (representative in Argentina), David Kaplan and Benjamin Shlomo Sussman. A. Ben Ezra was elected general editor.

After this, the following countrymen were added: Tzvia Greenglass, I. Greblovsky, M. Rubinshtein, Rav Shalom Podolevsky, Dr. I.Farber, Naftali Goldberg (representative for the southern states) and Yeshayahu Kastrinski (representative for Israel).

At the end of Shabbat, September 7, 1946, during a reception for our guest from Argentina in the Horodetz shul, we gave thanks to the writers of the various sections. Israel Sussman collected a fair sum of money to start publishing the book.

I must give special thanks to the Horodetz association, "Yehsuot Yaakov", who lent a hand to this effort. Also the Ladies auxiliary of the Horodetz association did not stand aside.

A special thanks I must give to our countrymen for their information and especially to Mr. Alter Elman, Mr. Ezra Kastrinski, Mr. Asher Kastrinski, Rav Mordekhai Greenberg, and to Eva Skavolev and to all those whose who donated their spirit and their substance..

Also we must mention with thanks, our countryman, Israel Sussman, the painter, who was also the art editor for "Horodetz", and the book committee, who brought this book to its completion.

A special appreciation goes also to the rabbi from Kobrin, Rabbi Baruch (descendant of saints), and to the well known folk singer, Moshe Natanzon, for the notes to Rabbi Moshe Kobriner's melody to the prayer, "Ya Akhsof".. Rabbi Kobriner is the founder of the Kobriner dynasty..

And finally, finally, I thank my friend, the Hebrew-Yiddish writer, Shmuel Berenholtz, for his helpful comments.

May this effort be blessed.

10th of Av, Year 1 of the State of Israel, 5709 (August 15, 1948)

[Page 1]

Map of Horodetz and Surroundings

[Page 3]

Horodetz: An Historical Overview

by Akiva Ben-Ezra

Translated by Eugene Sucov

A. The Geographic Location

Horodetz, in the Grodno gubernia, along which goes the Polesia railway, lies between Brisk (Brest) and Pinsk. It is not known when this village was founded. However, in the year 1142 Horodetz was mentioned in land registries found in old archives. In 1286 Horodetz was mentioned as a village, Horodel or Horodla, which the Duke, Valdimir Vasilevitsh, owned, among other towns, and which he therefore transferred to his wife, Olga Romanov.[1] Later, Horodetz was mentioned under the name, Horodnitzi, among other villages which belonged to Queen Anna, the widow of Stefan Batori.[2]

From contemporary drawings we can see how Horodetz appeared in those years when the entire area from Pinsk to Kobrin was overgrown with a thick forest and settlements were very few. In 1559 a forest path was hacked out from Pinsk, cutting through Tarakan and Horodetz, to Kobrin and Pruzhana.[3] In those times Horodetz did not yet have a river. Where now is a beautiful meadow, there were swamps through which the river Mokhavetz cut its way from Pinsk to Kobrin. Horordetz was then like an oasis in a desert; a settlement surrounded by forests and swamps in which roamed various wild animals.

The details of life in ancient Horodetz are not known. According to Babrovski, the historian of the Grodno gubernia, Horodetz contained, at the end of the 16th century, 5 streets: Kobrin, Freishibadske, Pinsk, Groshevski and Ilinske. In addition, there was a business market since there were 222 dwelling places, 15 taverns, 11 of which were beer parlors, and 23 breweries. In older official documents Horodetz was described as a town and not as a village.

It is worth while to examine more deeply the legend, which old Horodetz Jews and also residents of the nearby village of Antipolya (7 km from Horodetz), used to relate, namely, that in former years Antipolya and Horodetz were one town.

Ask yourself:

    a. Is it likely that several hundred years ago there was in Poland or Lithuania such a large town that was 7 km long? All the great towns of that time, and even in more distant centuries, such as Pinsk, Brisk and Grodno, were formed with only several hundred souls.[4]
    b. How did they arrange to put the cemetery in the suburbs? The old Horodetz "magilka" (the Christian cemetery), which was already lacking crosses, was already in the suburbs, on the way to the train station. If Horodetz and Antipolya were one town, how likely would it have been to find the "magilka" on the way to Antipolya?
    c. Only forty years ago there flourished a dense pine forest between Horodetz and Antipolya. Ask yourself: When did this forest grow up if both were part of one town?
    d. According to old Antipolya grave stones and an old synagogue marker, Antipolya already existed over 300 years ago.[5]

No, we must conclude that these legends, which circulated from mouth to mouth, are merely a product of local patriotism and are not grounded in any kind of historical fact.

It is worthwhile to remark on a major error, by now already printed in the Yiddish-English encyclopedia. There it says, "The small village of Horodetz was at one time a part of Kobrin, but it was destroyed in 1653, when it was overrun by the Swedish army."[6] This error is traced to a faulty translation from Babrovski's history book. He stated there that Horodetz was administratively and economically connected to Kobrin but that didn't mean they were one town.[7]

B. The Jewish Settlement

When did the pulse of Jewish life in Horodetz begin to beat? Exactly when, we can't say. It does appear that Jews lived in Horodetz from the very first years of its founding, that is, from 1142. In the beginning of the 17th century, the Horodetz Jewish community already was quite large and significant. In those years there were already in Horodetz, 8 Jewish taverns and hostels [8]. And in the middle of the 17th century, we find large warehouses, owned by the Jew, Missan (Nissan?) Yatzkevitsh and Avrashka.[9]

It is clear that Horodetz was, in those days, a central distribution point and people settled there to take advantage of the commercial activity. In summary, from the 17th century onwards, the Horodetz Jews were quite well integrated, according to the concepts of that time. This can be seen according to the accounting of the head tax which Horodetz Jews paid in 1673. They gave 51 zlotas. This was not a small amount in that time.[10]

Also, from another source, we learn about the Horodetz Jewish community and the role it played in Jewish life. This can be seen from regulations promulgated by "The Council of Four Lands"[11] in 1623. One of those decisions allocated a sum of money to Horodetz in order to renovate their synagogoue.[12] Horodetz is also included in the list of towns for which The Council of Four Lands worked out special regulations concerning wandering soldiers.[13]

According to various other documents, the Horodetz Jews joined with Brisk which was itself a part of the "Council of the Lithuanian Nation", which was composed of Brisk, Grodno and Pinsk.

It is worthwhile noting that the Jewish Chronicle, in writing about Bogdan Khmielnitzki's revolt in 1648, never mentioned Horodetz. However it does mention that in Kobrin, 200 Jews were murdered.[14] Is it likely, that if Horodetz was part of Kobrin, it would have escaped the massacre?

How did the contemporary Horodetz Jews live? How large was the contemporary Jewish community?

For these 2 questions we can get a partial answer from an old Polish document. From this document we can learn that the Horodetz community grew in numbers and in power. This document itself is not encouraging. It is a document which illustrates the helplessness of the Jews and their tragic condition even in the land where they had, as it were, national autonomy.

The Jew always lived in terror and all through those times he was exposed to the danger of expulsion and the confiscation of his property. How did the Jews survive the terrors at the end of the 17th century? Exactly what brought on the dark and evil decrees is not known. What we do know we learn from an old Polish document, a report of a legal ruling concerning Horodetz Jews, dated July 10, 1700.[15]

It deals with a Polish woman who had loaned money to several Horodetz Jews. On which terms they borrowed the money was not mentioned. All that we can be certain of is that they did not pay off the debt. The Polish judge in Horodetz ruled against the Jews. The decree was that the entire community must suffer. All Jewish property must be confiscated, even that which was outside the boundaries of Horodetz. And all the Jews, young and old, were expelled from Horodetz.

Was, indeed, the decree carried out according to the letter of the law or was it made less harsh? This is not known. But this is certain, that the protocol of the decree was saturated with hate for the Jews. The phrase, "The Untrustworthy Jews" was repeated in the protocol many times.

From the same document we can infer that Horodetz was then a town, since that is how it was described. Also the names of the 12 Jewish representatives can be confirmed. One of them is Missan (Nissan?) Haranovitz. It is worthwhile to ponder these strange names since it was not a small community. Concerning subsequent years there is very little knowledge. In 1766, we know, there were 254 Jews in Horodetz, a quite sizeable community for those years.[16] It appeared that the newly excavated canal, through which Horodetz became rejuvenated [17] also had an effect on the Jewish population. The population was nearly doubled; in 1847 there were in Horodetz 422 Jewish souls.[18] Unfortunately the Horodetz Jewish community did not hold on to its increase. We learn from a royal statistic of 1860 that in Horodetz were 295 Jews among 700 non-Jews.[19] Later, in 1878, again the community grew and in Horodetz were 567 Jews among 1264 residents.[20] And in 1897, the Jewish population numbered 648 among 1761 non-Jews.[21]

C. The Political Situation

The political scene experienced various revolutions and uprisings. In the years 1315-1341, the Lithuanian Grand Duke, Gedimin, took over Polesia. Later, in 1385, Lithuania united with Poland. And after that, in 1495, Alexander drove out all the Jews from the entire Lithuanian duchy.[22] In 1706 the Swedes conquered Lithuania. Of the fate of the Jews during those years, we know nothing. History is silent about this. The only vestige of this time remaining in the speech of Horodetz Jews was the phrase, "It remembers already Sweden", signifying an old story. Also, old Jews in Horodetz used to remember the Saxon war (end of 1705), but what kind of effect it had, we don't know.

In 1793 Horodetz was transferred to Russia and incorporated into White Russia (Belarus). From that time on a new chapter was started in the story of Horodetz. This chapter continued until 1914 when the first world war broke out and the Romanov dynasty no longer had any influence over Horodetz.

It is unlikely that the Napoleonic war (1812) had no effect on the Jews of Horodetz. All we know is that there were Jews siding with the French and others who were on the Russian side.

But we do have exact information about the Polish "povstanya" (rebellion), especially the second "povstanya" in 1863. Many Horodetz Jews sided with Poland. They provided the Poles with food and also with hiding places. But, when the Jew hides the Pole, is the chicken in the middle of the roosters, and the Pole does not forget to shout at his Jewish saviors, "Zshid Parkati, Zdeim Tshapki" (Filthy Jew, take off your hat).

The Russian regime settled scores with the Jewish "saviors" and one of the sacrifices was Devorah, the sister of Hersh Leib SSirota from Vigada, who was, for this sin, exiled to Siberia.

The suppression of the Polish revolt also overturned the political situation in Horodetz. Horodetz, with the surrounding villages, such as Rodetz, Vorotepolyeh, Tshelishtshevitsh, Ferekhreshtsh and others, had belonged to the Polish landlord, Voret. The Russian regime confiscated the property of the Jews and sold it for a small sum to the old man, Shter, who bought it from the Romanovs. The Horodetz Jews paid "platzveh" (land tax) to Shter and afterwards to his younger son, to whom Horodetz, Vorotepolyeh and Palayeh belonged.

Under the Tsar's regime the Horodetz Jews suffered all the evils and persecutions which the government dreamed up for Jews. Also the wave of pogroms which had raged in Russia for the past 80 years once again engulfed Horodetz Jews. In the beginning of the 80 years the Polesia railroad line was built from Zshavinke, near Pinsk, through Horodetz. The Russian regime brought Russians from the heart of Russia to build this raliroad line. In Horodetz were stationed some of these Russians who were working on the line. The air, which the Tsarist regime had poisoned, was full of hate against the Jews. The Russian ruffians had only to wait for an opportunity and they would beat the Jews.

This is how it was. One time, during the night, on the 20th of July 1882, the ruffians got drunk and began breaking windows, beating Jews and ravaging the Jewish community. It was a miracle that the Christians did not join them. The Uriadnik (Police captain), Shabnov, along with the Starshina (town elders), did not allow the pogrom to get any worse. Also the young Horodetz Jews were not sitting with folded hands and they fought back.[23]

A second time, in the summer of 1906, when the Russian ruffians rebuilt the iron bridge, another pogrom descended on the heads of the Jews, and we were overcome with terror.

D. Social Improvement

We have already seen that Horodetz was a distribution point on the route between Brisk and Pinsk. But a larger role began to be played after the canal was completed. The canal, which later was called Dnieper-Bug canal, used to be called Kralevski canal (king lover canal), after the Polish king, August Poniatavski (1764-1795), since he was the initiator of the concept.

This canal was opened with a great parade in the year 1784. In the great crowd was also the Polish king, Stanislav August Poniatavski, who made a special visit to Horodetz in order to personally witness the event.[24] The accomplishment was very great, and much was spoken and written about this at that time.

The canal, which ended here in Horodetz until 1841[25], joined the river Moklhavetz, near Kobrin, in the middle of the river Pina from Pinsk. In other words, this canal connected the 2 great rivers, Dnieper and Bug (consequently it was called the Dnieper-Bug canal). Thanks to this canal the Black Sea was connected to the Baltic Sea. The length of the canal was over 75 km.

Because of this canal one could ship through Kobrin, Brisk, Warsaw and Danzig various products such as grain, whisky, barley, hogs, candles, cloth, human hair, hog hair, tar, timber and ceramics.[26] Thanks to this traffic, Horodetz was called "Little Danzig", since Horodetz was transformed into a place for export and import business.

We read the following statistics for 1860: 23 ships and 69 barges were downloaded, carrying 29,315 "poods" (1 pood = 40 lb.), with a value of 104,438 rubles. And, in the same year, were loaded for export 32 ships and 9 barges carrying 28,393 poods worth 121,954 rubles.[27]

Above the canal was a primitive bridge which used to be opened with a rope when a "Berlinner" (wooden boat) or a "Parakhod" (steam ship) needed to pass through.. About 30-40 men used to pull the rope until the bridge opened. The crowds of travellers used to have to wait a few hours until the bridge got itself together before they could cross over. In 1883 a wooden bridge was made high enough that even a Parakhod could pass under it.

Horodetz became an important center because of its canal, and the Russian regime made Horodetz also a military stonghold. From about 1876, soldiers began to be stationed in Horodetz. In the beginning there was just one company of soldiers (about 100 men), but thereafter a total of 4 companies were stationed in Horodetz. The soldiers left Horodetz in 1888 but 5 years later they returned to stay until 1896.

With the outbreak of the first World War, the Horodetz canal lost its usefulness. We stopped exporting timber to Germany and the canal no longer carried commercial shipping; it became a simple local stream.

Commercial importance returned to Horodetz when the Polesia railway line was constructed (1882-1884). The line, which went behind the town, also required an iron bridge over the canal, so a train station to meet the canal was built a few minutes from Horodetz. Because of the importance of the canal, the local train station was called Dnieper-Bugskaya. Years later, under Polish rule, local citizens requested that the name of the station be made the same as the name of the village, Horodetz.

The canal and the railroad connected Horodetz with the outside world, and merchants with various businesses would come to Horodtz because of its markets. Along with the building of the train station, Horodetz also became the location for a central post office, from which was sent mail to Antipolya and other nearby villages.

Horodetz was much beautified when the highway between Horodetz and Antipolya was built (1908-1910). The main streets of the village were paved and mud was cleared away.

By 1928 Horodetz was linked to the outside world by telephone. The single telephone was in the post office from which we could connect to other towns.

During this time the highway between Kobrin and Antipolya was built (21 km) and an autobus route was established between Kobrin and Antipolya, passing thrugh Horodetz.[28] This traffic strongly connected Horodetz to her nearby towns and villages.

E. Culture in Horodetz

Jewish children in Horodetz received their elementary Jewish education in the traditional "kheyder" until age 13 -14 when they left the kheyder. Most of the boys continued learning in their own synagogues. Only a small number would leave Horodetz to learn in a yeshiva. Conversely, young men and Talmud students would come to Horodetz from strange towns and learn Gemara (Talmud) in our synagogue.

Occasionally the Rav (teacher) would study with several young men who were ready for advanced learning and preparing to be "Poskim" (experts in a branch of Talmud) and judges.

The Jewish children taught themselves Russian. Very few Jewish children attended the "Schola" (Russian folk school), which had only one teacher for over 100 gentile children. In addition, the sanitary conditions were not fit for the Jewish child.

When the enlightenment came to Horodetz, the young men of the synagogue would read "forbidden and false" books hidden under the Gemara. Some of these young men, who were corrupted by these stolen waters, never returned. They lost their father and mother and lost themselves in the outside world seeking "education". However, some were able to resist the pull of enlightenment. Only those with strong character stayed behind in the town, where they were able to satisfy their thirst for education and become famous personalities. One of these is the famous and learned Dr. Israel Michael Rabinovitz [29] who, himself, did not return to Horodetz. However, his nephew, Leyb (Reb Joshua Jacob's son), who had "gotten lost" with him, did return to Horodetz.

When Khassidism began to spread over the Jewish settlements, it also did not overlook Horodetz. Horodetz became a khassidic fortress of the Karlinner dynasty. Karlin, which is not far from Horodetz, in a short time found open hearts for the Karlinner doctrine. Many years later, when Reb Moshe from Kobrin began to spread his khassidic teachings, Horodetz Jews began to travel to Kobrin to be near Reb Moshe. After his death, they became his followers.

We cannot say that the khassidic way came in to Horodetz without wars and arguments. The opponents of khassidism were not quiet, but the sharpness of the arguments was moderate and did not inflame itself, as it did in other towns and villages.

Another movement which fought fiercely to take root in Horodetz, was the Zionist movement. In the beginning, when Dr. Hertzel emerged onto the Jewish arena, there were already several Jews in Horodetz who were inflamed by the idea of independence. Little by little this idea captured the entire Jewish community. Thanks to the Land of Israel movement, several Jewish families were saved from the murderous hand and they lived in and helped build the Jewish State.

F. Between Two World Wars

On Horodetz Jews was fallen the fate to drink a very large portion from the bitter cup, even though, because of the canal, Horodetz became strategically important. When the first world war broke out in 1914, the Russian government concentrated quite a large army in Horodetz in order to be ready to fight a battle against the Germans. Several Horodetz Jews began to be fearful of the results of the battle and they moved deeper into Russia, to relatives and friends. They left town and walked toward the train station. But not everyone had the good fortune to get into the trains and arrive in deeper Russia. Most of the Horodetz Jewish residents stayed in their neighborhoods till the end of the battles. And those Jews that did come back, returned to a destroyed Horodetz which was under the protection of German rule for the next 3 years.

The new rulers little by little began to introduce the German language into the folk school. Horodetz Jews, young and old, began to teach themselves German and learned how to get along with the German "Order". When the Germans lost the village, Horodetz became without civil government and various gangs terrorized her by day and by night. Finally Horodetz was included in the new Polish state. Then the terror became "legalized". The Polish regime quickly put the robbers and murderers under her protection.

It didn't take long before Horodetz was once again destroyed in the war between the Russians and the Poles. We prepared to escape but already there was no place to go. There was no longer the possibility of leaving and the Jews no longer had the strength to leave. The few Jews who still remained in Horodetz were the old and the children. The younger Jews had immediately gone to peaceful Brisk and began to escape to America.

Finally peace was secured and Horodetz became a part of Poland. The Polish regime introduced harsh laws about racial purity against those Jews who were not residents. The truth is, they were evil decrees specifically aimed against the Jews. The Polish regime also pased a law of compulsory public education for every child. Jewish children had to attend the "pavshekhne" (Polish folk school) till noon and only after this could they quench their thirst for Jewish studies.

The Polish government also introduced military service. The Horodetz Jews were not at all enthusiastic about this. But, many young men did their duty and went into the army. Some of them even excelled. But what does one do when one comes home after army service? What trade can be followed when the Polish regime has closed off all the ways in which a Jew could make a living?

The spirit starts to think about emigrating. But where should one go since all doors are closed? Two streams of immigration pulled them. One towrds Eretz Israel and the second to South America to countries like Argentina, Brazil, Cuba, etc. Horodetz gradually was emptied of its Jews and the Jewish pulse slowly weakened.

This was the situation until the outbreak of the second world war in 1939 when Horodetz was occupied by the Red army. Now, the Soviet regime began to rule the village. Subversive ideas came in on the backs of writers, whose books the Russian soldiers brought in, who promised "complete redemption" not only spiritual but also physical. The Russian army doctors were not burdened with soldiers so they lived very well in our town. But they spread rumors that the Soviet regime had exiled several Horodetzers and that a Horodetz girl had to poison herself.

After a short time Horodetz was captured by the Germans and Horodetz was wrapped in the embrace of the Nazis. Horodetz Jews were enslaved, tortured, killed and confined to a ghetto. The Horodetz Jews did not surrender but rather rebelled, sabotaged and escaped to the partisans in the forests, who were giving the Germans plenty of trouble.

But Hitler was stronger. He controlled everything and everyone. He smashed the houses to the ground and erased the memory of the cemetery. The grave stones were taken and used as paving blocks for the streets.

Horodetz became empty of her Jews. No more was there Jewish charm in the old Jewish village, no longer is heard the voices of children, Jewish hearts no longer beat there. A quiet cemetery atmosphere is felt in the air, which is soaked with blood. No traveller can stay there because of the sadness which hangs in the air. Even the extra-ordinary surviving Jew, David Volinietz, cannot stay there for more than 2 days. Every step reminds him of a martyr, every stride is bound up with memories of the happy past, which is no longer there.[30]

Horodetz once again became Russian in 1943. Did she also become Jewish? Do Jews live there? Does a Jewish life exist there?

As far as we know, no Jews live there now. It was a Jewish village and now it is no more. May her name be written in the history of Jewish martyrdom with golden letters!

Aharon Itche Leyzer's house
(about 200 years old) [since 1949 another 60 years have passed...]

This was drawn by Israel Zusman

References and Translator's notes:

1. P. Babrovski, "Russian Geographic and Statistical Materials, Grodno gubernia", vol 2, pg 922, 1953. Petersberg, 1863.
2. Slavar, "Russian Empire", vol 1, pg 668.
3. Vislok, "Records of Pruzhana City", pg 54, Warsaw, 1931.
4. The Pinsk Jewish community in the last 50 years of the 16th century measured about 300 souls. The Grodno Jewish community, at the same time, contained 600 souls. And Brisk (Brest) then had 85 Jewish families. (See "One Thousand Years of Pinsk", pg 32). Yet, in 1795, Brisk had a bout 1000 Jewish souls and 481 houses.
5. I. A. Shulrof, "Antipolya, Her Name and Her History", Jubilee Book of the Antipol Aid Society, Chicago, 1934.
6. Yiddish-Russian Encyclopedia, vol 7, pg 326 and also in vol 9, pg 526.
7. Babrovski, vol 2, pg 1053.
8. Rezesti and Nadpisi, vol 1, pg 237, Petersberg, 1910.
9. Yiddish-Russian Encyclopedia, vol 5 & 6, pg 707-8.
10. Kobrin had then given 139 zlotas more than Horodetz. See Ref 8, vol 2, pg 48.
11. "The Council of Four Lands" was a semi-autonomous institution of Jewish self government set up by the Polish crown in the middle of the 16th century. It originated in the meetings of business and rabbinical leaders at the annual fairs. It included the "Jewish" provinces of Poznan, Cracow, Lvov and Volhynia.
12. Records of the Council of the Four Lands, pg 116.
13. Ibid, pg 18.

14. See the "Book of Lamentations" in the Bible.
15. See "Records of the Vilna Community". vol 29, pg 267-270, Vilna, 1902.
16. Yiddish-Russian Encyclopedia, vol5-6, pg 707-8.
17. See the Chapter, "The Social Betterment Movements."
18. Yiddish-Russian Encyclopedia, vol 9, pg 575.
19. See reference 2.
20. Slavnik, "Polish Geography and Statistics", vol 3, pg 133, Warsaw, 1882.
21. See reference 18.
22. Vislok, "Records of Pruzhana City", pg 71, Warsaw, 1931.
23. Zalman Kamenetski in "Hamelitz", issue 29, 1882. Also in the nearby village of Drohitzin did the landowners start a pogrom. (See "Hamelitz", issue 40, 1882).
24. See reference 7.
25. Workers restored the Antipolya Jew, Yankel Shmulevitsh. (See Dr. Raphael Maller, "The Jews of Poland", vol 1, pg 366, N.Y., 1946.)
26. Slavar, "Russian Empire", vol 1, pg 76-77.
27. Ibid, pg 668.
28. Shammai Ravinski was the concessionaire of the autobus line between Horodetz and Kobrin.
29. See article by A. Ben-Ezra, "Dr. Israel Michael Rabinovitz".
30. Letter by David Volinietz.

Acknowledgements

Lucien Harris of Jerusalem, who kindly lent me his copy of Weinreich's Yiddish-English dictionary when I started to translate this yizkor book.

Ida Selevan Schwarcz and Roman Turovsky, who helped me understand obscure Yiddish / Russian expressions.

[Page 10]

"Once There Was . . . ."

A poem by Israel Sussman

Translated by Eugene Sucov

Dedicated to the memory of the shtetl of my birth, Horodetz

Translator's note: In the original Yiddish, the rhyme scheme for each 4 line verse was a-b-a-b. I have not tried to replicate that rhyming scheme in the English translation.

>Once there was a shtetl small,
>Horodetz was it known as.
>And what happened to it
>Is a secret known to one and all.

Not a word in history is written
About its people, secular or observant.
And from the houses and crooked alleys,
Only a trace is remaining.

Now I remember how I went to kheder,
Where summer and winter it was my home,
And where "Old Man Sender" constantly taught
Aleph bais with a whip.

In the cold winter nights
We would go together from kheder
Wrapped in an overcoat
With a lantern in our hands.

[Page 11]

I was taught by many teachers
In rooms with many children.
But inscribed in my memory
Is the melody of Shimon Isaacs when he chanted from the Bible.

Comes the snow and the frost
And everything immediately is frozen,
Birds stay in their nest
And kids slide on the frozen river.

Who doesn't think abut the cold shul
With a matza on the wall
To expel the old ghosts
With an invisible hand.

The study hall in its street,
And the small Hassidic shul in the market.
We used to become angry over an aliyah wrongly given
But we would still enjoy the service.

Where are you now, anti-hassidim and hassidim?
Jewish scholars and story tellers,
Jews working and toiling,
Jews ordinary and Jews remarkable?

Where is R. Itzik's guest house
Where every weary traveler
Would find a home
So he could rest his legs?

Where is the Rav R. Khayim's beautiful presence,
With his good attributes in his modest life?

R. Aryeh's ripe fruit became old,
His soul was freed from troubles and suffering.

[Page 12]

Where are Khayim Nissan and Naftali, the doctor,
Asher David, the ritual slaughterer as well as blacksmith,
And Shimon Isaacs roaring a sad song,
And the fire brigade putting out a fire?

Where are the young pioneer kids
With courage in their hearts and plows in their hands
Who had all prepared so rapidly
To travel and recover our land?

Where are the tailors, shoemakers and wagon drivers?
Where is Big Moshe in Karlinski's store?
No longer in Horodetz are there any Jewish shops,
All wiped clean from a black street.

And do you remember Fridays in the summer?
The Horodetz river would call us
And Jewish women and men joyfully bathed
In honor of Shabbat.

On the river's small waves
Occasionally would swim from Pinsk
A steamer and also row boats
With important merchants, as many as from Minsk.

Quiet would life flow there,
Quiet as the waters in the river.
Each one would to somethng aspire,
Whether children or whether wealth.

[Page 13]

Did Satan not envy
Our peaceful life and streets?
Did he not spin and contrive
A partnership with the Angel of Death?

The Bund was banned and locked up,
And immediately Horodetz overflowed with troubles.
From ten measures of grief and anguish
She drank in total, nine.

Said Satan to the Angel of Death,
"In serious Poland have some fun.

> Go down there and take a whip
> And give them there a life which is called Germany."
>
> "With this whip break every limb
> Of this difficult people, the Jew.
> And whoever is weak and is wailing
> Ever more strongly shall you strike him."
>
> Every Jew went to their slaughter
> With mute hearts, depressed and grieving.
> In the evening sinks the sun,
> Red faced and ashamed.
>
> In a mood like that of Yom Kippur
> From their depths emerged a prayer,
> "Ah, God of Abraham and Sarah.
> Why, from all the sinners in all the worlds,
> Did you select us to be a sin offering?"

[Page 14]

> We forget the heavens, the sun and earth.
> We will forge a sword,
> A sword of hate, iron and steel,
> Like the Maccabis did long ago.
>
> We will "Destroy the memory of Amalek from under the heavens"
> And then we will drink a l'khayim to us all.
>
> Once there was a shtetl small,
> Horodetz it was known as.
> And what happened to it
> Is a secret which everyone knows.

Final comment by the poet:

> Among the grievers sorrowful and stooped
> As a mourner during the 30 days of mourning,
> Stand I, with tear filled eyes,
> And recite the Kaddish for the Holy Ones who were murdered.

[Page 15 - 18]

The Shtetl

by Rabbi Dr. Jacob Bosniak

Translated from the Yiddish by Eugene Sucov, July 2000

Part A

This shtetl, which was encircled by fields and gardens, was divided into 2 unequal parts by the Dnieper-Bug canal and by 2 smaller canals called Free-canals on both sides. A large and high wooden bridge with smaller bridges on both sides of the river joined the 2 parts of the shtetl. The railroad line operated in the south side of the shtetl, not more than 300 meters from the houses. The residents would always know the time, from morning till night, according to the passenger trains which passed by the shtetl 4 times a day. The whistles of the locomotives were always a welcome noise and the trains with the colored wagons an unending source of interest. The train would cross the river over an iron bridge that was painted a deep green and would park about a mile from the shtetl, near the station which was named after the river, Dnieper-Bug.

On the Bridge

The river, with its 2 bridges and the railroad line with station gave the shtetl a certain prestige and an excuse to feel superior to the neighboring towns. Workers in Antopol, for example, which was much larger, would need to travel to Horodets. Antopoler coachmen would have to bring their passengers to the Horodets train station, which was quite far to go. When one had to write a "get" (bill of divorce) in Antopol, one had to come to Horodets because Antopol did not have a river.[1]

In general, the Horodets home owners felt themselves more cultured than the Antopolers. Because of the river and the railroad line, Horodetsers were in close contact with the outside world. Large and small lumber and wood merchants from all over Russia would stop over in Horodets for a few days on their way to the port of Danzig (today's Gdansk), during which time the lumber would swim in the Horodets canal. In the winter the peasants would bring the lumber to the river's edge. In the spring would start the feverish activity of assembling the barges from which Jews and gentiles alike made their living. During the entire summer barges would be pulled along the river carrying various people from Russia and also from other foreign countries. The foreign voyagers would patronize the Jewish merchants and the town was quite busy.

Along the 2 riverside parks which lined the river's edge, had grown a forest of beautiful trees. There, the youth of the town enjoyed themselvs. In summer they would sail off on a raft or they could bathe in the clean, clear water of the canal. It must be remarked that, for the sake of modesty, the men would bathe not far from the wooden bridge and the women bathed far behind the dam. In this way the dam served as a "mekhitza".[2]

It must be understood that, of bathing suits, Horodets was not yet acquainted. The gentile men would very often swim through the "mekhitza"… We must admit that the gentiles were better swimmers than the Jewish men. One of them used to bathe under the wooden bridge in the whirlpool and others of them would stand on the bridge and dive into the water.

The River

    In the winter the canal became the best place to skate. Even old people would enjoy standing on the bridge, contemplating the frozen river. From one side one could see the whirlpool which regulated the water level in the canal. And from the other side could be seen the green railroad bridge with the swiftly running trains. Under the bridge, floating barges which were loaded with long lines of differently clothed peasants, were slowly pulled. The gentiles who loaded and guided the barges down the river lived in cabins on the barges for weeks and months at a time. They would cook their meal over an open fire on the barges. This gave the pranksters in the town the opportunity to throw pebbles or spit into their target, that is to say, into the earthen pots. To actually get a pebble, thrown from the bridge, into a pot was considered to be an event about which one could boast. Sometimes it happened that one of the peasants could catch a prankster by the hand and then he would receive "broken bones". But this practise (of throwing pebbles) was finally stopped.

    Once in a while a steamship would pass through the shtetl. Then the entire town was turned upside down. Even the strongest teacher in the kheder (religious classroom) had the misfortune of not being able to keep the students in school. Young and old ran to the river to stare at this wonder. The ship was painted in many colors, with high smokestacks, with glittering brass all polished, with white hats and shiny buttons on the sailor's uniforms. Everything was wondered at, remarked about and discussed endlessly.

Part B

The riverside parks with the high, strong, fully grown trees on both sides of the river, were the shtetl's place for pleasure strolls. On Shabbat and holiday mornings many people, mainly the youth, met each other in the riverside parks and discussed their problems or the news of the day. In the hot summer's day, it was always cool there. Sitting on the grass and contemplating the twinkling waters of the river was a real delight. There the youth flirted or read a book, mainly from the government's forbidden list. That's how we spent our time.

And when the highway was built between Horodets and Antopol, it also became a place for strolling, especially on Shabbat afternoons. Then the young people would run onto the highway to meet boys and girls from Antopol.

But the river was the overriding reminder that the town was split into 2 unequal parts, "The Street" and "The Market", The "Street", that is, the Jewish street, extended for a distance of 4-5 blocks from Old Man Saul's tavern to Gedalya Yudel's shop. Beyond this shop began the Gentile street, or, as we called it, Kobrinner street

(since it led to the county seat in Kobrin). There, a Jewish child was afraid to take even one step lest the gentiles would throw stones at him, set dogs on him, or just plain insult Jews.

Only one Jew, Tsadok the hunchback, decided to live right in the middle of Gentile street with his wife and daughter. He was a small, lively Jew, with a hump in front and a hump in back. His throat itself was scarcely visible. He had black hair and sharp black eyes, with a black pointed beard and a face burned by the sun. He was always ready with a smile and a happy word for everyone. He was one of the regular prayer leaders in shul, standing near the furnace behind the bimah (prayer stand). He was by trade a plumber but he would also smooth fur pelts. Often he would also work on the river bank near the barges. He was a happy man, contented with however much he earned. Even though it was long walk from his house to the beit midrash (study hall), he never failed to pray with first minyan (quorum of 10 men needed to start praying) at daybreak.

The street was a long one. From one side it went toward Kobrin and from the other side it went toward the village Makhvedevitsh. On this street could be found the beit-midrash, and, on the side, in an alley, was the Great Cold Shul. In this place were also, forgive me for mentioning these in same sentence, the bath house and the cemetery. Between the study house and the Great Shul was the High Shul where the wedding canopy would usually be placed.

The greater part of the town was called the "Market". In the Market were located the Jewish houses as well as the shops, which were larger and finer and spaced over a larger area than those located on the "Street". The "Market" didn't have any pipe shops as, for example, were on Kobrin street. The shops in Horodets stood in an empty place, nearly 4 blocks in area, on which grew grass in the summer and was quite muddy in the winter. The houses on both sides of the "Market" were quite nice and large and were inhabited by several rich home owners. There, also would be found the Russian Greek Orthodox church and the Polish Roman Catholic church.

On the eastern side, opposite the Market, on the way to Antopol, not far from the Post Office, stood the Pravaslann monastery. It had a stone parking lot next to a great meadow which belonged to the priest. The walls were painted white and the roof with its cupolas were painted either blue or green. Never had a Jew ever placed even one foot inside the monastery, except for Aaron Leib, the miller. The monastery, with its trees surrounding it, generated a gracious charm to the the entire town.

Opposite the Market, on the southern side, stood the government public school. There, a few hundred peasant children of various parents went to study during the 3-4 winter months of the year. One individual teacher would teach all these children reading, writing and arithmetic at the same time, in one great room. The children would sit, crowded together on long benches. The little that they learned in the short winter session would be completely forgotten during the remaining months of the year when they would have to work with their parents in the field.

Next to the school stood the "Pazsharne" (militia) command and the police station from Volast, which had its own lockup for people who were arrested and needed to be held overnight or longer and then transported with other convicts to various parts of the country.

The Catholic church stood in a side alley of the Market which we called the Landowner's street. It was an old, high wooden building, unpainted and overgrown with weeds which gave the impression of neglect. In truth, at one time these neglected buildings belonged to the Russian Orthodox church and those which remained on the Market used to be Polish. But, after the Pavskanye (Polish insurrection), the Poles were removed and the Russians took over for themselves the nicer buildings. On this Landowner's street lived Shakhnow the Uriadnik (police constable), the Diak and a few Polish gentiles. At the time of the first World War there were hardly any Poles in Horodets. We could count them on our fingers, they were so few.

From the other side of the Market stretched a large Christian street. It was called the Pozmen street since it travelled to Pozmen. This particular Christian street was populated only by fervent Christians, so Jews very seldom went there, unless for business. From Pozmen street Jews would receive much trouble. Especially in the conscription weeks, when the Christian recruiters would get themselves drunk and generate a riot or start beating the Jews.

Usually the Market was empty, without shops. But when there was a holiday, hundreds of peasants would fill the street and sometimes also with horses and wagons. Then the Market became lively, and sometimes a bit too lively. The holidayers would show up on the first of each Russian month. Horodets had to thank the old landowner, Shter, and his wife, who had decreed that in Horodets there would be each month a holiday. The old Shter was the sole owner of Horodets. To him belonged the entire town and its surroundings. Everyone had to pay him rent money (Platzaveh). The old Shter had strong family connections; he was descended from the Romanov family and was a strong member of the high society of Petersburg. And for this we must give praise. Shter and his wife were very good Christians and had, for the Jews, a very friendly feeling. For example, one can mention the fact that when the old Shter would drive by the Jewish houses , he would throw coins for the Jewish children. (I don't know who learned from whom: the old Shter or the old Rockefeller)

And a thank you is owed to the Landowner by the first member of the Moyer family in Horodets.. That was Isaacs Moyer, the one to whom the landowner gave a goat. Especially we should remark on his friendliness in the summer when, after the midday shabbat meal, he would let the children into his palace grounds without restraint and allow the public to lie on the grass as a father under his vineyard and listen to music from a phonograph.

Part C

The cultural life of the Horodets Jews stood at a high level. In various houses came copies of the Hebrew periodicals Hamelitz (The Advocate), Hatsifirah (The Siren) and Hazman (The Time). Other Jews received Yiddish newspapers such as Yod and Friend. The custom was to have several partners share in the cost of one newspaper and to read the paper in sequence. Till the paper would reach the last partner it would either be torn or the news was already old.

A total revolution in newspaper reading was brought in during the summer of 1912. A newspaper was brought down from Warsaw, called Moment. It had installed Tsadok the hunchback as its agent. He used to carry the Moment every afternoon to his subscribers who were satisfied from day to day. The Moment would arrive every day on the same train. The public would buy the Moment as if it was water for making matza. The news and the romances were packed together just like dinner plates. Young and old, men and women would scramble to read this paper.

Many years have gone by; various rulers has Horodets had. People were born, people died. Dreams floated up, dreams were torn down. Only one dream still remains alive in the hearts of many Horodets Jews. To see once more the old town; once more to stand on the place where the crib used to stand, and even to see the grave of a father, a mother, a grandfather, a grandmother. And now? The Jewish Horodets is no more. Even a gravestone is not left standing in its place. Empty is the town, desolate, destroyed. In one's heart is a wound, a desecrated empty space. Let us fill up this void with the ideals of rebuilding our land, Eretz Israel.

Translator's note:

1. The get needed to specify the exact location where the get was written. A river was a permanent and easily identifiable geographical location, so it was preferred over a location without geographic markers.
2. The mekhitza was a curtained separation between men and women while they were praying in the shul.

[Page 19 - 23]

The Social-Economic Structure

by A. S.

Translated from the Yiddish by Eugene Sucov

Part A

The social and economic structure of Horodetz was varied. In her were represented various businesses and trades. And, while Horodetz was situated on the way between two well known cities, Brest and Pinsk, Horodetz was still one of the old time pass through towns which joined Poland to White Russia through a highway. Later on, Horodetz also connected to the afore mentioned cities through a canal.

Back in the olden times in 1563, without knowing whether there already was a Jewish community in Horodetz, we know that Horodetz was owned by an important land settler. In the beginning of the 17th century, Horodetz was a business town in which there were already 8 taverns, proof that many merchants traveled thought Horodetz and that many of them stayed the night. It was very fortunate that these temporary guests also did business in Horodetz. And there, where there was already a commercial center, there were also traveling salesmen. This we can see from the regulations, which the Council of the Four Lands established concerning travelers in Horodetz.

From the pieces of millstones and several houses which still remained, one can see that Horodetz at one time contained horse driven mills in which were ground meal and flour for Horodetz and its surroundings. From the ruins of a distillery, which were left behind in Horodetz, one can learn that, in past time, Horodetz had a still which produced whiskey.

There also had been, in Horodetz, an "oil press", in which was made oil. The only thing that remains in Horodetz is the family Allman, which took its name from "oil man", the grandfather of Old Sheppes (Allman), who had an oil press in Horodetz.

On the topic of industry was Horodetz backward. About 50 years ago, i.e. around 1900, an attempt was made by R. Yitzkhak Aharon to produce bricks, but it didn't succeed. Another brick maker who was located closer to the railroad station did indeed exist for several years until the First World War. At that time the brick maker employed 10 Jewish workers.

About 1907 Aharon Karlinski opened a clothing factory in Horodetz. He imported from Poland 2 tailors who taught the Horodetz girls how to do the work. However, the factory didn't have any longevity.

Alter, the Levi

A smithy

(Drawn by Israel Zussman)

Part B

With the opening of the canal from the Dnieper to the Bug Rivers, which connected Pinsk to Brest by water, new perspectives opened up for Horodetz commerce. From Pinsk and vicinity would be sent lumber to Danzig by way of the Horodetz canal. Thanks to the lumber, the wood merchants or their employees would stay over in Horodetz. They would buy food from the Jews for the gentiles who transported the lumber.

Horodetz also contained wood merchants like little Isaac (Israel), Khayim Nissel's grandson, who would, at the end of the summer store logs by the side of the river. In the spring we would assemble them and send them to Germany. From this came the nickname "Horodetzer with the logs".

Other Horodetz Jews dealt with rafts which would bring goods such as pottery, bark, linen, and other products and sell them to the large world.

The canal created another income for Horodetz Jews, namely the fish business, which became a very handsome source of livelihood. Another entire, special income did the canal bring to the Jewish world of Horodetz. This was the divorce decree (get) which was written in Horodetz because none of the surrounding villages had a river and traditional Jewish law required that a "get" could not be written without a river.

Horodetz was not only a center for writing divorce decrees, but also it was a center for marriages. How healthy Horodetz was as a central point, was a factor, since many rich marriages were performed there. The parents would outdo themselves and bring in the best musicians and entertainers such as Elikum Tsunzer and others.

The railroad, which was built in 1882 – 1864, brought the Horodetz Jew new opportunities for making a living, such as loading and unloading goods which were shipped to Horodetz, Antopol and surroundings. This created the bureaucratic "expeditor", who occupied much visible space in Russia and Poland.

As the train would stop a few times a day in the station, and people wanted to have a bite to eat or a drink, the wives would take a basket in hand, fill it with fruit, sausage, bagel, bottled soda water and go to the train to sell. The train selling became a permanent part of the station and Horodetz fell in love with this kind of business.

The train station was close to Horodetz, and thanks to this fact, the letters which were sent to Antopol came first to Horodetz. From there the letters were trans-shipped to Antopol. This was called "holding the gossip", That is, the government would pay a certain amount of money to those people who would transfer the mail.

The letters which came to Horodetz were carried there by a Jewish mailman and his daughter. The charge was: 1 postcard, 1 kopek; a sealed letter, 3 kopeks; and a money order, 10 kopeks. From carrying the mail he didn't make a living, so he had to come up with a second livelihood which was similar to carrying the mail. This turned out to be bringing merchandise to the merchants from the larger cities such as Kobrin or Brest (Brisk). These Jews were called "stage coaches". The "stage coaches" would carry a package of products which the merchant needed or which private people would order and he would bring it quickly. He would take a certain fee for his labor.

In the 1890s was stationed in Horodetz a battalion of soldiers. In the summer they were in the fields, but in the winter they stayed in town, and they were quartered in Jewish houses. This staying of the soldiers generated a fine income for the Horodetz Jews. Some added wood and foods, others would buy from the soldiers various products. That's the way the soldiers fulfilled an important function in the economy of Horodetz.

Alter the blacksmith

Part C

Horodetz was encircled by fields and gardens, which belonged to the landowners and the priests. Jews would buy trees from either the tree owners or the priests. Afterwards, in the beginning of spring, they would buy whole orchards or fields and depend on God's blessing. Buying orchards was a nice way of making a living for Horodetz men who were knowledgeable, but who wants to wait a whole year to sell the fruit?

Other Jews would buy land full of hay from the tree landowners. In the winter they would sell the hay to the homeowners for their cows or horses. Other men would buy from the tree owner a portion of the forest. They would hire gentiles to cut down the trees and later would sell to the Jews a few sticks or a bundle of wood to heat their homes during the wintry months.

Milk products, or as we used to call it, "pakhterai", used to be an outstanding livelihood, which high class men took up. The "pakhter" would, in the beginning, rent from the tree owner, the pasture; later on he rented also the cow, and the right to milk the cow, to make butter and Swiss cheese and to send it to Warsaw. Cheese production would cause the large pakhter to become an important person, a specialist in making Swiss cheese, a trade which bordered on needing expertise, and which was completely in Jewish hands.

The dairy products business or taking on lease an estate was bound up with investing lots of money. Not every one was able to get into it without a loan. From this was created the shady business of usury. The usurer would loan money to be paid back every week with high interest. Also the little shopkeeper or the peddler would very often approach the loan shark, who didn't have a nice reputation. More than one song or sarcastic anecdote was sung or told about the accounts of the loan shark.

The peddler, in contrast, was a sympathetic person, selling on the installment plan, calculating an extra profit. The peddler would fill his sack with various thing the women wanted, such as perfume, table cloths, shawls, needles, thread, buttons, crocheting needles and so on. And with the pack on his shoulders he would start his journey. That's how he would go from town to town, from gentile woman to gentile woman, and sometimes from one city to the next. And on Shabbat he would come home. Other peddlers would be on the road a whole month. And if God helped and he was lucky, the peddler laid down his pack and opened a shop, like Itshe the peddler (Jacob Polyak's father) and become a Horodetzer merchant.

But not every shopkeeper became rich. There was no livelihood for him in the village since in every house was either one shop or two. Some left the village. They traveled to America to work in the golden land. They would send their wives one US dollar; in Horodetz this was worth two rubles. These women who stayed behind created a special class which we called Americanikess. Thanks to these Americanikess there was prosperity in the village since they ate better, dressed better. Their standard of living was higher than that of those who stayed behind in Horodetz.

Part D

The immigration to America created a source of income for the agent. He was tied into the larger agent in Brest and in the border towns through which were smuggled immigrants. There were many kinds of immigrants, including gentiles and Jews who didn't want to or weren't able to get a passport. The agent would give advice on how to cross the border. But at the same time he would also take them across himself. Not just once was he caught with his living merchandise. Then it would cost him dearly in health and in money until he and his merchandise were too frightened to continue this trade. With the outbreak of World War I the agent's business died since the borders were shut tight. Also many other types of business closed down because of the war.

Another major source of income for the Horodetz Jews was the monthly fair which took place on the first day of each Russian month (and if it fell on Shabbat or other Jewish holiday, it was postponed). All of Horodetz, as well as the peasants from the entire surroundings would anticipate the fair days. The peasants would bring cows, horses, eggs, etc. and the Jews would buy them for resale. In addition to the monthly fair days were 2 larger market days; one in mid-summer when all the shopkeepers and tradesmen would , with anticipation, wait for the peasants to come to Horodetz.

Also the tavern keepers would wait for the market days. When the people had already had enough from the market day, the gentile would open his "kalitkeh" (purse) and say to his wife or his neighbor "paidim zapiti" (let's have a drink). And the gentile would drink until he lost a few rubles in the tavern. The "pivnieh" (beer hall) also gave a nice livelihood to the Jews of Horodetz. But this income was not so agreeable; they would have to deal with drunken men and women, not one of whom was not disgusting. But what won't a Jew do to make a living?

Between the shopkeepers, small dealers and workmen was another class which could not be counted among the above-mentioned groups. This class was the doers of holy work which included the Rav, the cantor, the beadle, the ritual slaughterer and elementary and advanced teachers, who were, in the modern idiom called "holy proletariat". This proletariat was a very useful element in Jewish life. Without them the religious community couldn't function. But their livelihood was not so easy. For their income they had to approach the more prosperous Jews who themselves were not so rich. Sometimes someone would leave a few rubles for the religious elders. That's how they passed the years, sometimes with more and sometimes with less.

We can't say that Horodetz didn't have any poor folk. There were in Horodetz also, destitute, needy Jews, who would appear at the butcher, but not in public. They did not go to the rich Horodetz houses asking for money. We sent them gifts in secret. And if one of them did not have the money for a wedding, we would make a wedding for a daughter. And it was not with what, or liking that, he would go out into the world with his pack. And when he had recovered the necessary amounts, he would return to Horodetz and become again a respectable homeowner, as before. In general, the Horodetz poor folk didn't go to the houses, not by themselves in the city and not to the stranger. And when they needed to approach people, they did this in a very discrete way.

Part E

With the coming of the Polish regime (after World War I, in 1920) the old ways of making a living went under and new ways rose up in Horodetz. With the new highway which the Polish built, from Kobrin to Horodetz, also came a new source of income, that is, driving an autobus from Horodetz to Kobrin and back. The bus carried passengers as well as packages. The autobus company was in the hands of Shammai Ravinski who hired special people to drive and occasionally repair the autobus.

In the times of the Polish regime was also a large steam mill which belonged to Todres Dubin and which gave livelihood to him and his family. With the growth of the Jewish community in Horodetz, also grew their income.

In Horodetz there were shoemakers, tailors, dressmakers, carpenters, drillers, smiths, butchers, wagon drivers and bricklayers. The shoemaker and the tailor worked alone or with 2-3 helpers. The same also for the smiths and the carpenters. But the drillers and the bricklayers would take on work and shared the work in a cooperative way, even though they didn't know the word.

The condition of the drillers was totally different from that of the other tradesmen. Their work started with sunrise and ended in sunset, summer and winter. The other tradesmen worked in their homes, alone or with workers in their workshops or forges. The work of the drillers would be mostly among strangers in the surrounding villages or large towns where they were more likely to find work. Occasionally one would need to overhaul a whole village or town. Mostly the drillers would work the tree canal where they would repair and overhaul the sluices and the "bodkes" (residences for the clerks and watchmen).

The drillers would very often renovate the station or overhaul the "bodkes" from Kobrin to Hitshin. And that's how things went. A "podrat" (project manager) from Pinsk or Brisk (Brest) would be authorized by the government to take over all the work. Parts of it he would let out for the drillers who would need to compete for a share of it. The oldest among them, by many years, was Shmerl the driller. Shmerl was a wise Jew and a good craftsmen. For a long time he was the chief of the Horodetz drillers. In later years Yossl Bantshok became the chief. Yossl Bantshok was a tall man, with a red beard, and was a specialist in his occupation.

The greatest income for the bricklayers was in repairing and rebuilding military barracks. But from time to time they would build an entire house or a palace for the landowner. The Horodetz bricklayer would work for a long time on the landowner's property and after finishing his palace and nearby houses, they would also work in helping to beautify the railroad station.

The Horodetz woodcutters would also work with the felt makers. Their work was to throw heavy blocks of wood on top of the fire. From dawn to dusk they would drag the saw through the wood. Alter, the Levite, Stone was above and Mattes was below. Year in and year out both of them made their living with the saw. And even though the work was very hard, Alter the Levite lived till he was 90.

The workday of the craftsmen in the summer would start about 8 in the morning after prayers and would continue the entire day till late afternoon prayers. After these prayers he would use the short time till evening prayers by going to the study hall or to the Chassidic synagogue where he would occasionally hear an itinerant preacher or he would learn some Torah. After evening prayers he would go home.

Also in the winter his workday started at 8 in the morning and continued till the evening prayers. After evening prayers he would sometimes go to the study hall. He would return to his work till 10 p. m. or 11 at night, especially before the Jewish or Christian holidays when there was much work.

Horodetz also contained a house painter, Aaron Leib, he was called. No work was for him too difficult. Summer he would join himself to the painters. Mostly he worked by the canal or the railroad, where he would paint the posts which marked off the versts (2/3 of a mile). The poles were pained in whiter and black stripes and had to be continually repainted. The work was assigned to a Horodetzer manager, either Khayim Berl or Isaacl Matyes. The manager would hand the work to Aaron Leib, so Aaron Leib and his 2 sons, Isaac and Noah, and his brother, Abraham, would paint the poles. They would also paint the tin roofs of the Horodetz and neighboring churches. The Tsarist regime didn't deny money to the churches, so every few years their roofs were painted.

On top of the roofs of the churches, Aaron Leib and his helpers didn't forget that they were Jews. It was very amusing to see, standing on the point of the church over the "kalakalnia" (attic in which were hung the bells for ringing) or over the cupola where a great cross stood, these Jewish painters with their yarmulkes and small tallis with the fringes showing painting the cross and singing Jewish songs. Winter, when no painters were around, Aaron Leib would take his sewing machine and his cutting machine and associate himself with the bookbinders. He would also repair galoshes. For Pesakh he would hang wallpaper in the houses.

The railroad and the river gave a livelihood to the Horodetz wagon drivers. In addition to carrying passengers from the train station and to the train station, they would also transport goods. They would sometimes travel with work bosses into nearby towns to get workers, or travel to supervise the transporting of the logs that would swim (float) in the canal.

The Horodetz craftsmen didn't visit any saloons as did the gentile population. Therefore, they were able to save from their outside earnings for a house, a garden, and 1 or 2 cows.

The cultural level of the Jewish craftsmen was also totally not that bad. They could study a chapter of the Mishnah, a bit of "the well spring of Jacob" and a few even understood a piece of Gemara. Several craftsmen also had quite nice voices and, during the High Holy Days, they would act as prayer leaders in Horodetz or in nearby towns. A few of them, who came to America, became full cantors. Some of them who stayed behind were considered as scholars.

With pride we can say: they did not bring shame to their village, Horodetz. Let us hope that their children will establish the traditions of their parents and their parent's parents.

[Page 24]

The Rabbis

The Rabbinic Context

By Rabbi Mordechai Greenberg

Translated by Eugene Sucov

In preparing to write a historical monograph about the Horodetz rabbis, which covers a period of about 150 years, I found it necessary to briefly review the general characteristics and features of the rabbis of those times.

Rabbi Mordekhai Greenberg

In the framework of religious living in those times, the rabbi was the greatest authority for the Jews. The rabbi was highly esteemed by everyone and ruled on every moralistic issue. He radiated an elevated influence on his flock. Nevertheless, what mattered most was that he stood outside the business interests, so he could have a dominant role in all the town's livelihood. His outspoken views had a desirable effect on all business problems.

Everyone related to the rabbi with great respect, treating him with great honor and affection. In his own congregation he was as if, in accordance with the Talmudic expression, "He was like a golden goblet". He was indeed the jewel of the village (shtetl).

A dramatic performance was played out when the rabbi entered the Study Hall. Jews are sitting around the table and studying. As soon as the rabbi opened the door and became visible, immediately everyone stood up and remained standing until he came to his place in front of the Holy Ark. In the Study Hall no one gossiped during the discussions by the rabbi. When they were not praying, each one held a book. One learned "Gemara", a second, "Mishna", a third "Ein Yaakov" and a fourth would be reciting Psalms.

> Gemara is the summary of discussions from the year 200 to the year 500 CE by generations of rabbis about applications of the statements of Jewish law presented in the Mishna in the year 200CE. The Gemara plus the Mishna make up the Talmud.
> Ein Yaakov is a collection of legends from the Talmud by Rabbi Yaakov printed about 1600.

Every Shabbat after services, everyone went to the rabbi and greeted him with a "Good Shabbes" and no one was absent. What were the reasons for this great respect for the rabbi? It was his great knowledge of Torah and his greater knowledge of the minutest detail of Jewish laws and customs. Everyone felt that the rabbi had a higher understanding of the Jewish wisdom in Torah and tradition. In those days, the rabbi was, more or less, an expert in "Shas" (an acronym for the six orders of the Talmud) as well as in rabbinic rulings and the general rabbinic literature. He was always sitting and learning, never wasting his free time. He had literally fulfilled the saying, "You shall learn Torah morning and night."

For the rabbi of those days, such dedication to learning Torah was an obsession, a basis for his moral principles and a source from which he derived inspiration and elevated wisdom. However, rabbis kept themselves familiar with the problems of their people so they could be wise leaders of their congregations. They did not leave any room for easily criticizing them.

For example. Rabbis very seldom gave sermons in their shuls (small synagogues). Traveling preachers, called story tellers would do this. They would give their sermons in simple language so that all could understand. They would include in their sermons examples and nice stories and would sing with special melodies, using the vernacular of the time.

Such a performance would be an insult to the rabbi. Usually the rabbi gave only 2 sermons a year. One on the Great Shabbat, the Shabbat before Passover, and one on the Shabbat of Repentance, between Rosh Hashana and Yom Kippur. These sermons were aimed at the learned ones. The other listeners only understood partially, but this was enough for them.

[Page 25]

Also, the rabbi did not refrain from teaching a lesson to Jews in foreign lands when he traveled to America. There was no lack of Jews studying in America. One of them gave a class in Gemara, a second Jew gave a class on a chapter of the Mishna, the third lectured on the Ein Yaakov and on the Torah with commentary by Rashi.

> Rashi (Rabbi Shlomo ben Itzhak), born 1040, died 1105 CE, was a great commentator on the Torah, using his detailed knowledge of Hebrew grammar to tease out subtle meanings from the text.

When the rabbi would, once in a while, give a lesson, he would present a subtle argument as a problem to the students. But, teaching had no interest for him.

In the larger towns the rabbi would have assistants who carried out many of the rabbi's functions. For example: ruling on a personal question, clarifying Torah laws, performing marriages and divorces. But the more difficult questions would be referred to the town's rabbi. In the small villages like Horodetz, the rabbi performed all these functions by himself.

The rabbi had a special helper, called a "shammes", but who was called the "court house shammes" because he was mainly used by the rabbi when someone had to be called before the rabbinical court or for any other important thing. In cases when the rabbi decided to call a meeting of the entire village for an important purpose, the shammes would go into every study hall and call out, in the rabbi's name, for all to come to the meeting. Everyone obeyed the call and immediately went to the meeting. Also the shammes would post notices in the study halls when the rabbi wanted to tell his people of some important ideas.

If there was a very serious matter about which he felt strongly, the rabbi would use his authority and send his shammes into every study hall to stop the praying. The shammes would yell out, "The rabbi has requested that you stop praying." The crowd would become confused. They would all need to come to the rabbi and then go to the meeting and decide what should be done. After the meeting they would all return to the study hall to study the Torah portion of the week and then end the service.

Among all of the other tools with which the rabbi of those times used to exert his influence, the ban (issur) or excommunication (herem) had the greatest force. To emphasize the importance of the decision for a meeting, the rabbi issued, through his shammes, a ban on the study halls during the time of prayers. Every Jew obeyed it with great respect and had great fear to ignore it.

The rabbi would use the "issur" when the ritual slaughterers in the village had an argument. The rabbi would use the "herem" very infrequently, only in exceptional circumstances. The word "herem" alone would generate so much fear that people were even afraid to say the word. In place of it they would say "hit", using the first letter of the dreaded word "herem."

Rabbi Moshe Tzvi

by Rabbi Mordechai Greenberg

Translated by Eugene Sucov

One hundred and fifty years ago, Horodetz became, with respect to rabbis, associated with the nearby village of Antipolya (7km from Horodetz) when the rabbi of Horodetz, Moshe Tzvi, also became the rabbi of Antipolya.

Rabbi Moshe Tzvi was the son of Rabbi Israel Rabinovitz, who had descended from a long line of great and respected rabbis. Rabbi Moshe Tzvi was considered to be one of the great rabbis of his time, great in revealed and in hidden things and was called a great master of Kabbalah (mystical Judaism). Rabbi Moshe Tzvi Hirsh was known not only in the local vicinity but even further away. Ordinary people would travel to him for a blessing, an amulet, or a remedy, while rabbis would consult with him on rabbinic or congregational matters.*

Rabbi Moshe Tzvi didn't produce any books, but after he died, his son and successor, Rabbi Yehoshua Yaakov, assembled a booklet called "Surprising Things in Halakha and Tradition", from his father's writings. In this small booklet we can already see the greatness of his learning.

Rabbi Moshe Tzvi didn't split hairs (during analysis of Talmudic arguments) in order to show his range of knowledge in the "sea of the Talmud", but rather would study a Gemara, a Rambam (Maimonides), or a Tosafot (later commentators on the Talmud) not according to its surface meaning (but rather according to its deeper or secret meaning). And, once in a while, he would take help from Ibn Ezra (medieval Jewish poet and philosopher).

An extremely clever concept is his unique explanation of the phrase, "Like a piece of pomegranate" (from Song of Songs, chapter 4, verse 3). The sages say of this phrase that "the simple Jews are as full of mitzvot (commandments) as a pomegranate has seeds" This phrase is very difficult and it doesn't interpret easily. (A simple interpretation is that the pomegranate is supposed to have 613 seeds, which are the number of mitzvot.) But Rabbi Moshe Tzvi interprets it this way (using Gematria, where Hebrew letters have numerical equivalents). "Pomegranate" (Rimon) has a value of 296. ":Piece" (pelah) has a value of 148, which is one half of the pomegranate value, and which has the same value as flour (kemah). Thus, the phrase means "The observant Jews give flour", that is, they support the Talmud sages. Therefore they will receive a half divine reward in the world to come.

Rabbi Moshe Tzvi stayed in Horodetz and also fulfilled his rabbinic duties in Antipolya. When his son, Rabbi Yehoshua Yaakov was 20 years of age, Rabbi Moshe Tzvi transferred the responsibility of Horodetz to him. Rabbi Moshe Tzvi moved to Antipolya in about 1822, where he remained as the rabbi until his death.

* A. Ben Ezra's comment: As an example, they brought Rabbi Moshe Tzvi from Antopole and Rabbi Yaakov Lifshitz from Minsk to certify the muddled signature on Rabbi Shaul Karliner's will.

[Page 26]

Rabbi Yehoshua Yaakov

Rabbi Mordechai Greenberg

Translated by Eugene Sucov

Rabbi Yehoshua Yaakov was man, small in stature but a giant in knowledge. Always he could be found in a happy mood. He would tell a joke mixed in with words of Torah. His jokes were very clever. Rabbi Yehoshua Yaakov was altogether happy. He didn't want to change his position of village rabbi to that of a town rabbi. He only wanted to sit quietly in Horodetz, learning (studying) and writing books.

Rabbi Yehoshua Yaakov was altogether happy. He didn't want to change his position of village rabbi to that of a town rabbi. He only wanted to sit quietly in Horodetz, learning (studying) and writing books.

Rabbi Yehoshua Yaakov authored the following books. "Yehoshua Yaakov" (1868), "Beautiful Sayings", "Generations of Yaakov", and "Tent of Yaakov" (all 1889), "House of Yaakov" (1892), "Dwellings of Yaakov" (1894), "Yakkov's Sources" (1896), and finally "Listen Yaakov" (1901). The contents of his books consisted of various commentaries and novel interpretations of Torah and Gemara.

He received no income from his books. He didn't even recover his costs. Where did he, nevertheless, get money for printing books? For this purpose he had a special source. Whoever brought him enough money could print his books.

Rabbi Yehoshua Yaakov was famous as a great tzaddik (saintly man). His name was known far and wide. He would receive many letters from sick people with pleas for help. Many sick people would come alone to him asking him to bless them and to pray for them. Some of them were suffering from epilepsy. He would give them amulets and for this he would get a donation. He used to have a special pushke (alms box) in which he would throw the money. This money was used to publish his books. He never took money from poor people. He would also announce everyone, so that he would not completely forget them. He would also go to a doctor. (This is a significant comment since his people were using amulets to cure diseases, not doctors.)

The writing of amulets he had taken over from his father, who had a very large following. What is the basis for amulets? They were well read documents which were written and signed with the initials of a posek (Bible expert) and certified with his sealing wax.

Here is an example of an amulet which was written and certified by the initials of a Bible expert. "If you will listen carefully to the voice of the Lord your God, and do what is right in His eyes, and will give ear to his commandments, and obey his statutes, I will put none of these diseases, which I had put upon the Egyptians, upon you. For I am the God that heals you."(Exodus, chapter 15, verse 26, weekly portion "Bo"). The sick person would hold the amulet in his pocket or hide it in his clothing.

It is interesting to note that both brothers, Rabbi Yehoshua Yaakov and Dr. Israel Michal Rabinovitz, both healed epilepsy. One with an old, traditional method and the second with a new scientific medicine method.

The rabbi's income came from selling salt. In later years he, as shopkeeper, changed over to yeast and candles. (The rabbi's wife was occupied with this). Further income for the rabbi came from responding to questions on the application of Halakha and from weddings. From each 100 rubles of dowry he would get 18 gilder. The largest dowry in those times was up to 300 rubles. He also got income from selling hametz for Passover. Jews would bring their hametz (bread or other forbidden to eat food) to the rabbi so he could remove it from their possession during Passover. The rabbi, in turn, would fictionally "sell" the hametz to a gentile, with the understanding that after Passover the gentile would return the hametz. It was customary to make a donation to the rabbi for handling each transaction.

Thanks to the railroad station which was near the village, many travelers came to weddings inside Horodetz from neighboring towns. And, thanks to the river which flowed inside the villages, there were many liberated merchants who would temporarily stop work and stop the rabbinic courts. Because of the river, people would come to Horodetz to receive a "get"(bill of divorce). A "get" must be written in a town which has flowing water. Not only "gets" but also marriage contracts (ketubot) had to be written in such a town. The reason is that the get or the ketuba identified the location of the marriage or divorce by a fixed, geographic feature, such as a river.

All these things were a source of income for the rabbi.. However, the rabbi was not a rich man. While the money did not stop coming in, his hand was always open for everyone who stretched out a hand to him.

The order of Rabbi Yehoshua Yaakov's house was like this. Get up every day and study. After studying came praying. In his house there was always a minyan (prayer quorum of 10 men). In his last years he was losing his sight so he would study less and less. In writing his books he would dictate to someone who would write it down.

He had large library, an inheritance from his ancestors. Among them were many books on Kabbalah and also rare books, among them, very old books. Some were several hundred years old, written by hand, and bound with parchment covers. For Passover we would take down the books and lay them outside, along the street, so they got plenty of ventilation. They would take up a lot of space on the street. Each passerby would stop and examine the books with awe and reverence and with pride in their old rabbi, who had so many books.

Rabbi Yehoshua Yaakov, of blessed memory, lived for 100 years and was the rabbi of Horodetz for nearly 80 years. To his funeral came rabbis from all the neighboring towns. They eulogized him and together with the entire village, accompanied him to his final resting place. On his grave was installed a memorial stone with a brick protection canopy.

[Page 27]

The Death of the "Old Rabbi"

By Alter Elman

Translated by Eugene Sucov

It happened on Wednesday evening of the week identified by the weekly portion "Life of Sarah", in 1902. The village was immediately aroused by shouts of "The old rabbi has died!" In truth there was no surprise since the rabbi was already very old. Some have said that he was 94 years old, while others said he was much older. In addition, he was already half blind and his nephew, Rabbi Yaakov Hayim Greenberg, was already performing his rabbinical duties. The world became speechless for the moment, as though it received a hard blow. For nearly 80 years he was rabbi of Horodetz, for 3 to 4 generations he had been their only rabbi, and now he was dead.

Beryl Rodetzer, the richest man in the village, immediately sent a carriage with a few good drivers to Kobrin to bring to the funeral the Rabbi Meyer Atlas and the Judge Rabbi Pininke (the son of Rabbi Eliyahu Shick). And from Antipolya came the rabbis David Schwartz and R. Hirsh.

[Page 28]

Meanwhile the village home owners gathered to discuss how to carry out the last will of the "Old Rabbi" who had requested the congregation to transfer everything to his nephew, Rabbi Hayim, after he died. Quickly, a letter inviting Rabbi Hayim to become their village rabbi was created for Rabbi Hayim and the home owners were satisfied.

On Friday morning, quite early, was the funeral. After the coffin was carried out of the rabbi's house, the shofar was blown, and the funeral began. Children and mourners all came to the funeral.

The first to speak was Rabbi Meyer Atlas. He began with a quotation from Jeremiah, chapter 9, verse 20, " For death is come into our windows". Just as a window shields us from cold and at the same time brings in light, so is a tzaddik. He is the shield of the generation. And when the tzaddik leaves us, we have no one to shield us.

When we reached the synagogue, we carried the coffin inside and Rabbi Pininke spoke. He started with a quotation from the portion of the week, "Life of Sarah", Exodus, chapter 24, verse 1."Abraham was old with many days." Just as Abraham was old with many days, so did Rabbi Yehoshua Yaakov come with his many days to his final rest at home where he had spent his days studying.

And at the cemetery, Rabbi Meyer Atlas handed to Rabbi Hayim the "invitation letter" and the crowd wished him congratulations and good luck. Pain and joy were intermingled in us. Everyone felt that the young rabbi, Rabbi Hayim, would not shame the village which was known for the high quality of it rabbis.

The congregation was not disappointed. After the 7 days of Shiva (sitting in mourning), the new rabbi gave a eulogy. Everyone came to the synagogue to hear the eulogy from the new rabbi. He chose to start with the quotation from Exodus, chapter 34, verse 9, "And Yehoshua bin Nun was full of wisdom because Moshe had laid his hands on him". This was a very appropriate quotation because the name of the "Old Rabbi" was Yehoshua and his father, who had certified him, was called Moshe.

The eulogy, which was filled with Halakha (directions for how to live an observant life) and Aggada (moralistic stories) made a very strong impression on the listeners. After this, one was reminded of the other eulogies. From then on, Rabbi Yaakov Hayim, whom we called Rabbi Hayim, became the official village rabbi till the month of Elul (September) 1915, when he and all the Jews of Horodetz evacuated the village. And we, the Horodetz Jews, have become unworthy of seeing him and warming ourselves in the warmth of his Torah. May he be a good defender for us (in the heavenly court).

The old Rabbi's Ohel

(Structure over the tomb of an important person)

Rabbi Yehoshua Yaakov z"l [Rabinovitz]
(painted especially for the book of Horodets
by Israel Zussman)

[Page 29]

The Wisdom Of The "Old Rabbi"

by *Ein haKoray

*This is a pseudonym

Translated by Eugene Sucov

If we want to know the face of a certain generation, we need to examine its rabbinic literature. In this literature is reflected the material and intellectual struggles of the people. From the rabbinic literature we can discern also the cultural level of the generation as well as its hopes and ideals. It is not futile for one to speculate about the histories in the rabbinic "Questions and Answers" from various times, because, in them, lay, wrapped up, entire life stories of the people. Through their words are vividly brought out the day by day life of all social levels, from the teacher to the simplest Jews and Jewesses for an entire year, with their various problems. And, not only in the "Questions and Answers" literature, which is established by the rabbis, the great teachers, but also in the rabbinic commentaries is there a lot of material with which the culture researchers and the historians can form a picture of the life and aspirations of the Jew, from his thinking and his anxieties. In the interpretation of a simple comment lies suddenly an entire chapter of the Jewish story, and from the analysis of a commentary, can we, many times, find out the ideals and threads of a certain epoch in Jewish life. In a Talmudic argument about a statement or a legend we see not only the thought process of the author, but also the intellectual position of the entire land in those times.

*"Each Generation and Its Interpreters". Each generation has its own commentaries and their analysis is, according to the next generation, a kind of sermon.

> *This is the translation of the title of a book (published in Hebrew in the early 1900s) that attacks the Wissenschaft (scientific) school of Bible analysis, in which study of the different styles of language usage suggests that there were 4 different human authors of the Bible.) In Hebrew, the title becomes a play on words, using "dor", which means "generation" and "dorshav", which means "its interpreters".

Each generation has its own commentaries and their analysis is, according to the next generation, a kind of sermon. It is not sensible logic to compare Talmudic arguments in a book of Halakha to an argument in a book of Legends. For example, the story of Bilham's donkey created an argument between 2 scholars of the Talmudic period, in which each of them argued according to a fixed method. But the story about the ring, with which Ahashverus decorated Haman, was analyzed according to the laws of buying and selling.

The 8 books by the "Old Rabbi" are an encyclopedia of all sorts of novel interpretations of the Torah, which rabbis from various generations have written. There is found in there, pure and deep Halakhic things, extracted according to the general principles of logic. In his books we find forceful interpretations of Biblical phrases and commentaries with which modern commentators can easily agree. But, we also find in there legalistic hair splitting, which would take a nice story and interpret it according to various methods from the Gemara. This last is clearly a small percent in comparison with the many intellectual pearls which lay hidden in the "Old Rabbi's" books.

The sources which the "Old Rabbi" consulted are quite simple and well known. They are: the Babylonian Talmud, the Jerusalem Talmud, commentaries by Rambam, Maharasha and Reb Nakhman, by Tosafot (later commentators) and a little bit from the Amoraim (last generation of Talmud rabbis). He also had some information about Ibn Ezra and grammar, although he never consulted a grammar book.

How is it then that explanations by the Dubner preacher had an influence on the "Old Rabbi"? Very often the Old Rabbi consulted him about his methods, which illustrated a maxim with an example. Immediately from the examples we can see that the Old Rabbi was familiar with real life in the world. He had eyes and ears which saw and heard what was going on in the world. And he was not such an innocent that one would be able to fool him.

From many examples in his books we see that he was skilled in Kabbalah and in Chassidic books. He operated with their methods of Initials and Gematria. It happens also that his straight forward wisdom prevented him from getting caught up in the various analyses by Initials. He said they were no more than "foolish ways".

The analytic wisdom of Rabbi Yehoshua Yaakov also captured errors in commentaries by Rashbam and in books of other commentators. His corrections were founded on his wisdom. We find also in his books, rationalistic clarifications. He says that the sages often times criticized too much, in order that we should keep ourselves from a sin. Many times have the wise ones extracted a ruling from a verse of the Bible (psok) which is true (in its setting) but the ruling of the sages is not found in there. They had clearly wanted to attach the ruling to the "psok" in order that it should be more easily remembered. The same is also the case with the popular conception of God which we find in the Bible. That God has feet, sits on a throne, and the like, is no more than a popularization of divinity so that the simple people should understand better.

Also we find the Old Rabbi giving a modern interpretation of a saying of the sages or of Rashi. And when a comment from the sages pleased him not, he says so, bluntly and undisguised. If he couldn't understand the simple meaning of a Tosafot comment he is not ashamed to admit it. The same applies to Rashi.

But knowledge alone is not enough. The central purpose of life is to perform mitzvot (God's commandments). In addition to this, one must educate ones self and learn Talmudic arguments. However, arguing for the sake of arguing is not so righteous; much better is it to perform mitzvot. Performing mitzvot is the purpose of living. And because of this (attitude) the Old Rabbi did not approve of flagellation or fasting because they hindered the performance of mitzvot. He goes even further to say that everything God created is only for the benefit of observant people.

What is the definition of observant? What shall a Jew do in order to become an observant Jew? Can a person really be a complete Jew?

Rabbi Yehoshua Yaakov understood that a world of pure tzadikim (holy men) is impossible because when all the faithful only sat and learned faith, the rest of the world did not have any observance. Therefore he held that work and learning should go hand-in-hand, since the one who works and simultaneously learns and also does mitzvot is a much greater person than the other learners and mitzvah doers who consider themselves more worthy than the others.

The Old Rabbi understood very well that it was impossible for observant people to do all the mitzvot, therefore he held that only through unity and peace can we be able to observe the entire Torah. He knew that not all people are the same. Some people can be corrected without being offended. But especially intelligent people can be more tainted than an ordinary person. One can be tainted even by one word which is not pure. The person may be a totally attractive teacher, but if his mouth is not pure, his teaching will also be not pure. Therefore, the Old Rabbi suggests that one should incorporate the following 3 good rules. 1. Modesty; 2. Keep yourself from speaking evil about others; 3. Jewish unity. Because we didn't cling to the way we should be in the above 3 rules, we are in exile.

Rabbi Yehoshua Yaakov held that too much modesty for a Talmud scholar is not worthwhile, since, if he takes for himself already too much praise for his modesty, he forgets that praise is only for the Torah.

Speaking ill of another does not bring peace, and if there is no peace, one cannot observe the commandments of the Torah. Therefore one must love the Jewish people, since loving the people is the foundation of the entire Torah. Who has hated a Jew is also grieving God, since it is impossible to have love for God and not have love for Jews. He goes further and says,"He who does evil to another is also grieving God even more, since he has sinned against God."

He was very forceful in his condemnation of those who guarded themselves against eating pig meat, other treif (non-kosher) foods and carrion, but made themselves unaware of "baseless hatred", even though this sin is equivalent to many sins. Rabbi Yehoshua Yaakov held that the sin of "baseless hatred" ranks above all the other sins together. And he provides a cure. If a person wants to cleanse himself of sin, he should love everyone, even the one who sinned against him. Instead of guarding ones self from sinning, says the Old Rabbi, guard against a good friend. And here he provides the proverb, "Protect me from my friends. From my sins will I alone guard myself", and the selection from Psalm 118, verse 8, "It is better to take refuge in the Lord than to trust in man."

The major principle of the Old Rabbi's way came to expression in a special booklet which contained 62 essays of appreciation. The number 62 is, by using Gematria, equal to "Very Good" in Hebrew.

Very Good = Tov M'Od; Tov = tet,vav,bet and M'od = mem, aleph, daled. The numerical values of each of the letters is as follows:

Tet=9, vav=6, bet=2, mem=40, aleph=1, daled=4.

The various essays were not only concerning God and man but also how a man should behave, even to an animal. He should not beat it and not load it too heavily. The Old Rabbi not only preached this ethical behavior, he acted upon it. It is told, that one time, going from the Beit Midrash with his tallit sack under his arm, he saw how a wagon driver was pulling his horse which had gotten stuck in the mud. The Old Rabbi went over and helped push the wagon. When helping another, he says, we have to help everyone, even the enemy. And we shall not make a distinction between Jew and Gentile. And, if one is insulted by another, he should keep silent and not respond. And, conversely, he should behave kindly to the enemy. And not only should a man not curse another, but even when he is alone he should not curse.

The Old Rabbi warned against anger, miserliness and depression. He worried about the A. D. Gordon (leader of a non-religious, Zionist organization) rules which embittered the people's lives. He always looked for ways to improve the people's fate. Thanks to his psychological point of view, he overlooked several conventionalities of his time. For example, he demanded that the parents should teach their children crafts and trades, in order that the children would be able to support themselves. "A trade is nothing to be ashamed of."

The Old Rabbi spoke out against a commonly accepted custom in his time, namely, taking dowry. He said, by way of explanation, "Look not at money, take not a wife with a defect just because she has money. Better to take a beautiful wife so that there will be love and peace between man and wife."

And the Old Rabbi also opposed laws and customs which were nick-named "from my generation to yours", as, for example, taking or giving presents with a business connection, or selling the "hametz" (food which was not kosher for Passover) through the rabbi. He held that it was simply deception.

Interesting is his opinion about praying. He held not with those who fool themselves in praying. He said, "Better to pray a little bit, but with focused intention, rather than praying a lot, quickly and hastily. God will fill in the letters and the vowel signs."

In the forewords to his books the Old Rabbi asks that we should not lay his books aside and that we should study them.

May this short appreciation of the Old Rabbi's works lead to increased studying of his books and following of the principles which he had inscribed in them. These principles come from a great humanist who the world didn't know. It is worth while to make a greater study of the life and work of the Old Rabbi, Yehoshua Yaakov Rabinovitz.

[Page 32]

The Rav, Rabbi Yaakov Khayim, of blessed memory

by The Rav, Mordekhai Greenberg

Translated by Eugene Sucov

The Rav, Rabbi Yehoshua Yaakov, obm, had 3 sons and 4 daughters, which his first wife, Bonya, had birthed. The oldest daughter was called Itke Rakhel, may she rest in peace. She had all the qualities of her father, obm, his natural humor, his intelligence and his cleverness. She interested herself in helping the ones living difficult lives in the village and in giving charity to the needy.

Itke Rekhil (that's how we called her) had a daughter, Esther, who married the Rav, Rabbi Yaakov Khayim, obm, the future heir of the rabbinical seat, on which Rav Yehoshua Yaakov, obm, had sat for 18 years.

The Rav Yaakov Khayim, obm, was born in Antipolya. His parents were observant Jews and philanthropic. In his early youth they died in an epidemic which had then raged. His grandfather, after whom he was named, was a great scholar and exceptionally zealous in performing the mitzvot. He always sat in the study hall and learned. He would memorize, every day, 40 pages of Gemara.

The Rav Yaakov Khayim had studied in his youth with the Antipolya Rav, Rabbi Pinkhas Michael, obm, who became very interested in him. After this, he was admitted to advanced learning of Biblical interpretation in the Kovne kollel (graduate school for older and better students). The Rav Yitzkhak Elkhanan, obm, the Kovne rabbi, wrote about him that he was a "genius" (ilui) Rav.

When he arrived in Horodetz, already betrothed to the old Rav's daughter, he became attracted to the rabbinate, rather than to full time study. The Rav Yehoshua Yaakov, was already old, and from the beginning helped only him. Soon all the rabbinical functions were given over to him. The old Rav had arranged a small salary for him. In his home, there was also a small business, which the rebbitzen (rabbi's wife) and her mother, would run. From all this, the rabbi eked out a marginal income.

The Rav Yaakov Khayim was a tall man with a patriarchal appearance. His beard was a little yellowish in his youth and middle age. From his countenance radiated holiness and goodness. He was loved by everyone, and influenced everyone with his friendly attitude and modesty. He was simply running away from empty honors.

He interested himself in everything, large or small. He developed feelings for each one of the unfortunate people who came through Horodetz.

> This comment is in reference to the disasters that befell the Jewish communities in what was called the Jewish Pale of Settlement at the beginning of World War 1. Jews were not allowed to leave the Pale without a special passport, so all the Jews of the Russian empire were collected there. The Pale lay between the western lands of the Russian empire and the eastern lands of the German (Prussian) empire. When the war started, the opposing armies would cross into the Pale, burning, scavenging and killing Jews on their way to meet the enemy. Jews ran from their homes to escape the scourge and traveled to nearby Jewish communities that had not yet been destroyed. These are the refugees that passed through Horodetz.

He did what was appropriate to help needy people. In the worst of times he would bring guests to his house, even escaped criminals, and give them food to eat and money. Afterwards, with his friendliest wishes and blessings, they departed. He followed after them, uttering blessings on their future travels.

The refugees were fallen people, outcasts who had lost their livelihood because of the war. They would travel from town to town and from village to village looking for help. They were unable to separate themselves and go alone to the small houses and ask for money. They felt themselves beaten and without purpose. A favorable word was, for them, a soothing balm, which strengthened them and uplifted their spirits. The Rav Yaakov Khayim, obm, understood this very well. He would occupy himself with them, asking about their problems, hearing them completely and showing them his sympathy.

His usual schedule was as follows: He would wake up every night about 3 am, when everyone else was still sleeping, to sit over a Gemara and learn. The whole village was sunk in a deep sleep but the Rav's house was lit up and the sound of his learning carried itself outside.

> Since the Gemara was written in Aramaic and had no punctuation, the correct intonation when chanting the passage in Yiddish or Hebrew, proved that you understood the flow of the arguments within the passage.

When it became day, the Rav began to prepare for praying. Coming out of the synagogue he sometimes gave to the townspeople a rabbinic commentary. As soon as he finished with "questions" he would immediately return to his studying. At no time did he sit idle and talk foolish or simple words to his friends. He always studied.

There were times when he was troubled about his eyes. But this didn't stop him from studying. When he was not able to look in a book, he would study from memory. Thanks are due to the village doctor, Naftali Weissman, who took him to Warsaw several times to a great eye professor and sat with him while his sick eyes were treated.

[Page 33]

In Horodetz there was a group of people who subscribed to the Hebrew language newspapers, HaMelitz and HaTsfirah. The newspapers circulated in a very tight circle of people, who transferred them from one to the other. These people would very often get excited about issues of the time and would have public discussions about them. The Rav, even though he was entirely involved in his studies, found it worthwhile to occasionally attend several of the discussions. He didn't consider it foolish words. He was accepting of each person's interests. He answered with quietness, and incidentally, as a guest, would throw in some words of Torah.

In the early years of the Zionist movement some of the people expected a quick establishment of a Jewish State in Eretz Israel. The Rav joined himself to the pessimists. His argument was that the hoped for salvation would not come for a while, but slowly. It would take many years. He had concluded this from the fact that the first aliya to Eretz Israel had taken 40 years till the Jews set foot on the Promised Land. And, afterwards, it took a very long time till they were able to exploit the entire land,

Furthermore, from a logical point of view, the moment had not yet arrived. The kings of Europe were hatefully opposed to the Jews so they would prevent it from happening.

Finally, his opinion was that the hoped for salvation would depend on the morals of the people, through which God's help would come. He had, to support this opinion, various verses from Tanakh, Talmud and

Midrash. But, with respect to the settlers already in Eretz Israel, he was very supportive. He would always say that we must buy what land we can and that more Jews should settle in Eretz Israel.

The Rav would give 2 lectures a year: one on Shabbat HaGadol (before Pesach) and the other on Shabbat Shuva (before Yom Kippur). Once in a while he would tell a story about a great Rav. Mostly his talks were filled with "pilpul" (Talmudic nit picking), and practically no one in his audience understood him.

Before he gave the lecture he would consult the Talmud portions and commentaries on which his lecture was based. Here is a summary of one of his lectures.

> A person who holds himself better than other persons is full of arrogance. He is better only in his own estimation. But it is an available resource for these people. When he just looks over those who are higher than him, he will quickly realize that he has not what to be proud of, and his arrogance will disappear.
>
> A person who contains the evil trait of jealousy, his jealousy is greater than him. Such a person, who is entirely for himself, needs to observe those he thinks are lower than him. He will quickly recognize that he needs to be satisfied with his own situation and that he has nothing to be jealous of.
>
> Now, what are his options? As the same person has both bad traits of arrogance and jealousy, he holds himself to be better than others and is still jealous of others. What kind of resource is available for these people? Where should he look? He should look above, to someone higher than him so he, in truth, can rid himself from this trait of arrogance. He would find out that he is not as superior as he thought. He will realize that he is nothing.
>
> Now that his arrogance is gone his trait of jealousy emerges. His jealousy strengthens and he will be envious of all those who are higher than him. He should again look above, to that which is higher than him, so that he will free himself from the trait of jealousy. Then he will not have anyone to be jealous of. But then the trait of arrogance will emerge again. He will, in his fantasy, continue to stay higher than everyone, and become a real "master of arrogance."
>
> For such a person there is no cure. About him, the verse from Psalms, 101:6 says: " Whosoever slanders his neighbor, him will I destroy; whoso is haughty of eye and proud of heart, him will I not suffer."
>
> A person whose eyes are full of jealousy and whose heart is filled with arrogance cannot learn. Such a person finds himself good and also wants everything that other people have. He has a dilemma. Theory is not appropriate for dealing with such a problem. Therefore the aforementioned person can only find a way out through controlling himself."

In the year 5671, on the 27th of the month of Menahem Av, (Aug. 21,1911) the rebbitzen died. This created a very bad situation for the Rav, but in his studying he found consolation and encouragement. And this is how he filled his life in Horodetz till the onset of World War 1.

It was a Shabbat in the month of Elul (September), 1915, when the entire village became full of Cossacks. Heaven and earth and Cossacks. A great fear enveloped all the Jews. All the houses in Horodetz were burning. The village was surrounded by fire on all sides. The grenades were crackling. We heard strongly the shooting of the cannons. It stopped in one barrage, but the war had already caused the end of the village. An order arrived that all its residents must immediately leave Horodetz on account of the anticipated joining of the hated armies.

[Page 34]

In spite of the tragic situation everyone came to pray on Shabbat, early in the morning, just like always on Shabbat. On Sunday, early in the morning, all the Jews left the town. The journey was terrible. The Rav and his family traveled 3 weeks until they came to Katerinaslav.

In Katerinaslav were only 2 shuls which prayed in the Ashkenazi style. One of these shuls immediately named the Rav Yaakov Khayim their rabbi, with great pride. He would lecture on Mishnayot and Gemara and occasionally give a commentary for a particular purpose. His schedule in Katerinaslav was the same as it had been in Horodetz. All day long he sat and studied.

In honor of the arrival of the Rav, the leaders of the shul created a charity fund, greater than those of the other shuls. It had a special help committee for the entire city. For those shuls that had no committee, this shul became the model for all the other shuls in Katerinalsav.

Rav Yaakov Khayim died in Katerinaslav on Shabbat morning, the 7th of Elul, in the year 5679 (Sept. 22, 1919) at the age of 103 years.

The funeral was the next morning, on Sunday. The rabbis of the town, along with all the out of town rabbis, gathered to pay him their last respects. They gave eulogies in his shul and in the cemetery. All the businesses from any town in which he had lived were closed. All were able to come to the funeral. But only the rabbis busied themselves with his body.

"May His Soul Be Bound Up in Eternal Life"

Facsimile of the Rashi section from a sermon by R' Khayim

Author's note:

I thank the Horodetz group "Yehoshua Yaakov" from New York for installing a stone over the grave of the Rav Yaakov Khayim. The grave is located in the cemetery of Katerinaslav at section 25, row 5, #33.

Does the grave still exist? Haven't the Germans (cursed be their name) demolished his grave just as they have demolished all other Jewish graves?

Only in the future world will we know.

The children who survived him are Dr. Tzvi Greenberg, a writer of various articles, who was killed at the Russian front, and his daughter, Reyzl, who lives in New York.

[Page 35]

The Last Rabbi

by the Rav, Shalom Podolevsky

Translated by Eugene Sucov

The last rabbi of Horodetz was the genius rabbi, Ari Greenman. He was from Antipolya, son of a blacksmith and son-in-law of a rich man of Brisk (Brest-Litovsk). When he first came to Horodetz, right after the first World War, as a temporary refugee, he was quite young. But he soon remained in Horodetz permanently. He was a great genius and a holy man. His interpretations would amaze the greatest people. His memory was so good that as soon as he saw something he already understood the thought. He was really an expert on Shas (an abbreviation of the "Six Orders" (shisha sederim) of the Talmud). He had also a very sharp mind which would amaze the rabbis and yeshiva students of the nearby villages with his questions and learning. Also, he was zealous in his practice of the commandments. He would learn day and night. His holiness was so great that he obeyed every law in the Shulkhan Arukh ("The Arranged Table", an organized collection of the 613 commandments in the Bible). He was a man pure and of sterling qualities. And our village was very satisfied with him.

The rabbi had no children so he arranged for a neighbor orphan to be with him in his house. She became like his only child. Later, when his wife died and the orphan married and moved away to Argentina, he was again alone. His home was the greatest and most beautiful in Horodetz. It was facing the plaza, where had stood, before World War 1, the small synagogue for the Jews of Kobrin. After the war the Korinner Jews bought it back using money they got sent from America. But the Horodetz Jews determined that it rightfully belonged to the Rav. His house was a home for wise men. Whenever a rabbi or a traveler who was a Rav or a good Jew came to the village, they all stayed at the rabbi's house.

The rabbi received no salary from the village. His only income was from buying and selling khametz (food not kosher for Passover), selling gifts for Purim and once in a while he received a gift from his American brother.

The Rav behaved in a very unusual way which generated wonderment and amazement in many people but mainly from the rabbis of the surrounding villages. Namely, he had a cow which he alone would drive to pasture early in the morning, at the same time as did the town leaders. They would stay and look while the Rav himself milked the cow. He would also raise does. He loved very much living animals, but mainly he loved small children from whom he would get much enjoyment.

Our Horodetzers respected and honored him greatly, knowing what kind of genius and holy man he was, and how other rabbis consulted with him.

His plainness and simplicity only increased the love and closeness of the village towards him, feeling that he was one of them. They felt, without a doubt, the same as all the other Jews of the village.

The Rav is no more, even his house is gone. May, at least, be immortalized his handwriting and the official stamp of the last rabbi of Horodetz.

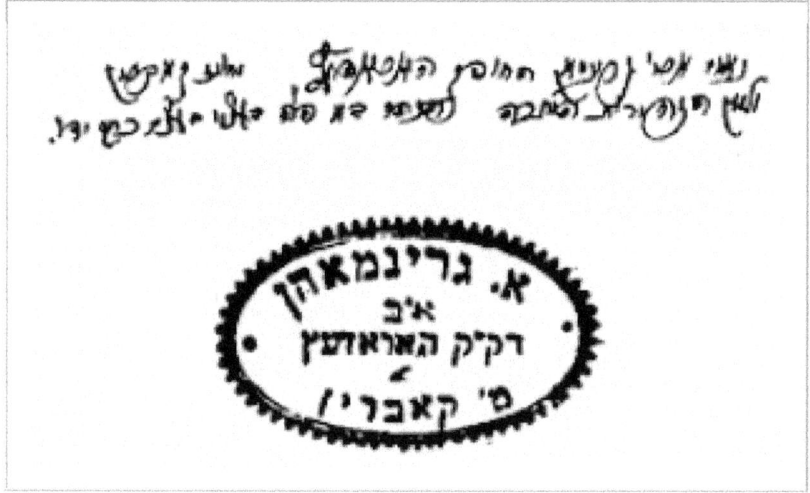

Facsimile of the last Rabbi's handwriting

Stamp translated:
A. GREENMAN
of Horodetz village
Province of Kobrin

[Page 37]

Synagogues

The Cold *Shul* [synagogue]

(Memories)

by Rabbi Dr. Yaakov Bosnyak

Translated by Hannah Kadmon

[Translator's notes in square brackets]

The Cold Synagogue
(drawn by Israel Zussman, based on guidelines of the old Jews of Horodets)

My shtetl Horodets boasted about its old cold *shul* [synagogue]. Passing by wood-merchants who stayed for Sabbath in Horodets - to ferry their merchandise to Danzig through our river - never missed praying in this *shul*, regarded as a real holy place. The Staliner Chassidim use to boast that R' Aharon Karliner or R' Aharon the Big, when they visited town, they went with all the Chassidim from the *Shtibl* [small house of prayer] to pray in this *shul*.

The *shul* was famous not because of its architecture which was quite simple, but because it was old. Nobody knew when it had been built. The dominant opinion was that it was eight hundred years old. It was truly imposing with its antiquity and simplicity, inside and outside. I remember it quite well from the time before it was renovated. As a child, when my parents used to come from the village to the city [the author considers Horodets a city] for The Days of Awe [High Holidays, ten days from Rosh Hashanah to Yom Kippur], we prayed in the *shul* where my father had a "shtot" [reserved place] which he shared with my uncle Zalman, an inheritance from grandfather Menashe. I was enchanted by the *shul*'s appearance, as well as by its atmosphere of holiness and dignity. The *shul* was the tallest building in the city, about 50 foot tall from its base to the tip of its roof, and the windows were about 20 foot above ground level. The walls on the outside were grey-black because of old age. The external planks were cracked like the wrinkled face of an old man. In many spots moss and grass grew in the cracks and under the cornices of the shingled-roof there were many bird-nests made of the black greasy dirt from the surroundings.

Inside, the *shul* left a different impression. Since the windows were high above the heads of people, and the panes were of quite thick and unclean glass, the light of sun was never strong inside. People felt as if withdrawn from the world outside. A thick silence dominated the inside of the *shul* and created an atmosphere of awe. From time to time we could hear a faint hum of a dove or the squeal of a bird under the cornices. It seemed to me that what I heard was the "still small voice" that Elijah heard on Mount Carmel. [Kings I 19;12].

The walls were covered with various paints, but already quite blackened. On a background that was once white, but in my time was already yellow or blackened by dust, there were paintings of the four animals mentioned in a saying by Yehuda Ben Teima. [Mishna Avot 5;20 he said: "Be..."] strong as a tiger, light as an eagle, swift as a deer and brave as a lion [to serve the will of your father in the heavens"]. Some very well known prayers from the *sidur* [prayer-book] were inscribed within painted frames of various colors such as *brikh shmaya* [bless heavens], blessings of the Torah, *yehi ratzon* from the first of the month prayer, *yehi ratzon* read on Mondays and Thursdays, and other verses and graces. On the eastern wall, there were paintings of vines with big grapes. In my childhood I was certain that this was the bunch of grapes that the spies brought from the land of Canaan. On both sides of the Holy Ark, the motif of the vine with large leaves and bunches of grapes was carved of wood of various colors,

Large, heavy chandeliers hung on chains from the ceiling which was made up of thick yellow-grey planks resting upon heavy beams. The ceiling had never been painted. It looked as if the community did not have enough money to complete the work of decorating the ceiling.

The *shul* was approximately 50 foot wide from south to north, and about 75 foot long from east to west. The pulpit was positioned not in the middle – as is the custom of the Ashkenazi Jews - but rather in the first third from the entrance, in accord with the Sephardic Jews. * [see author's footnote at the end of the article] in the area between the pulpit and the lectern, on the two sides of the Holy ark, there were two big chests, about 3 X 5 foot, containing white sand. These chests had a twofold purpose: 1. on Yom Kippur, the landlords used to stick into the sand big *strinave* or wax candles. 2. The whole year round the two circumcisers of the shtetl used to hide in the sand the cut foreskins from the *bris* [circumcision ritual].

Around the walls, as well as around the chests, and near the pulpit area described above, there were benches made of thick boards, separated into "*shtet*" [sections, seats] above which were inscribed the names of the landlords to whom these sections belonged. Behind the pulpit there were no benches in the cold *shul*. Props, big and small, of various forms and colors, filled the *shul* close to all the benches.

The floor was made of hardened clay, or cement. It looked like a stone floor.

When I asked why they spread hay or straw for Yom Kippur, I got the explanation that it was to avoid bowing, or kneeling *kor'im* [kneeling in awe], on the stone-floor. If the floor is not covered, it [bowing or kneeling] would be just like idolatry.

In the past, there was no separate women's section. Only, the southern wall had an added *falush* [also pronounce *polish* = an anteroom or corridor in a synagogue] where some old women use to come to pray during the summer month, and on the Days of Awe. The *falush* was narrow, half-murky, and very dirty. The women could not hear the cantor in *shul*. There were only four square holes about 6 X 4 inches. When a woman would stand on the bench, she could peep in and catch a word said by the cantor.

A second narrow *falush*, adjoined the western wall, had right in its middle two heavy doors that led into the *shul*. That *falush* was divided into three parts. The middle part was the ante-room that led to the entrance. On its left and on its right, there were two small rooms that were never used. "*Sheimes*" [stray leafs of sacred books] and torn old *taleisim* [the prayer shawls] were scattered in the two rooms. The dust and dirt of tens or perhaps hundreds of years had accumulated there.

The area between the *shul* and the *Beit-Midrash* [the study house, where people used to pray as well] – about half an acre ground – was named the *shul*-yard, the place where all wedding ceremonies of the *shtetl* took place.

Before the end of the previous century [that means: the 19th century] this place was neglected. In a rainy weather it turned into a "sea" of black mud. In dry weather – full of holes, small pits, and dust. However, in the nineties a rumor started circulating that the old *shul* was about to collapse, God forbid, because of age. Many people thought that the walls started to curve. The landlords decided to strengthen and recondition the *shul*. That is when the *shul*-yard was also salvaged.

The head of all the workers of the community was Berl Rodetzer, the *gvir* [the richest man] of the shtetl. I remember him quite well. He was an elderly heavy Jew, of medium height, with hoary-grey hair and quite broad hips, adorned with a heavy silver chain on the *kamzelke* [vest; waistcoat]. He always used to carry a long fine caftan [worn by observant Jews], with a black common cap. For a man of his age and heavy figure he was quite lively and energetic. He threw himself into the job of renovating the *shul*.

I never knew from what source the shtetl got the needed sum of money for the job. One morning, I noticed with joy the piles of new logs – long wide boards – thrown around the *shul*. Ziske, the carpenter, with some helpers, started working. Work continued a whole summer. On Rosh Hashanah we already prayed in the renewed *shul*. The four walls, inside and outside, as well as the floor and the ceiling, were covered with new boards - The old *shul* in new clothes. Indeed, it had become cleaner and had more light, but the atmosphere of holiness was gone. The four animals and the blessings of *yehi Ratzon* as well as the heavy hanging chandeliers and the props, were no more there. The sand chests remained as before. The walls were bare. The eyes could not find anything to fix one's gaze on. Personally, I felt like in a big crate, made of plain boards stuck together, and the fragrance of fresh resin impregnated the atmosphere.

The *falush* next to the southern wall was completely removed. Only a tall cabin, with a roof above the stairs that led to the balcony, was left. It became the women's section. The *falush* next to the western wall stayed the same. Only one of the rooms was cleaned. It was used as a "*Kheder*" for a few *Gemore* children during the summer months.

The best and most beautiful improvement in the renovated *shul* was, in my opinion, the fence that Berl Rodetzer had built around the *shul*-yard. It was made of round patches all of one size, sturdily built, with broad gates leading to the left side of the *Beit-Midrash*. The gates were always locked. They were opened only for a wedding. Now, the *shul*-yard had a quite aesthetic appearance. The chickens that used to peck in the sand and the pigs that used take a nap in the mud – all disappeared. Fresh grass started growing and some dozens of trees were planted. Together with the tall wall of the *shul* it looked festive.

The access to the *shul* was through a side small street. In front – a run down fence of a garden that belonged to Uncle Benjamin., on the right – the fence of the *shul*-yard, and on the left – an old fence of a garden that belonged to the city bathhouse. The small street which had only five or six small old bunks, across from the bathhouse and the *"hegdesh"* [poor house; place where things were gathered for the poor], led to the cemetery. All funerals used to proceed past the *shul*. When the deceased was from among the distinguished landlords, they used to stop at the shul for the *hesped* [funeral oration].

The fact that the small street led also to the cemetery, left a strange psychological impression. The locals were sure that the dead from the cemetery got together to pray collectively in the *shul,* during the night, wearing their white shrouds and three-tasseled prayer shawls. [The dead are exempt from fulfilling religious rituals. The *talis* has four tassels on four corners. It is possible that in Horodets they used to bury the dead in the prayer shawl with only 3 tassels. It is also a common custom to cut off all four tassels for the burial…]

Of course, nobody saw the dead. However, everybody was sure that it was so. At night they did not walk past the *shul* but rather ran past it. Many men and women from the shtetl would, at all times, swear that they had heard all kinds of sorrowful sounds from the *shul*, when they walked past the *shul* in the darkness of night.

Even as a child I did not believe in the legends about the dead in *shul*. I craved to spend an hour alone in that holy place. It was so still and relaxed, so secluded from the world, so close to God. However, my strict mother never allowed me to do that. She strongly believed in the fantastic and "tall stories", and was quite adamant that the *beit midrash* was good enough and I was not allowed to go alone to the *shul*.

Not always could I resist the attempt to go and study an hour in the *shul*. From time to time I would steal in, when nobody was looking, lock the door and spend some hours with a *Gemore* or with another book. It was not difficult for me, because a relative of mine, Yedidya, son of Zalman, was the official attendant of the *shul*. On Fridays he used to come a bit earlier to stick the candles in the hanging candle-sticks and light them up. He was always the last person to leave the *shul* in order to lock the door. During the winter months, in the worst cold, he was the first among the "volunteers" - together with other young people - who, wearing a pelt, would form a *minyen* [ten men for the prayer] every Sabbath morning, so as not to shame the *shul*. I found out where he used to put the big key. Very quietly I stole the key, and through side ways I would steal into the *shul* when nobody was looking.

I did so many times and I was quite successful. However, in the end, a thief must be caught. One summer day, I woke up quite early and went to *beit hamidrash* to pray, while the key to the *shul* was left in my pocket from the previous day. I craved for the stillness and seclusion of the old *shul*. I knew that my mother was expecting me for lunch a few hours later. I believed that I was safe.

I had made a mistake in my estimate. By accident, I was caught red handed, and that was the end of my seclusion in the old *shul*. When I had already been engrossed in studying and chanting heartily: "Raba said… Abaye said… "[Two distinguished names in the *Gemara*], I suddenly heard a sharp blow on the door, followed by frightened sounds: "Open…open…". When the door opened, I saw my mother in front of me, scared, breathless and her face as pale as lime. Next to her, stood my uncle Aharon, son of Itche-Leizer, burning with anger. I don't remember what they told me because I was very shocked from the sight of my mom. I remember only that she, herself, locked the *shul,* stuck the key in her pocket, and said: "Don't ever dare to take the key in your hand. Come.…"

Disgraced, my head bent down, I was walking between the two of them, like a real thief caught red handed. Walking past the *beit hamidrash*, my mother said harshly: "Go in and pray, and return straight home."

I ran swiftly up the stairs of the *beit hamidrash*. My mind wasn't set praying. I was thinking of the punishment awaiting me at home, and figuring what measures to take so that my friends in *kheder* would not discover the whole story. Had they known what had happened, I would have been put to shame and humiliation.

I entered my house quietly. Aunt Foygel, (Yedidya's mother. We lived together in the same house) cast a sharp glance at me, but said nothing. To my great amazement, my mother also kept quiet. While she served me a good lunch, she said: "Will you never more do such things?" "Never", I answered in a low voice.

In the evening, my mother told me what had occurred previously. It so happened that just that particular early morning, uncle Aharon, son of Itshe-Leizer, came to pray in *beit hamidrash*. In the middle of the week he seldom came there because he traded in the villages and used to pray in the marketplace. From the *beit hamidrash* he walked behind the bathhouse, and passed by the *shul*. By chance, he heard my voice. He knocked on the door, but I did not hear him and did not respond.

Actually uncle Aharon was a nice Jew. I had a lot of respect for him. However, he liked to stick his nose in other people's matters. He loved to scold others and very often used to raise his voice to very high tones.

When he knocked quietly on the door and I did not hear, he was frightened because of his own fantasy and superstition. All the yarns about the dead, ghosts and spirits came to his mind, and he ran to my mother. Breathless, he arrived in the house and this is what followed:

– Where is Yaakov?

– He went to pray in *beit hamidrash*.

– This is what you think, but he is not there. I know that he has locked himself up in *shul* and is studying there all alone. I heard his voice. I knocked on the door and he did not open it for me. Is this how you neglect your son? You are his mother and father. (my father was already then in America). Alone in *shul* – he is in the greatest danger. God knows what can happen to him, God forbid…

My good mother felt, pitifully, very guilty. Very frightened, she ran with uncle Aharon and using all their strength they knocked on the door until I heard and opened it.

This episode put an end to my seclusion-visits to the old *shul,* but not to my love for that holy place. The key to the *shul* was strictly hidden away and I did not look for it anymore. Not long after that I left Horodets and traveled to study in a Yeshiva.

All my life in America, I hoped and dreamed to travel again to Europe, to see my shtetl Horodets and once more lock myself in the old *shul*. Now it is too late. Neither the shtetl nor the *shul* exist any more.

Honored be their memory.

Author's footnote:

It seems to me that the facts indicate that the original builders of the *shul* had a Sephardic tradition, and perhaps came from the eastern lands or were of the Spanish expelled Jews. My family name, Bosnyak, means in every language "a man who is from Bosnia", where the Jews were all descendents of the Spanish expelled Jews.

[Pages 41-42]

Comments about the Cold *Shul* [synagogue]

by A. Ben-Ezra

Translated by Hannah Kadmon

[Translator's notes in square brackets]

We cannot know how exactly old was the Horodetser Cold *Shul*. However, it was already an old *shul* in 1632. We learn that from the "Register of the State of Lithuania". In that register (side 116) we find that at the session of "The Council of Communities" in Khomsk, 6th of Tevet 1632, they assigned 25 gildn for the renovation of the Horodetser *shul*. It was a great deal of money for those times. At the same session they also assigned the same sum of gildn for the Pinsker *shul*.

Another fact can establish the antiquity of the Cold *shul*: in the old times there was no women's section like in the very old European *shul* in Worms, etc. [Worms= וורמיזא is a German city on the banks of the Rein. Rashi was active there].

Also, the old Holy Ark [where the Torah Scrolls are deposited] had a past history. When they renovated the *shul*, they noticed the following script on the Ark: אל הקדש " "בזאת יבוא אהרון [with this will Aharon come to the holiness] and above certain letters there were drawn marks from which it could be learned that the Ark was already 190 years old.

Also, at the end of the last century [19th century] there was still an old metal plate [in the *shul*] on which the following was inscribed: "לפ"ק....זרח ר' התורני "אלוף [Torah champion R' Zerakh... the year ...], from which it could be established that R' Zerakh donated this plate to the *shul* 170 years previously.

The last renovation, or what was called; "*geshalevet*" [sparing, salvaging] was done in 1904, and it ended around the *Shvues* holiday. The money for the renovation came from Shmuel Kaliker's bequest, as he had written in his will that a big part of his money should be spent on the renovation of the *shul*.

The Horodetser *shul* served as a fortress in time of war or attack, like the *shul*s of Lutzk, Ostra, Tulchin, and others. Also, almost the same legends were woven around the Horodetser *shul*. Namely, in the time of one of the wars (Zaksish?), the Jews hid there. The enemy fired at the *shul* but did not hit anybody, except burning holes in the *shul*. These holes could be seen before they renovated the *shul*, where new boards disguised them.

The boards were placed high. Children used to say that it reminded them of the Ark, the boards of which were also elevated. The *palush* [also pronounced *falush* or *polish* = an anteroom or corridor in a *shul*] of the *shul* served in the old times also as a jail for Jews, like in other communities. When someone committed a sin – they placed him in the *palush*, his feet stuck in small wood blocks, (according to a piece of news that R' Alter Shefes had heard).

A dispute arose around the last renovation of the *shul*. The *Misnogdim* [opponents of the Chasidim] wanted to pull down the old wooden *shul* and build a new *shul* made of stone. However, the Chasidim who were very influential in Horodets were against it and they won. They held, by tradition, [orally passed on from the elders] that R' Aharon The Big, the founder of the Karlin-Stalin dynasty (1739-1772) prayed in the Horodetser *shul*. R' Zusha from Hanifalye and R' Elimelekh from Lizensk also prayed in the Horodetser *shul* when they observed [accepted willingly] exile (around 1747). When the old Staliner (1802-1872) used to visit Horodets, he, too, prayed in the *shul*. He was so fond of the *shul*, that once, when he came to the shul to pray, he kissed the walls and exclaimed: "How do we get this *shul* for the High Holidays in Karlin?"

As for the location of the platform –it merits to dwell upon it a bit. The honored R' Yaakov Bosnyak speculates that since the platform was near to the door, it confirms that the *shul* was build according to the Sephardic style, and that the first inhabitants in Horodets were our Sephardic brothers. This is a fine assumption, but it has not been investigated. Also, in the old *shul* of Vilna the platform was near the door (according to a letter from Prof. Levi Ginsburg to R' Bosnyak), and the *Gaon* of Vilna remarked about it in his interpretation about "Orah Haim" [=lifestyle], in "rules of a *shul*", mark 140. The *Gaon* relies upon "*Kesef Mishne*", *Yad Hakhazaka,* rules of prayer, chapter 11, matter 3. The "*Kesef Mishne*" gives a reason for placing the platform near the door. In the past, when the *shul* was very big, they were supposed to place the platform in the middle of the *shul* so that people could hear the cantor or the Rabbi. However, nowadays, when the *shul* is small, it is more fitting that the platform is not in the middle.

By the way, it is worthwhile to note that legends about phantoms around the *shul* are not specific to Horodets. Such legends circulated in other towns that had owned old *shul*s, as well. (see Liberman-Viner's legends about the old *shul* in Fohrbishtza region of Kiev, "Reshumot" d' page 394; Philological script 2, 328, Vilna 1928, Yiddisher folklore side 154 Vilna YIVO).

The *shul* belonged to all Jews of Horodets, without exception, whether they were Misnogdim or Chasidim. Every home-owner had a "shtot" [=reserved seat] in the *shul*, and the "shtot" was passed on by inheritance from father to son.

In the *shul* the folks used to pray only on Sabbaths and Holidays even in winter. In order to have a *minyen* [=ten men] on the wintry Sabbaths – they used to come to pray by turns; every Sabbath – other home-owners. They used to pray in fur coats and in a hurry.

This is how the cold *shul* joined together all Jews of Horodets until 1915, when the Germans entered Horodets. The Russian troops were directed back to their posts, and left scorched earth before they retreated, to obstruct the enemy. One of the posts was in Horodets, where a horrible battle took place.

All this happened in the month of Av, the month of disasters [destruction of the Temple] when the Russians were forced to retreat from Horodets. As grandmother Shifra used to tell (she and grandfather Aharon-Yossl were the only Jews who remained in Horodets when the Germans entered the town) the Russians set the *shul* on fire once, but the *shul* did not succumb to the fire. Eventually it went up in smoke, and together with it, also, the fantasies of Jews who for generations wove legends around this remarkable *shul*.

[Pages 42-43]

The *Besmedresh*

By M. Rubinshtein

Translated by Hannah Kadmon

[Translator's notes in square brackets]

[the word *Besmedresh* is from the Hebrew: Beit Midrash = literally: a house of study (of Bible and Gemara). It is distinct from a synagogue. It did serve also as a place of prayer in the Jewish communities]

Regrettably, we don't have any photograph of the *besmedresh* which was built in the seventies of the last century [19th] (see the old Rabbi's sermon at the dedication of the building, "Yeshuot Yaakov" 82-86, Warsaw 1878). It was burnt down during WW1 like the synagogue.

As we do not have any photograph – I will try, at least, to describe that *besmedresh* which played an important part in the life of the Horodetser community for tens of years, the way it was imprinted in my memory.

The base of the *besmedresh* was high. All four walls were painted white and had big windows. The roof was pointed on all four sides. In front, in the roof, there were two circular small windows.

The entrance to the men's *Besmedresh*, on the northern side, faced the street and had a big high platform with steps on three sides. The steps led to double doors coated with triangular panels, and strengthened with nails especially made by a blacksmith that looked like buttons. Upon opening the doors, one entered into a lobby with a window and a bench. From the lobby one was led into the entrance to the *besmedresh*. The entrance had a double door.

Inside, in the north-western corner, opposite the door, a wash-stand was installed, for hand-washing.

At the southern wall - where the door was - stood a long table and two long benches; one was close to the wall and the other opposite it, with an iron-rest. The wall had three windows overlooking the street. Two plain lamps hung above the table.

Close to the eastern wall, in the middle, there was a platform encircled by fence-pickets [paling]. The Ark was on the platform and it was reached by a step in front.

The pulpit was located on the right side of the step. Moshe-Mordechai's "*shtot*" [reserved seat] - a chair and a reading-prop - was on the left side of the step, close to the eastern wall.

On both sides of the Ark there were long tables. The benches facing front had iron-rests, and the ones close to the wall did not have them. That was the eastern wall, where the Rabbi and the "*pney*" [elite] had their "*shtet*" [reserved seats]. The walls on the north side had two windows, overlooking Pinye the butcher's house. Two lamps hung on chains above the tables and could be pulled up and down.

The western wall also had three windows, overlooking the synagogue, and had two long tables with benches the same as near the southern wall. Plain lamps hung by the tables. A long pendulum clock hung up high, in the middle of the wall. Moshe Mordechai used to wind this clock every Friday in his own way, making it run a bit fast so that people would get up earlier for prayers...

In a corner of that wall, leading to the women's section, stood a cupboard with shelves, and up above the cupboard there were some more shelves. That is where the great books were arranged such as old six books of the *Mishnah* and new ones, as well as *mishnayes, Ein Yaakov, Midrashim* [interpretations] and other such books.

Two tall ovens stood in the middle of the western side where there was a partition between the men's part of the *besmedresh* and the women's section. The ovens almost reached the ceiling. Between the two ovens there was a door, through which it was possible to enter the women's section of the *besmedresh*.

On the side of one of the ovens, facing south, there was a low wall and on its top –a wooden grid to enable the women to hear the cantor.

Opposite that wall, there was a small table with a drawer, where *tehilim* [psalms] books were stored. By the table there was a cupboard without doors, with lots of shelves on which were arranged *khumashim* [first 5 books of the bible] "*sfarbes*" (twenty four) [24 books of the bible] and other such books.

Next to the second oven, facing north, there was another wall with a wooden grid, the same as on the southern side. On that wall they used to hang their coats.
Opposite the two ovens there stood tables with benches only next to the ovens. Plain lamps hung above the tables.

In the middle of the *besmedresh* there was a platform. Steps led to it from the northern and southern side. In front of the platform, on the eastern side there were benches with props. On the platform opposite the Ark there was a table for reading the Torah. Under the table in the floor, there was a hole to stick into it the "*shemes*" [non-kosher *mezuzes* and torn pages of holy books].

On the platform, behind the table, facing the women's section, there was a box with wine for *kidush* [blessing over the wine] and *havdala* [ceremony when Sabbath is over], a tray, a *yad* [hand = a pointer used to read the Torah] etc.

Opposite the platform to the side of the Ark, three flash bulbs were hanging to throw enough light.

The women's *besmedresh* had two entrances. One was from the street, on the west, with many steps, and the second was from the men's *besmedresh*, that is: from the lobby of the men's *besmedresh*. On the western side there was a room full with wood ready for winter - to heat the ovens. Upon opening the door to the room, one could see on the southern side three windows overlooking the synagogue. The western wall faced the street that led to the synagogue. By the eastern wall stood the two ovens that separated the women's from the men's *besmedresh*.

The women's *besmedresh* was full of benches and with small railings on both sides. Next to the benches there were props. Each woman had her own fixed reserved seat, like in the men's *besmedresh*. The seat reserved for the Rabbi's wife and other distinguished women was near the wall that separated the sections.

[Pages 43-45]

The *Daveners* in the *Besmedresh*

[*Daveners* = those who pray, the congregation]

By Rabbi Dr. Yaakov Bosnyak

Translated by Hannah Kadmon

[Translator's comments in square brackets]

The spiritual and, to a certain degree, the social life of the *shtetl* was reflected in the *besmedresh*, through the Sabbath day. The most beautiful and spiritually rich hours during this holy day, were before *Minkhe* [the afternoon prayer], when the folks came to study. In our *besmedresh* we did not have props except in the women's section. Only two men sat near a prop – the Rabbi and Moshe Mordechai, the *bal koyre* [Reader of the Torah in the synagogue]. They had their *"shtat"* [reserved seat] in a corner, to the left of the steps that led to the Ark. On the right, there was the prop for the leader in prayer. The inside space of the *besmedresh* was occupied by four long tables and benches; two by the eastern wall on both sides of the Ark, a third one near the southern wall and a fourth one near the northern wall. There were also two short tables next to the two brick-ovens and two narrow tables in front of the platform. All the tables were taken by men who were studying or merely browsing through a book. In one corner, Gedalya-Yudl the shopkeeper studied *Ein Yaakov* [a compilation of all the legendary material in the Talmud together with commentaries.] He was chanting it in his own manner, with 20-30 men sitting or standing around him, listening attentively to every word. In another corner, Shimonke – Gdalya-Yudl's father – was bent over a *Gemore*, twirling his beard and uselessly laboring to delve into a Talmudic issue. His son's chanting reached his ears and a smile of pleasure spread over his face. Not far from him, his neighbor, Shmuel the cobbler, was sitting, exerting himself over a big *Gemore*. He often derived pleasure from his son Moshe who used to drop in sometimes to study a page of *Gemore*. In another corner sat Berl-Leib the butcher and Ovadia the baker, learning together *midresh* [post Talmudic literature of Biblical interpretation] sharing the same book. Sender the *melamed* [teacher in *kheider*] was reading aloud the *Zohar* [the holiest mystical book of the Kabbalah]. Aharon, son of Itche Leizer, used to study *mishnayes* [collection of post Biblical laws and rabbinical discussions – part of the Talmud]. Here and there, at every table, folks were studying. Some studied the first 5 books of the bible with the interpretations of Rashi [11th century interpreter], others used to recite psalms with *meymedos* [added interpretations] or just a chapter. It was really a spiritual pleasure to spend those hours before *Minkhe* [afternoon prayer] in the *besmedresh*. \Something quite different took place in the hours before *Mayrev* [evening prayer], at dusk, when it got dim-dark before the *shames* lit up the lamps. All the local folk of the *shtetl* assembled to pray *Mayrev* at those hours. Most of them used to say *Tehilim* [psalms], verse by verse, with enthusiasm. A mood of yearning and spiritual soul-searching got hold of every person who repeated the verses of "אשרי תמימי דרך" ["blessed are the righteous"]. However, not all those present were under the spell of chanting the psalms in the traditional melody. The young children became impatient waiting for the stars in the sky [to mark the end of Sabbath]. To pass the time, they used to throw *"peklakh"* [wads] quite lavishly. Quietly, in the dark, they formed a lump from a hard, wet, handkerchief, and threw it at somebody's head. This started angry voices, clamor, brawls and led even to a scuffle in the *besmedresh*.\Something even worse took place early on Sabbath at the time of reading the Torah. The cause was Moshe Mordechai, the Reader of the Torah. That man had a peculiar character. He insisted that only he must be the Reader of the Torah, although the whole congregation did not want him. He used to read with great ecstasy and devotion, but his voice was utterly hoarse. It irritated everybody and it was unpleasant. People asked him kindly and then threatened.

They entreated him to allow another Reader to approach the reading table, but nothing helped. The everlasting Jewish stubbornness was reflected in Moshe Mordechai. Not once was he hit with a wad on his head while he was reading. Not once were people challenged to throw him out of the platform, but they could not carry it out. He used a belt to bind himself to the reading table that was built into the platform and they could not move him from the place. Not once was he beaten and even bled, but he stayed the only and permanent Reader in the *besmedresh*.

Often, he also ran to the pulpit wishing to pray only there, but he was held back. When he was asked, frequently, "R' Moshe Mordechai, why are you so stubborn?" he would give in and smile. However, when it was time to read the Torah, he forgot all and did as he wished. He could not restrain himself.

Moshe Mordechai had an additional weakness – blowing the shofar. Only he deserved to blow the shofar and no one else. The congregation was against his blowing the shofar. However, can one fight with him on Rosh Hashanah High Holiday when even a fish trembles in water? Moshe Mordechai actually took advantage of the opportunity knowing that on Rosh Hashanah nobody would quarrel with him and nobody would throw him out from the platform.

Well, Moshe Mordechai had already finished reading out, in his hoarse voice, "למנצח" [*lamenatzeakh* - prayer preceding the blowing of the shofar], took the shofar to blow, but no sound came out. He did not have any choice and called out: "*Nu, Nu*" which meant: "Someone help me, let somebody else mount the platform and blow the shofar". It did not take long and Se'adya, a healthy young man with broad shoulders, climbed to the platform, took the shofar in his hand, brought it to the right corner of his mouth and blew the shofar – *t'kiye* [a medium length sound] *shvorim* [a series of broken sounds], *tru'a* [a long sound]. It was performed smoothly by him and the congregation breathed freely. They told each other: "Not he who reads out "למנצח" – can also blow the shofar". In fact, these words had become a saying, a proverb, in the *shtetl* and were used to describe a person who finishes only half a job…

[Pages 45-46]

The *Besmedresh* and its Visitors

By M. G. K.

Translated by Hannah Kadmon

[Translator's notes in square brackets]

Meshulokhim and *Magedim*

[Messengers and Preachers]

The *besmedresh* was not a place where only the folks in the *shtetl* derived satisfaction. Visitors from the whole world found in the *besmedresh* a place to introduce their activities.

In the old days the young men of Horodets used to sit in the *besmedresh* and study. They met there a few foreign young men with a great desire to study the Torah, who had left their birthplace and settled to study in the Horodets *besmedresh*.

Among the students, there were some *"Prushim"* [recluses; devote themselves exclusively to the study of the sacred books]. They left behind a wife and children, their livelihood and worldly pleasures and sat down to study Torah for its own sake.

All these foreigners knew that the Jews of Horodets would not forsake them and would provide them with *"teg"* [= days; eating as guests at a certain house at given days of the week], night's lodging, and even give them some pocket money.

Horodets was a gathering-point for messengers, preachers and poor people. The exchange was in the *besmedresh*. Almost every day another *maged* would present his sermon. They chanted and read out the Torah, but not all of them could attract the public. Some of them were already well known to the people of Horodets so that they were referred to by a nickname. For example: the "pedestrian" *maged*. One was nicknamed "the sheepish" *maged*. He was short with a reddish beard. He used to come for a wintry Sabbath. His "audience" was very small but he did not leave the *shtetl* empty handed.

If the mediocre *maged* gave his sermon in the middle of the week, the congregation would place a plate at the exit of the *besmedresh* and everyone used to throw in a coin, according to one's means.

On the other hand, when a renowned *maged* or *meshulekh* [messenger] arrived, all the Jews of Horodets would assemble in the *besmedresh* to listen to their sermon. After the sermon they provided them with food and lodgings. Someone would invite the renowned person to his house, or the *shames* would lead him to the house of one of the *balebatim* [home-owners]. Two *balebatim* would go from house to house to collect donations for him or for the Yeshiva that he represented. Thus he would make more money. However, if the sermon was not a success, or if he did not give any sermon at all, the congregation provided a helper to accompany him. They did not let a *maged, meshulekh* or any other important visitor, walk alone from house to house, but provided them with an escort. That was considered more respectable, and it also helped in getting larger donations.

The Kovner [from Kaunas] *Meshulekh*

The *Meshulekh* from Kaunas was one of the prominent *meshulokhim* that frequented Horodets. He dressed like a Chasidic Rabbi and wore a *shtreimel* [a fur hat]. He was famous in Horodets for being a saintly man and a miracle worker. When he arrived, it was a festive day for the *shtetl*. The richest home-owners in the *shtetl* wanted him to stay in their house over night and have his meals with them. Those who got him had the rare honor and felt privileged. Two of the finest home-owners used to round up the annual contributions for his institution.

He spent his day mostly in the Rabbi's house. All the folks used to come and greet him. They would come with their children so that he could bless them. Wives would come for blessing. The house was full with people as long as he was staying in the *shtetl*. He was a wise man and used to adorn his speech with biblical vocabulary.

The Three Yeshiva Boys

Around the year 1900, Horodets supported three yeshiva boys in the *besmedresh*. They did not stay in Horodets at the same time. One of them left and the other arrived. Later on, the third one arrived. They used to sit alone all day long, studying *gemore*. They would finish one tractate of the Talmud and would start another one, and so on.

They did not eat *teg* [= days; eating as guests at a certain house at given days of the week]. However, the women of Horodets used to take care of all their needs. They brought them the best of food to the *besmedresh*. They treated them like "the apple of their eyes."

These were great scholars. In addition, they were wise and understood how to manage their affairs. They were more or less worldly. When, in the end, they got married, they left the *shtetl*.

The third and last young man was interesting. He was an odd person. He was altogether detached from this world. He made the *besmedresh* his home. He studied there and he slept there, too. However, he slept very little, constantly studying. His language was mostly Hebrew or Aramaic-Hebrew. A small crowd used to stand around him listening to his reading out or commenting on what he was studying. He was quite versed in the six books of the Mishnah. He studied Zohar [the holiest mystical book of the Kabala] and other books of Kabala.

For the women he was an "occupation". They used to bring him the best of food, but he did not eat everything. He was a vegetarian. He did not eat any meat. He liked cookies most of all. If he wished for cookies without sugar – he would get them. At day time he used to walk about, come back to the *besmedresh* and resume his studying. He did not stay for long in Horodets. He left and no other yeshiva boys arrived after that.

A "*Shabtai Tzvi'nik*"

[A self-proclaimed Jewish Messiah - http://en.wikipedia.org/wiki/Sabbatai_Zevi]

It was winter of 1912. The news spread that an eccentric man was in the *besmedresh*. He did not eat for a whole week, except for a potato baked in the oven of the *besmedresh*. The time of the arrival of Sabbath, as far as he was concerned, did not correspond to that observed by all Jews – Friday in the evening. He greeted the Sabbath on Friday, around midnight. His Sabbath meal was entirely different from that of all Jews: twelve Hallahs, twelve pieces of fish and all kinds of dishes that the Jews of Horodets were not accustomed to. There were several people who provided this eccentric man with all these "delicacies", and nice home-owners such as Zeidl the butcher and Chayim son of Rasel used to fuss over him.

It cannot be said that all the folks of Horodets thought alike about this man's queer customs. There were others who were of the opinion that he was an adherer of Shabtai Tzvi and he should be thrown out of the *besmedresh* and that they should not cater to all his idiosyncrasies.

The eccentricity of this man caught my interest. Once, on Saturday, after the meal, I went into the *besmedresh* to look at this odd man. I saw a man of middle stature, quite fat, with a black beard, covered with a *tales* [tasseled shawl], who ran many times to the bookshelves to take out a *gemore*, *mishnayes*, a *midresh* or a *kabala* book, turned the pages looking for every passage that dealt with the Sabbath, emitted some sounds and returned the book to the bookshelves.

The congregation had already gathered for the afternoon prayer. He climbed to the platform and held a sermon in Hebrew or Hebrew-Aramaic. Some people shouted: "Get down, you Shabtai Tvi'nik" Others said: "Let him speak". So this Jew kept on with his sermon as though not he was mentioned. The congregation fixed ears and eyes on him but they did not understand a word. The Hebrew of this strange man was very queer. He finished his sermon, descended the platform, made a *kiddesh* [benediction over the wine], resumed praying and went back to studying once again.

After *havdole* [the ceremony at the close of Sabbath to differentiate between holy and profane] this strange man was still covered in his *tales* as if he did not want to part from the *tales* and from the Sabbath. For him it was still Sabbath. The people of the congregation were already smoking – some had a cigarette and others a pipe – but he kept doing his thing. For him it was still Sabbath. Why did he carry on like that? Why did he withdraw from the congregation? Who would ask him these questions? Even if someone asked him, would he understand Yiddish? And even if he understood what one asked him, would the one who asked understand the answer? He used such a Hebrew that nobody understood…

All that was left to do was – watch and keep quiet. However, how long could one sit in the *besmedresh* without dinner? And what about going to sleep? Did he plan to sleep in the *besmedresh* on a hard bench?

I decided to go home and return to the *besmedresh* early the next day, to see when Sabbath was over for this "Shabtai Tvi'nik".

On Sunday, early in the morning, I was there. The congregation had finished praying and took off the tefillin and went home to their routine daily life. The "Shabtai Tvi'nik" was still saying the evening prayer preceding the close of the Sabbath. He had time. Why should he hurry? Thank God he finally finished the evening prayer. It was already noon time. He started the *havdole* to close the Sabbath.

I was the "lucky" one. I saw the big *havdole* candle over which the "Shabtai Tvi'nik" said the *havdole* prayer.

Thus the eccentric Jew carried out his whims for a few weeks, until he left Horodets.

It is worthwhile to ponder about that man. Perhaps there are other such Jews in the world.

[Pages 47-50]

The Stoliner Shtiebl

[The prayer house of the Stolin Hasidim]

By Israel Zusman

Translated by Hannah Kadmon

[Translator's comments in square brackets]

[Unlike a *shul*=synagogue and *besmedresh*=a house of studying but also of prayer, the *shtiebl* is a small Hasidic prayer house.]

R' Israel, the "Stoliner Rabbi"
Under the photo: a facsimile of his signature

[**Karlin-Stolin** is the name of a Hhasidic dynasty originating with Rebbe Aharon the Great of Karlin (today a suburb of Pinsk, Belarus). Karlin was one of the first centers of Hasidism. In the 20th century the Karlin Hasidim were divided into two courts. The bigger was called the Karlin-Stolin court. Stolin was the town close to Karlin, where R' Asher, son of the founder, served as Admor (acronym of "our master and teacher"). The smaller court was called the Pinsk-Karlin]

The Stolin-Karlin Hasidim occupied a distinguished place in the life of Horodets. Although they amounted to around a quarter of the Jewish population, they played a significant role both in the cultural and social life. It is enough to note that they composed about half of the *melamdim* [kheider teachers], elders, ordinary non-orthodox rabbis and fine *balebatim* [home-owners].

The Stoliner *shtibl* included very great scholars such as: Yankl the Hasid, Eliyahu Yankl the butcher, Israel Leib the *melamed,* Shefe, Yehuda Ozer, and in later years the very distinguished R' Shalom son of Itzik, Asher David the butcher and others.

The *shtibl* was in the back of Motye Hillel's house. In order to get there, it was necessary to go through a narrow alley, between Motye Hillel's house and Chana's house, daughter of Pelte and later Chava' house, daughter of Aharon-Yosl. Despite the fact that this *shtibl* was on the side – it was at the head of the *bosey-medroshim* of Horodets.

In the *shtibl* itself there was a very lively and joyful atmosphere. Here they studied a page of *gemore,* here they learned a chapter of *mishnoyes* [collection of post biblical laws and rabbinical discussions], or just told stories about rabbis and especially about the Karliner dynasty that descended from R' Aharon the Great, who was one of the Mezeritsher's disciples. [R. Dov Ber, the Maggid of Mezritch]

A few weeks prior to Rosh Hashanah, the Hasidim became very cheerful. Some Hasidim used to gather and hire a wagon to travel to Stolin for the Holy Holidays. It cost them three or four rubles per person. That was before the railroad was constructed, and in those times - three or four rubles were quite a sum. Other Hasidim such as Reuven-Meir the Pilgirm, who actually performed the mitzvah of "making a pilgrimage" [=originally, to the Temple in Jerusalem by foot]. He used to walk to Stolin. It took him, indeed, two weeks, but he got the taste of pilgrimage to Jerusalem, praying in the Rabbi's *shul* felt as if he were in the Holy Temple, and Rabbi R' Aharon, then R' Asher and later the "Yenuka" [=infant] were the Big Cohen. [High Jewish priest].

[A. Ben Ezra commented that R' Aharon was also named "the old Rabbi', R' Ahser was also named "The Young Rabbi" and the "Yenuka" was named R' Israel.]

The travel to Stolin was to fill oneself with spirituality and influence the surroundings. The elderly had influence over the the youngsters who bound themselves to the way of life of the Karlin Hasidim. It was especially marked by a *hilule* [hilarious celebration] during Holidays, in which the Hasidic children participated with their elders. They danced together with their fathers and grandfathers and ate with them at the table.

The spirit of togetherness was very noticeable among the Hasidic children when R' Aharon's *hilule* was celebrated. The boys used to make clay candlesticks and lit 256 candles in them, the numerical value of the name אהרון = Aharon. The boys were instructed on other occasions as well. For example: sitting at the last day of Passover at the table, attending the Passover, Yankl Kadliner would start with the renowned Karlin melody "והיא שעמדה". [Our faith has strengthened us against all enemies trying to destroy us]. Each child was honored by getting a part in reading out "אדיר במלוכה" [praising the name of God].

* * *

Yom Kippur was very inspiring. They used to spread straw or hay on the floor and the observant Jews used to sit a whole night in their white stockings.

Moshe, Chantshe's son, was granted the right to participate in the morning prayer of the High Holidays, despite his annual mistakes such as שעוה (wax) instead of שועה (cry) and יורקע instead of יוחקו ... Itizikl was granted the right to sing the "היום" [Hayom =today] after "ונתנה תוקף" [U'ntane tokef], [parts of the Yom Kippur prayer] with the help of his children: Israel, Yudl and Nyomke.

"V'hi she'amda"

(Song for the Passover Seder)

The text is from the traditional Passover Haggadah:

This is the promise that has sustained our ancestors and us.
For it was not one enemy alone who rose up against us to destroy us.
In every generation there are those who rise up against us and seek to destroy us.
But the Holy One, blessed be he, saves us from their hands.

Caption at bottom:

This is an old Karlin melody, which the Karlinner khassidim sing till today.

Translation of song by Eugene Sucov

This was a melody that Itzikl had brought from Stolin. He heard it himself from Yankl Telekhaner, the chief composer of Stolin.

The most beautiful celebration observed by the Stoliner Hasidim was "*Simkhes Bes Hasho'eva*" ["שמחת בית השואבה" = the rejoicing of the drawing of the water during Sukkot], the leading event during the intermediary weekdays between the first and last days of Sukkot. The Hasidim used to assemble in the *shtiebl* after dinner, raised a toast *lekhayim* [to health] and ate fruit that each Hasid used to bring. They were not contented with eating fruit. They sang and danced the real dance… and Shimon Eizik accompanied the dance on a drum. Yankl Kadliner with his stately appearance started first with a sedate dance, and even the allegedly rigid Motye, son of Hillel, also hummed to the beat. The celebration lasted long into the night. This celebration attracted a big audience and the Stoliner "*Simkhes Bes Hasho'eva*" earned a great and well deserved fame.

"*Simkhes Bes Hasho'eva*" was a prelude to "*Simkhes Toyre*" [Simkhe=rejoicing], where first they danced and sang separately [only men] for the "*hakofes*" [circular procession with the Torah scrolls around the reading platform]. People from the whole *shtetl* came to watch this, and this was the only case during the year when the doors were open wide even for women and girls. The folks came to see with what enthusiasm the Stoliner Hasidim danced and sang in honor of "*Simkhes Toyre*".

The next morning after prayers and after the "*hakofes*", they used to go for the "*Kiddush*" [=benediction over the wine], from one Hasid's home to the next, and not just "go" but rather walk dancing. By the time they finished with the last "*Kiddush*", it was already time for attending the afternoon prayer…

* * *

Saturday before praying everybody is busy. Near the window, north east, sits Itshe, son of Binyamin who is also nicknamed "Itshe the Walker" [peddler], as he uses to peddle with a bundle around the villages, selling the gentiles needles, yarn, kerchiefs/shawls and other small items.

On the other side of the table, opposite Itshe, sits his son, Yaakov, and studies with him *Mishley* [proverbs] with interpretations of MLBI"M [= R' Meir Leibush son of Yekhiel Mikhal]. Itshe is crazy about MLBI"M. He finds in this interpretation all the tastes of the world, and it to makes him chant them. He actually licks his fingers, as if he derived pleasure from eating something sweet. All the other interpretations are, in his eyes, nothing in comparison with MLBI"M. When Yaakob's children grow up – they will inherit the place of their father and will also rock over Proverbs with MLBI"M.

However, before Itshe teaches his grandchildren Proverbs, he studies with Simkha Yudl *mishnoyes*, telling, in passing, stories about his wanderings in the villages as a peddler and also about heroes of the past.

"Once upon a time", he tells, I enter an inn and I see how the *melamed* teaches his pupils an interpretation. When everybody was asleep, I sprang out of bed, went to the table where the interpretation was left lying. I took it and threw it into the garbage…

By the oven sits Khayim Leib, a renowned rich man. He studies "*Khumesh*" [the first 5 books of the Bible] with Rashi's interpretation and at times fills his nostrils with tobacco and studies further.

Khayim Leib is an irate man. If one remarks that the literal meaning he draws from Rashi is incorrect, he becomes so angry, as though, God forbid, they are doing horrible things to him! And when one says to him: "R' Khayim Leib, you should read "יוצר המאורות" and not "יוצר המיורות" [bad pronunciation of the word meaning sun, moon and the stars], he shouts: "Get out you brat"!

Across, near the window, east-south, sits R' Shalom, son of Itsik, holding a *gemore*. He studies it for his own pleasure. A whole week he teaches the public "Ein Yaakov" [collection of the legends in the Talmud] between the afternoon and evening prayers. However, on Saturday he isolates himself with the *gemore* and enjoys Rashi, and *Tosfos* and "מהרשא"

[Rashi – an acronym of: Rabbi Shlomo Yitskhaki - a distinguished interpreter. Tosfos – a collective commentary of rabbis on the Talmud-Bavli. – מהרשא acronym of Rabbi Shmuel Eliezer son of R' Yehuda Idelsh, interpreter of the Talmud].

For three-meals [Saturday eve, Saturday morning, Saturday afternoon], they sit at the long table near the northern wall. On the table there is a piece of hallah and a tail of herring. They take a bite, they tell a miracle, and for dessert they sing a Karliner melody half sad and half merry. It is already quite dark but the people do not want to part from the Sabbath queen. However, it is necessary to go to the shop and to their other occupations. They say the evening prayer and honor the Sabbath with songs accompanied by Shimon Izik's drum.

Aware that tomorrow is already Sunday, that they are no longer princes and that it is necessary to worry again about the next day, they go home with a heavy heart.

It is remarkable how the Karlin Hasidim become lively again and resume their soulfulness even in the middle of the week, when the Rabbi is about to arrive. This is how it was indeed when R' Israel, the "Infant" arrived in Horodets on a plain Wednesday. [see illustration on page 47 of R' Israel]The common everyday mood vanished and a mood of festivity embraced the Stoliner Hasidim in their *shtiebl*. All of them rejoiced together with the Rabbi, who honored them with his visit. R' Israel did not behave as a Rabbi who comes every year to visit his Hasidim who lectures and lengthens the prayer. On the contrary, his prayer of "*Shmone-Esre*" was the shortest. He carried himself like a merchant, was dressed as a merchant and here and there scolded in Russian like a Russian merchant.

* * *

The Stoliner Hasidim lived in unity, devoted to each other, always ready to do a favor to each other, always full of enthusiasm and kindness to people. When the heart was heavy – they took a sip of liquor /whisky and gained faith and confidence. When the sorrow of the world oppressed them too much, they started singing and then dancing.

Hasidim dancing
Drawn especially for the book of Horodets
By Dvora Zusman, Israel's daughter
(this drawing won the second prize from the "Scholastic" exhibition)

[Pages 51-53]

The Kobriner Shtiebl

By Shlomo Podolevsky

Translated by Hannah Kadmon

[Translator's comments in square brackets]

R'David Shlomo (The Kobriner Rabbi)

The Hasidism in Horodets differed from that in the neighboring *shtetles*. Hasidism did not take strong root in our neighborhood. In most *shtetles* there were no Hasidim, and if there were any of them – they were only tens. *Shtiebles* of their own they did not possess.

Horodets, through it was smaller than other *shtetles*, had, in addition to a *shul* and *besmedresh*, two *shtiebles* – Stoliner and Kobriner. The Stoliner Hasidim were mostly the elite of the *shtetl* – such as Karlinski and others, while the adherents of the Kobriner Hasidim were mostly craftsmen, butchers, some shopkeepers and some *melamdim* [kheider teachers].

Until some years prior to WW1, they did not have their own *shtiebl* but held their prayers in private houses. For some time they prayed in Pinye The Butcher's house on the other side of the bridge. Later they prayed for a long time in Yitskhak Aharon's house near the river. Finally, they bought the house that Binyamin The Doctor built for his daughter Perl, opposite the Rabbi's house, and turned it into a *shtiebl* to hold prayers in it.

I remember the joy of the Kobriner Hasidim when they celebrated the house-warming of the *shtiebl*. It was Purim 1910. That Purim fell on Friday and the son of Moshe The Klezmer [musician] from Kobrin - a klezmer himself – was then in Horodets. The folks marched into the *Shtiebl* accompanied with singing and flute. Young and old were happy that finally the Kobriner Hasidim would have an equal status, and not use somebody's apartment even without pay.

Thanks to becoming independent house-owners, the Kobriner Hasidim felt pride, elevation, and lifted their heads high because the Kobriner dynasty was still young – only 75 years old.

[Ben-Ezra comments that the founder of the Kobriner Hasidism was R' Moshe, Who was a disciple of R' Mordekhai Lekhevitsher. R' Moshe served as a Rabbi 26 years, He died the 28th of Nisan, 1858. His Hasidic beliefs are found in his book "אמרות טהורות". See also M. Buber "אור הגנוז" pp. 447-462, Jerusalem 1947. After his death, his grandson – Rabbi Noakh Naphtali - succeeded him. His teachings appear in the book "אמרות טהורות". He died in 1889. His son, R' David Shlomo, succeeded him and he died in 1918.]

The Kobriner Rabbis did not have many Hasidim and their way of life was very simple and modest. They did not have any stables with horses, nor palaces. The "court" of R' David, third generation, was a small brick fenced court in Kobrin, on Ratner Street, and was not much different from the courts of the other house holders. Therefore, the internal conduct of the Kobriner dynasty was entirely different from the other Hasidic dynasties, especially in their way of praying, as if one is out of breath.

Every year after Sukkot, the Rabbi used to travel around the *shtetles* where he had his Hasidim. Into Horodets he came for the Sabbath of "ויצא" portion of the Torah. The Rabbi was dressed in white, with white stockings, a white housecoat and a *shtreimel* on his head. His face was noble, white, with a reddish beard, sprinkled with grey spots. For the welcoming of the Sabbath and the evening prayer, some of the Hasidim would eat in a hurry the Sabbath dinner, and return to the *shtiebl* when the Rabbi started to set the table. From after the evening prayer, the Rabbi used to sit in a closed room to study. Later, when the crowd of Hasidim assembled, he would come out of the room and go to the table and the folks would stand up.

The *shames* [Rabbi's attendant] – who was also the *gabe* [manager of affairs] - a short man with a black beard, used to serve the Rabbi a container with water. The Rabbi washed his hands and immediately started reading out "אתקינו סעודתא" ["have the meal ready"] together with the Hasidim who had not gone home to eat. They said the words with heat, with zeal. Later, the Rabbi washed himself, read: "שאו ידיכם" ["raise your hands"] and made a *Kiddush*. After each course of the meal, the Hasidim used to snatch leftovers. The children of Aharon Leib The Painter – Noakh and Izik - were especially remarkable in snatching the leftovers. I can still see Izik in front of my eyes holding a hand full of noodle-pudding that he had snatched, eating from the handful and singing…

R' David used to sit in a closed room, early on Sabbath and pray alone until "נשמת" [the soul of] and for the prayer of "נשמת" he would go into the *shtiebl*. This prayer said by the Rabbi, sounded strange. From one sentence to the next, he used to "pass out" and the folks would stand amazed. When they heard him again uttering a word, it sounded as if the Rabbi wanted to return to life again.

Besides Friday evening, the Rabbi arranged meals on Sabbath after praying and Sabbath night "מלווה מלכה" ["accompanying the queen", the Sabbath, on her way out…this was done with song and a meal and the meal was called the fourth meal]. During the three Sabbath meals the Rabbi delivered a *"d'var Torah"* [sermon/lesson on topics relating to the weekly Torah portion]. The listeners were attentive. It was already well into the night when the Rabbi finished the three meals and started the evening prayer. Not only Hasidim attended the rabbi's meal, but also Stoliner Karliner Hasidim and many *Misnodgim*. At each meal the Rabbi delivered a sermon/lesson. The listeners would fix their eyes and ears to hear the Rabbi's lesson.

The overcrowding was indescribable. People stood tight trying to raise their heads above those of the others to catch some of the Rabbi's words. The Rabbi spoke silently, rolled up his eyes, swallowed a word, "passed out" and held back.

Musical notes for Moshe Kobriner's melody to יה אכסוף ["Ya Ekhsoof"]
A poesy written by R' Aharon the Great [Admor of Karlin]
(Recorded by R' Barukh "Kobriner Rabbi" andapted by Moshe Natanzon)

    The Kobriner Hasidim, amazed, swallowed with thirst every word they could snatch. Although they did not understand – still every word that came out of his holy mouth was precious to them. After every piece of lesson, they commenced with a merry song or dance in which the Kobriner Hasidim excelled.

    The arrival of the Rabbi in the *shtetl* was refreshing, a continuation of *Simkhes To'yre* = [joy of finishing the year's reading cycle of the Torah], and it brought a festivity to the monotonous life of the *shtetl*. Very quiet and calm people became lively during the week that the Rabbi stayed in Horodets.

Moshe Burshtein, or as he was nicknamed "Moshe the Big", a noble man, a scholar, of the Old Rabbi's family, a quiet man, was transformed into a different man when the Rabbi arrived. A whole year he kept quiet. Only twice a year he was talkative – when the Rabbi arrived and on *Simkhes To'yre*. At the Rabbi's table he was leading the singing and on *Simkhes To'yre* he collected around him all the children and he sang "The Savior will come soon, Elijah will come soon". Then He asked the children: "When will he come?" and they answered him: "Soon in our time, our Messiah" etc., On *Simkhes To'yre* they permitted additional jargon songs such as "what we are, are we – however, Jews we are" and so forth.

The Kobriner *shtiebl* was a quite beautiful small *besmedresh*, in the middle of the market, not far from the cloister, surrounded by trees and with a small garden. The mason Avraham Ezra, son of Shmerl, was the *shames*. They allocated to the *shames* a separate apartment. They did not name his wife *shames'te* but nicknamed her *shtiebli'khe* because she kept the *shtiebl* very clean.

Once, a Jew-hater sent a paper claiming that the *shtiebl* was placed in too close proximity to the cloister. The Tzar's law demanded that between a church and a building used for another religion there should be a large space. I remember how they used a long cord to measure the distance from the church to the *shtiebl*, and although it was according to the law, they paid some rubles to let the *shtiebl* stay where it was. It seems that a tavern/pub close to the church was kosher. Piece of evidence - Shmuel Khayim's pub was very close to the cloister… [The Yiddish index of names adds his family name: Sirota]

During the day on Sabbath, Alter the Shmid used to teach the congregation *Ein Yaakov* [a compilation of all the legendary material in the Talmud together with commentaries.] In addition, older children used to study *gemore*, all by themselves.

Besides the Kobriner Hasidim, R' Khayim, who lived across the road, used to pray in the *shtiebl* during the week days. This fact added more importance to the *shtiebl* and its Hasidim. The fame of the Kobriner *shtiebl* kept growing until the break of WW1. When most of the *shtetl* was burnt down, the Kobriner *shtiebl* was also consumed by the fire, and with it the sweet loved memories.

[Page 54]

Institutions

Translated by Hannah Kadmon

[Translator's notes in square brackets]

Translator's introduction:

The term *gabe* in Yiddish or גבאי in Hebrew, needs some special clarification. The dictionary defines the *gabe* as a warden of a public institution, especially in a synagogue and also manager of the affairs of a Hasidic Rabbi. The truth of the matter is that the role of the *gabe* as well as his rank or status, was, and still is, determined by circumstances and by the characteristics of the synagogue, community, societies and leaders. This chapter about Institutions illuminates the various tasks and social standing of the *gabe*. I will use the Yiddish word *gabe* in my translation.

The same goes for *shames* in Yiddish שָׁמָשׁ in Hebrew. The dictionary defines the *shames* as a beadle, sexton in synagogue, Rabbi's personal assistant. His tasks are various – from knocking on the wooden windows to waking up people for prayer, to lighting the candles in the synagogue and to closing up after the last men has finished praying. Therefore I will use the term in Yiddish - *shames*]

The "*Khevre Kadi'she*"

[The voluntary burial society]

By A. S. Horodetser

Introduction

One of the oldest, most influential and richest societies in town was the "*Khevre Kadi'she*". It was a great honor to belong to that society, especially to become a *gabe* in that society. Very few could reach the level of becoming the *gabe* of the "*Khevre Kadi'she*", who was a kind of a president. Only chosen ones, the learned of the town, such as R' Israel Yosl Mazursky, R' Hillel and R' Shalom Kostrinsky, were privileged to be thus honored.

It seems that this society did not confine itself only to burial ground, or cemetery lots, and to the dead. It included in its activities other community functions. All these activities were entered in writing into the register of the "*Khevre Kadi'she*".

Regrettably, the old register where they registered many important events was destroyed. The new register that dealt only with society-matters, is missing. It got lost during WW1, when the residents of Horodets fled away and many houses were burnt down.

We will have to be contented with the recollections presented to us by R' Alter Alman, R' Mordechai Greenberg and other Horodetsers.

The duties

It became a custom that when someone wanted to join as a member of the society, he had to pay 25 rubles. In addition, he had to prepare the annual banquet, the eve of the month of Shvat. If the banquet was not so fine, it was possible to compensate the members of the "*Khevre Kadi'she*" with another, better, banquet.

The new member was obliged to serve as the society' *shames* for the next three years. The role of the *shames* was to call the members of the "*Khevre Kadi'she*" to perform their duty when someone died.

[Editor, A, Ben-Ezra, noted: Almost the same requirement appears in the "*Khevre Kadi'she*" of Zablodov (in the region of Grodno) : "For three years the new member must remain in the lowest rank of a servant of the society… and for three years he must prepare the banquet for the society". (look up Yerukham Bakhrakh's *materialen tsuder geshikhte foon byalistoker gegent*, "YIVO bletter" vinter 1946, band 28, no.2 z.323 and also z/325, 326)]

"*Khevre Kadi'she*" members were exempt from paying burial-fee. However, if a death occurred among non-members, the society with its *gabe* fixed the sum of money to be paid for the burial.

The Horodetser "*Khevre Kadi'she*" excelled in its unique and various practices and customs such as praying in *Beit Hamidrash* every first of the month, practicing together "Small Yom Kippur" and arranging the yearly banquets. [Small Yom Kippur was the custom of fasting and praying for atonement, the evening preceding the first of the month. The prayer was said even by those who did not fast].

The big banquet

Among all the other practices of the "*Khevre Kadi'she*", the practice for which they were foremost noted was the winter banquet. [The editor comments: in Zablodov and in Grodno they held the annual banquets during *Khol Hamoed*. In other communities the banquet took place on the following dates: 14th, 15th, 19th of 20th of Kislev]. Before the banquet, the members observed the fast [of Small Yom Kippur] and prayed for atonement in the *Beit Hamidrash*.

The banquet took place in the *gabe'*s house. If there was no new member to prepare the banquet according to the rules of the society, the members of the society prepared the banquet by themselves. It was really like a "King Solomon banquet". They baked special large Hallahs, served big portions of fish, meat, chicken, *tsimes* [vegetable stew] and fruit-dessert. The banquet was not short of wine and whisky. It was quite a joyful and high spirited event. They used to sing aloud all kinds of melodies. At that annual banquet they chose the candidates for the following year and almost always the same candidates were chosen. The folks, then, went home joyful, taking with them parts of the food wrapped in cloth for their wives and children.

The *Simhath Torah* Banquet

This second banquet, smaller, took place on *Simkhath Torah* [joy of finishing the year's reading cycle of the Torah] also took place in the *gabe'*s house. It started on *Shmini Atzeret* [eighth day of Sukkot] in the evening and continued until late evening. The banquet consisted of fruit, cakes and whisky. The banquet was held in a very festive and joyful mood. After the banquet, all went out to the street and led the *gabe* to the synagogue. They carried lit candles in their hands and sang aloud Chasidic and Misnagdic melodies. The town-children preceded them and helped with the singing. Upon entering the synagogue, they continued the jubilation with songs and dance, while making the *Hakofes* [circular procession with the Torah scrolls around the reading platform] around the platform.

All the folks, be they *Hasids* or *Misnagdim,* came to the synagogue to participate in the *Hakofes*.

A Rebellion

The *"Khevre Kadi'she"* had relatively high expenses: fencing in the cemetery, paying the grave-diggers, meals arranged for the purpose of boosting the society and other similar matters. Where did they get the money to cover the expenses? The society sought to cover the expenses by means of requiring a fee for the dead, according to the financial situation of the close family. A committee was chosen for the purpose of assessing how much to charge for every dead person's burial. The assessors saw to it that the society would not lack money to cover all that was needed. The truth must be said that the assessors were not too accurate in their assessment.

In the years of the sprouting revolution-movement in Tsarist Russia, the trend of liberation that spread all over Russia permeated Horodets as well. The first signs of this trend were reflected in the *"Khevre Kadi'she"* which possessed a good deal of bureaucratic tendencies. A rebellion started rising against the *"Khevre Kadi'she"*. People came out in the open with complaints about the management of the society. They demanded more acceptable handling of burial fees. The society, however, had its own justified considerations and was not willing to give in to the "rebels". Thus a real feud started in town, the notorious feud concerning *"Khevre Kadi'she"*.

A group of young, strong and capable men united and founded a new *"Khevre Kadi'she"* and started competing with the old society. When someone died, they came earlier to "snatch" the dead, without charge, brought the body to the cemetery and that was it. The old society remained without a stitch of work: no dead and no money. However, they did not keep quiet either. When they realized that things were worse and they were almost "bankrupt", they kept vigil and started also to make haste. It actually happened that the two societies would stand waiting to "snatch" the dead body. It became a matter of ambition: who will defeat whom, which society would prevail and which would discontinue.

The anarchistic situation continued for three years. Both sides became weary. When the feud cooled off, the two societies decided to bring the case to *din-Toire* [lawsuit before a rabbinical court]. They sent for Rabbis from Korbyn and Antipolye, and they sat as court, together with the old Rabbi, R' Yehoshua Yaakov. After having heard the claims of both sides, the Rabbis declared the following verdict that contained 4 points:

1. The old *"Khevre Kadi'she"* would prevail and the young *"Khevre Kadi'she"* would be dissolved.
2. A uniform fee of three rubles would be charged for each dead, and not more than that.
3. People who had no means would not be charged at all.
4. People of means may be charged a higher fee after the Rabbi, not the society, had assessed their means and fixed the fee.

Both societies were satisfied with the verdict. The old society was satisfied that it prevailed and would continue to exist. The new society was satisfied that it had won in essence and carried out its agenda. There was again peace and quiet in town.

[Pages 56-57]

The Small Societies

By A. Alman

Besides the very influential *"Khevre Kadi'she"*, there were other societies in Horodets that stimulated the communal cultural-life of the Jewish inhabitants of Horodets.

We know that there was once, in Horodets, a society by the name of "Ein Yaakov". [Ben-Ezra refers the reader to the article "Dr. Israel Michal Rabinovitz" pp. 94-97 of this book]. We neither know how long this society existed nor when it was discontinued.

Seventy-five years ago [around 1875] there was also a *"Shas* society" [ש"ס = ששה סדרי משנה = the six Mishnah books = oral Jewish laws]. The members used to assemble once a year in Yosl Lieber's House (of the Mazursky family) allocated the *Shas* parts to the members and also celebrated the conclusion of the yearly study. This society was also discontinued. However, though there was no more a *Shas* society belonging to the whole community, there was a small *Shas* society in the Karliner *shtibl*. On Hanukkah or on the 15th of Shvat the members gathered in *shtibl* to celebrate the conclusion of the yearly study and have a feast.

There was also a *"Mishnayes* society" that functioned quite a number of years and was discontinued because of a feud amid the slaughterers. [Ben-Ezra refers us to the article "The feud" pp. 71-72 in this book].

The celebration of the "commencement" was in the form of a feast, not a big one, on Hanukkah or 15th of Shvat, in a member's house such as Alter Shoel's. The cost of the feast was covered by the membership fee of 3 rubles paid by the new members. If there were not enough new members, the old members used to chip in. At the "commencement" they used to read the introduction to the register of the society that had been written by R' Moshe Tzvi. They also read out the names of the new members. The secretary was R' Shalom Kostrinsky, and I was once the writer. This was the text: "today …. in the year…..we have gathered in the house of alter Rabinovitz, and a new member has joined the society, R'…..and has paid 3 rubles to the appointed for the society."

At the "commencement" they also voted to elect five arbitrators, as well as a *gabe*. I was elected, once, as an arbitrator and I was also the one who kept the register. I kept the register several years, and then passed it to R' Mordechai Kostrinsky.

One of the finest society was the *"Talmetoyre* society" [Hebrew: תלמוד-תורה = Talmud Torah= learning of Torah]. The objective of this society was to pay tuition fee for poor children. The *gabe* was R' Shalom Kostrinsky and the trustee was R' Israel Yankl Kamenetski, or Yudl the *melamed* and at one time – Zeidl Yarmok.

The income of the *"Talmetoyre* society" came from the following sources: membership fees, *"hallah-fee"* and "paying off *kapores"* [paying money to redeem the necessity to buy a hen for observing the custom of atonement.] Every housewife was required to contribute one groshn a week as *"hallah-fee"*, which she put in a separate box. The intake would render three rubles a month. The town's *shames* or somebody else used to collect the few groshn.

On Khol Hamoed of Passover and of Sukkot, they used to meet together in the *gabe*'s house. There, they decided how many children they would support, and how much money they should pay this or that *melamed*. [Ben-Ezra comments: there was also a *"Gmiles-khe'sed* society" [charitable loan-without-interest society]. Its cashier was Motye Hillel's. Apart from the community's *"Gmiles-khe'sed* society" there were some Jews who handled a private *"Gmiles-khe'sed"*, such as for example Khayim Itsik's, and they used to lend a few gilden.]

This is how it proceeded until the outbreak of WW1, when all the elements of old societies were shaken up and new societies were not founded. With sound of the cannons, many ways of life disappeared together with the old dear institutes.

[Pages 57-58]

Hakhnoses-O'rkhim

[Shelter for poor wanderers]

By Y. Yitskhaki

Actually the *Hakhnoses-O'rkhim* was not founded by the community. It was a private institute. It was referred to as "Itsik's *Hakhnoses-O'rkhim*". Officially it was founded before WW1, when Itsik became a "Gevir" [rich man]. [Ben-Ezra refers us to "Fanye Shaf" pp. 107-108 in this book].

In previous years, there was a *"hekdesh"* [a poor-house] near the bathhouse. It was very cold in there, like in all other poor-houses. It was wet and there were some torn cots. R' Itsik's *Hakhnoses-O'rkhim* was more of a home than an institute. People felt there like at home.

Itsik's *Hakhnoses-O'rkhim* was a distinct chapter in the history of Horodets for the last 50 years. Even before he turned his house officially into a *Hakhnoses-O'rkhim,* the tradition of his family was to open his house for all the poor. There was hardly a day when there was no poor man in the house. On certain days, 9 or 10 poor people spent the night in the house. Each of them got a cot with a pillow and a dish with cooked food. They used to sleep on the cots, in the alcove, in the parlor and in summer they slept in the cellar [the word here was unclear] and in the attic. In making the "beds" for the poor, the children used to compete who would make the "beds" in a quicker and better way.

It was said that once, on a hot summer day there was, somehow, a big "crop" of poor men, about ten of them. One of them was dressed like a dandy with lacquer shoes and cap. One of the poor men pulled Itsik to the side and said: "Do you know, R' Itsik, the poor man with the cap is a thief, a murderer and possesses every possible evil. Beware of him." It was late at night and Itsik was still sitting, bent over a book, and studying. Everybody was already asleep except for the dandy. The dandy then approached R' Itsik and asked him why he did not go to sleep. Itsik answered him: "I will tell you the truth, young man; I have heard that you are….. I am afraid of going to sleep." The dandy said: "Yes, R' Itsik, It is true that I am a thief and a murderer, but I will not do you any harm. You can go to sleep." R' Itsik went to sleep and in the morning the young man had already left and nothing was missing in the house.

R' Itsik used to draw a great deal of pleasure from disguising himself and listening to what people had to say about him and about his *hakhnoses-o'rkhim.* It is worthwhile to relate the following incident. Once he travelled through some small town and went in to the synagogue to pray. A Jew approached him, greeting him with *"Sholem aleykhem"* and asked him where he came from. Upon hearing that he was from Horodets, this Jew asked him if he knew the hospitable R' Itsik Zusselman. R' Itsik responded: "You call him hospitable? He is a *sheigetz* [insolent person]! He drives out every poor man from his house and lets nobody cross his doorstep!" – "How can you say that?", said the Jew, "you are slandering the name of a precious person. He has a very high reputation here. All the folks rave about him." – "I know better!" said R' Itsik, I know him better than you. I tell you that he is a *sheigetz*. He cannot even face a poor man…"

Itsik could not keep up playing the comedy for long, and he admitted that he, indeed, was R' Itsik. "If that is so", said the Jew, "You are indeed a *sheigetz*"…

When we talk about R' Itsik's "*Hakhnoses-O'rkhim*" we must not neglect to mention the wonderful figure of the righteous Alte Zusselman, Itsik's wife, who was the soul of *Hakhnoses-O'rkhim*. It is worthwhile to recall a few events that illustrate her radiant personality that became almost legendary.

Every evening, before going to sleep, she used to leave a small kerosene-lamp burning on the window sill. She wanted the small lamp to serve as an indicator, to guide the way to a place for the night, in case a poor man came late at night, when the whole town was asleep and it was dark outside.

More than once, she gave her dinner meal to a hungry poor man, telling him that she had already had her dinner, and later she could be seen in a corner, somewhere, eating a piece of bread with tea.

When there were more poor men than pillows in the house, she insisted that only she would offer her pillow. When something was missing in the house or when someone was caught red-handed, she was never angry, but would say: "He probably needed it."

She even died in the service of the poor and needy, like a soldier on duty, taking care of the horrible typhus disease at the time of WW1. She said: "When God above needs me – He can always take me away".

It really happened that way. She caught the disease and God took her away. May her memory be blessed!

Alte Zusselman
(drawn by her son Israel)

Itsikl in front of his *Hakhnoses-O'rkhim*

[Pages 59-61]

The Town Autonomy

By Shlomo Libers

Translated by Hannah Kadmon

[Translator's notes in square brackets]

A. The "Oprave"

The *"meshtsanske oprave"* ["residents-management"] of Horodets, was made up entirely of Jews: A Rabbi, a *starosta* [distinguished elder of town], 13 Jewish representatives, a scribe and an administrative office with a big list of registered, missing and departed. Despite the fact that the *"meshtsanske oprave"* was entirely Jewish, the town-elder was, for about 10 years, Afen the *feldsher* [old-time barber-surgeon]. He was the only gentile resident in Horodets who was a *meshumed* [a Jew who converted to Christianity].

How does an apostate become a leader of Jews? Here is the story. Sixty years ago [in 1889] R' Shalom Kostrinsky was the town-elder and his brother Motye was a Rabbi. Both were distinguished Jews who inherited from their father, R' Itzik, the active participation in community affairs. The two brothers were Karliner Chassids. The mere title of "Chassids" cast a shadow on them. The "Misnogdim" of the town started to grumble: "what is going on? The Kostrinsky have gotten hold of everything for themselves, just like Moses and Aaron in their time." [The two leaders of the people of Israel in the desert after the departure from Egypt].

They continued the gossip and "fermented" it until Shalom was forced to flee to America, and Mendl the miller was elected as town-elder. Mendl was a very honest Jew. He could learn and write, but only from right to left [Yiddish]. Unfortunately, he could not write from left to write [Polish or Russian]. Here, the governor himself interfered and offered a compromise: Afen would be the town-elder. Afen was quite a good person. People said that he was originally a Horodetser, one of the kidnapped Jewish children during the reign of Nikolai I.

[Russian Tsar Nicholas I issued the "Statute on Conscription Duty" in 1827. Jews were subject to military service at a quota (four conscripts per each thousand subjects all over Russia) and were required to provide conscripts between the ages of 12 and 25. These under 18 were sent to "cantonist" (pre-military) schools, were converted, in the process, and at the age of 18 would serve in the army for 25 years. The main goal behind the compulsory military service was "Russification" of Jews and other non-Russian minorities. The unpleasant task of implementing conscription quota fell to the community. Since many of the males eligible for recruitment did everything to run away, hide or bribe, orphaned children were lured or snatched with the help of informers and kidnappers – indigenous members of the community, skilled in deception, appointed by the leaders of the community]

Leibl, son of Israel, became the scribe. He was a tall person, with a "Franz Yosef" beard – one part pointing to the left and one to the right – as if meaning to say: "when I wish - I go to the left and when I wish - I go to the right. I still waver where to turn."

As mentioned, Afen was a baptized Jew. It was distasteful to the Jews of Horodets that an apostate would be their town-elder. They saw to it that their town-elder was again a Jewish Horodetser. They actually succeeded and R' Motye Kostrinsky was installed as town-elder. In 1899 Tsar Nikolay II granted amnesty and R' Shalom returned from America and became the Rabbi of the town until 1915, when the Germans conquered Horodets. After Motye Kostrinsky's death, Izikl Motyes (Izrael) became the town elder. He was a Jewish lumber merchant, who knew very little about community affairs and hardly knew the *ispravnik* [police officer]…

Izikl's office did not last long – only a couple of years - until the "*oprave*" stopped existing under the occupation of the Germans during WW1.

What were the functions of the "*oprave*"? According to the laws of the Russian Tsar, many people were registered in the location where they originally lived. They could reside in Warsaw, in Petersburg or in any other place but they were registered in the place where their fathers or grandfathers were born, while they themselves were never in that place.

When they needed a passport, they had to ask for it in the location where they were registered, where they were unknown. Naturally, they had, therefore, to pay the scriber, town-elder and the rest of them [where they were registered]. They were not allowed to report for the draft where they were residing. They were forced to travel to that place were they were registered and report there. All payments that applied to the inhabitants of the town had to be paid also by those who were registered there, even thought they were residing in another state or town. Thus, the registered people who were actually living in a different place, had to carry a bag of troubles. Those of the registered who were living far and had the means, used to hire somebody, a cripple, who traveled and reported in place of the real person to be conscripted. Thus, by such means, the rich freed themselves from serving in the army. Of course, only the rich could accomplish such measures.

In the past, Horodets - together with Divin, and afterwards together with Antipolye - had to deliver only one soldier a year. In other words, Horodets had to deliver one soldier every two years.

The period of "abduction" [Tsar Nicholas 1] left a great deal of heart-break in Horodets. The "kidnappers" often used to get off badly. In retaliation, people burned their houses or created other troubles for them. "*Lovshtzik*" (kidnapper) became a nickname to imply malice, lack of pity or compassion, evil and malevolence. This nickname accompanied the "kidnapper" to his grave and followed his children and grandchildren.

To manage that difficult situation some order was introduced. There was a custom to buy a soldier, paying him 500-600 rubles. When they had already bought the "victim", they used to feed him well until he was drafted.

They collected the money from various towns in the region and every Jew was committed to donate to the recruit fund [*rekrutave*=recruit].

Later, it was ruled that everyone must report to the draft, but not all were conscripted. There were "*pravilne*" (*gezetslikhe*) [according to the law], third, second and first status. The first status included single sons. They were exempt from service. The *gezetslikhe* hid themselves so that those of the other two statuses would pay them, and if not, the ones exempt from service would be drafted as well. Therefore the males of these two statuses used also to hide until the quota of recruits was filled. A soldier would get 200-300 rubles as a prize from those who were released.

The Tsar's government saw that this hiding would not recruit too many soldiers, so they proclaimed that if someone did not report for the draft, his closest family had to pay a fine of 300 rubles. This rule applied only to Jews.

Then the Jews once again found a solution. They did not want to serve the Russians for various reasons: it meant eating non-kosher food, being subjugated to coarse, ignorant and impudent gentiles and being humiliated as Jews, as the Tsar's authority always thought up new inhuman decrees against Jews.

B. The "Korovke"

The "*korovke*" [from the Polish word for a cow], a tax on meat, was an old law, that operated in the Polish and Lithuanian Jewish communities. The Council of Four Lands had already dealt with various problems pertaining to the "*korovke*" and its role in Jewish life, and it was mainly known as *mendele's "tax"* [tax on kosher meat]. However, what role did it play in the life of the Jews of Horodets?

The "*korovke*" was a fixed tax on meat that they had to pay for slaughtering – from an ox to a hen - and the payments were to be spent on the needs of the Jews in the town.

Was it really like this? Did the Jews benefit from the "*korovke*" payments? How did they handle the payments?

First of all, there was an official government transaction once in three years. The price was 400-500 rubles a year. Whoever "bought" [a sort of lease] the "*korovke*" had to deposit that price at the hands of the "*oprave*". It was customary that no one was permitted to advance the money except the representatives of the "*oprave*", who knew the price. Afterwards they used to "sell" [the lease] over the pulpit in *beit hamidrash* [study house and also place of prayers] to whoever offered more. However, it was not "allowed" to offer too much, because anyway the money was not used for Jewish purposes, and if someone bid too much, the community excommunicated him. [The editor, A. Ben-Ezra, comments that an excommunication pertaining to "*korovke*" was practiced more than 300 years ago according to the register of the Lithuanian states. Page 210] – nobody was permitted to visit the banned person's home or speak with him, and he could not slaughter in the town.

Whoever bought ["leased"] the "*korovke*", used to open a register with receipts and the slaughterer was not allowed to slaughter without a receipt from the holder of the "*korovke*". The price for a hen was 2 kopeks, and for a cow- 2 rubles. If a housewife wanted to have a hen slaughtered for a sick person (no healthy person in Horodets would eat any hens), she had to go, first, to Jews who held the "*korovke*", get a receipt, bring it over to the slaughterer and then pay the slaughterer for his work. The same applied when a butcher slaughtered cattle. The "*korovke*"-money was meant to be spent on the upkeep of the *beit-midrash*, the bathhouse, etc. However, things were somewhat different: the cloisters stood on the town's territory and therefore they belonged to the town and had to be maintained by the "*oprave*". Even though there was not even one gentile in the self-governed community, the Jews with their meager money had to pay for the maintenance of the cloisters. The priest was appointed by the authorities and got his salary from the government. When the government claimed the money from the Jews who had the lease on the "*korovke*", the first payment went to cover the needs of the cloister, and the gentiles were exempt from this duty. In truth, a small sum was spent to pay for the "*oprave*"'s scribe and town-elder and there was nothing left for the synagogue and *beit-midrash*. Thus the synagogue and *beit-midrash* were maintained thanks to private donations.

As was mentioned above, they would "ban" from time to time when there was over-bidding on the "*korovke*". Such a case actually happened in Horodets. Once, S.H. who knew the real price of the "*korovke*", sent a closed envelope with a down payment of a higher price than was fixed by the representatives, and the "*korovke*" was actually granted to him. That S.H. had a partner, a Jew from Kobryn. In short, the Horodetser community declared a ban on him, and made his life difficult until this buyer relinquished the "*korovke*" and lost his down payment.

That incident was engraved in the minds of the land-owners of Horodets and from that day on nobody bid more than the accepted price of the "*korovke*" and the "*korovke*" remained almost always in the hands of the same people.

[Page 62]

Holidays

(memories)

Translated by Hannah Kadmon

Rosh Hashanah

By Tzivia Greenglass

[Translator's notes are in square brackets.]

[Tzivia also belonged to the Kostrinsky family. Her name in Hebrew is pronounced Tzvia and means "a gazelle". However, she was called by all: Tzivia…]

The greater the distance from my childhood, the stronger are the memories of the Holidays imprinted in my memory, with the tradition and customs observed in my home. I wander in my thoughts from "Street" to "Market", from house to house, from person to person and from one Holiday to the next Holiday – my thirst for them unquenched.

It is the first of the month of Elul. The sky is clear, bluish beauty, but the trees, the grass – their green has turned to yellow. The leaves on the trees, weakened by age, cannot withstand the slightest Elul wind – they fall to the soil and cover with yellow the dry grass and soft sand around it.

The sound of blowing the Shofar is heard, the first reminder of the approaching Rosh Hashanah and The Day of Judgment. Soon the Shamash will wake people for "*Slikhot*" [a collection of prayers the best known of which is *Avinu Malkenu* — "*...Our Father, our King, We have sinned before you. Our Father, our King, we have no sovereign but you... Our Father, our King, Deal with us a with loving kindness and mercy ..... "*]. His voice – so mournful, melodious, cites the few words: "wake up for *Slikhot*".

In the middle of night, Jews get up, run to Slikhot, rushing to unburden themselves of the weight of sin. A feeling of fear, mixed with reverence, inhabit even children's hearts.

It is the eve of Rosh Hashanah. Wagons crowded with men, women, children, beddings and food arrive, one by one, from Mekhvedevicher small street, and from the Gentile's side, from Kobryner street. Jewish villagers arrive in the shtetl to observe Rosh Hashanah, pray to God, and ask forgiveness together with the shtetl folks.

The Jews of Horodets are very hospitable. They share with their neighbors berths and bunks, sleep on the floor and host these village people with brotherly love, smiling faces and embraces. Soon I see myself in the "Cold" Old Synagogue, by the east wall, besides my mother and grandmother. I peep out of the openings in the wall separating the women's gallery from that of the men's hall.

The synagogue is crowded with Jews – old and young. All of them standing wrapped in their Talit [a prayer shawl]. Three, four, Jews are standing on the middle of the pulpit and the "*Ba-al Tki-a*" [the man whose task is to blow the shofar] is ready to blow. A holy stillness grasps the synagogue. An intense chill runs through the body. The sound of the shofar is carried throughout the whole street. The tones produced by the shofar feel like an effusion – outpouring of a desolate spirit of hundreds and hundreds of years of "*Galut*" [living in the Diaspora], mixed with the closeness to God.

And the *"Shliakh Tzibur"* [public emissary], Rabbi Yankl Kodliner, begs God and, weeping, sends his prayers to heaven.

Yes, my longings for you, dear shtetl Horodets, will never subside.

Yom Kippur

By Tzivia Greenglass

The Holidays of my childhood are so deeply rooted in my heart and soul, that when a Holiday approaches, the sights I remember arise to life. One after the other they fly through my mind, like light clouds in the sky.

It is the eve of Yom Kippur [day of Atonement], one or two years after WW1.

We are refugees, living in Yekaterinoslav. The family is smaller as some died and some were lost. We hope to share the fortune of those whom the Soviet government sends back to their destroyed homes. It is difficult for me to tear myself and leave my new home where I matured and where my cognition was nurtured.

The nearer the possibility to move back to our real home, Horodets, gets, the more difficult it is to think of tearing away from the new home. This, despite the fact that the old home is so dear and close to the heart, and our soul longs for it so much. A mixture of longing, pain and desolation gnaws at my heart. It seems to me that it is a heavy trial. Hiwever, heavier trials await us.

A few days before Yom Kippur, we get a note from the government that we must be ready to the move back home. Our transport of refugees sent out of Yekaterinoslav is scheduled two days hence – exactly the evening of *Kol Nidrei* [special prayer on the eve of Yom Kippur].

There is a racket in our house. Everybody is distraught. We don't know what to do. If we don't travel – it means hunger and who knows if there will be another opportunity to get away. In addition, the expectation to get to America will be extinguished. And if we do leave for home, does it cross one's mind that a really devoted Jew, my pious old grandfather, R` Shalom Kostrinsky, will not observe Yom Kippur?

My grandfather, happy and joyful by nature, always satisfied with his lot even in the biggest times of distress, could not accept this last tribulation.

A cloud covering his good looking and wise face – my grandfather walks around like a shadow. Meanwhile time flies. The Day of Atonement approaches nearer and nearer. My grandfather consults friends and the Rabbi. Early on the eve of Yom Kippur, my grandfather comes from the synagogue and says: "Children, I will not sacrifice you life by exposing you to hunger. We are going to travel!" we, the grandchildren, feel relieved when we hear our grandfather's resolute decision.

It is evening, time for Kol-Nidrei. We are at the train station of Yekaterinoslav. The freight car is full with packs and bundles, Jews and Christians. Filth is also there. A gloomy candle lights the train windowless wagon. Ten Jews are standing mournful in our wagon that functions now as a synagogue. Some wear a *Talit* and others are without a *Talit*. They stand bent over the gloomy candle. The sad mood presses our hearts and minds. Then, in this fearful atmosphere we hear Kol-Nidrei sung in its traditional heart-stirring melody.

We swallow tears, we cry spasmodically. However, Jews are not allowed to cry. A soldier comes in, and in the middle of Kol-Nidrei he sends away the praying people to their own wagons, while the train is about to start its voyage. In the wagon, near the dull candle, only my grandfather remains with a couple of Jews who ride in the same wagon. Our Christian neighbors sit still in the corners, on the bundles, and conduct themselves with great respect to the Jewish prayer to God.

I look at grandfather and I cannot bear seeing him sad. I close my eyes. Sitting with closed eyes, the memory of the evening of Yom Kippur and Kol-Nidrei in my home, Horodets, arises before me.

Here, I see Jews from the "Street" - old, young, children and women – wearing white clothes. All are rushing to the synagogue, to the Beit-Midrash, or to the Shtibls of the Chassidim, to snatch a prayer, a plea, before Kol-Nidrei.

Almost every one of them carries with him a candle - a long or a short one, a thick or a thin one. Hurriedly, they wish each other "*Khatima Tova*" [to be signed in the book of life]. People who have been cross with each other, pause to beg forgiveness, wishing each other a good year. It seems to me that the wind in the street is full of holiness.

And here is our old, old synagogue, around which many legends are woven. I see the synagogue lit with extra bright lamps and scores of candles. On the pulpit, in the middle of the synagogue, R` Yankl Kodliner, completely wrapped in white, sings with a sweet sadness his prayers and pleas. I hear his crying as he implores God: "*Al Tashlikhenu Le-et Zikna*" [Do not forsake us when we are old"]. And simple Jews wrapped in white robes and Talit fill the old holy synagogue with holiness and reverence.

I forget where I am – I find myself totally in the synagogue of my childhood. A strong shake brings me back to reality. I open my eyes – we are on the train. My grandfather is standing, bent over the dull candle that is about to expire. His countenance and his eyes express sadness, longing and exile of many generations. That sadness, my grandfather, I will never forget. In the depth of my soul I hold his pain and will carry it to the end of my life.

[Page 63]

Sukkot [tabernacles]

By Tzivia Greenglass

Summer is over. Mild winds blow and pluck off the trees the yellow, weak, leaves, carrying them on their wings and throwing them at the feet of passers-by. Autumn is moving in.

The passing of harvesters with wagons full of grain has ceased, but the wind still carries the reverberation of their hearty singing the song of field, harvest and joy. In truth, our Jews did not experience this feeling of joy of field and harvest, but we celebrate the Holiday of nature with the *Sukkah* [tabernacle], *Etrog* [citron fruit] and *Lulav* [palm branch].

The morning after Yom Kippur, Jews carry old boards, tables and shutters to build the *Sukkah*. I was always jealous of the children and grandchildren who helped built the *sukkah*, dragging boards, bringing nails, etc., In our house and in my grandfather's house, there was a built-in *sukkah*. We only had to wash and clean it up and adorn it with fruit. We just had to open its "wings" and the *sukkah* was ready to welcome this important Holiday. However, the temporary *sukkah* had another taste to it. It was set up with effort and then you could sit in it in comfort. The *mitzvah* of "*leishev basukkah*" [to sit in the *sukkah*] was really felt in the temporary sukkah. On the other hand, when rain started pouring into the *sukkah*, we would close up the "wings" of our built-in *sukkah* and get rid of the nuisance. In the temporary *sukkah*, a race would start. People would rushto snatch the candles, tablecloth, pillows and blankets so that they won't get wet, and would ran with all the utensils into the house. Still, this running added some Jewish charm…

Who does not remember the delight of *Khol Hamoed* [days in between *Sukkot* and *Simkhat Torah*]. There was a great deal of travelling to stay as guests with family, or host guests coming over. Our train station was thriving on *Khol Hamoed*. The government became rich thanks to the Jewish *Khol Hamoed* travelers. The joy and delight of the Holiday reached its peak on the last day of *Sukkot – Simkhat-Torah* [the joy of having finished reading the Torah and starting a new round of reading the Torah till next year].

My grandfather's house was full of joy. Tables are set with wine, sponge cakes, nuts, candies and fruit. My grandfather, the *gabbai* [the secretary] of *Khevra Kadisha* [the burial society] invites the shtetl for a *Simkhat –Torah- Kiddush* [blessing over the wine]. People drink, sing and dance. Soon they lead the *gabbai* to the old synagogue. The "Street" is lit with scores of candles that have been mounted on the windows' sills and on porches along the whole length of Kobriner Street, up to the synagogue. Children are carrying flags with a lit candle on top – a real illumination. They sing through paper-honks and beat copper saucers and pots. A mixture of sounds reverberate in the stillness of the night. To the tones of singing, flares a *Simkhat –Torah* dance around the *gabbai*.

The synagogue is lit by extra bright lamps and candles and the light blinds the eyes. They dance again, they dance around the Torah scrolls that are being passed from hands to hands, and they kiss the scrolls. Ah, how the cold synagogue warmed up the hearts of Jewish children.

Now, the *sukkah* is burnt down, singing is muted and dancing has stopped. A longing gnaws at the heart.

[Page 64]

Hanukkah

By Tzivia Greenglass

It is Hanukkah. I look at the Hanukkah-Menorah with the burning candles and I long for Horodets. I long for my childhood, for my home, and for Horodets. ----

[Tzivia continues with an almost verbatim description of her longings found in the pervious chapters about the Holidays, so I skip the passage.HK]

It is cold outside. The frost "stings". The "Street", the "Market", the river and the fields around – up to the horizon - are covered with a shawl of white snow. Trees are white, roofs are white, everything is white, except for the grey smoke that winds over the whiteness.

I am sitting in Khana's *Kheder*. He tells us the story of Hanukkah and the revolt of the great leaders, the Maccabees [father and five sons led the revolt against the Greeks in the 2nd century B.C.]. He tells the story of Hannah and her seven sons – moving us, kids, to tears. The Rabbi finishes telling the stories of Hanukkah and in honor of this bright Holiday, he sends us home earlier than at other times.

Wrapped in coats, shawls and kerchiefs, the children run home. I don't go home, I run to my grandfather, where my good mother, my sister and brother are waiting for me. I run and the snow squeaks under my feet and the frost nips my nose and ears.

I run on, out of breath, and reach my grandfather's house. Grandfather, grandmother, mother and the whole household are there. My grandfather is waiting for me to say the blessing over the Hanukkah candles.

The Hanukkah lamp is on the window sill. My grandfather lights the *Shamash* [the serving candle], sings the blessings with a hearty sweet voice, and the first candle is lit.

The lit wicks of the Hanukkah-Menorah, on the window sills of houses, light up the street around them and warm the hearts of children. I stand and watch the burning candle and Hannah and her seven sons march before my eyes. They paid with their life because they were not tempted to betray their belief and their people. Then I see Matityahu the Cohen and Yehuda Maccabee with his soldiers and it seems to me that the Hanukkah candles are in fact *a yortzeit* [memorial candle lit once a year] candle for the soldiers killed in the revolt. I keep on watching, unable to tear myself away from the Hanukkah candle. Then, a warm, loving hand wakes me up to reality. My grandfather says: "My child, here, this is your Hanukkah money." I quickly forget Hannah and her sons and the Maccabees. I grab the Hanukkah money, hug my grandfather and kiss him with all my childish strength, I take out from my pocket the tin *dreidl* [spinning top] molded for me by my brother Moshe, and we start playing the *dreidl* game.

We actually play the game using buttons that we have torn out of our own dresses, pants, coats and shirts. Suddenly – wow, the smell of fried potato *latkes* [pancakes] reaches our nose. We quickly count our winnings, in buttons, and sit down ready for the *latkes*. It does not take long before grandmother comes to the table with a bowl full of *latkes*. The house becomes full of merriment; eating *latkes,* playing cards and Chinese checkers, and the children renew their *dreidl* game.

And, the Hanukkah candle flickers and flickers until it is no more.

Now, whenever I watch the lit Hanukkah candles, I visualize the revolt of our brothers and sisters in the ghettos, visualize our martyrs enveloped in flames of fire in the crematoriums and I seem to hear their cry: "*Shma Israel*" [Here o, Israel]. Yes, I watch the candles and I see memory-candles for our martyrs and dear ones.

[Page 65]

Fifteen of Shvat

(The Rosh Hashanah of the Trees)

By Tzivia Greenglass

The forest rustles on Rosh Hashanah
Murmers prayers with fervor
Trees wrapped in snow
Stand in Talits.

Not a forest – well, well, what do you know – a synagogue
And with holiness it is full
And the old tree of the community
Is the Khazan, in charge of prayer

And the wind – listen:
The shofar blows Tru-ru-ru
And the trees beg God
That he will grace them

With a good year they should be blessed:
Sweet fruit for the people
Silently bent they stand
Outside, a white snow is falling

Purim

By Tzivia Greenglass

It is the end of winter. The sun heats more intensely. The days become gradually longer. The frozen earth starts emerging out of its coagulated state. The water from the melting snow and ice flow in the ditches, and then farther to the canals. However, enough water stays on the plane, and the process of mixing – water and earth – produces fresh soft mud. The mud bothers nobody.

If one wants to walk from one house to the other – one lays a board, a broken shutter or some bricks and walks over, or one jumps over and is already on the other side. Children are very delighted. They are not bound to be cuddled next to the ovens. The sun is smiling and the *liyuz'kes* [puddles] water winks at them to come outside to the street and play freely. Purim is already near. *Ester Ta'anis* [Fast day prior to Purim] feels already like a Holiday in the village. Smells of fresh baking are drifting in the air from here and there: *HomenTashn* [triangular cookies with sweet filling such as poppy seeds, plums, etc], Purim cakes, *lekech* [spongecake] *tortn* [*fruit pie*], *fladn* [fruit layer cake], *and strudels.* Children are having fun. They lick from one bowl and form a second bowl, they taste the cut edges of the fruit cakes, and they wait impatiently for the *megile* [the scroll of Ester] reading, to deafen Haman's name with the rattles.

The *Beit Midrash* [small orthodox synagogues], the Karliner and Kobriner *shtiblekh* [small Chassidic houses of prayer] let people in for the reading of the *megile* - almost the whole of the population of Horodets - and the rattles are active with gusto.

The main Holiday is nearing. However, first we have the *se'ude* [the Holiday dinner]. Several hours before the dinner, one can see in the street people with covered plates. These are the *shalakh mones* [plates with sweets cakes and fruit sent from one to the other]. When I saw through the window a plate with a white cover, I would feel like tearing away the cover and then peeping to discover what is there on the plate.. When the messenger of the *shalakh mones* entered our house, he would not have to wait for mother to receive it from his hands.

When I saw a candy in the form of a pony, puppet or bird, I would immediately grab it not to put it back. For that, mother had to "pay dear" by replacing the bird with three big marmalade candies, the puppet - with a big piece of strudel, and the pony – with an apple… While doing that, she would remove the lemon and replace it with an orange. [called "China apples" in Yiddish] (oranges were more important than lemons). She would pay the messenger for bringing the *shalakh mones* and for carrying back the *shalakh mones* with the alterations.

It is already evening. A very long table is ready in the dining room at my grandfather's house. A very tall cake adorns the head of the table. Candles burn in the decorated brass candle sticks. Bottles of wine have small glasses around them. Friends are invited to the dinner. There is again a feeling of a Holiday. The marinated herring and the Purim cakes have all heavenly tastes. However, how can we sit at the table and eat, when all the time more *shalakh mones* keep arriving, and we must peep to see the contents of the plates and even grab a *nash* [some sweets]. When my poor grandmother becomes too tired to exchange the contents of the plates, she takes the *shalakh mones* that Motye Karlinski has sent and sends it over to the Rabbi, and the Rabbi's *shalakh mones* she sends over to Karlinski. Uncle Khayim's *shalakh mones* is sent to uncle Aharon-Yossl, Aharon-Yossl's *shalakh mones* is sent to uncle Motye, and that of uncle Motye, is sent to aunt Mindl. And that is how the *shalakh mones* are being exchanged one plate for the other, and are sent without adding to them even a small bit of the sponge cake. My grandmother was a bigger economizer than my mother.

Then, in the middle of exchanging, the Purim-actors come in. They are adorned with brass buttons and their faces are smeared with soot. They position themselves and play-act the story of Purim – from beginning to end. The red Haman used to scare me. I can visualize him now with the glittering buttons, the soot and the twisted ends of his whiskers, wearing a red hat.

Thinking of Haman and the Purim actors of my childhood, tens of Hamans creep into my mind, the tormentors of my people and my relatives. Is there a sigh that can relieve my heartache?!

[Page 67]

[*Peysekh*] Passover

By David Kaplan

[Translator's notes- in square brackets]

Right after Purim, there was a great deal of commotion in Horodets. People started right away to prepare for Passover. As you know – it was necessary to have matzo for Passover! There were *shvalniyes* [sewing workshops] in the "market" and in the "street". The furniture from those houses were taken out and replaced by big tables and other tools that belonged to the sewing workshops. Generally this work was done cooperatively: one would help the other to bake the matzos. Everybody knew how to roll the matzos. That was done by the women. However, only a few men knew how to make punctures in the matzos. It was a great honor to make the punctures in the matzos. I was also privileged to puncture, at Israel Yankel's *shvalnie,* thanks to the grown up children who gave me this opportunity. When the matzos were ready, they were stacked, right away, in a big *bodniye* (a sort of barrel) and locked until Passover. Nobody was allowed to get close to the matzos, for fear that there would not be enough matzos for Passover. It was impossible to buy or bake other matzos. All the women were busy both by day and by night. In every house, the fire was burning all night, for fear they would oversleep and miss getting up to bake the matzos.

And what about whitewashing the house? And who will scrape and scrub the benches/chairs, beds and other household furniture? In short, the women were busy day and night. Is it a trifle? The joyful Passover is drawing near.

Children were also busy: they have to help their mothers – some would hand the *derkatch* (a worn out broom), some would hand the white-wash or just bring down the Passover table-wear from the *boydem* [attic]. Right after Purim we would suffer exile. The tables, chairs and beds were put away in the backyard and in the middle of the house they put a barrel, and on top of it – a board, to serve as a table. And what about sleeping? Some slept on the floor and some on the oven. Food was not so hot. Therefore there were other good things as a reward: we ran to the tailor to be fitted with new clothes, and to the shoemaker to be fitted with new shoes.

Thank God, we made it to Passover's eve. There is no Kheder now. We are free as a bird, we can go wherever and whenever we wish. The house is clean, tidy and white-washed. Yellow sand was poured on the floor and we prepare for the Seder. There is joy in our hearts and also in our pockets (as they are full of nuts). We are wearing a new garment and on our feet – new shoes or boots. Truthfully, our toes are somewhat squeezed in there but the shoemaker said: "until after Passover it will be OK". Nu, we have to believe him…

On Passover, after the festive midday meal, the young men would go out to the highway, all of them bragging about their new garments and about their pockets full of nuts. The moment they were farther away from the shtetl, all of them would start cracking their nuts. All were merry and in good spirits.

On *khol Hamoed* [intermediary weekdays between the first two and last days of the holiday], the *melamdim* [*kheder* teachers] started preparing their *kheders* before summer. Each of them made an effort to look well groomed. They combed their beard, twisted their whiskers, and with a pretty cane in hand they went into the houses to recruit their pupils. This visit was not so agreeable for the boys because the teacher would interview-test them and not all children knew or remembered what they had learned.

However, the teacher had found a way to make it appear that the child answered well. After all, he had to have them in *kheder* before summer. The children barely breathed before the teacher was gone. Then, all boys set out together on the way to the train station. That was an old custom in Horodets, to walk to the train station on *khol Hamoed*. All of them returned together from the station to the shtetl with a song on their lips. In a word - it was lively and joyful.

As soon as the holiday was approaching its end, the heart felt gloomy. We had to go back to the *kheder* and nobody liked it. However, what could we do? It had to be like that! Therefore we got some compensation: we helped carry up the Passover table-wear to the attic, and that, in a way, was a continuation of Passover.

Where does one obtain a Horodetser Passover?

[Page 68]

Lag B'Omer

[33rd of the 49 days between Passover and Shavuot]

[L = 30 = ל   G = 3 = ג]

By Shlomo Gar'in

[Translator's notes – in square brackets]

A Holiday resembles a person. It changes and it is affected by the environment and time. Each Holiday has its own character and local color.

They say that Lag Ba'omer in Horodets was quite different from the one I remember from my Kheder-years, in the twenties of the twentieth century. In the past, so they tell us, the Kheder-children used to make bows and arrows and "fought" the children from another Kheder. They had generals, field-marshals and all the paraphernalia of an army. In my Kheder-years, so it seems, the Horodets-boys were already fed up with wars. They had already seen the wars between the Germans and Russians, *Pietlortzes, Balakhovtzes, Poznantshikes, Halerttshikes*[1] and finally the Russian-Polish war. The children of Horodets said: "Enough with wars".

It is also told that already prior to WW1 they used to eat dairy food, such as cheese, and in the aristocratic houses they used to pull down the shutters and eat blintzes… Why pull down the shutters? This is to avoid gossip. [perhaps envy?...]

Why did they eat dairy food? This is not my specialty. The expert who can answer this question is the editor doctor Akiva Ben-Ezra. He deals with folklore – let him provide the answer to this puzzling question. [Ben Ezra's answer is in a footnote: "It is very simple: Lag b'Omer occurs in spring, when there is a sufficient amount of milk; for who among the Horodets Jews did not have a cow? Blintzes are prepared on a festive occasion."] [I wonder whether he meant it seriously that most Jews of Horodets had a cow.HK]

When the Stoliner *shtiebel* existed, the Chassidim there used to prepare a real feast, with fish and meat, as it is clearly a joyful celebration of Rabbi Shimon Bar Yokhai [spiritual leader. Opposed the Roman rule after the destruction of the Temple and hid from execution in a cave for 12 years, studying the Torah]. The Kheder-children taught by the Stoliner teachers, benefited from that feast.

There was another sign that Lag b'Omer was already here. A barber appeared, quite early, from the neighboring shtetl, Antipolye, to trim the hair of the Horodets Jews, who did not have a haircut in the days of the *sfira* [betweem Passover and Lag b'Omer]. In my days, this sign no longer existed. Instead of the Antipolyer barber we used to wait for the host of children from the kheders of Antipolye, who used to come to Horodets, on foot, every Lag b'Omer.

A whole year, we, kheder-children, looked forward to that day. On that day we were in high spirits and we were full of joy and strength. We were not afraid or the *shkotzim* [Gentile fresh lads] anymore. We outnumbered them!

Besides feeling free and proud against the *shkotzim*, we simply felt free: first – there was no learning in the kheder. Second, we could do whatever we wished. There was no "forbidden!" like on other Holidays. We were permitted the pleasure of bathing in the river of Horodets, and indeed together with the children from Antipolye who had come especially for this purpose.

On account of our guests, we used to wake up quite early, when the cows were going to the pasture. This in itself was an experience. When did a child have the opportunity to see the shepherd going from house to house to goad the cows to the field?

The "street" children left out with bow and arrow in the hand. And indeed, while marching over the wooden bridge, they tried shooting the crows that had their nests on an old oak – which according to our childish fantasy, had been standing there since the six days of creation.

The assembling point was near the "*Pozharne*" [fire station] in the market. The "street" children would also gather there. We would position ourselves like the orchestra of the firemen brigade of Kobryn, who visited Horodets, every year, on the "third of May". [when the Polish parliament in 1971 adopted its constitution]. We would hold in our hands tin sheets, cymbals and whistles, made of *la'ze* and then march to the beat of a Polish marching song, from one corner of the shtetle to the other, stopping at the alley where once stood the Polish cloister. Why indeed in that alley?

People said that a woman who converted to Christianity lived there and apparently it was an instinctive protest against that woman.

When we left the alley we marched to the Antipolye-road, to welcome our guests. We stopped at a small grove, not far from "*Mogilkes*" (Gentile cemetery). That was by reason of Lag B'Omer that we got as far as the "*Mogilkes*" where the "not good ones" were located – whether dead or alive…

We spread on the grass and waited for the coming guests. While we were resting there, our Yaakov Hershl, son of Meir, used to tell wonderful tales about Jewish heroes.

However, not everybody had the patience to listen to all the tales about the Jewish heroes. So, what was to be done? We let ourselves out to frighten the *bushanes* [storks]. Upon seeing a *bushan* we call out: "bushan, bushan, pojar" [run away]. And, indeed, the *bushan* rose on its long legs, with its white wings, and fled.

Other would occupy themselves with the bows and arrows, shooting birds and small forest animals.

And here we start catching glimpse of the host of kheder-boys from Antipolye. A real army: hats with a "magen-Dovid", rucksacks on their backs, marching like real soldiers. To judge by their walk and their looks, they felt quite proud in comparison to the Horodets children. We let them march forward in front, and we marched behind them, until we reached Itsikl's orchard. They sat down and started enjoying all the good stuff that they had brought from Antipolye. We watched with envy and kept quiet. Therefore we had our revenge when we reached the river. There, we showed them what we, Horodets-children, could accomplish in the river.

We showed them such tricks that they had never seen before, because there is was river in Antipolye. We swam standing, we lay "*klafter*" [crawl-swimming], and we sprang into the river again and again.

It was a day of heroism and bravery and a whole year we looked forward impatiently to the next Lag b'Omer.

Footnote from Zvi Gitelman:

1. The first term refers to Ukrainian nationalists led by Semen Petliura. "Balakhovtses" were a military group in Belorussia under the command of Stanislaw Bulak-Balakhovich, who managed to fight in the Tsarist, Bolshevik, Polish and Belorussian armies. Poznantchikes were the Armiia Wielkopolska, a military group that fought the Germans for control of what is now western Poland (including the Poznan area). Stanislaw Haller was a Polish officer who fought the Bolsheviks in 1920 and was the military's chief of staff in the early 1920s. As the memoir states, all of these units attacked Jews at one time or another.

[Page 69]

Shavuot

[Pentecost. Holiday celebrating the gathering of the first fruits and the giving of the Torah to the Jews]

By Tzivia Greenglass

[Translator's notes in square brackets]

Sabbath and Holidays awaken in my memory vivid pictures from my childhood. In front of my eyes, they are alive – rising from the dead.

Not only people have their own luck. Holidays have marked luck as well. I think that the luckiest of all Holidays is Shavuot. (Although Passover cannot complain of its luck). Surely, what other Holiday occurs in the midst of bloom and green like the Holiday of Shavuot?

Young, fresh grass sprout in the courtyards, in the small gardens and in the surrounding small parks. The trees next to the houses spread with pride their wing-like branches, painting in green the streets and decorating the small houses.

The sand under our feet is soft and dry, without any trace of mud. The sky is blue and clear as if transparent. The two small canals (side-brooks), that stretch parallel to the two sides of the river, are covered with green *tsherot* and *flisniak* (sort of grass), and various kinds of water-flowers and other flowers. And right in front of my eyes burst forth light-blue field-flowers of great variety, the *"nyezabutkes"* (forget-me-not).

I would have given anything to be able, one more time, to hold a twisted bouquet of these flowers - from the fields around my shtetl.

We, children, observed very devotedly the custom of decorating the houses with branches of trees, grass and flowers in honor of Shavuot. We walked in groups, barefoot, to "ravage" the canals. With dresses pulled up and trousers folded up, we risked *bradzshen* (crawling) in the muddy water to snatch and pluck a flower. Few hours later, we returned home with large bouquets of flowers, taller than ourselves. Upon reaching home, we sorted the flowers to put them in vases, jars, bottles and glasses – to fit their size and placed them on the window-sill and on tables. Thus we beautified our hearts and houses.

Now that we already had flowers for the Holiday, what is to be done about getting green branches in honor of Shavuot? That, you should know, was a more complicated matter.

Who would allow us to cut their trees? The Poritz of the shtetle had a grove, not far from the iron bridge, that looked untended and abandoned. Our small "commando" set forth to that grove to cut branches. Sometimes we were lucky in our first attempt - bringing home whole branches adorned with green leaves. However, more often, the Poritz's hounds smelled the mischievous group and would drive us away and chase us with wild cries. The youngsters fled home, some through the *batchvenikes* (river edges), and some through the iron bridge and the railway tracks. However, the cries and growling abuse did not frighten us too much and did not deter us from coming to the grove again and again. It was a must to have green leaves for Shavuot.

[Page 71]

Episodes

By A. Kostrometzki [=A. Ben Ezra]

Translated by Hannah Kadmon

[Translators comments in square brackets]

A. The Dispute = [מחלוקת]

[*Shoykhet* = *ritual slaughterer*. *Shokhtim* = ritual slaughterers.]

[*Misnogdim* = *opponents to the Hasidic movement*. See: http://en.wikipedia.org/wiki/Misnagdim]

[*dintoyre* =lawsuit before the Rabbinical court]

When one asks an elderly man from Horodets: "Do you remember the dispute?" he would understand immediately that one means the well known dispute in Horodets about the *shokhtim*. This dispute continued for about a year (1892-1893), left an impression on the surrounding towns and *shtetls* and reached even R' Yitskhak Elkhanan. [a Rabbi from Kaunas]

This was not a regular dispute like the disputes that took place in Jewish communities. It was not about this or that *shoykhet*. That dispute was the climax of the old hatred between Hasidim and Misnogdim in Horodets.

Horodets was a Hasidic stronghold for the Karliner-Stoliner dynasty. Their Rabbis visited Horodets quite often as they had there absolutely fervent adherents. As a result, the Karliner Hasidim had a strong influence over the community-life in Horodets. Their influence was mostly marked in the arrangement of the *klekoydesh* [he religious personnel]. Admittedly, the Rabbi was not a Hasid but nor was he a fighter against the Hasidim. Therefore, the Hasidim were in charge of half of the slaughtering. In other words: the Hasidim had a Hasidic *shoykhet* and all that was slaughtered in the *shtetl* was in cooperation with the "municipal" *shoykhet*-cantor.

At least there was an understanding. However, the Misnogdim showed contempt for this agreement. The Hasidim, on their part, looked for flaws in the Misnogdim's *shoykhet*. I was told that a hundred years previously there was a *shoykhet* by the name of Shmuel. Shmuel used to give out lucky charms, for which he charged money. The Hasidim used this fact as a pretext and the *shoykhet* had to resign.

Later on there was a *shoykhet*-cantor by the name of R' David. He was a quiet and honest man who kept himself at a distance from the dispute. For a while it was quiet in Horodets. 70-80 years ago, there was a *shoykhet* by the name of Yirmiyah Zerakh, a zealous Misnoged who extremely despised Hasidim, and naturally a dispute could not be avoided.

It is told about Yirmiyah Zerakh that when he heard that his son, Itshe Meir, had become a Hasid, he made a *krie* [tearing of clothes as a sign of mourning over the dead] and sat *shive* [seven days of mourning]. That son, some years later, became a Rabbi in Retsitse, in the Minsk region. God "punished" Yirmiyah Zerakh, and his second son, Pinye, became a Kobriner Hasid – Pinye the Butcher…

A clash arose between the Hasidim and the Misnogdim. One day, the Stoliner Rabbi, R' Aharon (the "Old Rabbi") arrived in Horodets. The Misnogdim damaged the *mikve* [ritual bathhouse; pool for ritual immersion] so that the Rabbi would not be able to immerse himself for purification.

On the Hasidic side, the *shoykhet* R' Eliyahu Yankl is well remembered. He was a great scholar and knew by heart the entire ש״ס [six books of the Mishnah – the Talmud]. When he was seventy, a "rebellion" started against him actually from among his own followers, that is: his own Hasidim. The leader of that "rebellion" was the young man Asher David (look up the article about R' Asher David), Yankl Khasid's son-in-law. He claimed that R' Eliyahu Yankl was too old and should not be permitted to slaughter.

In the end, the Hasidim sent away Asher David for a year to study slaughtering in Pinsk, at their expense. Until his return, they supported his wife and children.

When Asher David returned from Pinsk with a diploma for ritual slaughtering, the real dispute flared up. The Misnogdim seized the opportunity to reckon with their enemies: "How is it possible that a young man should share in equal part with the town's old *shoykhet*"?

The "municipal" *shoykhet*-cantor was then Moshe Meir. He could teach well but he also knew very well the business of creating a dispute. He led a campaign among the Misnogdim that the Hasidim should get a third of the income from slaughtering.

What was the income based on? Besides a payment, the *shoykhet* got a *kishke* [guts] with *shmalts* [fat] from every slaughtered cow.

The Misnogdim influenced the non-Hasidic butchers not to engage the Hasidic *shoykhet,* guided the cantor to defeat the Hasidic "whims", and, of course, see to it that he also got the *kishkes*. When they gave Asher David the opportunity to slaughter a calf, the *kishke* was quite small. It was the small *kishke* that ignited the fire: "Why shouldn't Asher David get the same part of *kishke* as the cantor?"

The Kobriner Hasidim were caught between the two fires and it is safe to say that they were neutral. The reason was as follows: they did not occupy the appropriate peak in Hasidism. The dynasty of their Rabbis was quite young, only the third generation of Rabbis. Their first Rabbi, R' Moshe, was neither a Rabbi's son, nor a Hasid. In addition, the number of the Kobriner Hasidim was small. They were not deeply rooted Hasidim and many of them were former Misnogdim. They lacked the pride and devotion that the real Hasidim possessed. It was only natural that they did not join the Karliner Hasidim. The Kobriner Hasidim were entirely confused. It posed for them a grave problem whom to join. Therefore they took a passive stand.

The Hasidim clamored, came to Rabbi Yehoshua Yaakov Rabinovitz and demanded justice, to return to the old agreement. The Rabbi found that the Hasidim were right about this issue. He sent the *shames* to the *shul* to declare a ban on the cantor's slaughtering, as well as a ban on imported meat to Horodets, until they arrived at a settlement.

There was a great commotion in the *shtetl*. Women came to ask questions about what to do with the dishes in which they ate the banned meat. Many people threw out their pots and plates that they had used when they did not know about the ban. There was no meat in the *shtetl*. The Misnogdim became vegetarian, for the time being, and the Sabbaths dinner were dairy.

Melancholy descended on Horodets. The Sabbaths were marred. Fathers and children sat at the Sabbath table to sing songs and suddenly there was no singing. What was the matter?

How could they sing "Meat and Fish" when it was not permitted to look at meat, and instead of meat they ate sour-milk with cheese, sorrel [a vegetable] and the like? Where could one get a piece of meat?

The fire of the dispute was re-kindled. The Misnogdim realized that the Rabbi supported the Hasidim. The more extreme Misnogdim called everybody to a meeting, just to spite in the Rabbi's house, to pressure the Rabbi to revoke the ban. In their excitement they lost their moral balance. The Rabbi, aware that he was representing the function of justice, did not want to yield to the heated assembly.

Many Rabbis with R' Yitskhak Elkhanan intervened in order to bring peace. Only when the Misnogdim agreed to *dintoyre* [lawsuit before the Rabbinical court], did the Old Rabbi call off the ban. R' David'l from Antipolye attended the *dintoyre*, from which the Hasidim came out victorious.

Afterwards, when the verdict was published, the Misnogim's leader came to the Rabbi to apologize and ask his forgiveness. The Rabbi calmed them with some sharp Torah-jokes and gave them his blessing.

With time, the stain between the Misnogdim and the Hasidim in Horodets disappeared entirely and peace and quiet prevailed.

[Page 72]

B. The *Ta'are Bret*

[The board on which dead bodies are laid for cleansing before burial]

[Parts of this chapter, the dramatic ones, were written in the present tense by the author and I prefer to translate these parts using the present tense as well. HK]

In the second half of the 19th century, there lived in Horodets a Jew named Shmuel Kaliker [cripple]. He was nicknamed so because he on his two legs were crippled, almost paralyzed. He walked with the aid of two crutches. Mostly, he used to sit in one place. His hands were also not normal, distorted, Heaven preserve us. However, his mind was clear like crystal, and his natural understanding to analyze things was famous in the whole neighborhood. It is said that he was also versed in ש"ס [ש"ס =the six Mishnah books = oral Jewish laws; the Talmud]. He knew by heart the tractates of *Baba-metsi'a, Psakhim and Khulin* with the interpretations of *Rashi* and *Ma'harsha*. In addition, he knew grammar, Russian, Polish and knew a bit about medicine.

Not in vain was his house a center for people of various classes. From various towns people used to come to him for advice, to consult with him about various problems. For example: A Jew got a lease on an estate from a *porets* [gentile lord; landowner] for a certain price, naturally after a down payment of a certain sum, but the Russian government does not let him hold the lease. The Jew is perplexed: he gave the *porets* the down payment, believed him, and he does not have the lease. What should the Jew do? He comes to Shmuel Kaliker and is helped by his good advice. Or, a Jew sits in a village, manages an inn and makes a living. He pays the *pristav* [police commissioner in Czarist Russia] to be allowed to stay in the village, which was against the law. One bright morning he is told to get out of the village. It is bad. The Jew runs to Shmuel Kalike and gets some advice.

Wood merchants, grain merchants and merchants of other branches, all used to come to consult with Shmuel Kaliker. His advice helped all those who had heavy problems, and Shmuel Kaliker, with all his keen senses, familiarized himself with the problems of each individual. He received each and every person with kindness, and without any charge, as he himself was a man of means. He had a grain-store.

Shmuel Kaliker's house was a societal get together place. People talked to each other, there, and discussed local and worldwide questions. Whoever wished to read newspapers, could do it in Shmuel's house, both in Hebrew and in Russian. Besides Jewish books he owned book of science and literature. If a person wished to know whether his son had a good head, whether he understood *tosfos* [collective summation of Rabbis elucidation of issues in the Talmud] and *Ma'harsha* [interpreter] or if someone's future son-in-law was really something special, he would bring him to Shmuel Kaliker to test or appraise him.

Appraising or testing children made Shmuel Kaliker come alive, as he did not have his own children to test. He was childless.

* * *

Shmuel Kaliker left a will in which he bequeathed the larger part of his wealth for various charitable purposes. He appointed 7 guardians to carry out the will. After his death, when they opened the will, the guardians found out that the greatest part of the wealth was composed of promissory notes, debts from various places. They demanded from his wife to give them all that was left. However she handed them only a small part of what was left, and avoided handing over the rest, claiming that she did not know of any other articles except the ones she had handed over.

The guardians brought over the Antipoler Rabbi, R' David, to help the Rabbi of Horodets. The two of them sent the *shames* to the woman to summon to a *dintoyre*. She came with her nearest friend to the rabbinical court.

The Rabbis are sitting there, talking to each other: "A good name is better than precious ointment, and the day of death than the day of one's birth" (*Kohelet;* [=Ecclesiastes] chapter 7;1). This verse fits well the deceased – during his life he was notable for his good name and now for his will. They read out the will: a part for his wife, after her - the *shul,* the *besmedresh,* the Hasidim's *shtiebles,* the *talmetoyre* and other institutions.

The Rabbis call the *shames* to bring in the two sides in the dispute. The wife, Gutel, comes in. R' Hillel Karlinski rises to his feet. He is the eldest guardian, their representative, also the *gabe* of *Khevre Kedi'she* [voluntary burial society]. The *dintoyre* began.

R' Hillel presents his claims. The Rabbis listen to him. Then, they turn to the woman to hear her response and at that they comment to her that the wishes of the deceased must be fulfilled. The woman answer that she knows of nothing else in addition to what she has already handed. The Rabbis speak to her again and say that if she does not remember, they will grant her time to try to remember. They take a break from the *dintoyre* for a few hours. The two sides and all others who are present come out of the court house. Yisrael Moshe, the cemetery attendant comes in. R' Hillel calls him to the side and commands him to go to the cemetery and bring from there the *ta'are Bret* to the Rabbi's house. Yisrael Moshe hears this command with great surprise. R' Hillel notices the effect on the man's face and says: " Yisrael Moshe! Don't ask any questions! The *gabe* of *Khevre Kedi'she* is talking to you, bring the *ta'are bret* and put it in a side room so that no one notices it, and wait until I tell you what to do."

Yisrael Moshe carries out the *gabe*'s command and brings the *ta'are bret* to the Rabbi's house. Women in the street notice it and one of them asks: "Who has died?" Another woman answers: "Nobody died in the *shtetl*. He is carrying a soul from the cemetery on the *ta'are bret*." "Whose soul? What soul?", all the others ask in unison, and they follow Yisrael Moshe's to the Rabbi's house.

The Rabbis resume the *dintoyre*, tell the *shames* to call in the litigators, saying something to each other. The litigators come in. The Rabbis turn to them and say: "If it is difficult for you stand up, you can sit down. Only the two litigators can sit down. It is not allowed that one stands and the other sits." The two sit down. Then the Rabbis ask the woman: "Do you have anything to add to what you said before?" The woman answers: "No, I don't know about anything else".

Once again the Rabbis say something to each other. R' Hilled turns to them and says: "Allow me, gentlemen, to pose one question to the woman and address the question directly to her." Again the Rabbis consulted each other and answer: "You can talk to her but do it very calmly, not with anger".

R' Hillel starts: "Gutel, did you hear what the Rabbis said before, that the will of the deceased as he put down in writing is holy and must be fulfilled?" "Yes," she retorts, "I heard". R' Hillel continues: "Do you know that the deceased is present here in court and is waiting for your answer? You should know that Shmuel is here! Here, he comes!" then he calls out: "Yisrael Moshe!" Yisrael Moshe comes in with the *ta'are bret*.

All the people present get up bewildered, not knowing what is coming next. R' Hillel shouts at the woman: "Quickly, run home, bring everything here, Shmuel will be waiting here until you return. However, don't linger, don't let him wait too long."

Gutel runs home. R' Hillel tells Yisrael Moshe: "You can take away the *ta'are bret*". Whispering, he continues and tells him: "Hold the *bret* in the street and wait until Gutel returns."

Gutel returns from her home with a bundle in her hands. She glances swiftly at the *ta'are bret* in the street, and runs into the Rabbi's house. The Rabbis are sitting waiting. She places the bundle on the table, says goodbye and goes home. Yisrael Moshe takes the *ta'are bret* back to the cemetery.

The guardians confer among themselves. They reproach R' Hillel for not having asked the Rabbis whether to do what he did. R' Hillel retorts: "Where there is a question there is also an answer. The Rabbis would surely not have dared to take such a step against the woman." In the meanwhile the guardians sit and open the bundle, check everything inside and find it fits the sum of the will.

In the course of time, the Horodetser community leader collected all the debts, through it took a few years. With a part of the money they renovated the *shul*, repaired the *besmedresh*, sent children to *melamdim* and they divided the rest to cover various charity-matters. Shmuel Kaliker's name remained famous and glorified.

[Page 75]

C. A *Blut-Bilbl* [Blood libel]

Did you get to know Tshernetski? Do you remember that there was a gentile in Horodets, a cobbler, who spoke Yiddish like a Jew?

If not, I will provide you with additional signs: He had flecks on his face and he was a… drunkard. If not for his drunkenness he could be mistaken for a Jew.

One day the Kobriner Rabbi came to spend a Sabbath in Horodets, and Tshernetski came to the Rabbi to "celebrate" saying: "Bless me, Rabbi, that I should stop drinking". The Rabbi smiled and said: "May God help you".

I don't know whether God helped Tshernetski to stop drinking because Tshernetski did not help himself, like the saying: "God helps he who helps himself".

Tshernetski did not stop drinking. He was drunk day and night. However he should be commended as good gentile and even when drunk he did not hit any Jew like the other drunken gentiles in the *shtetl* whom it was frightening to encounter.

It seemed that Tshernetski did not have a family. He was always seen in Jewish homes. During the day he used to work for Nakhum the cobbler and at night he used to sleep in the attic of Alter the Blacksmith's house.

* * *

One day, or rather one night, between Purim and Passover 1912, Tshernetski slept, as drunk as Lot [from the Bible], in the attic at Alter's house and suddenly there is a bang! crash! The household wake up 'neither-dead-nor-alive', jump out of bed, light a candle and start searching for whoever caused the loud crash. They discover that Tshernetski is lying at the entrance of the house. Not anybody else, but Tshernetski has fallen from the attic. They approach the man; they touch him as if they do not believe it is him.

"Lea" shouts Alter with restrained mood to his wife, "He is dead".

– "What should we do, Alter? The gentiles will say that we killed him."

– "Keep quiet, go over to uncle Lieber. He is a wise man. He will advise you what to do", calls out to her their son, Moshe.

Without uttering a word, Lea covers herself with her shawl and leaves to cross the bridge to her brother Lieber.

– "Open, open, it is I, Lea", she calls out as she knocks on the window of Lieber's bedroom.

Lieber slides down from his bed and quietly opens the door, not to wake up the children, and whispers: "What is the matter?"

– "Oy, we are in a mess; Tshernetski fell from the attic and was killed. What should we do? Where do we put him? All his life the gentiles did not want anything to do with him, and now they will all become his relatives and stick up for him, and that will fall on us and on all the Jews of Horodets. What should we do, my dear brother?"

– "Calm down, my sister. Pack him in a sack and Moshe will move him somewhere near a grove and leave him there. Moshe is a healthy young man. He can manage it on his own and the less people – the better. The night is dark and nobody will see or hear."

– "OK, we will do that"

– "And you know what else, my sister, travel straight to the *Kholoz'shiner,* and God be with you and with all the Jews.

Lea went home immediately, to deliver the advice. Indeed, on that dark night a sack with a dead body in it was left in a grove, and Lea traveled to the *Kholoz'shuner* to get his blessing

Things fizzled out. The floes melted. The smell of freshly baked matzos in the *shvalnyes* or *talakes* was carried to the street and market. Carrying the matzos one person commented to the other: "Have you already heard: Tshernetski was found dead. "It is said that he was in a sack. The gentiles say that the Jews killed him to use his blood in baking the matzos."

– "He is lying in the market near the administrative office until the police commissioner from Antipole and a autopsy will be performed on him"

– "God will help us that it will be done and that all will end well. It is not a trifle: the world is full of blood libels. The Beilis trial [**Beilis** was a Ukrainian Jew accused of ritual murder in Kiev in a notorious trial] has poisoned the minds of even the best gentiles."

And everyone hurries to his home as if he has committed some crime. It is better not to draw attention. Man and wife wish each other "May we eat our matzos with joy".

Small kids feel that the days prior to Passover of that year are not like those of any other year. The joy of baking the matzos is missing. People walk with bent heads and the Rabbi has a melancholic mood more than ever."

– "Have you heard", asks Yudl the *melamed* his wife Sarah Beile, "The gentiles say that the Jews strangled him and others add to it that we drained his blood and put it in our matzos."

– "Tell me the truth, Yudl, is there no law to put blood in the matzos?"

– "What nonsense, don't you know that we are not allowed to eat meat that has even a drop of blood in it? How can you even think of such a thing? What does a Jewess know? How to pray *teitch-Khumesh* [A Yiddish version of the Pentateuch] and write down a short Yiddish letter.

– The police commissioner is already here, as is also the doctor from Kobrin. Tshernetski is lying on the bare ground in the market near the administrative office, and gentiles – young and adults are standing around him. All of them watching the deceased and moaning over him.

– "These dirty Jews", cries one gentile.

– "They killed our Tshernetski", cuts in another gentile.

– "They drank his blood", helps him a third gentile.

– "Jewish Passover", screams a gentile woman.

The doctor attends to his job, cuts the abdomen, looks into the intestines, opens the skull, taps it, weighs it and measures it. At the same time the fate of the Jews of Horodets is being weighed and measured – for death or for life. Their life is now in the hands of the doctor. The gentiles sharpen their ears to hear the doctor's verdict. What will he say? Will he say what they say, or something different? Will they have a fling or will they return to their cabins and fields?

The doctor puts away the skull on the ground and sedately declares in Russian: "He was a drunkard. He fell down and battered his brain."

The gentiles bowed their heads. One by one, ashamed, they dispersed. Only the deacon and Shakhnow the *uriadnik* [religious personnel] were left by the post-mortem examined body of Tshernetski. The deacon - to perform the 'rights' and the *uriadnik* – to see to it that no unholy event takes place.

In truth, nothing unholy took place and the Jews of Horodets breathed freely, went out of their houses again to prepare themselves for the beloved Holiday of Passover, for which they had waited a whole year.

[Ben Ezra comments that this event was reported in the American press at the time]

[Pages 77-84]

Gute Yiden = Good Jewish People

Translated by Hannah Kadmon

[Translator's comments in square brackets]

[*Yid/Yiden* = Jew/Jews. However, when Jewishness is irrelevant it means a person/ people, persons, men. I will use in my translation the original Yiddish word, in the singular and in the plural]

Horodetser Rabbis

By K. Rushevsky

[In this chapter the author differentiates between **Rov** plural: **Rabonim** = orthodox rabbis and **Rebe** plural: **Rabeim** = Hasidic rabbis]

It is accepted: A *rov* is not a *rebbe* and a *rebe* is not a *rov*. The *rebbe* performs miracles by remedies and cures and his Hasidim are plain, uneducated people. However, the *rov* is a scholar who "swims in the sea of Talmud" [=thoroughly conversant with the Talmud], the one who weaves into his teaching some hairsplitting, asks difficult questions and with his logical thinking and great proficiency answers every question.

This is what people believe. However, historical facts contradict the above mentioned "axiom". In the Jewish history we find many great *rabonim* who were, in some degree, also *rebeim,* who mastered not only a lot of knowledge of Talmud, but also had philanthropic feelings for the community and for every individual.

Before the *Besh"t* emerged, there was R' Yehuda Khasid, the *Maha"ral* from Prague and other great *Rabonim* in whom all the qualities of the great *rov* and *rebe* were fused. And even after the *Besh"t* became famous in the Jewish world – there were other great *Rabonim* to whom people used to travel to get their blessing, a cure or an advice. Among them were R' Zekil Leib Varmesser ("the Miracle

Worker from Mikhelshtat"), R' Yehoshua Gootmakher from Greydits, and others like them. There was a very good reason why these great *yidn* were given the name "good *yidn*". People obtained from them a good word, a good advice, and mostly found in them a Jewish heart that ached for the unhappy and afflicted and strove to alleviate their pain.

[*Besh"t* =Ba'al Shem Tov - Rabbi Israel ben Eliezer, a mystical rabbi. considered to be the founder of Hasidic Judaism *R' Yehuda Khasid* - a preacher who led the largest organized group of Jewish immigrants to the Land of Israel in the 17th century *Maha"ral* - Judah Loew ben Bezalel - an important Talmudic scholar, mystic and philosopher; a leading rabbi in the city of Prague in Bohemia for most of his life; known for creating the *golem* of Prague].

Horodetser *yidn* were not an exception. The "good *yid*" was part of the Horodetser *yid*, both in sorrow and in joy. If, God forbid, there was some trouble in a home, somebody fell sick or the *Poritz* wanted to throw a Jew out of his possession – they ran to the "good *yid*". When something good happened such as an opportunity to gain the right to cut wood in a forest or get hold of some other merchandise – in this case, too, they went to the "good *yid*" for a blessing or a good advice.

More than a hundred years ago, a Jew from Horodets did not have to travel to get to the "good *yidn*". He had them in his own *shtetl*. However, for unforeseen emergency, they ran to *rov* R' Moshe Tzvi, and later to his son R' Yahoshua Yaakov, who offered a blessing or an amulet.

Not only Horodetser *yidn* used to come to their *rabonim* for a cure, but also foreign *yidn* from other towns and *shtetl*s used to bring their sick people to the *rabonim* mentioned above, who were renowned as great cabalists, especially the quite old *rov* R' Moshe Tzvi. (The many books of Kabalah found in his house bore witness to this fact).

People also came to them with an "evil spirit" and epilepsy. The story goes that *rov* R' Yehoshua Yaakov was a great specialist in healing the epileptic. He had a certain remedy for this specific illness and from near and far people used to travel to him for that remedy. Many *yidn* remember even today, with a blessing on their lips, the old Horodetser *rov*, who had saved them, or a member of their family, and thank this saintly man for having been saved by him.

[Pages 78-79]

R' Pinkhas Mikhael

By Akiva Ben-Ezra

One of the "good *yidn*" who had a great influence over the Horodetser *yidn*, was the *rov* R' Pinkhas Mikhael from Antipolye (seven kilometers from Horodets). This great *rov* and saintly man had become a legendary figure and won a place in the Yiddish-Hebraic literature.[1]

R' Pinkhas Mikhael was an outstanding pupil of R' Asher Hakohen, the *rov* from Shershev and Tiktin (Grodno district) and author of the famous books: "ברכת ראש" about the tractates of "ברכות" [blessings] and: "Nazir" [hermit].

Like his great teacher he, too, did not want to use the rabbinate as the source of his livelihood. Actually, he sat day and night and studied and his wife was the provider. Many towns offered him to sit on the rabbinate-throne but he declined and continued studying, bit by bit adding his own *khidushim*[innovative approaches to religious issues]. His proficiency and profundity were inexhaustible and his modesty and piety were boundless. He was respectful of every person and was polite even to a child. If someone was in distress – he was first to help, both spiritually and materially.

When R' Asher Hakohen passed away, and in Shershev they had to choose a *rov* – the *balebatim* [house owners] of Shershev approached R' Pinkhas Mikhael to convince him that he must take upon himself the rabbinate in their town. He finally accepted and became the Shershever *rov* (he was already more than 40 years old).

R' Pinkhas Mikhael served as *rov* in Shershev all in all 6 years. Afterwards, (in 1864), he was summoned to Antipolye as *Mara D'atra* ["the master of the locality" = the rabbi as the sole religious authority of the locality in which he serves]. He served as *rov* in that capacity until his death 1890.

As soon as he settled in Antipolye, Antipolye became a center of attraction for thousands of people, both rich and poor. For each one he had a good word, consolation, a blessing or a cure. Therefore people left Antepolye very contented.

R' Pinkhas Mikhael did not want any pay. His meager income was from selling yeast. He used to say: "For Jews every rouble is important" and therefore he did not want to charge those who traveled to come to him. If someone insisted that the righteous man should take some payment from him, the *rov* donated it for charity.

From the same standpoint, so it seems, this great genius was lenient in his judgments. Many stories were told about how R' Pinkhas Mikhael used to rule leniently. He understood how difficult it was for people, especially Jews, to earn some money.

R' Pinkhas Mikhael was popular not only among Jews, but also among gentiles, educated or uneducated, because his heart was open wide for gentiles as well. He used to say: "A gentile must also live".

There is a fire in *shtetl,* and people rush to save the houses of the rich, forgetting all about the houses of the poor. However, R' Pinkhas Mikhael does not forget them. What does he do? He climbs to the roof of a house of a poor man and sits there. The firemen see him there and are aware that the fire is about to burn him with the house. The *rov* refuses to come down until they save this house.[2]

R' Pinkhas Mikhael was not narrow minded in his outlook. He delved into the various problems of the Jewish situation with his sharp eye. He saw that Russia was already lost for the Jews, and across the Atlantic Ocean new horizons opened for Jews. True, Jewishness over there was quite weak, but America was still a shelter for thousands of Jews. Therefore, R' Pinkhas Mikhael approved the plans of those who came to him to ask if they should depart for America. His answer was: "Go away to America. You will be able to make a living there. Only don't forget to observe the Sabbath"

Early welcoming of the Sabbath was one of his elementary principles. He would have sacrificed himself for that principle. Every Friday, towards evening, he used to go, ahead of time, to the bathhouse with a small broom in hand, to chase out the people from there, because when a *yid* observes the Sabbath as he should – he is protected from offenses and God guards him from troubles.

Even though R' Pinkhas Mikhael stammered, great *rabonim* and scholarly *Yidn* used to travel to him. They wanted to discuss with him Torah issues and learn from him something new, either in the literal interpretation of *Gemore* or in the commentators.

R' Pinkhas Mikhael was very keen on *Rashi*'s interpretation because *Rashi* is short and sharp and consistently logical. He believed in proficiency and not in brain-gymnastics.[3] If he did not understand a commentator he was not ashamed to admit that he did not understand[4] and when with his awesome proficiency he discovered a mistake in *Rov* Asher's ben Yekhiel [one of the most regarded commentators] he did not hesitate to announce it clear and sharp.[5]

No wonder his analytical logical mind led him to publish "*Leket Hakotsrim*" to *Nazir, Tmura, Meila* and *Tamid*. [tractates of Mishnah and Talmud], an interpretation which is sharp and clear, right to-the-point and without hair-splitting. Most learners did not understand those tractates because they were hardly studied. This fact urged R' Pinkhas Mikhael to collect and assemble from the old and new commentators, add to them his own short interpretations and make those tractates intelligible to the ordinary learner.

"*Leket Hakotsrim*" commentary resonated loud among scholars, and we find agreements with it and also praise of it from R' Tzvi Hirsh Arenshtein from Brisk, his mentor R' Asher Hakohen who also interpreted the "*Nazir*" and others.

His book "*Divrey Pinkhas*" [=sayings of Pinkhas], printed many years after his death (1929-30) by his grandson, R' Izik Rabinovitz, is full of *khidushim* [innovative approaches] and interpretations of ש"ס, תוספות, רי"ף, רא"ש, ר"ן and other interpreters of ש"ס. [six books of Mishnah]. This book was also written using the same R' Mikhael's method: no hair-splitting, logical explanation, proficiency and sharpness.

That book was also acknowledged by many *rabonim* such as R' Yaakov Meir Padva from Brisk, R' Khayim Soloveitchik and others.

In addition to books pertaining to legislative part of the Talmud, there is also a testament that R' Mikahel Pinkhas wrote ("Testament of the famous Genius *Tsadik* Pinkhas Mikhael Z"l". Pinsk, 1914-15). [*Tsadik* has two meanings: a saintly man and a Hasidic Rabbi]. That testament reflects the ideals of this great *tsadik* who not only preached but also realized in his life, and wanted his family and followers to observe these ideals. In that testament we can see his great soul. Blessed be his memory.

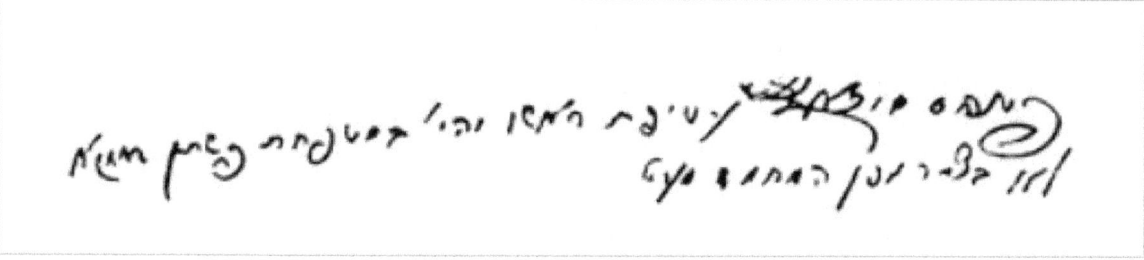

Facsimile of R' Mikahel Pinkhas' "prescription"

Footnotes:

1. Moshe Stavski "*Lekever Israel*", Moledet, volume 3 issue 2 Jaffa 1912-1913
   M. Lipson "*Midor Dor*" part 1 pp. 135-6 143-4; "*Di velt dertseilt*" 53, 105-6. Also "*otsrot foon yidishn humor*" by R' Yitskhak Ashkenazi, 47-8
   The last years, A. Rabinovitz wrote in the Tel-Aviv Rabbinical Journal "Haposek" some anecdotes and

episodes about R' Pinkhas Mikhael.
In "the Registry of the Town of Pruzshene153 there is an interesting legend about this virtuous man.
2. This episode was printed by E. Ben-Ezra under the title: "The Righteous On the Roof" [in Hebrew] in the "H*aivri Hakatan*" [for children in Hebrew] batch 3 pp. 3-4 1941-2 Chicago.
3. See for example "Words of Pinkhas" p, 41, Warsaw,1929-30
4. There, 37, 44, 53, 58
5. There, 72, 74

[Pages 80-82]

R' Mordkhi'le

By M. Mishkin

Translated by Hannah Kadmon

[Translator's comments in square brackets]

R' Mordekhy Veitzel-Rozenblat, renowned all over the world under the name "R' Mordkhi'le Slonimer", or "R' Mordkhi'le Oshmener", was of the most distinguished geniuses of the last generation. R' Mordkhi'le was born in 1934 or 1836 in Antipolye, district of Grodno. His father was a miller and R' Mordkhi'le adopted his first surname: Veitzel. He died in 1915.

In the field of *Halakha* [Jewish religious laws] he left behind a condensed book with questions and answers as well as manuscripts that exhibit his stature as a world-genius. However, while as a genius he was appraised only in the world of rabbis and Jewish scholars, because of his other rare qualities, great virtues and personality exhibited in his treatment of day-to-day people, he was acclaimed one of the most distinguished in his generation.

R' Mordkhi'le Slonimer was famous as a miracle worker. His fame spread from person to person as a saintly man whose blessings or promises were sure to be fulfilled, and whose advice and council were always sensible and proved right.

The hundreds of stories and anecdotes about the miracles he worked and about his words being able to heal and affect - were wondrous and mysterious. Naturally, many of these stories were exaggerated and magnified. Many of the miracles are similar to those told about the "*Baal Shem Tov*" [R' Israel son of Eliezer, founder of Hassidism], R' Levi Yitzkhat Berditshever, and other great Hassidic rabbis. However, the fact that miracles performed by those Hassidic rabbis were attributed to him only proves that he was really a great man.

There were records of the fact that when R' Mordkhi'le scolded someone, that person forgot his habit of winking repeatedly with one eye. Others who came to him bent-over emerged walking erect, and half-insane became sober.

R' Mordkhi'le
(drawn by Israel Zussman)

Those were indeed miracles, but they could easily be explained by the hovering influence that his radiant personality had on them.

When still a child he stood out with exceptional intelligence and good virtues. His father, a plain observant Jew, sent him to study in *Yeshives* and Mordkhi'le emerged from there well versed in *Shas* [Acronym for Hebrew *Shisha Sidrei Mishna* - The book of six parts of the Mishna together with Talmudic commentaries] and *Poskim* [Hebrew: "deciders" – post Talmudic legal scholars who decide the Halakha="law" in cases where previous authorities are inconclusive or in those situations where no *Halakhic* precedent exists.]

When he was 14 years old, as was the custom in those days, a rich *Balebos* [house owner] in the *shtetl* "snatched" him to be his son-in-law on "*kest*". [room and board offered by a family to its new son-in-law to enable him to continue his studies without financial worries.] Thus, with no worries about making a living, R' Mordkhi'le dedicated himself to study with more zeal. He traveled to *Yeshives* as a "*Poresh*" [Hebrew: "*Parush*"="recluse" – one who devotes himself exclusively to the study of the sacred books] and was renowned as prominent scholar of Torah.

R' Mordkhi'le returned to Antipolye and became a regular house-owner, although neighboring and far away towns offered him to occupy the Rabbinical post. In those days Antipolye's Rabbi was the world known miracle-worker R' Pinkhas Michael, to whom people came from all over. R' Mordkhi'le became R' Pinkhas' main assistant, helping him in rabbinical matters and learning from him his proceedings.

R' Pinkhas Michael gave him the first push to the awareness that it is a "gmilas khesed" [deeds of charity] to help the unfortunate with a blessing, a good word and encouragement, and that it is a duty to take upon himself the burden if he feels that he can do something to alleviate the suffering of the unfortunate.

R' Mordkhi'le's name grew famous over time and he could not turn away from the Rabbinate. House owners from *shtetl*s and towns approached him and offered him the rabbinical post. They persuaded him that occupying that post would enable him to serve the Torah and strengthen Judaism. R' Mordkhi'le accepted the offer, but Antipolye did not want to release him.

In 1870 some house-owners from Buten came during the night to Antipolye and practically "kidnapped" R' Mordkhi'le, took him out of the *shtetl* stealthily and paraded him to Buten, proclaiming him "*Mara De-atra*" [Arameic: "the master of the locality" = the local rabbi in his capacity as the sole *halakhic* authority of the locality in which he serves].

As a Rabbi, R' Mordkhi'le became even more famous. Legends and tales of wonders were woven around him, and people started traveling to him for blessings. Buten was proud of its R' Mordkhi'le, but what it did to Antipolye came as a boomerang to Buten. House-owners from the *shtetl* Karlitz arrived in Antipolye, harnessed to a wagon instead of horses, carried R' Mordkhi'le to the wagon and took him by force to Karlitz.

In Karlitz, again, R' Mordkhi'le did not stay for long. Oshmene was a bigger town, and he became their "*Mara De-atra*". A few years later, when the Gaon R' Yosef Shloper died in Slonim, he was taken with great reverence to Slonim and stayed there as Rabbi until his death.

R' Mordkhi'le had his own ideas that brought him to Slonim and did not neglect to carry them out. Although he was busy answering requests, he found time to be attentive to town issues. He saw to it that the Yeshiva of Slonim expanded, and that Sabbath was strictly observed.

It was a pathetic sight every Sabbath: the old R' Mordkhi'le with the fur *shtreimel* on his head and the long silk *kapote* [coat], accompanied by the *shames* [servitor, personal assistant], striding quickly, quickly, like a young man, around the market place, his eyes searching all corners, lest there should be an open crack in a door in the long line of stores, and lest they were still working stealthily.

Naturally, everywhere doors and shutters were closed. However, once, a barber was found leaving his barbershop open on Sabbath. The quiet R' Mordkhi'le then screamed murder and did not leave the place until the rebellious barber was forced to close his barbershop. From that day on the name of that barber became a byword for many years.

In his biography R' Mordkhi'le nearness to R' Pinkhas Michael is noted. In this connection it is worthwhile to tell the wonderful miracle that stirred people.

The tale, or legend, goes like this:

> In the night of the eve of Yom Kippur 1879, R' Mordkhi'le saw in his dream a fine man accompanied by two other men on both sides. The accompanying men told R' Mordkhi'le that they were witnesses, and that it was not merely a dream but a real thing,

a truth to remember, and they vanished. Then the man who was left, told R' Mordkhi'le that he came from the realm of the dead, and that a punishment from heaven would befall him. R' Mordkhi'le woke up with a heavy heart and in the morning, Yom Kippur, prayed with a great dread, and cried a lot.

On *Shmini Atzeret* [eighth day of Sukkot] he saw again the man in his dream, wearing white shrouds, and he told the Rabbi: "You ought to know that you have done a lot with your prayer and tears, but the punishment is not totally annulled." R' Mordkhi'le beseeched him with tears to reveal to him the contents of the punishment and what sin deserved that punishment. Then the man told him this story: He himself was Mahari Ben Lev a Rabbi in a town, who left after him a book of replies [Rabbi Yoseph Ben Lev was a famous Rabbi in Saloniki 1500-1580 and author of "replies" – Halakhaic laws]. One day, when he was a "decider" and ruled on a lawsuit before a rabbinical court, one of the persons in question whom he found guilty broke out in anger and he, the Mahari, slapped his face. From then on that man's soul cannot survive, and he wants to help it. Since R' Mordkhi'le was a descendent of that man, he must rectify his soul, because he carried now the man's sin.

Shattered, R' Mordkhi'le asked, stuttering, what he could do to rectify the soul and cleanse it from any blemish. The Mahari Ben Lev told him to buy his book of replies and learn by heart what the rectification must be. R' Mordkhi'le asked him, then, where he could get hold of his book. The Mahari Ben Lev directed him to send R' Pinkhas Michael, in Antipolye, money for the book.

R' Mordkhi'le obeyed the call of his dream, and wrote a letter from Buten about his secret to R' Pinkhas Michael. R' Pinkhas Michael used to empty his pockets every Friday evening and hand over all the letters to his grandson, Alter, to burn, except for those dealing with *Halakha*.

This is how R' Mordkhi'le's letter fell into Alter's hands. However, instead of burning it, as his grandfather ordered, he gave it to R' Moshe the writer to copy it, and this is how the secret was revealed to all and sundry.

When Pinkhas Michael found out that the secret had been revealed, he was angry at his grandson and, indeed, a short time afterwards the grandson suddenly died. When R' Pinkhas Michael learned of his death, he said: "He should not have acted foolishly".

As mentioned before, we cannot vouch for the truth of the story, though there are copies of the letter and they are dated "Buten, sixth of the month of Shvat, 1885.

(Comment of Editor Akiva Ben Ezra to this letter:

The complete letter was published for the first time in "a group of pamphlets", first issue by Yitzkhak Hirshenzon, Jerusalem. The letter got into the hands of the editor of that issue through a student of "Shnot Eliyahu" ["years of Elijah", A book written by the Gaon of Vilnius]. This student traveled through Antipolye and stayed with R' Pinkhas Michael. When he opened a book there, to browse through, he found the letter mentioned above, which he copied. The letter was also inserted in the following publications: "*Hamora Hagadol*" by David Veissman, 1903, "*Mosdot Ha-emuna*" by

Mordechy Arie Nisenboim, second edition, New York 1923-4, "*Khalom Nora*" printing house Talpiot, Tel-Aviv 1938-9.)

All sorts of people sought R' Mordkhi'le: rich Jews wearing in winter the expensive fur coats over their shoulders, mixed with wrinkled talkative Jewish women carrying parcels and bundles. Young women, barren, who came asking for a blessing to have children, mixed with crippled, humpbacked, lame people who were carried by their family to the Rabbi. Those multi-colored crowd of Rabbi-seekers used to fill up, daily, all hotels and inns in town. Special coachmen used to travel to the train station to drive R' Mordkhi'le's visitors. A big part of the town's population earned their livelihood from these visitors. Not only Jews traveled to seek the Rabbi. Quite often one could meet Christians, rich and poor, who took themselves off to the Rabbi to pour their suffering hearts to him. And those who came, never left disappointed.

R' Mordkhi'le did not charge for his blessings and advice. When a rich guest wanted to give a "*pidyen*" [= "ransom"= payment for the advice], he would show him the sealed metal alms-boxes of yeshivas, or other institutes, where one could place a copper or a silver coin.

Moreover, many stories were told about poor people whom R' Mordkhi'le used to help out of his own pockets. When poor people came asking for an advice how to help themselves after a fire or another disaster, he would stick in their hands some money and move quickly to bless others, thus not enabling them to thank him.

R' Mordkhi'le believed that a great part of the people were miserable only because they talked themselves into being unfortunate. Others suffered anxiety and thought that they were sick. Others were very nervous, melancholic, weak and broken down. Such people needed only encouragement, confidence, and hypnotic belief in someone who would bid them to revive, to pull through, and they would obey him. Thus he directed them to a helpful way of life.

R' Mordkhi'le sensed that he possessed the art of gaining trust and confidence and this prompted him to take upon himself to act as their doctor and help them. It indeed was the case and this explains the secret of his working of miracles. Equipped with new strength, those people who sought the Rabbi emerged from his house with courage and resolution. As if touched by a magical hand, they got well and became productive members of the community.

[Pages 83-84]

The Kholozshiner

By Gedalyahu Kaplan

Translated by Hannah Kadmon

[Translator's comments in square brackets]

The Kholozshiner

He lived in a small village, not far from Pinsk. During the day he labored industriously in his smithy, hitting with his hammer on the anvil, and at night he sat engrossed in studying *mishnayes* [collection of post biblical laws; part of the Talmud] till dawn. In his daily life he was a pious honest Jew all year round, with black eyebrows over his lively eyes. He was the well known

"Kholozshiner" [Kholozshin was the name of the village] or R' Eliya Mordekhay son of R' Khayim Levinson. Quite often he walked to Karlin to study Torah with the Karliner Rabbi. He was greatly influenced by the Rabbi's teaching that had to do with matters not only between man and God but also between people. The "Kholozshiner" believed that the way a person behaves to others is as important as the way he behaves towards God. Therefore he was an affectionate loving friend to every person - a Jew or a Christian.

He was respected and revered by Christians as well, and when a farmer came to sharpen his sickle or scythe he knew deep in his heart that when the "Kholozshiner" held the tools in his hands, the year would be blessed with a rich harvest in his field. Not only the Christians believed so, the village Kholozshin was always full of people in distress who turned to R' Eliya for a blessing.

His blessing was very simple: "R' so and so, you should only have faith in God and imagine "מלא כל הארץ כבודו" [the whole earth is filled with his glory- Psalms 62;19], He is the pillar of fire. Don't forget "שיויתי ה' לנגדי תמיד" [I have set the Lord always before me - Psalms 16;8] and God will help you. Don't worry, dear brother. Love God and God will love you and all the Jewish folks."

He often comforted people with King David's saying: "גול על ה' דרכך ובטח עליו והוא יעשה" [commit thy way unto the Lord; trust also in him - Psalms 37;5]. Follow the ways of the Torah and you will be saved from all evil. Our father in heaven does not forsake us because:

"הנה לא ינום ולא יישן שומר ישראל" [Behold, He that keepeth Israel shall neither slumber nor sleep- psalms 221;4]. "We have gone through the worst perils and He helped us overcome them. We are like trees in winter that grow anew and blossom when spring comes"

How was the "Kholozshiner" discovered? It was told that when thousands of people travelled to Slonim [southeast of Hrodna, Belarus, of significant Jewish population under Polish and Russian rule] to the famous R' Mordkhi'le [of the Hassidic court], the Rabbi, in his old age, refrained from admitting visitors who came to pay their respect and told them: "Why do you travel to come to see me? Better travel to the smith in Kholozshin! The blessing he will give you will be fulfilled". And, when the rush to Kholozshin increased and thousands of people overcrowded the small village of Kholozshin, the gentiles thrived because the visiting guests bought their food-provision from them. So, the folks travelled to the "Kholozshiner" - some for a blessing, others for advice. He modestly looked into a small book titled "Mikhael and Uziel" which contained medications and charm-remedies and from the list he chose one or the other.

The popularity of the "Kholozshiner" soared mainly at the beginning of WW1 when the Jewish youth did not want to die fighting for the anti-Semite Tsarist government. They visited him for a blessing and, they say, the blessing proved itself. The "Kholozshiner" sometimes gave also a mascot. His mascot was on a small paper in a very popular style. Here is the text written on the paper given to a Jewish soldier:"שומר ישראל שומר שארית ישראל ואל יאבד ישראל האומרים שמע ישראל" [from the prayer book: "The keeper of Israel, guard over the remainder of Israel and they will not be lost those who recite: 'Hear O Israel: the Lord our God is one Lord'" Dvarim 6;4]. The following is another text that contains a phrase from Psalms: "קרוב ה' לנשברי לב ואת דכאי רוח יושיע" [God is near to those of broken heart and saves those of a contrite spirit - Psalms 34;18]. He also gave a "*firerel*", a Russian 2 kopeks coin, a charm to lead one along a road with no obstructions.

During WW1 he left Kholozshin and settled down in the neighboring town of Drohitichin. The Polish government seized the opportunity to build a special station for the Polish railroad at the edge of town. The station was named "*stantzye rabina*". Through this station people arrived in great numbers to receive a blessing from the good Jews.

The "Kholozshiner" was the good Jew for the masses, to whom he was very close and spoke their language. The following is a characteristic episode to show his popularity. Once, a tannery was burned down and the tanner was left stark naked. Just then, a rich city-man came to receive a blessing from the "Kholozshiner" to ensure that his horses would not be stolen. The "Kholozshiner" told him to go to the tanner and give him 100 rubles to build a new house in exchange for the tanner's dog which would protect the horses from being stolen. The town-man gave the poor tanner 100 rubles and the tanned gave him his black dog. The town-man left very satisfied since from then on he did not have any more trouble with thefts.

One day, it was during Passover, the city-man's black dog brought home half a loaf of bread. The man was beside himself and on *Khol-Hamoed* [the intermediary weekdays between the first two and last days of the holiday] he travelled to the "Kholozshiner". He fell down before him crying hysterically: "My dear Rabbi, I have sinned gravely, I should be punished by *karet* [shorten one's life]. The dog ate *khometz* on Passover." [leavened bread is forbidden on Passover]. The "Kholozshiner" calmed him down and said: "Dear friend, do not be so distraught, the punishment of *karet* is meant only for people and not for dogs. Don't be so frightened, the dog will not get hurt…"

When the writer of these lines, before leaving for America, started saying goodbye, I met him, deep in thought and distressed. Contrary to the distinguishing quality of this remarkable man, known for his simplicity, he said to me: "Farewell and stay well in your new land America". He pushed into my hand the book of Dvarim [from the Bible] and showed me a verse in it:

"תמים תהיה עם ה' אלהיך" [Thou shalt be perfect with the Lord thy God - Dvarim 18;13]- "be a wholesome Jew." Then he told me an anecdote about a city-man who heard that if you buy a deluxe *esreg* [ethrog - citron fruit for Succoth] - God will you will give you a good year. This city-man hurried to the Rabbi and said: "Rabbi, let me have a deluxe ethrog". The Rabbi answered him: "I would surely give you, but it is already too late. I have only one left but it has already been ordered for the rich R' Shmulke." The city-man said: "Dear Rabbi, let me just have a look at it to see what a deluxe ethrog looks like." When the Rabbi showed him, the city-man pulled out of his pocket a pocketknife, cut the ethrog into two halves and said: "I should get a half and Shmulke should get a half". The Rabbi screamed "The ethrog is trashy, because an ethrog is *kosher* only when it is whole…"

When the "Kholozshiner" died, *khol Hamoed* Succoth 1929, 90 years old, the greatest Rabbis came over from all towns and villages around Drohichin to have the right to carry his bed. Jews from Antipolye, Horodets, Khomsk and other places, came to pay him the last respect.

When the Germans, their names be erased, removed all the headstones from the new cemetery at Drohichin, a survivor from Drohichin told that the headstone on the "Kholozshiner"'s grave stayed in its place. May this headstone be an eternal acknowledgement, in memory of the illuminating spirits that lit the way to our folks in their suffering and in their happiness!

[editor's remark: see about the "Kholozshiner" also in "My Town Motili" written by the well known Hebrew-Yiddish author R' Mordchai'le (Khayim Tzemerinski) pp. 81-82].

[Pages 85-87]

Cultural Awakening

The Revolution

By A. S.

Donated by Esther R. Buchsbaum

Edited by Hannah Kadmon

The free winds of change that had blown in Russia in the beginning of the 20th century had also reached the small town of Horodetz, but, in a small way. The reason was plain. There weren't any factories in Horodetz, and consequently the working class didn't exist. There were a few hired workers in town: at the men's and women's tailors, the shoemakers, carpenters, and smiths, where there were one or two workers. The owners worked together with them from morning to night.

According to the system of that time, they used to hire a worker for 1 year or 3 years, with meals and a pair of work boots (at the shoemaker) or a suit (at the tailor). That way, the worker became a son of the house like their own child. The worker used to also do housework like taking out the slop buckets or taking care of the owner's children. So the owner was not an exploiter according to the modern way of thinking. Many times the owner had to use his wits to get the few rubles he needed to pay his workers.

The only true worker who understood the revolutionary movement in Horodetz, and did everything he could to advance the revolution, was Feishe, Yankel Rosenbaum's son.

Pashe Rosenbaum

Feishe had been a shoemaker hired by a landlord who was a shoemaker in town. He was a true proletariat;.a son of generations of "horopashnikes", that is, people who lived by the labor of their own hands. He was ready for anything. He wasn't afraid of anyone, not even a police officer (a uriadnik) or the priest.[1]

Potentially the Horodetz workers were ready for revolutionary work. They, however, lacked organizers. But this element was soon to come to Horodetz in the form of two young men, Avraham, Chaim Hersh Nadritchni's son and Itche, Shiah Farber's son, who had studied in Pinsk. During Passover vacation in 1905, when they came home for the holiday, they took it upon themselves to revolutionize the Horodetz workers.[2]

Itche Farber (Dr. J. Farber)

Avraham Hersh Nadritchni

Avraham and Itche were very close to members of the S. S. party. [in Yiddish: ס.ס] This party was a mixture of Labor Zionists and of Territorialists. In 1905, Pinsk was an important place in the S. S. movement.

Soon Avraham and Itche came to understand that the world is not only for Jews. There were also gentiles who had to be pulled into the cause. That was a hard piece of work and also dangerous. You don't play around with gentiles. Finally, they did organize a large group of non-Jewish youth. For this, they received high praise from Vanya Sverdyuk, the younger son of Maxim Sverdyuk, a Horodetz gentile, who was very wealthy and a secretary of the village council.

When they invited Vanya to address a gathering, he quickly accepted. But, because he was not a speaker, he suggested that he would read out something appropriate. The gathering met behind the sluice gates of the river. The meeting was a great success.

Avraham and Itche were dissatisfied with this reading-out. They approached people directly, personally. They brought proclamations. One of the gentiles hooked up his horse and wagon and both organizers put on gentile clothes. Feishe had made glue (*pap*). In the middle of the night they rode around the village neighborhoods and glued the proclamations on the crosses which stood at each end of the village and on the offices of the A. D. Gordon Zionist organization. The neighborhood talked about this action for a long time.

A little later, Aaron Karlinski joined the two organizers. He was the son of Mottie Hillel Karlinski, one of the real big shots from Horodetz.

Aaron was a Zionist who was pulled toward practical and cultural work. Through his initiative were founded free evening courses in which one could learn to read and write Yiddish and Russian. Naturally, those who were learning were mostly girls since the boys had already learned in Hebrew school (*cheder*).

All the poor seamstresses studied there. The teachers were Ruhama, daughter of Isaac Israel, and Maita, daughter of Shimon Isaac Glantzer.

Aaron Karlinski had also dreamed of founding a cooperative in Horodetz. His argument was as follows. In Horodetz, many young women loiter without a stitch of work. Therefore cooperatives have to be organized, so that the Horodetz folks can become productive.

Very often the Pinsk Central Committee of the S.S. sent agitators to Horodetz. One of these young men was the 18 year old Aaron Asher Weinberg who, in 1906, was a traveling agitator. He is now the current New York advocate and Labor Zionist worker.

The first lecture which Aaron Weinberg read in Horodetz was in a grove behind the brick making factory. He lectured about historical materialism, that in essence must lead to territorialism. That was on a summer Sabbath. On that Sabbath all the youngsters - the worker's children and the employer's children - disappeared from the village. Fathers and mothers ran around the village wondering what had become of their sons and daughters. No one realized the reason for this disappearance. In the evening, when the young people finally came home, not one of them was punished.

The second lecture which Weinberg gave in Horodetz was about the concentration of capital and its leading directly to materialism. I think that the second lecture took place in Chana Pelte's house. This lecture made a big impression on the listeners, whether because of the rich topic or because of Weinberg's outward appearance. He had grown a patriarchal beard (for various political reasons).

Besides the S.S. being in Horodetz, there were also the Bundists, but they were a small group. The Bund, whose program was to nurture a Jewish working class, had, as was pointed out before, no working class in Horodetz to work with. That's why the Bund did not have a future in Horodetz. It wasn't entirely unrecognized though. It called out strikes and campaigned for fewer working hours, better conditions and higher wages, similar to the program of the A.D. Gordon Zionist group.

The speaker for the Bund was Jeremaiah Aaron, son of Asher Rudetski, who was a land owner and a rich Jew. In addition to the practical revolutionary work, daily educational-work was required. This enlightening work could not be done adequately by either a visiting or local lecturer. For this task, a library was organized which was filled with Yiddish books with a socialist orientation by authors such as Karl Marx, Kutski, and A.D. Gordon. The library was kept in the home of Shlomo, son of Moshe Burshtein. Shlomo was also the librarian. Sadly, the library did not exist long because, little by little, the readers kept the books for themselves in their homes.[3]

Shlomo Burshtein

By the end of 1906, the important members and leaders of the revolutionary group had gone away, some to America and some to Warsaw or other towns. With their departure, the revolutionary spirit also drifted away and new winds started to blow in the village.

Footnotes:

1. After the revolution, Feishe went away to America. In New York he was a worker. After that, he relocated to Atlanta, Georgia where he opened a shoe business. Feishe died June 17, 1940. Itche, son of our dear countryman, became Dr. J. Farber.
2. Avraham later went to Warsaw and learned to be a dental technician. After that, he had a dental laboratory in Lodz, until the Nazis murdered him and his family. "May the Lord avenge their blood".
3. A few years later Shlomo became a teacher of Russian in Horodetz and in America he became a worker till he died on August 8, 1934

Comment by Hannah Kadmon:

The (ס.ס) S.S. party mentioned in this article deserves some clarification. In the conference of Poalei Zion in Minsk, 1901, the following issues were disputed: the linkage to Eretz Israel, the connection to the International Socialism of non-Jewish workers, and the connection to the Russian revolutionists. In 1905, following the Uganda Plan presented in the 6th Zionist Congress, the Territorialists (those who wished for a territory for the Jews not necessarily in Eretz Israel) withdrew and founded the ס.ס (S.S) The Zionist-Socialist Workers Party. The initials should therefore be Z.S. rather than S.S…

[Pages 88-89]

Zionism

The First Step

by A. Tzioni

Translated by Hannah Kadmon

[Translators comments in square brackets]

[the word *Besmedresh* is from the Hebrew: Beit Midrash = literally: a house of study (of Bible and Gemara). It is distinct from a synagogue. It did serve also as a place of prayer in the Jewish communities. The *shtiebl* is a small Hasidic prayer house]

We can open with a question: Who in Horodets was not a Zionist? Who, in Horodets did not go to *Besmedresh* three times a day and repeated each time the same prayers in which there is a plea to God to return to the holy land? And who in Horodets lived so well that he or she was so contented with daily life that Horodets could occupy the place of the land of Israel?

The difficulties that the former Russian state heaped on the Jews, turned all Jews in Horodets into Zionists. However, Zionism in the modern sense of the term, the political Zionism of Dr. Hertzel, was quite unfamiliar to the general public in Horodets. Only few, who read Dr. Hertzel's literature, had an idea about his Zionism.

When Dr. Hertzel appeared on the Jewish arena and the whole world started discussing political Zionism, the echo of this blowing-of-shofar reached Horodets as well, calling to free the Jewish people and return them back to their own land, the land of Israel.

Chaya-Dvorah

In those years of national awakening, the house of Chaya-Dvorah was the spiritual center where the Zionists used to gather and discuss the issues of Zionism. At her house they could hear a Hebrew song sung by her talented young daughter, who knew Hebrew very well and had a very beautiful voice.

Ester and Avraham Bartenboim

Chaya-Dvorah's house became, later, the only house where one could hear Hebrew spoken in daily life. Ester and her well known husband, Avraham Bartenboim, used to talk Hebrew even to their dog, whom they called *"Navkhan"* [Hebrew: one who barks], and when Ester gave birth to Hertzel and then to Chayim – the children were brought up in Hebrew as a mother tongue.

(Ben Ezra's comment: Avraham Bartenboim collaborated with "Hatzfira" [a Hebrew newspaper in Warsaw to spread enlightment and Zionism]. He helped production of textbooks "Talking Hebrew" and "Hebrew Style" [in Hebrew]. He died in Warsaw, 1907. Ester, his wife, was a teacher for many years in Warsaw, in a Hebrew school established by Krinski, S.L. Gordon, Pugatchov and others. Ester and her sons were murdered by the Nazi beasts.)

Aharon Karlinski, son of Motye-Hillel played an active role in the small Zionist group. He was a very consciencious and idealistic young man, who plunged with all his zeal into the Zionist movement. When Dr. Hertzel set forth his slogan "recruit the communities", Aharon immediately hitched himself to the task but stumbled against the opposition of the orthodox Jews who did not want to relinquish their post to the younger people. They considered the political Zionism a danger to the traditional Judaism. In Horodets, like in the big world, a struggle took place, but in Horodets the Zionists did not attain victory. In the *besmedresh*, near the oven there was a great commotion: should they wait for the messiah to arrive, or should they, to the best of their ability, hurry the steps of the messiah.

Few did not wait for the messiah, bought *shkolim* [membership dues to the Zionist movement] and shares of the colonial bank [financial instrument of the Zionist movement], but it did not become a popular trend. Aharon Karlinski did not rest, lectured in private, held sermons in the *besmedresh*, but when a *maged* [preacher] arrived there, people preferred to listen to him than to Aharon.

Yaakov Hersh Helershtein

This is the opportunity to remember another great idealist, with a heart full of love for the land of Israel – Yaakov Hersh Helershtein, the shipper who lived near the train terminal. Helershtein was a chasid. He used to pray in the Stoliner *shtiebl* but he was an enlighted person. He had in his house a nice Hebrew library and when somebody wanted a Hebrew book he visited Helershtein. Helershtein used to participate under a pseudonym in "Hatzfira" and "Hazman" [two Hebrew newspapers of the time], and his house served as a gathering place for scholars.

Helershtein was not an orator, he was rather a writer. Once when he stood up to deliver a Zionist speech , he remained silent, could not speak and sat down again. However, in his quiet modest way he did a lot to clarify issues and he helped prepare the hearts to be ready, later, to absorb the seeds of national renaissance.

Honor to his memory!

When the small group of Zionists dispersed and the clamor of the revolution was heard in Russia – the voice of the national movement became silent, in Horodets, for the time being.

Aharon Karlinski started getting closer to the revolutionary movement and Hellershteyn, in the meantime, withdrew, and dedicated himself to Hebrew literature that was the only comfort in his life.

[Pages 90-91]

A "Political Criminal"

by Naftali Goldberg

Translated by Hannah Kadmon

[Translator's notes in square brackets]

Between 1905 to 1912 Horodets kept very quiet about Zionism. There was no active movement there. The older generation entertained the hope that messiah could come any time except on Sabbath, Holidays, Sabbath-Eve and Holiday-Eve. The younger generation were busy either in business, or being "externists" – a term well known among young Jewish men in Russia, who were not allowed to attend high schools.

Kive

All of a sudden, a mature young man of fifteen, with red hair and temperament, started to set up a Zionist movement in Horodets. The name of this redhead youth was Kive, son of Tzeitl, so named as his mother's son because his father was in America. (today he calls himself Akiva Ben-Ezra) [His father's name was Ezra Kostrinsky]. (He is the editor of this book).

This young man, Kive, started reading various books and brochures about Zionism. He was not contented with his own personal Zionism, but started to spread the ideas of Zionism in Horodets in general, and in particular among his three friends with whom he was studying.

The first friend was Liber Polyak, who was murdered with the six million victims. The second was Motl Vinograd, who later studied in Belgium and became a professor of chemistry in the University of Yasi, Romania, and in the last years assumed a very high office in the Romanian government. I, the author of this article, was the third friend.

Kive believed that the future of the Jews lay in the land of Israel. He used to get a great deal of material, books and brochures, and would gather his friends who used to read and hold discussions together. Little by little, we also started to understand the spirit of Zionism, and we hoped that when we grew up we would go to the land of Israel.

Kive took advantage of every opportunity to stir the youth of his age to Zionism. In summer, Yankele, son of Motye who was son of Itzik Kostrinsky, came for vacation. Kive invited him to give a lecture to the youth, in Itzik's orchard, or in his own house. He was not satisfied with just lectures for young boys and girls. He arranged lectures for the grownups. Once on a summer Sabbath night, he brought over a lecturer from the neighboring *shtetl* of Antipolie. The lecture took place in Chayim Nisl's house where wandering troupes used to give concerts and where other various entertainments were held.

Kive busied himself not merely with the task of offering information. He did with his friends some practical work such as selling national-fund stamps of *shkalim* [the coins for membership dues] and on the Eve of the Day of Atonement they placed in the *bote-medro'shim* collection-containers for the Odessa Committee [a charitable pre-Zionist society in the Russian Empire which encouraged emigration to the Land of Israel and the developing of agriculture there]. If somebody did not have the sum of half a ruble for a *shekel,* he would pay it little by little. From year to year the takings grew.

Kive was not contented with that, too. He started to get the Horodets Jews interested in a library that would offer spiritual food to the old and young. Thanks to his initiative, a committee was established to collect money and buy books. Many *balebatim* took part in this enterprise. You must understand that this library was established illegally. The books were stored in Isaacl's (Israel) house. A few times a week, people used to come there to read books. The selection of books was quite nice: in Hebrew, Yiddish and in Russian. Ester-Chaya, daughter of Dvorah, helped a lot, living in Warsaw in the center of the Yiddish-Hebrew culture.

Kive's name became very popular not only in Horodets but also in the neighborhood, and from near and far people corresponded with him as with a grownup. His correspondence was very substantial and it drew the attention of the police. Besides letters from Zionist centers, he used to get letters also from 'Poalei Zion' central committee [movement of Marxist Zionist Jewish workers], as they were interested in him and wanted to get him to join their activity.

How did his address reach the Poalei Zion? This is how it happened:

Shlomo, son of Liber, (Podolevsky) was a member of the Poalei Zion, an activist in Brisk [Brest]. He gave them Kive's address.

Under the Tsar's regime, the Poalei-Zion members reeked of revolution, while, actually their movement had to do with the workers' movement. The authorities considered the Poalei Zion members as revolutionists.

As far as Zionism is concerned, the authorities pretended not to notice it. After all, it was an organization that was not connected officially to present-day local work, that collected money under the heading of "A Society to help the Jewish farmers in artisans in Syria and Palestine" known as the "Odessa Committee".

One morning in the month of Heshvan (ה' חשון תרע"ד)[November 5th 1913], a gendarme arrived from Brisk [Brest], placed policemen around the house where Kive lived, carried an *abiske* [search] and found whole packs with forbidden "merchandise": prayer books, Torah books, books, journals brochures, national-fund stamps, letters from the whole world…and letters from the Central Committee of Poalei Zion. In the midst of the search the mailman came in, bringing two additional letters from Poalei Zion. In short, the result was that they arrested Kive and carried him away.

There was a big commotion in Horodets. The fear of further arrests was in everybody's mind. On the third day they found out that Kive was brought to Kobryn and from Kobryn to Brest and put in prison there, locked in a room all by himself. All of Horodets took to heart Kive's destiny. They started approaching the high "windows" looking for a way to release Kive from prison. It was very easy to fall into the hands of the Russian regime but very difficult to get released. Weeks passed and Kive, the big "criminal" was still behind bars.

On the tenth week of his arrest, the authorities let us know that they would send to Horodets the *prokuror* [prosecutor] for an interrogation. One morning we, the three friends, were called to the *zemstva* [the regional authority of Tsarist Russia], and policemen on horses rode behind us, as though we were criminals. After waiting a few hours, a prosecutor from Grodno came in and also the colonel of the Brest gendarmerie, wearing his uniform with the golden epaulets, and they started the interrogation. The policemen guarded us sternly the whole time so that we would not speak to each other.

Frightened, I entered the room where the prosecutor and the colonel were sitting. I actually shivered, but did not lose my head. Besides what they knew about Kive, they also knew that there was a library in Horodets. (However, my father and some other people packed the books in crates, dug a deep pit and hid them in). They asked me about the library and whether I was a Zionist, and mainly whether Kive belonged to the Poalei Zion. I answered right away that Kive was not a member of the Poalei Zion but only a common Zionist.

The questions asked of my two friends were of the same character. By night we had become the heroes of the day.

After the interrogation, it took a few weeks and a great effort of well-known Zionists in Grodno, Brest and Petersburg until Kive was freed (י' שבט) [February 6th], but only for a short period, until his trial. In the meanwhile, he was under the supervision of the police. Kive and his mother did not lose any time and started to prepare for a quiet escape to America. One night, Kive came, his head wrapped in a hood, to say goodbye.

Not long after that, WW1 broke out and with it, temporarily, the Zionist activity in Horodets halted.

[Pages 92-93]

The National Revival

by Shmuel Hoizman

Translated by Hannah Kadmon

[Translator's notes in square brackets]

In 1919, when the detainees and "*bezshentses*" (refugees) started returning to Horodets, Zionist cultural life pulsed again in the *shtetl*. A non-partisan culture- committee was organized and it renewed the library and established a choir.

Shlomo Burshtein was the librarian, Hershl, the teacher, led the choir and Israel, son of Itsik (Zussman), was the chairman of the Culture- (read: Zionist) Committee.

The gatherings took place in the "shkole" (Polish school), and in "pakai" (palace) that was half ruined. Musical plays were held there, to which people used to come from Kobryn and Antipolye, and the takings went to the Zionist funds such as "*Keren Kayemet*" [Jewish National Fund - to buy and develop land in the land of Israel] and "*Keren Hage-ula*" [preceded the United Jewish Appeal and collected money for the Zionist organization]. In the spring of 1920, when the Balfour declaration was confirmed in San Remo, Horodets celebrated. Everybody put on festive clothes and went to the *besmedresh* to pray *hallel* [a Holiday prayer reciting from Psalms 113–118, to praise and thank God]. In the Afternoon a parade was organized for the whole *shtetl*, young and old, with the blue and white flag at the head, and they marched to the palace. In the palace the small children of Horodets were singing, sitted in half a circle. Israel lectured about events of the day and all the folks showed their enthusiasm by throwing coins into the blue and white collection box [of the *Keren-Kayemet*]. Even gentiles and Polish soldiers threw coins into the box.

However, this enthusiasm did not last long. Israel and others of the group departed for America and for a while Horodets was at a standstill. Only one institution, the library, was still active but it was very unsatisfactory.

After some time, Liber, son of Yaakov (Polyak), returned from Russia and applied himself to the library, recruited some of the young people who were still in Horodets, and they built up the library both spiritually and materially. In a short time the library became richer with books, including Yiddish books. Later it became rich with Hebrew books as well and with a collection of children's Hebrew books.

The small group also revived the national fund and the "*Keren Hayesod*" [United Jewish Appeal fund] in Horodets, and established a "*He-Khalutz*" group ["The pioneer" Zionist youth movement to promote agricultural settlement in the land of Israel] that included 14 members (boys and girls). Liber himself became a teacher of general studies and saved every coin for his travel to the land of Israel.

(comment of A. Ben-Ezra, editor: "It is interesting to note that already then, Liber was mentally a citizen of the land of Israel, and instead of signing his name as Liber Polyak, he signed: Khaviv Ben-Yaakov [חביב בן-יעקב])

Liber was joined by a young man from Pinsk, Yaakov Adrezinsky, who finished the secondary school with natural sciences trend, in Pinsk. This young man became a teacher in Horodets and stayed to live there.

Thanks to these two idealists, the national feeling was stirred and added color to the still and monotonous life of the youth in Horodets. Naturally it was merely in a miniature form because the youth in Horodets were small in number and possessed little intellectual strength. Liber and Yaakov also organized a "*He-Khaluts Ha-Tza-ir*" ["the young pioneer"] for the younger children, who were to take the place of the "*He-Khaluts Ha-boger*" ["the grown up pioneer"] at the age of eighteen.

They also organized courses and gave lectures about Jewish and general history, political economics, the Zionist movement and Hebrew and Yiddish literature.

It was quite a difficult task to organize and establish the "*He-Khaluts*" in Horodets, and even more so to lead the organizational and cultural activity, because of various disturbances imposed both by the authorities and by inner local difficulties.

Still, the "*He-Khaluts*" movement in Horodets was very esteemed by the Zionist Committee of Warsaw. Representatives from Warsaw and Pinsk came many times to give lectures and highly praised the members of "*He-Khaluts*" in Horodets. Many of the members went for training in the Polish *kibbutzim* [collective farms] and occupied administrative positions.

Besides the cultural activity, the members trained in Horodets proper. They rented a plot, plowed, sowed and planted and prepared themselves for farming. After a short while some members settled in the land of Israel. Liber was also ready to be on the road but he was not destined to fulfill his life-long dream.

In summer they used to gather on the banks of the river [called locally: *Botshveinikes*. בוקוגמטך is a towpath; path along a river or canal that is traveled by men or animals towing a boat[or in the grove near the station-building. However, it was difficult in winter. They were forced to switch their meeting place from the house of one member to another member's house.

There were also times when each chapter of "*He-Khaluts*" had to be legalized wherever it was located. In order to get this legal recognition, they had to have a minimal number of members and own a their own meeting place. This was difficult for the youth of Horodets to achieve. Therefore, they had to carry their activity illegally with additional hardships for "*He-Khaluts*".

The library, the inspirational-spiritual source for the youth of Horodets, had also undergone a crisis. In 1936, the representative of the public administration in Kobryn led a search in the library and resolved to close the library under the pretext that there were too many radical books around.

The Horodets youth were not discouraged. They made an effort to re-open the library and carry on the preparation activity for *aliya* [settling in the land of Israel]. That was when the clouds of the second world war started hovering above. Simultaneously with the liquidation of the Polish identity, the Jews of Horodets and their dreams came to an end as well.

God above, curse the Nazi murderers! Utterly erase these modern *Amalek*! [see Exodus 19;14]

We honor you, martyrs. We will never forget you!

Standing from right to left: Sender London, F' Hoyzman, Blume Rikhter, Libe Ganilski, Zlate Orlovski, Reizek Yarmetski, Yosk Mantak.
Sitting: Yaakov Hersh Hoyzman, Rive Kuprianski, Prume Eaminski, Ruchama Volinietz, Yudl Podolevsky

[Page 93]

Personalities and Characters

[Pages 94-97]

Dr. Israel Mikhl Rabinovitz

by A. Ben-Ezra

Translated by Hannah Kadmon

[Translator's comments in square brackets]

One of our people's greatest shortcomings is that we are either not acquainted with our scholar sages and great brothers, or underestimate them. Then, when we start bringing them to our minds, understand them and appreciate them, it is after they are dead, like the profound proverb: "After the death of the saintly, say" [Hebrew: אחרי מות קדושים אמור]. It reflects a norm that you don't talk negatively about a person after his death and you only enumerate his virtues. The proverb is composed of the names of 3 consecutive portions of the book of Leviticus: אחרי מות, קדושים, אמור. [Another possible ironic interpretation of the expression is: after death, even the most ordinary person turns into a saintly and righteous person ...] And after some scores of years they are entirely forgotten.

Dr. Israel Mikhl Rabinovitz belongs to these less known during their life and forgotten after their death. To asses any great personality, it is necessary to use the familiar three criteria: the family from which he stems, the country in which he grew up, and the period in which he lived and was active. These three factors throw light on Dr. Israel Mikhl Rabinovitz's life.

The name "Rabinovitz" already informs us about the family. The name stems from the word Rabin (Rabbi in Russian) and, indeed, he was a descendent of a family of Rabbis, a whole chain of Rabbis. There is a belief that this chain of Rabbis goes back twenty four generations.

Dr. Israel Mikhl Rabinovitz

Israel Mikhl was born in Horodets, county of Kobryn, province of Grodno, in 1818, to his father, the Rabbi and Cabalist Moshe Hirsh who was a Rabbi in Horodets in place of his own father, and in his last years of life was also a Rabbi in Antepolye (8 versts away from Horodets. [Verst=Russian measure of distance: 0.66 of a mile].

While still a small child, Israel Mikhl stood out with his excellent memory and comprehension. Whatever he learned stayed with him for life.

In the records of the Horodets Society "Ein Yaakov" of that period, we find Mikhl registered as a member with the following comment: "ילד שעשועים" [a boy, the joy of his parents] Israel Mikhl son of Rabbi Moshe Tzvi". This small comment tells us a lot. This particular Society was founded for the purpose of studying "Ein Yaakov" [a compilation of all the legendary material in the Talmud together with commentaries], which is not a very complex material for studying. Still, only grown-ups belonged to this Society and not children, not even the Rabbi's children. If Israel Mikhl belonged to the above mentioned Society, he probably won this exception by right.

In the early years of his life, he studied in his town of birth - Horodets, and while still a young boy he already travelled to the Brest [Brisk] *Talmetoyre* which was famous in those days. Later, he studied in the *Yeshive* of Grodno, where he started to demonstrate his genius and one could forecast the future Dr. I.M. Rabinovitz. In the context of those years, he had absorbed the whole *Talmud* and its auxiliary books. Naturally, he was ordained as a Rabbi when he was very young, but he did not practice as a Rabbi.

In 1877 he published a book about ritual slaughtering and non-kosher food based on the principles of medicine. This book was an eye opener to our enemies who wanted to forbid the Jewish ritual slaughtering, submitting various reasons for that.

We would like here to list the main books that he had published in French: "Medicine and Talmud", "The Jewish Religion", "Criminal Laws in the Talmud", "Introduction to the Talmud" – translated also into German and Hebrew. He also published French, English, Russian, Latin and Polish grammar books.

In his Polish grammar book he endeavored to draw a comparison between the Polish Language and the Hebrew and German language. He also published a scholarly grammar-book that he wrote in German, as well as various articles in various journals.

Dr. Rabinovitz's activity did not stop at researching and translating the Talmud. He was also a fighter in the nationalist movement in the eighties of the 19th century. Those years were a new epoch in our life in the Diaspora. Our intelligentsia in Russia who attached themselves to Nihilism - with the belief in brotherhood and in enlightening the *muz'ik* [Russian villager] - gave up hope. The Russian villagers slapped them in the face and refused to learn from them. The wind of nationalism blew in the world. It was after the Balkan war. The Balkan countries became independent with Russian help, naturally. The idea of independence, having one's own land, started invading the Jewish community. The pogroms in Russia, which topped all Jewish troubles in that land, had their effect in this matter.

All that influenced the rise of the "Khovevey Zion" movement. [Khibat Zion/Khovevei Tziyon = a Zionist organization with the land of Israel as its goal]. This movement spread to all parts of the world like the rays of the sun and reached Paris as well. The movement found in Dr. Rabinovitz one of the most dedicated adherents. In November of 1884, when the first Zionist world conference assembled in Katovitz, Dr. Rabinovitz was there, old and weak but young in spirit and cheerful. He participated very actively in the debates and was a member of one of the committees.

Later, when the old Visotzki was about to sail to the Land of Israel, he negotiated with Dr. Rabinovitz to become the secretary of the commission. However, because of various reasons Dr. Rabinovitz did not accept this offer. In 1888 he was president of the Society of "Dorshey Tziyon" in Paris. He was then 70 years old. The Russian Jews celebrated his jubilee, sending him telegrams and… buying his books. This buying of his books was for him probably dearer than congratulations, because his whole ideal was to spread his books so as to enable him to publish new books and continue his translation of the Talmud. Therefore, he travelled to Russia, his homeland, where the greatest part of the Jews were living at that time. With their help he would be able to fulfill his wish, and at the same time see his family to whom his heart was bound.

In 1889, before *Shavues* he arrived in Horodets. They greeted him with honor near the *shtetl* with the Rabbi, his brother, and brought him to the *shtetl*. On *Shavues* Holiday he gave a sermon in the synagogue. It was in German because his Yiddish was not fluent enough anymore. The story goes that he said in that sermon that he was finishing the sermon he started just before he left Horodets. The same story runs also in Antepolye saying that when he was there on a visit and spoke in the synagogue, he said that it was the missing end of the sermon that he did not finish when he disappeared.

Israel Mikhl died in the summer of 1892, poor and lonely materially, but leaving behind him rich spiritual legacy and a long list of books that were his companions on the hard rocky road of his life. In these books he found consolation for his poverty and solitude.

If our brothers did not understand how to appreciate Dr. Rabinovitz in his life time, an honest Frenchman did understand. He was the owner of a Parisian coffee house. He set for Dr. Rabinovitz a special table in a corner with all the comforts so that the doctor could do his work undisturbed. At this table, Dr. Rabinovitz created his work that opened the doors of the Jewish culture and enabled every educated Christian to gain a better understanding of the Jews.

[Pages 98-99]

Motye Hillel's [Motye, son of Hillel]

by A. M. Tzeitlezon

Translated by Hannah Kadmon

[Translator's comments in square brackets]

The Mazursky family was one of the most branched out and influential families in Horodets. People said that Binyamin Mazursky who lived 150 years ago [prior to the date of this book 1949] was the landowner of the *shtetl* and the vicinity and collected taxes for the government [probably having a concession for that]. The story goes that he had barrels full of gold.

R' Binyamin Mazursky, the rich property owner, had to relinquish his estate and the concession to collect taxes. [The writer does not explain the reason for that]. Wishing to hold to his possessions, he looked for a Polish *shlakhtshitz* [in Polish: a nobleman] whom he trusted and registered all his possessions under this man's name. This *shlakhtshitz*, however, was loyal to himself more than to Mazursky and took everything for himself. Thus, Binyamin Mazursky was no longer a rich man. He lost all his possessions. He sued the *shlakhtshitz* and spent the rest of his money on that.

He bequeathed one thing to his children - the pedigree of the Mazursky family.

R' Binyamin Mazursky was a *parnes-khodesh* [elected once a year by the community for a public office]. Such an office was could also be inherited: members from the Mazursky family took hold of the office of *gabe* [manager of affairs] of the *Khevre Kedi'she* [voluntary burial society] and officiated high handed. It should be noted that, to their credit, they married into scholarly families.

The granddaughter of R' Binyamin married a young man from Pinsk by the name of Hillel Kaplan. He was a fine scholar with a head on his shoulders. He even got a taste of the Enlightenment and to top it off was an ardent *Misnoged* [opponent the *Hassidic* movement]. Hillel used to say: "The fact that among the *Hassids* there was equality and the high-in-rank *Hassid* is equal to the low-rank *Hassid* - this is good. However, when the lower-in-rank is equal to the higher-in-rank - that is bad." Nevertheless, his own sons became ardent *Karlin Hassids*. One of the sons, Motye, out of utter devotion to the *Karlin* dynasty, changed his name from Kaplan to Karlinski.

Motye Hillel's, or as he was called later Motye Karlinski, was the son-in-law of the old Rabbi of Horodets, a status that greatly suited him both owing to the Rabbi's pedigree and knowledge of Talmud.

In his youth, Motye was very pious and conducted himself like a great *Hassid*: He wore white long stockings with loafers, prayed with enthusiasm while walking back and forth in his house or in the synagogue raising his right hand upward and snapping his fingers - meanwhile singing in a high voice some verses from the prayer such as: "You are until the world was created and you are since it was created" "You created the sky and the sky beyond" "and you give life to all", and so forth.

In his old days, Motye Hillel's became a bit "aristocratic". Thanks to his educated children, he used to wear shiny modern shoes, a white "*hertzl*" [vest] with a nice necktie and cuff links. On Holidays he used to wear a top hat with a long coat and like a dandy used to walk into the *shtibl* [Hassidic house of prayer]. The congregation is already deep in praying, but Motye Hillel's is not in a hurry. He browses in a book as if the prayer does not concern him. The congregation has already reached "*Nishmat*" [part of the prayer] with might and main and R' Motye is still engrossed in his book - who would dare take a look and see what book it is. Already Khayim-Leib calls the "*Barkhu*" [another part of the prayer]. Here, R' Motye grabs his *talis* [striped tasseled shawl worn during prayer] and in a flash it is already on his shoulders. He hurries across the *shtibl*, his handkerchief in the air and at the end of *shimenesre* [18 blessings said quietly, standing up with legs fastened] when the congregation have already gone through the prayer, R' Motye catches up with them and the whole congregation waits for R' Motye to finish his *shimenesre* and then they hear him hum with a special melody "*o'se shalom...*" [The last verse of the prayer: God will bestow peace on his people]. This is the sign for Khayim-Leib that he has to start the loud recitation of *shimenesre*.

Motye Hillel's was considered a scholar with a sharp intellect. He often came to R' Khayim - the chief Rabbi of the community - to study with him chapters of *gemore* [the part of Talmud that comments on the *Mishna*].

Besides *gemore* he also used to browse in other books from his fine library.

Motye Hilel's had a stately appearance: a tall straight figure, a long well groomed yellowish beard and sharp eyes that pierced whoever came near him. On every subject Motye had a joke or an anecdote. His humoristic tales reflect the way of thinking of this phenomenon Karlinski.

For example, he told this story: Once there was a really ignorant person who became very rich, and associated with the greatest people and scholars of his time. At the end, this rich illiterate person became a big knowledgeable person and started expressing his opinions about rabbis, cantors, and the like. One day, someone asked him: "You know worldly things because you meet educated people, and you can learn because you associate with great Rabbis. So, I ask you, where from do you know the silent *shimenesre* prayer?..." [that, naturally, one does not learn just from associating with learned people...]

R' Motye wise answers were famous: Once R' Israel, the Stoliner Rabbi was in Horodets and stayed at Karlinski's place. When the Rabbi saw the beautiful Sh"s [six parts of the Mishna together with Talmudic commentaries] each of the books tucked in a separate case, he asked Motye: "Motye, how many "backs" do these books have? Motye answered immediately: "not two" (because two would have meant that he never opened the books). [Some people had dummy books with two "backs"...]

Motye Hillel's house which was the most beautiful in *shtetl* was also a bit of a guest house, as wood-merchants, gentile landowners and intellectuals stayed there overnight. The house was a meeting place for the learned. They used to discuss politics, various problems -both secular and Jewish - and incidentally drop some biblical quotation, a joke or a witticism. Motye Hillel's house was the most aristocratic house in *shtetl* and when the children grew up one could hear some Russian in the house. The house was no longer Motye Hillel's' House but the Karlinksy's house and the Karlinksy's house called the tune in *shtetl*.

Besides the guest-house, Motye Hillel's had a fashion store that very little catered to the inhabitants of Horodets. It was a store more for gentile landowners than for Jews and it held more beautiful cases than merchandise.

This is how Motye's house functioned until WW1. When the Germans drew nearer to Horodets and the community started to move out, R' Motye Karlinski with his wife fled too and settled in Yekaterinoslav until their death.

Motye Hillel's wonderful house in Horodets was burnt down immediately, like all other Jewish houses, and this marked the departure of the last "Mohican" of the Mazursky family that played a significant role in Horodets.

[Pages 99-101]

Rabbi Yitskhak [Isaac] Aaron

by Rabbi Mordechai Greenberg

Translated by Hannah Kadmon

[Translator's comments in square brackets]

R' Yitskhak [Issac] Aharon had a personality with contradicting traits. He was a pious Jew like all pious Jews, had a deep knowledge of *Talmud*, "*Yad Hakhazaka*" [alternate name for the *Mishneh Torah*, the code of Maimonides], *Zohar* [holiest mystical book of the Kabbalah] etc., At the same time he read scientific books, was interested in general education and knowledge, Bible, grammar and mainly in Eugenics. The vegetables in his garden were entirely different from the regular vegetables. They were extraordinarily big. His cucumbers, radishes and potatoes, were famous for their size and juiciness.

His hens were tall, almost reaching the table top from where they picked their food. Even in his daily life R' Yitskhak Aharon was different. Every morning he used to take out from a cupboard his small box with scented herbs, shake it and have a good sniff. Then he would take a little of the herbs in his mouth and sprinkle herbal scent. The house filled with a scent nobody could ignore…The smell was too strong to bear and it filled the house the whole day. From time to time, R' Yitskhak Aharon refreshed the fragrance by taking out his small box, again, shaking it and sniffing.

Besides his mastery in Eugenics, with which he experimented on his hens, geese and turkeys at his home and in the garden, he was also an architect.

Once he had the urge to do something in the art of architecture. It occurred to him that the vegetables in his garden were wonderfully big and tasty but when they lay a few days in the house, they were no better than other vegetables and he had to throw them away. He walked about, deep in thought and finally came up with the idea: since he has a workshop for production of bricks (the truth is that they were not acknowledged as better than other bricks, he considered them the best in the whole world), he planned and built a small brick-cellar. What he built was not an ordinary cellar. He did not use any wood or iron in the construction – just bricks. In the walls he inserted bottles [for decoration?].

The main art of the cellar was inside: thick painted walls with a ceiling painted sky-blue. It was so painted that it looked in the dark as beautiful as the sky. Only the sun, moon and stars were missing in that sky.

The depth inside was the same size as the outside height of the building. There were no steps to go up, except for a long kind of a ramp.

In summer it was cold in the cellar, like in a cold winter day. He stored there the vegetables from his big garden. He sold them to certain house-owners only.

R' Yitskhak Aharon found in this creation satisfaction for his thirsty soul which was yearning for knowledge and art. That cellar did not last for long. It existed only a few years. It became clear that something was lacking in R' Yitskhak Aharon's architecture. That construction with the thick walls and thick ceiling caved in all of a sudden, luckily with no casualties.

R' Yitskhak Aharon's *sukke* [the erected Sukkoth booth] was also famous. His *sukke* was different from other *sukkes*. A few boards, a broken door, a part of a window, branches to cover above – this is a traditional Jewish *sukke*. However, R' Yitskhak Aharon's *sukke* was constructed of other materials: patches of twisted straw coated with lime, the cover above was of corn-sticks that grew in his garden. That was something different, imposing. All the folks came to examine his *sukke* and the *sukke* proved to be without fault – according to religious laws.

In addition to all his "inventions" and occupations, R' Yitskhak Aharon also taught. Teaching for him was not a source of income but an ideal. Grown-up youth used to come over to him to learn Hebrew, grammar and Russian.

His mode of teaching his pupils was unusual. He did not believe in any method or in textbooks. He had his own method in teaching grammar: he opened the prayer book, analyzed a few sentences and that was it.

However, on his table one could find the *"maslul"*, and *"Talmud Lashon Ivri"* [two traditional textbooks for teaching Hebrew]. He took a look at them only rarely.

When he taught the Bible, he explained to the pupil the context of the chapter and then let him read on his own. He wanted the pupil to find independently, all by himself, what he knew and what he did not know. That was his personal method.

He was different in his praying, too. Even though he was a Kobryner Hassid, he used to pray alone and in certain places in the prayer he would stand up and sing in a unique way. For example, the verses: [in translation from Hebrew:] "all eyes are raised to you and you provide for them food when needed", "you humiliate the proud and lift the humiliated" and "and you help the poor". Through these sung verses, he expressed his ideals in connection with the suffering of people and as a protest against the misery and social order of the world.

R' Yitskhak Aharon was unlike others in his eating habits as well. At a period in his life he led a life of a vegetarian. For six years he did not eat meat and his nourishment was bread and vegetables from his garden.

His statements about food were very peculiar, not alluding to his leading a vegetarian life. He used to say: "If you want to be a really pious Jew, take an earthenware vessel, go to the river, fill it with pebbles and eat them"…

R' Yitskhak Aharon's outlook on life was unique. He did not yield to public opinion and never had any regard to prevalent opinions concerned with either life or death.

The following remarkable story is a sample of his strong character. It was before Passover in 1888. The river had thawed and overflowed. Those who lived near the river moved to houses that were not affected by the flood. However, R' Yitskhak Aharon refused to move from the place. His family evacuated the house because it stood near the river and he stayed in the attic and observed the Passover *seder* by himself...

No wonder the people of Hotodets regarded R' Yitskhak Aharon as a *meshugene* [crazy] and this is how they nicknamed him. Yet, they respected him. Especially they respected his opinion about *eiruvim* [the religious rules about carrying things out of the house on Sabbath only within an enclosed area, such as a wire strung on the circumference of a town.] Every Friday afternoon, he used to go out with his blue eyeglasses, a stick in his hand, to inspect the *eiruvim*, if they were not torn and if they were set according to the Jewish rules. He had the last word on the *eiruvim*. If he said that it was forbidden to carry on Sabbath – they immediately announced in the *Bote-Medro'shim* [study houses where people used to pray as well] "It is forbidden to carry" and there was nothing you could do about it.

Neither *eiruvim* nor his "inventions" were the essence of his life. In the last years of his life it was clear what the essence of his being had been for many years. On a particular day, in the year 1907, we heard that R' Yitskhak Aharon was going to the Land of Israel. He sold his house, garden, all his tools and even his books. He exchanged all for money, sat on a wagon with his wife and rode to the train station, on his way to the Land of Israel.

However, fate was not in favor of R' Yitskhak Aharon spending his last years in the Land of Israel. In Odessa he got paralyzed and had to return.

He stayed, paralyzed, at his daughter Reizl's house in Kobryn, the rest of his life. Although he was paralyzed, blind and could hardly utter a word - even then, it seems, grammar occupied his mind. If he had a young man around who had some knowledge of grammar, he immediately started "teaching" him grammar in his particular way.

* * *
*

R' Yitskhak Aharon was a potential great inventor who did not have the opportunity to cultivate his extraordinary aptitudes, a man with ideals which he could not realize. He has been forgotten but not by those who knew him well.

[Pages 101-102]

R' Shalom Kostrinsky

by Yaakov Kostrinsky (Rekhovot, Israel)

Translated by Hannah Kadmon

[Translator's comments in square brackets]

Of the four brothers, uncle Shalom was the most distinguished, both owing to his name and to his Jewish and worldly knowledge. He was also respected for his tolerant attitude towards people with opposing ideas. I remember him as a short man, clear and smiling face and the looks of a scholar. This is the figure of R' Shalom: knowledgeable in Talmud and *poskim* [post-Talmudic commentators] and in the Rabbinical literature, expert Bible scholar and familiar with the Russian language and worldly matters. Basically of a soft nature, he exhibited a strong character in known cases. Appearing as a worldly man, he at the same time was a great observant Jew and had very deep religious feelings, though far from being fanatic. The youth used to feel very comfortable in his company. Until today I cannot forget his awe-bearing image. This strong impression was due to the strong religious feelings and strict character of uncle Shalom.

He had four daughters: Henye, Chaya-Dvorah, Rachel-Hadas and Chava, the youngest. Though I was a small child, I remember well the following: The youngest daughter, Chava, died in infancy. She died Friday evening. Uncle Shalom was welcoming the Sabbath at the Stoliner *shtiebl* and kept on praying as though nothing happened. Early next morning, he came again to the *shtiebl* as was his custom, and he did not show outwardly the awful tragedy that had happened and that hurt him inwardly. After praying he returned home. He then entered the room where the baby was lying and approaching the corpse he said loudly: "Good Sabbath, my daughter!". I can remember even today the shudder that ran through my body, when I heard the bold and confident traditional "Good Sabbath" at such a moment. Until now, I cannot stop wondering at uncle Shalom's firm belief, at his spiritual strength and powerful self-control. All this Shalom did because according to שולחן ערוך [the *Shulchan Aruch*, the Jewish code of laws] you are not allowed to mourn the dead on Sabbath. However, after הבדלה [*havdala;* ceremony when Sabbath is over], out of his awfully aggrieved heart burst out his quiet lament.

Uncle Shalom was not only embraced by his family. He was embraced by the whole *shtetl* and the surrounding *shtetles* both for his personal merits and for his status as an established Rabbi. Many people approached him for an advice because of his lucid and logical mind.

This was probably the reason for appointing him as *gabe* [manager of affairs] of *Khevre Kedi'she* [voluntary burial society], after Hillel's death. Such an appointment was reserved for the most distinguished in Horodets.

Because of a denunciation in connection with a legacy, he had to flee to America in the nineties of the 19th century. In his new home he was also active in public matters. He was one of the founders of the Stoliner *shtibl* "Beit Israel" in New York. Seven years later, he returned to Horodets, and became again the established Rabbi. In 1915 he fled from the fire of war [WW1] deep into Russia, wandering from town to town until the end of the war. After WW1, he went to America to join his daughter. He settled in Springfield, Mass next to his daughter Rachel-Hadas. There, too, he was immediately highly regarded by Jews and Christians. Every synagogue wanted him as a member.

R' Shalom Kostrinsky

Just as in Horodets, uncle Shalom held study-groups with Jewish people who derived a great pleasure from his way of teaching, which was seasoned with proverbs, witticisms, or tales.

Uncle Shalom had a very strong passion for writing of letters. He used to write letters to all his relatives and acquaintances, to urge one person to support a relative in Europe or remind another person of an article or of a story that happened at one time. His language was Talmudic and his handwriting was clear – every letter was a pearl. It was delightful to read his letters. From his handwriting one could learn about his obvious understanding. When uncle Shalom was sitting without writing any letter, he used to lead his forefinger over the table as if he was about to write, as if he wanted to express his feelings and thoughts that filled his heart and mind. That was the reason for his writing many letters.

The anecdotes that he told were very popular. As an example, he used to say to someone: "Why do you hate me? Have I done you any favor?" Or something like this: "After all, the smallest district in Russia is Grodno and the smallest county in Grodno is Kobryn, and the smallest shtetl in the Kobryn county is Horodets". When someone reproached him: "R' Shalom what are you talking about?" he would answer: "You mean to say that I am lying. Better say: 'It seems so to you'. Never say 'you are lying, you are telling a lie'. Say: 'It seems so to you'. It is nicer and more gentle".

That is how uncle Shalom used to speak until close to the age of hundred years. One day apparently blind and frail, he unintentionally fell off the window and died.

[Pages 103-104]

Motye Itsik's

[Motye, son of Itsik Kostrinsky]

by A. Katrosy [a pen-name of A. Ben-Ezra]

Translated by Hannah Kadmon

[Translator's comments in square brackets]

There were two "Motyes" in *shtetl*. One was Motye son of Hillel (see article about him) and the other was Motye son of Itsik. The latter was the youngest of the brothers Kostrinsky - sons of Itsik, son of Chayim – who occupied a distinguished place in Horodets.

Motye Itsik's, besides being an important *balebos,* was for many years the "starosta" [town-elder], the official head of the Jewish community – a very demanding position. It entailed obligations and responsibility concerning the Jewish residents of Horodets or Jews who were living in other towns and villages but were registered with the community of Horodets . [*balebos (pl: balebatim)* = proprietor, owner, host, master, landlord. It has also the connotation of a man of means.]

Motye Itsik's (Kostrinsky)

There were Jews in Czarist Russia who got involved in various illegal dealings. What Jew, wishing to survive, did not break the law from time to time? These Jews came running to Motye Itsik's. He is acquainted with the *pristav* [police commissioner in Czarist Russia] from Antipolye who is a good brother to the *ispravnik* [police officer] of Kobryn and has tight connections to the *natshalstva* (administration). Well, he would advice what to do and with whom.

Motye Itsik's was very busy especially right after Succoth, when it was conscription time and an order was issued to serve in the Russian army. This order terrified the Jewish young men because the length service in the army was four years under most difficult conditions. Discipline was very harsh and work was hard and uninteresting in the company of illiterate *muzshikes* [Russian villagers]. On top of that, they could not eat kosher food. And who wants to be in *slozshva* (military service)? Even gentiles looked for advice how to be exempt from military service.

R' Motye is busy. He must "see" the police officer, he must "converse" with the doctor and with some other eminent people who sit in the *prisotstva* (military committee). Actually, Motye does not speak Russian so well, but what he cannot say in Russian he says with a pat, a smile, etc. The administrator "understands" him and all is straightened out… the administration is satisfied, the candidate for conscription is exempted and R' Motye derives pleasure, too.

It cannot be said that he always succeeds. Naturally, a rich conscript manages to be exempted faster, but this has always been so. The rich are lucky.

However, his intercession did not make R' Motye rich. He was just a *balebos*, had a nice house, not bad furniture, clean and tidy. He wore quite elegant clothes and that is all.

R' Motye had quite a big family, sons and daughters, but they lived in the big city such as Brest and Yekaterinoslav and occasionally came for a visit in summer. That is when the house became alive and there was a lot of noise. Friends came to visit the big-city-dwellers and discussions were carried of various problems. Motye, with his wife Feige-Rive were purring with pleasure: It is no a trifle! They speak fluent Russian!

A special heart warming was the visit of their youngest, Yankele. He came from the Yeshiva of Meer or Telz and the whole *shtetl* was excited about him. Even R' Chayim, the Rabbi of Brest, loved him very much.

Fathers and mothers in the *shtetl* remarked: "Truly, this is *nakhes* [a proud enjoyment] for father and mother". Even later, when Yankele became a pupil of the Yeshiva of Odessa and finished high school with distinction, there were quite a number of people who felt jealousy in their hearts. However, R' Motye did not like Yankele's "buttons". After all, he is a Stoliner Hasid, travels occasionally to the Rabbi, sits in *shtiebl* and studies a page of Gemara and here his son wears brass buttons…A way out was found: Whenever Yankele comes home for vacation, he takes off his gentile's clothes and he looks as Jewish as the other Jews.

In addition to Motye's belonging to the whole *shtetl*, he was the "father" of the family. If there was some misfortune – uncle Motye was at hand. If there was some happy event – of course he was there. If something happened and this or that member of the family deviated from the traditional way, uncle Motye was there, shouting, abusing and when necessary beating as well. He intervened and expressed his views not out of wickedness, God forbid, but out of devotion. He was the chief leader of the Kostrinsky family.

This is how Motye led the *shtetl* and his family until his death in 1912.

[Pages 104-106]

Berl Rodetser

By Itke Podolevsky

Translated by Hannah Kadmon

[Translator's comments in square brackets]

Berl Rodetser

Berl Rodetzer was, for many years, a well known person in Horodets and surroundings. No ancestral-merits were credited to him and he did not stem from an important lineage. He was a self-made Jew, whose toil and brains helped him win a place among the rich and those of aristocratic descent. Under more favorable circumstances and not at the Tsar's period, such a person would have played a national role because he had all the qualities and skills of a leader.

In his youth, Berl Rodetser was a blacksmith in the village of Rodets (near Horodets). In those days, many gentile land-owners started neglecting their property. It was right after the Farmers' Liberation. For many generations, the landowners were accustomed to live off the cheap slave-like labor of the farmers and to lead a parasitic libertine life. When they were forced to start paying the farmers and to manage their own estates, the landowners could not or did not want to do so. So, in most situations they leased their property to a Jew. The Jew with his economizing and hard toil drew from the property enough income to pay the farmers, to draw his own pay and also to pay the landowner. In those days, the number of Jews "possessing" property by lease increased.

The first piece of property that Berl Rodetser possessed on lease was Rodets, the same village where he was living. Through hard work he soon got rich, very quickly leased a second farm and in no time was in the possession of seven pieces of property. This is something to be especially noted: the person who could not read and write in any language other than Yiddish and could not sign his name in Russian, became a land-owner of a great part of the Kobryn County -hundreds of acres. Later on, he bought for himself a small farm named Dvorishts. According to the decrees of the Tsar, Jews were forbidden to possess property on-lease or buy any piece of land. So, all buying and leasing were registered in the name of a gentile from Horodets - Maxim Sverdyuk. He was rich and very smart.

From year to year Berl Rodetser became richer, and with his riches grew his Jewish taste. His daughters were wedded to scholarly sons-in-law of important descent. The dowry was in the form of settling each son-in-law on a farm of his own. As for Berl, he moved to Horodets. He bought a large piece of land on the main street near the wooden bridge and built there two big houses. In those days, these were the most beautiful houses in town. In the back of the houses there was a big garden in which various vegetables grew, of the best sort. On Sundays, all his children and grandchildren from the farms would get together in Horodets with their horses and carts and domestic helpers - a whole kingdom. In town people were delighted and proud of Berl Rodetser, especially the craftsmen and the ordinary people who considered Berl Rodetser one of their own. When he settled in Horodets, Berl Rodetser acquired four reserved-seats near the east wall of the synagogue and of the *Bes-Medresh* [which was a place of study and also for prayers]. Having a good income and free from managing his business which was taken care of by his sons-in-law, he dedicated himself to community activity. He renovated the synagogue which was close to collapse and - no similarity implied - also the bathhouse which was old and neglected. Berl paid for those two renovations. He was supposed, later, to collect money from the *shtetl* but a large part of the money he never got back.

He also took upon himself the "*korovke*" [tax on meat; see pp. 60-61], the handling of which involved a great deal of swindling. He saw to it that whatever little money remained after taxes was used for the good of the community instead of finding its way into the pockets of the officials of the "oprave" [town autonomy]. He also introduced order into the *Khevre Kedi'she* [voluntary burial society]. Naturally, he acquired many enemies. However, the "public" was always on his side. All the others kept quiet out of awe and respect, being aware of his connections to the landowners and especially to Shtern, the landowner of the *shtetl*, whose farm he had on lease. Shtern was a *statski savetnik* (a high official) in the Tsar's government and he was also a member of the *prisotstve* [military committee] that conscripted people to the army. Berl Rodetser took action to free a great number of Jewish youth from military service. That was a very important matter in those days. Berl never charged a cent for these favors procured through Shtern.

Berl Rodetser's conduct was like that of a very rich man humane to his folks: donated generously, helped marrying poor relatives and orphans.

Berl Rodetser lived to the ripe old age of eighty four. Until his death he was full of energy and zest for life. When he was seventy years old, he married, for the third time, a rather young woman who bore him two children - a girl and a boy. It was striking to see Berl Rodetser, an old graying man, playing with these two children like a young man married only a few years.

Berl Rodetser died around 1915. Thirty years have passed since, but his name is remembered and will be remembered a long time from now.

[Page 106]

A Wedding in Horodets of Berl Rodetser's grandson

(The beginning of the 20th century)

First row standing from right to left: Yirmiyahu Rodetski, the contractor, F/P. Burshtein, Butche Burshtein, Sander Shtshopak, Yirmiyahu Shub, Yosef Roytkopf, Aharon Asher Volinietz, Leibe Shub,
Avraham Ravitsh, Binyamin Lifshitz, Khayim Dines, Tante Mindl, Beile Shtshopak and a Jew from Brisk.
Second row: Tzirl Rodetski, Sonya Rodetski, Itke Bregman, (two unknown) Sheine Novoselker, (unknown) Sarah Feshe Dubin, Etye Shub, Binyamin Burshtein, Khaya'ke Rodetski, Tzirl Lifshitz, Neima Dines, Tzivya Stavski, Rivka Dines, Bashke Shub.
Third row, sitting from right to left: Shakhna Rodetski, Beile wife of Yankl Kodliner, Mrs Shtshopak, Itzikl the carpenter, a Jew from Brisk, Mashe Burshtein, Aharon Asher Rodetski, Berk Rodetzer, Golde Dines, Ester Dvora Lifshitz, Khaya Tzirl Shub, Gitl Ravitsh, Meir Lifshitz
Fourth row: Freide Rodetski, Yehudit Rodetski, Avreml Rodetski, Menashe Rodetski, Moshe Dines, Itzil Lifshitz, Moshe Lifshitz, Kalman Ravitsh.

[Pages 107-108]

"Panye Shaf" [Mr. Sheep]

(Itzikl)

by I. Zis

Translated by Hannah Kadmon

[Translator's comments in square brackets]

"Panye Shaf" – this is how the Horodetser *Poritz* [Polish land-owner], Shter, called him. However, the Jews of Horodets called him simply "Itzik the carpenter" or in short: Itzikl.

Actually Itzikl was a zestful person rather than a carpenter. He used to accept work as a contractor and hired craftsmen to do the job according to his planning.

Plain work Itzikl did not take upon himself. He dealt only with Polish land-owners, and especially with Shter, who was on intimate terms with Tsar Nicholas I. The palaces (or *pokoyes* –as they were called in those days) that he constructed were renowned in that region.

Itzikl not only dealt with Polish land-owners – he also built the houses of the Stoliner Rabbis, in Stolin, and thus he became 'one of the family' in Rabbi Israel's Stoliner "court". However he was not a fanatic Hasid. He liked everybody; Hasidim and *Misnogdim*, pious and non-observant, young and old, poor and rich. He liked to hear and tell a good joke, but mostly he liked to help people. There were two kinds of people, however, that he disliked: the fanatic and the stingy. These two types of people used to arouse his anger and sometimes he quarreled with them.

R"Yizhak Zusselman - Drawn by his son Israel

As mentioned before, Itzikl was a zestful person rather than a craftsmen. Once he had the urge to convince Shter to sell his court. Itzikl was actually the middleman and accordingly was to get a commission of a few thousands of rubles and would have become a rich man. However - slow down Itzikl, don't be hasty! Shter paid him indeed a thousand rubles, but Andronovsky, the land-owner who bought the court did not want to pay the five thousands rubles that he owed according to the agreement. Itzikl sued him in court and after a few years of trial that cost him a lot of money, he gave up the hope of collecting this money. What did Itzikl do with the thousand rubles that he got from Shter? By one Sabbath eve the money had evaporated. How come? Quite simple: he donated for charity left and right, to whoever asked. He founded a fund of some hundred rubles to hand out loans with no interest, improved the shelter for wanderers, renovated the Karliner *shtiebl* [Hasidic house of prayer], made new cupboards for the books and brought in a new Talmud from Vilna. With the few rubles that remained he started acting like a land-owner. He planted a grand orchard with all kinds of fruit trees ordered from abroad, and… and took the saw, the plane and the hammer and with his own hands built a… pigeon coop.

"What are you building, R' Itsik", asked his neighbor.

"A pigeon coop", answered Itzikl

"A pigeon coop?"

The neighbor walked away confused and nodded his head; "what is the matter with Itzikl, has he lost his mind? What does he need the land-owner's whims for?"

Itzikl's pigeon-coop

What Itzikl called "a pigeon coop" became "seeing" and "hearing" and all kinds of "chirping sounds" – a "pigeon coop" with 32 small rooms for 32 "pairs", the likes of which the Jews of Horodets never saw or heard before. There was a lot of excitement in the *shtetl*. When he had a visitor for Sabbath, he would slaughter some pigeons to treat his guest in honor of the Sabbath.

This "riches" of Itzikl did not last long. His legs withered. He lay a long time in a hospital in Warsaw until the Stoliner Rabbi helped him travel to Vienna where they amputated both his feet up to his knees in order to save his life. He came back from Vienna (with his righteous wife, Alte, who constantly took care of him) with prosthesis. When he walked supporting himself with a cane, it was almost unnoticeable that he had prosthesis. All of that cost a lot of money and he was no longer rich.

Shortly before WW1 he travelled to Moscow to consult an expert doctor and he stayed there until the end of the war. Over there he earned some thousands rubles and started again to conduct himself lavishly like in former years.

(comment by A Ben-Ezra: "about his other communal activities look up the article 'Under the Polish Rule' by Rabbi Shalom Podolevsky.)

In the meantime, his children immigrated to America and they steadily sent him a few dollars to enable him to carry on his activities of doing good.

This is how he led his life until the Germans, curse them, occupied Horodets.

The money that his children used to send, to support him, stopped coming completely and his communal activities were cut off abruptly.

A tragic day arrived. The Germans, their name be erased for ever, were not only cut off all his sources of income but also used him as a target for mockery and ridicule, until he - together with his house, his *besmedresh* and books - met his tragic death. May God revenge his spilled blood.

(comment by A. Ben-Ezra: "look up the article 'The End'")

[Pages 109-110]

A Community Leader

By S. Ben-Haviv

Translated by Hannah Kadmon

[Translator's comments in square brackets]

When I mention the name Khayim-Itche to a Jew from Horodets or Antipolye and also to many people in the entire surroundings of Horodets who lived there in the years 1925-1941, it evokes in them love, respect and pride. If you ask a village Jew: "Do you know Khyaim-Itche?" He would tell you legends about him and would recite many of Khyaim-Itche's witticism and jokes that he used to tell; and, rolling up his eyes would say: "He was an extraordinary man, with outstanding wisdom, and primarily - our fellow-man". The name of Khayim-Itche was well-known among store keepers, workmen and peasants. Each of them claimed him as one of them.

Who was Khyaim-Itche? How did he become so well-known? Where did he come from? Khyaim-Itche was really a Horodetser - Lieber's son. He was the second of Lieber's twelve children.

As a child, Khyaim-Itche's talents did not stand out. He attended the *kheyder* like all other children. At the age of 14 he became a *melamed* [teacher in *Khyeder*] in a village. Later on, he left for Antipolye and learned to be a quilt-maker. When Lieber's wife, Tzivia, died at the age of forty, he helped his father raise the children. Afterwards he worked in the fields, with horses and cattle, enjoying telling jokes and witty stories. He was fond of politics, read books and behaved like all the young men of Horodets. When WW1 was over, Khayim-Itche experienced his first thrill. He left for Brisk [Brest], started working for the greatest leather-merchant of Brisk, became acquainted with the local worker's movement and gave himself body and soul to organize the workers union, forbidden at that time in Poland. He hid under a false name and became the secretary of the workers of Brisk. In his free time he read a lot and studied the life of the workers.

Khayim Itche

The police in Brisk got wind of Khayim-Itche, and searched for him as a political criminal and a founder of a union. Khayim-Itche hid for some time in Brisk and when he could no longer hide there, he left Brisk and the workers movement and returned to Horodets, where he married one of the most beautiful girls of the *shtetl*. The young couple settled in Antipolye and Khayim-Itche opened there a leather business.

This is where Khayim-Itche's career rose. At first, he started on a small scale. He established his store on Pinsker Street. However, very soon he drew closer to all the cobblers and farmers of all the villages and built a big house with a big store close to the market near the brick-built *besmedresh*. [The study-house, where people used to pray as well]

Later, he bought an additional store in the stores-section of Antipolye and also a great piece of land on the outskirts of Pinsk and began to play a great role: He did not commit himself solely to his business. He gave himself body and soul to the life of the community. When the community in Antipolye was established, he became the leader of the community and set the tone for the *shtetl*. When a bank was founded in Antipolye, he was the administrator of the bank and played an important role in the establishing of banks in Poland. He went to Warsaw for conferences and his opinions carried weight. When people from Horodets needed a loan, they knew that their landsman would help them get it from the bank in Antipolye. From day to day, the name of Khayim-Itche became more eminent in the neighborhood. He became very friendly with the Rabbi R' Yitzkhak Valkin, and together they built a big *Talmeytoyre* [tuition free religious public school] not just for the children of Antipolye but also for the children of Horodets and the surroundings.

Every evening one could see people coming to Khayim-Itche for an advice. Khayim-Itche had always a smile for all and gave them wise advice. Khayim-Itche traveled to the high officials in Kobryn and Brisk to intercede on behalf of his poor fellows. It happened a few times that an official came to collect taxes and started writing a formal document. Khayim-Itche tore up the paper and smashed the pen. It took, then, a great deal of effort until the incident was hushed up. When the worker needed to implement something, Khayim-Itche was their spokesman and advisor.

When WW2 broke out, Khayim-Itche was very active on the side of the Soviets (we have no idea what kind of role he played there). When the Nazis, their name be erased, attacked Russia, Khayim-Itche left for Russia. Nobody knows about his fate there. Is the clever Khayim-Itche still alive? Is he active for the good of humanity? Does he read, whole nights, Russian, Polish, Yiddish and Hebrew books? Will we ever hear from him again? Or perhaps the Nazis captured him on the way and killed him? And, even if he is still alive, is he alive only as far as we are concerned? Will the Russian government release him?

Only God knows.

[Pages 110-112]

The Town's Joker

By David Kaplan

Translated by Hannah Kadmon

[Translator's comments in square brackets]

Every town and *shtetl* had their own joker. Vilna [Vilnius] had Motke Khabad, Ostropolye had Hershele, and so forth. The Jewish joker was different from the gentile court-jester. The court-jester belonged to the king, to the landowner, to the rich. His job was to make his master merry, and incidentally make fun of the people around. His jokes were restrained, masked. His humor was covert. However, the Jewish joker gave free rein to his humor. He did not spare anyone. He sent all away with a flea in their ear: from the Rabbi to the bathhouse attendant.

The Jewish joker became the mirror in which one sees the reflection of ghetto-life with its petty notions and outlooks. The Jewish joker also expressed the sorrow and distress that accumulated in the heart of the oppressed Jew against his tormentor - whether a gentile or a Jew.

Not in vain did the Jewish town Joker become the darling of the town, as he became the *shofar* [the horn blown in Synagogue] through which people wished to proclaim their complaints and pain with sarcastic humor.

Tevye the shoemaker was an independent man. He was a short fellow with thin legs and a hump in back and in front. When he walked in the street, nobody could follow him so quickly, because he did not really walk but ran very fast. He always looked pale and his pointed small beard was quivering all by itself. He lived on the main street with his wife Beyle and six children in one room. There he had his workshop with his tools and he worked hard. He did not make many new shoes. First of all, he did not have enough money to buy leather. If someone gave him in advance the money to buy leather to make him new shoes, he did not live to see his new shoes, because Tevye had a preferable mission for the money. He immediately went to Abramke the butcher - who was his neighbor - and right away bought a large piece of lung and spleen, brought them to his wife, told her to cook a good meal and enjoyed eating it. When he was asked by the customer to show him the new shoes, he said that he did not have any reason to buy the leather. The buyer would say: "Is this possible, Tevye, where is the money that I gave you in advance?" Tevye would answer briefly and bluntly: "In my stomach!" and that was the end of it.

Summer evenings, after work Tevye took off the apron and the patched trousers, put on a different pair of trousers with new patches, and went out for a stroll. He used to walk in the market where he would stop near Motye Karlinski's store, one of the finest house owners in the *shtetl* and perform his pranks in front of the girls of the market. His best joke was that he had to sell them buttermilk in straw mats. The girls started laughing and he stuck out his tongue, extended two figs [rude gestures] with his finders and ran back to the street.

Moshe Burshtein, the grocer, resided in the Market. Tevye used to enter his store when nobody was watching, snatch a herring, tear its head and tell Moshe: "How much is the herring without its head?" Moshe would become angry and shout: "Get out of the store, you hunchbacked crook". Tevye would not be alarmed, would snatch the herring and run home. It was futile to run after him. One jump and he was gone. Sometimes he knocked, in the middle of the night, on the window of Abremeke the butcher shouting: "The goats are coming, go slaughter them - the sooner the better - I have already milked them." Abremke cursed him properly: "A dark dream on your head". Tevye stuck out his tongue and ran away.

Near Tevye was the house of Khayim-Hersh. Once, the latter's son, Abreme came over from Lodz with his wife. He was a dentist's technician. His wife's name was An'yute. She was a fragile woman and therefore they cooked sheep's meat for her. Tevye got wind of that dish and stealthily entered Khyaim-Hersh's house, took the pot with the cooked dish, brought it home and told his wife: "Beyle from now on I name you An'yute, because you, too, are eating sheep's meat"

Tevye stole once into Yaakov Polyak's textile-store. The store was full of customers. Tevye seized a piece of white cloth and said: "Look, I and Yaakov's heir will lie together in the same cemetery in the same shrouds."

Another time, Tevye snatched a herring in Shamai's food-store, broke its backbone and said: "No longer privileged, it has a hump like Tevye's"…

On the whole, Tevye came to life in the fair, when the farmers from the surrounding villages used to come with their cattle, horses, chicken and eggs; and where shoemakers and tailors used to come to sell their merchandise and small merchants used to come to bargain and mediate. That is when Tevye left his workshop with the gentiles who used to come for their boots, and headed to the market. There, farmers dealers and children used to gather around him and Tevye told his wise and sarcastic jokes. Not one farmer broke his eggs while laughing hard. Many merchants took advantage of the incident to strike a deal.

Then, Horodets had something to tell and something to laugh at until the next fair.

Tevye the hunchback went through all the calamities of WW1 and its outcome. It was tragic-comic that the Poles who invaded Horodets arrested Tevye as a "communist". Horsemen rode in front and in back of Tevye while small agile Tevye was forced to run after the horsemen who led him to Kobryn to be executed.

What did Tevye think of? How did he react at that time?

It is difficult to answer and his "communist friend" Hershel the teacher [editor's note: look up the article about Hershel the Teacher] were not allowed to utter a word. Surely if he had been allowed to speak he would have cracked a joke about the Polish government and its order.

Tevye also went through the hell that the Germans, their name be erased, brought to Horodets. What did Tevye "the cold lung and liver" say then? Who did he make fun of?

Praise the jolly pauper Tevye.

[Page 112]

Melamdim and Teachers

[Melamed = teacher in the *kheder*]

Sender the Melamed

by Ami

[Ami is one of the pen-names of Akiva Ben-Ezra]

Translated by Hannah Kadmon

[Translator's notes – in square brackets]

Sender the Melamed

When a Horodetser hears the name Sender mentioned, his earliest childhood flicks in his mind like a cinema-movie. He was then wrapped in a praying shawl and brought to Sender's *kheder*. Sender was a short Jew who wore a *talis-ko'tn* [four cornered tasseled undergarment] and its tassels got tangled in between his legs.

One picture follows another: here he sits by a long table, in front of him the Aleph-Bet. The "angel" throws sometimes a coin and sometimes a candy, honey-cake or sponge-cake. Here he is a small *kheder*-child playing with other children in the garden, sometimes getting lashed with the "noodles", sometimes getting "sick" not willing to go to the *kheder*. It seems like only yesterday: it is winter, it is cold outside and slippery, the children don't go home to eat dinner. Sender brings their small pots with food from their home, puts them in the oven to heat, they eat the barley soup, nibble on a piece of *khale* or bread, and they continue their lessons: *komets aleph o, domets bet bo*. Towards evening, Sender himself returns the children back home. A picture fades away and another appears instead: the children begin learning the *khumash* [five books; Pentateuch]. The book is *Vayikra* [the third book]. Why *Vayikra?* Because it starts with sacrifices that purify. If a Jewish boy starts with sacrifices, he becomes pure as well. Then there is eating, drinking and all are joyful.

Who among the Horodtsers did not go through Sender's *kheder*? Sender himself was very satisfied with that, although he often said: "Dear God, let me have at least one year without being a *melamed*." His wish was indeed granted. The last year before his death, he was already weak and old (he was about eighty years old when he died).

I don't know whether Sender really meant it or rather joked about his wish, because he was a joker by nature. He used witticisms and used to joke even about himself.

Sender loved small children very much. He used to say: "When die, I want to be buried among the small children." When he was asked: "Why among the small children and not near the Rabbi?" he would answer with a smile: "Simple, I want to be able to cheat them of the Friday *bandes* (*boolkes*) [baked rolls]."

Sender used to say about *melamdim*: "If a melamed does not get *tshekhatke* (tuberculosis) after one year of teaching – he is not a melamed…" Of course, he included himself among all the *melamdim*. It seems that Sander was a *melamed*, a *baal-poel* [with ability to convince, affect] because if not, he would not have stayed a teacher of the youngest children in Horodets, and have twenty children to teach without an aid.

Sender was also a distinguished person in the eyes of the State, and he was bestowed the rank of "*dyesyatnic*" whose duty was to notify who would be on guard, to watch that no fire broke in the shtetl, God forbid. Sender cherished that role quite strictly and did not discriminate between rich and poor. All were equal in his eyes. He had a very strong sense of justice and therefore he felt a strong hatred towards the Romanov [the Russian Tsar's family] government and love for the Poles. He was a great supporter of the Poles and hoped to live to see their independence.

As mentioned, Sender was a man of justice. For example, he could not stand it when a rich person would beg for a sniff of tobacco from a poor man. For this purpose he had two boxes – one for the rich men and the other for the poor. When a poor man asked him for a sniff of tobacco, he would offer him a box full of tobacco. However, when a rich man asked him for a sniff of tobacco, he offered him an empty box…

Sender also strove to help the economy of the Horodetser Jews – in his own way. If a cow stopped producing milk, or if she was doomed, people used to come to Sender, to "talk" her out of it. Sender did it willingly and was very happy with his good deed.

When Sender became old and his beard started to be grey, he said: "It is already spring. It is blooming. My beard is also blooming."

Because of his making jokes, many things were ascribed to Sender. Thus they said in Horodets that when thunder is heard - Sender hides in a heap, or drinks castor oil with bread. There is no limit to what was said! Who then saw it all? Let us rather say things that we, ourselves, have seen or heard from Sender, the *melamed* of small children in Horodets, forty years ago. May he be an intercessor on behalf of all of us. [that is, in heaven].

[Page 114]

Shmuel the Cobbler

by Ami

[Ami is one of the pen-names of Akiva Ben-Ezra]

Translated by Hannah Kadmon

[Translator's notes – in square brackets]

In Horodets, one's importance was not based on wealth or profession but on scholarship, especially Jewish scholarship. If one was a learned man it did not matter where he came from nor what his occupation was. In other words: Importance in itself was the main thing – composed of piety, honesty and being a man of letters. Actually, what Jew in Horodets was not a man of letters? If he did not know a page of Gemara, he knew a chapter of *mishnayes* [collection of post biblical laws; part of the Talmud], or at least a verse in *khumash* [first 5 books of the bible] with Rashi's commentary. Everybody understood the meaning of the words in the prayer book, except for one Jew who was not from Horodets who mumbled his prayer.

That is why there were no separate *Bote-Medro'shim* [study houses where people used to pray as well] for craftsmen like in other *shtetles* because all people were almost equal.

That was indeed the reason why in Horodets the Rov [Orthodox Rabbi] could be a cobbler's son, or the son of a blacksmith, as long as he was a great scholar and an honest Jew.

For the same reason it was possible that a Jew who was a cobbler for many years, became later a *melamed* [teacher in Kheider], and that was not a drawback. One remark – he was called "cobbler" to the end of his life.

Shmuel the Cobbler was born in Pinsk. His father was a Jewish scholar and a merchant of grain. His barges sailed with grain on the Dnieper to many big towns. Once, a big storm sank his seven barges with the grain. He became poor. He ate his heart out and died. Shmuel was then still a child. As an orphan, without a father, he walked about in the town. From time to time he went into the *besmedresh* where the young men were sitting and studying and they let him study with them. He had a head on his shoulders and a good memory and these came in handy. When the young men learned to read the Torah, he would hold the *Tikun Korim* and this is how he learned how to read the Torah. [*Tikun Korim* is a book showing a sample of the text as it looks in the Torah Scroll, with the special font and all the traditional vocalization signs, and by its side the transliteration showing how the text should be read.]

When Shmuel became 20 years old, he figured that he should make some living and plan for his future. So, he studied to become a cobbler. After working with a cobbler for 12 weeks he soon became an independent cobbler.

Shmuel the Cobbler

In Horodets, Shmuel had a half brother from a different father, whose name was Tankhum Ber. He found Shmuel a match - Lipshen, daughter of Mikhl the tailor. Shmuel married her and settled in Horodets as a cobbler, was in charge of some workers and made a living. However, Shmuel the cobbler was drawn to the *besmedresh* more than to cobbling and since his house was opposite the *besmedresh*, he used to drop in, every day, before prayers, to study a chapter of *mishnayes*. In between *Minkhe* [afternoon prayer] and *Mayrev* [evening prayer] he studied a small part of *Ein-Yaakov* [a compilation of all the legendary material in the Talmud, with commentaries]. When he had some free time he would drop in midday too, and take a look at a book. He knew the Bible by heart.

On Sabbath, it was a great pleasure for him to entertain a guest, a well-read Jew, have some learned discussion with him, hear from him a good word – a literal interpretation or a non-literal interpretation – and celebrate real enjoyment-of- the Sabbath. After all, regrettably, could he learn anything from the cobbler's thread?...

This is how Shmuel the cobbler did his job. He was more in the *besmedresh* than by the cobbler's last and he was more adept at studying than at cobbling. Younger cobblers, better craftsmen than him, sprang up and he found it difficult to make a living. These younger cobblers held Shmuel in respect and approached him with an offer to become the *melamed* of their children. Naturally, he accepted their offer and became a *melamed*. He taught the children from the *Aleph-Bes* to *Khumesh* [first 5 books of the bible] with Rashi's commentary. This is how Shmuel became a *melamed*. Term after term, year after year, he was teaching the children of Horodets, until the death of Yosl Pines, the *shames* of Horodets. It occurred to the landlords of the community that there could not be a better *shames* than Shmuel: a Jew who can study, read the Torah, knows how to keep books in order, can also pray at the synagogal lectern and lives exactly opposite the *besmedresh*. Thus, Shmuel became a *shames* in his old age. Here he felt at home (*like a fish in water*).

He could actually sit and study as well.
[The dictionary defines the *shames* as a beadle, sexton in synagogue, Rabbi's personal assistant. His tasks are various – from knocking on the wooden windows to waking up people for prayer, to lighting the candles in the synagogue and to closing up after the last men has finished praying.]

This was the small world in which Shmuel the cobbler-*melamed-shames* lived until the first world war. When the *besmedresh* was burned down, Shmuel left for Antipolye where his two daughters were living. He died at the age of 76, 10th of Sivan תרע"ז [1917]. May he rest in Eden.

[Pages 115-117]

Chayim Itzik's

[Chayim son of Itzik]

by Ami

[Ami is one of the pen-names of Akiva Ben-Ezra]

Translated by Hannah Kadmon

[Translator's notes – in square brackets]

[Yiddish words used in the text: *melamed*=teacher in *Kheyder*; *kheyder*= traditional Jewish religious school; *rebe*= Hasidic rabbi; *balebatim*=plural of *Balebos*=proprietor, owner, host, master, landlord. It has the connotation of a man of means.]

Chayim Itzik's

When a child, aged 6-7, from Horodets, was asked "where do you learn?" He immediately answered: "by Chayim-Itzik". The truth of the matter is that this *melamed*'s name was Chayim Itzik's, which means in Yiddish: Chayim, the son of Itzik. The small children mistakenly distorted the name Chayim Itzik's into Chayim-Itzik, and this name prevailed over fifty years. Old and young knew Chayim Itzik's, the short Jew with the long reddish beard: Cheerful, lively with a heart full of warmth for children and adults.

Chayim Itzik's, was a Kobriner Hasid, and truly a fervent Hasid. Without the Rabbi he did not make a move. He traveled to the Rabbi for Rosh-Hashanah and Yom-Kippur and just like that - in the middle of the year.

In Chayim Itzik's *kheyder* the pupils had already learnt *Khumesh* [first 5 books of the bible]. It was also possible that they began "*Lekakh Tov*" [homiletic interpretation of the *khumes*h]. Chayim Itzik's used to teach according to the portion of the week, sometimes more and sometimes less.

In Chayim Itzik's *kheyder* the children used also to write. They started with the Aleph-Bet, and at the end, when a pupil had already mastered all the letters, back and forth, he wrote on a *fir-ksav* [practice sheet with written text] with the following text: "God willing, after Sabbath, portion 'life of Sarah' there would be a fair". The pupils copied, tracing the written text for many weeks, until the practice sheet was torn. Afterwards, the Rabbi would write another *fir-ksav* similar to the first one, and again the pupils would trace the written text again and again.

Chayim Itzik's never learned pedagogy, but to a certain degree he was a pedagogue, who understood the physical and mental structure of the child. For example, he nailed a strip of wood between two legs of the table so that the children could rest their feet on it. He set the inkwells in sardine-cans and fastened them one to the other so that the children would not overturn them.

Chayim Itzik's teaching was done sweetly, with singing. (Chayim Itzik's had a beautiful voice. He was also a cantor.)

The children are sitting around a long table. There are noodles on the table. The *rebe* himself prepared them. A small lamp hangs over his head and Chayim Itzik's teaches the portion "*vayekhi*". Here comes the verse: "And as for me, when I came from Padan" [Genesis 48;7]…where Yaakov apologizes to Joseph for having buried his mother, Rachel, in the middle of the field. The *rebe*'s eyes become misty and in a low voice he begins: "Ve'ani" – and I, "Yaakov" – Although I bother you with my burial, I did not do the same for your mother Rachel. I did not bury her in "me'arat ha'makhpela' [cave of Machpelah], and she was not even carried to Beth-Lehem. But all this is according to God's order. When Nevuzaradan will expel and exile the Jews, they will pass along Rachel's burial place, and Rachel will rise up crying out and weeping and asking for mercy. A voice from heaven will answer: "Yesh sakhar li'fe'ulatekh" – [Jeremiah 31;15-16] thy work shall be rewarded, and thy children shall come again to their own border." [see the musical notations at the end of the article]

At the last words the eyes of the *rebe* become moist and the children start crying. The childish hearts know why they are crying; They and their parents are in exile.

Upon entering the *kheyder,* children already knew that the Jews were in exile. It was not permitted to rejoice like non-Jews. Inside the *kheyder,* above the door, there was a naked part of the wall – stripped oft the wall-paper that covered the walls of the room – a dark area, a reminder of the destruction.

At every opportunity, the *rebe* introduced the subject of the exile, and that the Messiah son of David would come and the Jews would return to Eretz-Yisrael, and we would have again kings such as King David and his son King Solomon.

King Solomon was the symbol of wisdom, wealth and prophecy. This, the *rebe* explained clearly when he taught "The Song of songs" before Passover. Chayim Itzik's raised his voice and chanted: "The Song of Songs" – that is: the song of all songs. All the songs are holy but this song is even holier. All songs are from a king. This song is from a king, son of a king, a prophet son of a prophet, a wise man son of a wise man. *"Asher Li-Shlomo"* [of Solomon] – that means: that *shalom* [peace] of the whole world belongs to him. [Solomon in Hebrew is *"Shlomo"* and the word "peace" in Hebrew is *"Shalom"*].

Chayim Itzik's loved peace like life. If someone offended him, he did not quarrel with that man. He was only cross with the offender, and did not talk to him. There were several *balebatim* with whom he was cross. One of them was Ephrayim Itzel. What was he sore about?

This is the story: Poor men frequent the *shtetl*. When you give them a *groshen* it is quite a big sum. However, not everybody is *"a gevir"* [rich-man] who can afford to give a whole *groshen* to every poor man. So, what is the solution? That a poor man will be given nothing?.. The old Rabbi, R' Yehoshua Yaakov, devised the following solution: He wrote on small pieces of paper "half G"P [half *groshen*] charity for the poor, here in Horodets". People used to buy from the Rabbi the half *groshen*s in order to be able to give charity to the poor. When a poor man finished begging from door to door he would come to the Rabbi with the "coins" to exchange them for real *groshen*s. When the old Rabbi passed away, Chayim Itzik's took upon himself this "bank-business".

[Ben-Ezra's comments: G"P (ג״פ) means "Polish *Groshen*" (look up "Registry of Council of Four Lands" by Y. Halpern, p. 538; "Registry of the Land of Lita" by Shimon Dubnov p.342). One *gilden* equaled 30 *groshen*s. In short: half G"P means: half a *groshen*. Such half *groshen*s were in circulation also in the neighboring *shtetl*s such as Motele (look up R' Mordkhe'le "My shtetl Motele" registry B' p. 23). In the old times they used to give the poor a *pru'te* [small change coin] that was drawn on a piece of parchment or engraved on tin and its value was equal to a third of a *groshen*. In later years they "upgraded" it to half a *groshen*]

Ephrayim Itzel envied Chayim Itzik's "bank-business" and produced coins as well. This "competing" ended in their not being on speaking terms.

Facsimile of Ephrayim Itzil's coin

A Currency Stamp:
[Line 1] Half a Polish Grush;
[Line 2] Charity Learning;
[Line 3] Horodetz currency.

*[**Translators note**: When wandering, destitute Jews would come through Horodetz they were too proud to ask for money directly. So they would give a lesson in Torah. The richer people in town would give them a grush (a basic Polish coin worth about 25 cents). But the poorer people couldn't afford to give a grush, and yet they didn't feel right in not giving them anything. So the rabbi devised the currency stamp. It was stamped on a piece of paper and distributed to the poorer residents who then gave it to the wandering, destitute Jews. With this piece of paper they could buy what they needed from the local merchants.]*

Chayim Itzik's held these coins in a separate small box and this box was stored in a locked desk drawer. So, in the locked desk drawer a whole treasure was stored. The drawer contained also separate boxes: for cheap tobacco, paper for rolling cigarettes, money collected for Eretz-Israel, a few wallets with documents and a pocket knife that Chaim Itzik's used for carving pointers. Chayim Itzik's was a master producer of pointers. On the side lay a bone-pointer that he carved all by himself. This pointer was flattened almost like a knife and was used for a different assignment, quite dignified. The pupils preferred this pointer to the one that Chayim Itzik's held in his hand, because with this particular pointer the Rabbi used to scrape the halva that got stuck to the paper and give to the kids, so that it did not go to waste. It is after all Jewish money. Let a child have a taste of halva with bread…

Chayim Itzik's did not want to benefit from what belonged to others, even the light of candles. Every child, by turns, used to bring a pound of gasoline so that there would be enough light during learning in the winter nights. Right after 8 o'clock in the evening, when the children put on their clothes to go home – he would light his own lamp and put out the lamp that was filled with the gasoline that the children had brought.

Chayim Itzik's did not let the children go home alone. He used to accompany them to their homes. And, if a child happened to be sick or when the snow or mud were deep, he would come to the pupil's home and teach him so that the child would not waste Torah-learning-time, and so that Jewish money would not be wasted.

The kids learned – some more and some less – day after day, in winter from 9 o'clock in the morning till 8 o'clock in the evening and in summer from 9 in the morning until the cows returned from the pasture. Then the children were free to go home. However, on Friday, the children were free from 12 noon. They had to wash their hair and prepare for the Sabbath. Chayim Itzik's, on the other hand, did not become free even on Friday after midday. That is when his real work began. He ate a bite, changed his clothes, took his white clean sack on his shoulders and went from door to door. Everybody knew the purpose of his coming: for *khala*s [twist bread] for the poor. When the housewives were baking their *khala*s, they baked a *bulke* [roll] for Chayim Itzik's and Friday, after midday, they put that in his sack. He carried the rolls to whoever was in need, quietly and discreetly, somewhat like charity given in secret.

Jokers used to say that Chayim Itzik's walked with the sack because he wished to secure for himself a *hesped* [funeral oration] after 100 years. However destiny was such that he died in the midst of the flaming WW1, when people died like flies, without funeral orations or even an honorable funeral for such a quiet unassuming man such as Chayim Itzik's. May he rest in the Garden of Eden.

[Pages 117-118]

Yankl Kodliner

by Ami

[Ami is one of the pen-names of Akiva Ben-Ezra]

Translated by Hannah Kadmon

[Translator's notes – in square brackets]

[*kheyder* =traditional Jewish religious school.
"*Yenuka*" [from Aramaic: baby. It was the nickname given to the chief Hasids when they earned their status before 13 years of age, such as Rabbi Shlomo from Karlin.
Besmedresh =the study house, where people used to pray as well
Shtiebl = a small Hasidic prayer house
Misnogdim = opponents to the Hasidic movement
Shimenesre=18 blessings said by Jews in the three daily prayers]

Kodlin was a village not far from Horodets. A hundred years ago Jewish families settled in that village. Because of the mean gentiles who occupied the village of Kodlin, the Jews moved away from that village. Indeed, that village was known for its mean gentiles, and Jews used to steer clear of that village. They would rather lengthen their way than travel through Kodlin. So, Kodlin became devoid of Jews. Kodlin became a synonym for cruelty and hatred of Jews. Since Kodlin was devoid of Jews, people used to say of someone who was growing up an ignoramus: "He will be a Rabbi in Kodlin".

Yankl Kodliner was born in Kodlin when Jews sere still living there. However, he lived most of his life in Horodets. Since he came from Kodlin, he was called Yankl Kodlinder. However, the name Yankl Kodliner was mentioned with respect. Both *Hasidim* and *Misnogdim* had high regard for Yankl Kodliner. He knew how to study a page of *Gemore* [part of the Talmud]. He was blessed with a beautiful voice and was a man about town. In addition, he was good looking. He was tall, chubby, with a silvery-white beard, had a pair of clever eyes and a smile on his lips.

However, in *kheyder* his smile was gone. There he was completely serious. He sat at the head of the long table and on his two sides sat ten children. On the table there was a long *polke* [shelf] to enable him to reach to the far end of the table as well. He taught children-*khumesh* [first 5 books of the bible] and also other books of the Bible, such as Joshua and Judges. He also taught how to write "*azbuke*" [Russian Alphabet], write down a Russian address, and a letter in Yiddish. Yankl Kodliner was considered a strict *melamed* [teacher in Kheyder] but good and successful.

Having finished teaching, he became a different man – a sweet, loving man. He liked to coin a phrase, tell a story about the old Stoliner Rabbi, the "young Rabbis" and sometimes about the "*yenuka*". When Yankl Kodliner finished his work at the *kheyder*, he took his cane and walked slowly along "The Street" and thus, strolling, he reached and entered the *besmedresh* and sat down to study.

Yankl Kodliner was a distinguished person in the Stoliner *shtiebl*. He was the reader of the Torah and often was the reader of the extension of the morning prayer [*Musef*] on Sabbath or Holidays, but not on the High Holidays. On the High Holidays he used to read the extension prayer in the *besmedresh* and in the synagogue of the *Misnogdim*. In truth, he was not so fond of praying with the "crowd" as they did not blow the shofar during the silent *shimenesre* and they lacked the Stoliner enthusiasm. However, what doesn't one do to make a living? The few rubles will be useful.

Yankl Kodliner's *Misnogdim*-like conduct was not to the liking of the Stoliner Hasids. However, it is not allowed to speak ill of a Jew. He probably needed it. Who would dig into somebody else's pocket?

Indeed, the *Misnogdim* derived pleasure from the fact that Yankl Kodliner prayed with them on the High Holidays and they had a taste of his *"ke'vakarat"* [from the prayer of "*Netaneh Tokef*", eve of Yom Kippur] or "*l'el orekh din*" [from a hymn on Rosh Hashanah], etc.

When Yankl Kodliner started chanting during prayers in the *Misnogdim's besmedresh*, he used to jump a bit, instinctively, like a Stoliner Hasid. The congregation really liked it. Not just one of them came home and told his wife: "How did you like Yankl Kodliner's "*Ha'okhez b'yad*" [hymn on High Holidays]?

Others tried to imitate Yankl Kodliner's gestures, bounce, and hand-swing. Mostly, he impressed the children who used to pray in the *besmedresh* and they imitated him quite well.

The notes for "V'Ani";
Left hand side (in Hebrew): Rashi's Musical Teachings

Yankl Kodliner

When a child returned home from the *besmedresh*, he would take a handkerchief, cover with it his head, like a praying shawl and "pray" like Yankl Kodliner. His parents would watch him melting with delight: "He is growing to be a Yankl Kodliner".

Yankl Kodliner's name is indeed engraved in the memory of many Horodetsers. May he put in a good word for us.

[Pages 119-120]

A *Melamed*-Merchant

[*melamed*=teacher in Kheyder]

by Ami

[Ami is one of the pen-names of Akiva Ben-Ezra]

Translated by Hannah Kadmon

[Translator's notes – in square brackets]

[*Besmedresh* =the study house, where people used to pray as well
Ein Yaakov =a compilation of all the legendary material in the Talmud together with commentaries
kheyder =traditional Jewish religious school.
Misnogdim = opponents to the Hasidic movement
Shtiebl = a small Hasidic prayer house
Shimenesre=18 blessings said by Jews in the three daily prayers
"*Yenuka*" =from Aramaic: baby. It was the nickname given to the chief Hasids when they earned their status before 13 years of age, such as Rabbi Shlomo from Karlin.]

In the shtetl he was called Alter Shefe's. [son of Shefe]. Old and Young knew him as Alter Shefe's. Not only Jews associated with him. Even gentiles of Horodets and the surroundings had dealings with him.

First of all he was a *melamed*. Not just a *melamed* of small children, but rather of *Gemore* [part of Talmud]. What child did not at one time or another come to be Alter Shefe's' pupil?

It should not be forgotten that the page of *Gemore* had to be mastered by Friday. Really, who can forget such an event?

And what about the portion of the week [in the Bible], with two portions of Rashi? All in all, they all knew Alter Shefe's the *melamed*.

And who did not know about Alter Shefe's' kvass? They called it "*khlyevene*", but it was not produced from bread. Eight ingredients went into the production of the kvass. (what ingridients? That was Alter Shefe's' secret). Owners of taverns as well as inhabitants used to buy this kvass, and gentiles also came on Sundays or during fairs to revel with Alter's kvass. It was dirt-cheap – only two kopeks for the bottle. And who did not taste Alter's kvass during his lifetime?

Alter Shefe's was not satisfied with merely producing a cheap drink. He produced also a quite classy drink, a drink proper for *Kiddesh* [benediction over the wine] and for *Havdole* [ceremony at the close of the Sabbath]. This drink he made from raisins. Business was at peak before Passover. That is when he brought into his house the wine that he had made in other people's houses, so that he would not be caught. There were three types of wine: 80 kopeks for cheap wine, a ruble and 20 kopeks for medium grade wine, and a ruble and 50 kopeks for the selected wine. There was much noise, fuss and commotion in the house and storehouse: tasting the wine, passing criticism or judgment, bargaining, collecting '*bunkes*' [Russian: *banka* = jar] bottles, paying some money, registering the rest in the log book, and business goes on.

R'Alter Shefe's (Elman)

However, Alter Shefe's did not become rich from all these sources of income. He had a wife who endowed him every two years with a boy or a girl, and he needed money. What should he do?

He opened a small grocery store: a little lime, brushes, salt, herring, and a roll with kvass – all the items that a gentile cannot do without.

However, where does one get the gentile customer, when every other house has one or two grocery stores?

A Jew always manages: more fairs should be held in Horodets. The two fairs – one before Shavuot and one in the middle of summer are not enough. A fair should be held once a month so that the gentiles would come to Horodets from the surrounding villages and it would be possible on this occasion to charge some money. Alter and Shmuel Chayim hit on an idea, got a signed document that they must have fairs, got a loan from the *Karovke* [from the Polish word for a cow, a tax on meat] (never to return) to give the *ispravnik* [police officer] of Kobryn, the *pristaw* [police commissioner in Czarist Russia] of Antipolye, and the *uriadnik* [police constable] of Horodets. A fair was held. Indeed, every "*perve*" [first of the month], and Horodets came to life a little bit.

In truth, before the fairs were established, people clamored: 'It will be worse, they will be in charge of footwear, tailoring, etc., and the local craftsmen will be affected". However, Alter Shefe's was right. The fairs were sources of income to the shtetl.

Despite that, there were not yet enough livelihoods: one must have clothes, a child grows up and must be sent to the bigger town to learn some trade. Alter searched for an additional income. Admittedly this income was not a daily income, but it brought in a few rubles, and even though it was once a year, it was clean, neat, and truly Jewish – handling of *esrogs* [citron over which blessings are said during the Sukkoth holiday].

Alter Shefe's already had a "monopole" [exclusive control] over the citrons. The whole shtetl knew that Alter had the citrons, the *Lulav* [palm branch] and a variety of myrtle branches.

The business of the citrons was a blessing for Alter Shefe's pupils. It was not unusual for some pupils to want to study with Alter Shefe's just because of the citrons. Right after Yom Kippur, Alter Shefe's travelled to Kobryn and stayed there until the eve of Sukkoth. All this time they were exempted from studying. Anything goes: they could go wherever they liked, they could do whatever they felt like doing, and had the time of their life.

It can be said that even in the middle of the year it was also not so bad to be Alter Shefe's' pupils. He was not a strict teacher, he did not beat them like other teachers and discipline was not so intense. From time to time the *rebe* goes out for a few minutes to take down something from the shelf to hand to his wife Dvoyre, or help her in the grocery store. All of a sudden he is told that the collector of tax on spirits is around, and the wine must be cleared away, and the children are having fun.

Alter Shefe's prayed in the Karliner *shtiebl*, but it cannot be said that he was a devout Karliner Hasid. Well, he honored the Rabbi but he was far from traveling to Stolin.

Was he just estranged from Hasidism or simply did not have the time or money for the travel to Stolin? Possibly – both… He was always occupied, never had the time. He barely made it to the *shtiebl* for the evening prayer. It was quite dim when he hastened into the *shtiebl* and his mind was whirling*. It is not a trivial thing. A wife, children, a cow, a *kheyder*, a shop, kvass, rolls and so on. Here he must go to the *kheyder* to study with Kive'le [Akiva Ben Ezra, probably] *mishnayes, Ein Yaakov* and here this "only son", Kive, desires to study Daniel with interpretation of the Melbim [acronym of R' Meir Leibush son of Michal – a great interpreter of the Bible]. He has this urge because the Melbim discloses the end of the exile, the coming of the messiah and Kive craves for the end of exile. He wants already to know when the Temple will be rebuilt. Browsing the Melbim must be a prerequisite before sitting with Kive to study. Kive is likely to raise questions and he must be prepared to answer them.

All in all, Alter Shefe's is very busy. He was always in a hurry as if in a race, until WW1 outraced him and he was left without a livelihood. He barely pulled through during the years of the war and came with his family to America. Here he continued teaching for his living, and had more time to study a page of Gemore.

We wish him that he will live many more years in health and derive pleasure from his children and pupils.

*[The Yiddish idiom used in this context was: "Oon der *Kazirak* iz fardreit" = and the eye-shade of the hat was turned the other way"

I found only one man, 90 years old, who remembers this idiom from his youth in Belarus. The word *Kaziriok* in Russian means the eye-shade part of a hat (casquette) and it was pronounced in Yiddish as *Kazirak*. The old man told me that when someone mixed things up, or acted in a confused way, they said that he wore his hat with the Kaziriok turned the other way, to the back…]

[Page 120-122]

R' Shimon Izik

by Ami

[Ami is one of the pen-names of Akiva Ben-Ezra]

Translated by Hannah Kadmon

[Translator's notes – in square brackets]

R' Shimon Izik

Shimon Izik was famous. When one said: "he is a pupil of Shimon Izik" it meant that the pupil learned also writing, Hebrew and grammar. He was the only *melamed* in *shtetl* who taught "*Pakod Pakadti*" [Exodus 3;16] and translation into Hebrew. This was program for each day: 9 o'clock in the morning the pupils - around 10 or 12 - sit down around the long table. R' Shimon Izik sat at the head of the table with the pupils on both sides. Along the length of the table lay the long "*falke*" (stick). They started studying *khumesh* [5 first books of Bible]. In Izik's *kheyder* they learn it in the regular order, and with a melody that pervaded all organs. It simply made the pupils crave to learn and learn. R' Shimon Izik had a separate melody for the Bible and a special one for Isaiah. Whoever once learned Isaiah at Shimon Izik's *kheyder* - possibly had forgotten the words, but the sweet lovely Isaiah-melody he never forgot. It became dear to the heart and to the soul and it accompanied him wherever he wandered or migrated to new lands.

After having studied a few hours *khumesh*, singularly or in pairs or the whole class together - they went to have lunch. This also took an hour. The pupils went to their homes and so did the Rabbi. The Rabbi walked slowly, watching how the pupils walked, or perhaps ran. Running is not a Jewish trait, and especially when you go out of a *kheyder* because it may seem as if you run away from the Torah. This is not showing respect.

When the pupils had already finished their lunch, they returned soon to the *kheyder*. However, the Rabbi was not back yet. R' Shimon Izik was not in a hurry. The hour was not over yet. Meanwhile, he chatted with Motye Karlinski on the latter's porch. Sometimes another man was there on the porch, and they chatted about politics.

Shimon Izik was wholly politic-oriented. He reads the "*bleter*" [= newspaper]. Politics was his life. Here he expressed his knowledge and experience. He presented facts from the far and near past and especially from *Perekrest*. First and foremost - *Perekrest*. *Perekrest* here and *Perekrest* there. "In *Perekrest* they said so and so", in *Perekrest* this and that is doomed". One might think that *Perekrest* was a large city, somewhat like Warsaw or Paris. The truth, however, was that *Perekrest* was just a farm near the river, a few miles away from Horodets and Shimon Izik was a *melamed* over there for a few years, and over there he had acquired "the seven wisdoms" from the various merchants who used to come to trade.

After having talked about this farm for half an hour on the porch, R' Shimon Izik returned to his "rascals" (that is how he nicknamed his pupils). When the pupils heard that the Rabbi was approaching, they sat down around the table as usual, pretending that they had been rehearsing diligently. Truly, they had been turning the room upside down before the arrival of the Rabbi, or had been playing with sticks or another game in the alley next to the *kheyder*. One of the children was on guard, turned the eyeshade of his hat to the back and lying down stealthily by the entrance to the alley, could hear whether the Rabbi was approaching. The moment he saw from far off that the Rabbi was approaching the alley, he ran back as swiftly as an arrow. That was the signal that the Rabbi was coming and the pupils must appear disciplined.

Afternoon was the time for writing. Shimon Izik had two classes - a bigger and a smaller one. When one class was learning, the other class was writing, and vice versa. Here the Rabbi taught how to write Hebrew. He held in his hand the "Translator" by Inditzki, and said in Yiddish: "The horses stand in their stall" and one of the boys translated it into Hebrew. Then the Rabbi said in Yiddish: "My brother is big and your brother is small" and another pupil, next in row, translated it into Hebrew. All the pupils of this class wrote in their notebooks the translated sentences.

Leaving one class to write, the Rabbi turned to the second class to teach them from a Hebrew book. Shimon Izik was not a big picker of books. All books were fine as long as one knew how to use them for teaching and learning. Sometimes he used "A Living Language" and other times he used "Talking Hebrew" by Krinski, or the "Hebrew School" by Grazovski. Every story or poem the children had to learn by heart, word by word, or else they might get a smack. Shimon Izik was not one of the *melamdim* who hit children. However, one could not get off cheaply. What for was the long stick lying there on the table? It was not there for decoration. And for what purpose did God give the *melamed* a pair of hands? - Hopefully not for actual use. Shimon Izik had another kind of a punishment (to avoid hitting them). It could not be called a slap and it was not a smack with the stick. It was dealing with the boys "in a calm" way. However, whoever was lucky to "get it" from the Rabbi, and especially those who sat near the Rabbi, felt the taste of it. In plain language, they called it a poke. Shimon Izik's poke had a taste of its own. Here is the reason:

When Shimon had to enlist, he had himself maimed. They removed/dislocated part of the middle finger of his right hand so that this finger - usually longer than the rest - became the same length as the fingers on both sides. When Shimon Izik used to close his right hand, the middle part of the middle finger protruded above the other fingers. With this he poked the children.

Still, they loved being in R' Shimon Izik *kheyder* because it was organized. Every unit of studies lasted one hour. The best hour was when they learned Isaiah. Shimon Izik had a special love for Isaiah and he transferred this love to his pupils. This "highlight" they learned in summer in the early evening and in winter evenings until 9 o'clock. When God helped and the watch was slow, they went home around half past nine without any word of complaint. Between the first of the month of *Kheshvan* up to first of the month of *Adar* [approximately between October and February] learning took place in the evenings except during Christmas and Hanukkah. During Hanukkah the Rabbi was not very strict. He used to play Chinese checkers with the children, "goats and a wolf", and pretended he did not see when someone made his dreidl spin. However, on other days they learned, exercised and rehearsed or practiced writing. In winter there were almost no days off, except half a day on *Ta'anit Ester* [Fast of Esther and on Purim eve] and Purim. Therefore, in summer the pupils got a few days off that other pupils in other *kheyders* did not have such as: 15th Sivan - the joyful jubilation of the old *Karlins* [the Hassids of Karlin], the 15th of *Av* - the joyful celebration of the younger Rabbis when the Hassidim of Stollin were throwing their banquets. Shimon Izik was very honored at such celebrations. First of all he was a Hassid of Stollin and what Stolliner would not attend the banquet? Second, Shimon Izik was a drummer. Stollin-Hassidim were not content with just eating and drinking and telling stories about their Rabbi. They sing and at the same time dance. How could a dance take place without a musical instrument? And if no other instrument was available, a drum was also good enough. Shimon Izik had a claim to the drum at every Stolliner celebration such as: Saturday night after *havdole* [ceremony at the close of the Sabbath], after the prayer for the "renewal" of the moon, at the close of a Holiday, a jubilation, etc.

When Shimon Izik held the drum in his hand, he forgot everything: his sick wife, his daughter who should already get married, his "rascals", the world politics and even *Perekrest*. He hit the drum with concentration performing a composition by Mendelssohn.

I don't know if Shimon Izik knew about the composer Mendelssohn, but he did know a lot about the composer's grandfather - Moshe Mendelssohn - the father of the Enlightment movement. In the *kheyder*, in a corner near the door, stood a cantor's desk. Below, under the topmost books lay Isaiah and Jeremiah with commentary. One could find there also "The Study of the Hebrew Language" by Ben-Ze'ev, a Hebrew-Yiddish dictionary and a few annual publications of "Small World" that he had brought along from his pupil in *Perekrest*. Besides the cantor's desk and the long table with the benches on both sides, there was nothing else in the room. As a matter of fact, it was the women's section of the Stolliner *Shtibl* [a small Hasidic prayer house] that was separated from the *Shtibl* by a small screen between the stove and the window. This screen did not reach the ceiling so that the voice of the cantor would be heard by the women. Across the length, in the middle, another screen enclosed an apartment for the *shames* [attendant]. There, in the narrow *kheyder* Shimon Izik taught his "rascals" who grew up to be fine and proud men who remembered with respect the name of their Rabbi Shimon Izik.

[Page 122]

R' Asher

by Ami

[Ami is one of the pen-names of Akiva Ben-Ezra]

Translated by Hannah Kadmon

[Translator's notes – in square brackets]

[In this article, in particular, the author often moves from the past tense to the present tense. I follow his way of writing]

It can be said about Asher that he was a born *melamed* [teacher in Kheyder]. When he was quite young, twelve years old, he was already a *melamed* in a village. He was the only small kid to study together with grown up youth, twice as big as he was. He was still a student and yet had to continue learning, but he was already a *melamed*. Who was to blame for that? Not his father, R' Aharon-Yosl, and not his mother, Shifra, a descendent of *melamdim*, but the bitter economic circumstances.

Asher was thirsty for learning. He wished to become a scholar like his brother, R' Chayim-Mendl, who was well known as a great scholar and a Stoliner-Hasid and who, because of his great Hasidism did not accept a rabbinate-position. If he could not be like his older brother, he wished to be at least like his other brother, Ezra, who taught Gemara to the Rozenblatts, the manufacturers of Lodz.

What did Asher do? He tied a rooster to his bed and early in the morning, when the rooster crowed, he sprang off his bed and started studying. Asher devoured all that fell into his hands, from a portion in the Bible with Rashi's commentary to a page of Gemara - all by himself. When he did not fully understand a certain issue, he used to re-read it and go over it several times.

Year after year, village after village, good and bad pupils, Asher studied by himself and with others until he was completely familiar with the whole Bible, could learn quite well all by himself a page of Gemara with *tosfos* [collective summation Rabbis elucidation of issues in the Talmud] and commentaries by the Maharsha [מהרש"א] and won a name for himself as a good *melamed*, not fooling around or letting his pupils fool around. [that is, treating his teaching very seriously].

R' Asher

Asher got married, his wife opened a grocery and Asher became a shop-keeper. However, Asher could not stay a shop-keeper. He was a descendent of scholars and not shop-keepers. So, he became a *melamed* in Horodets. He got ten or twelve children, rented a "*kheyder*" in Itsik's house - quite a large house - and started teaching. However, Asher is not like other *melamdim*. First of all, he drops the name Rebe and calls himself Reb Asher. ['Reb' means 'Mr.' while 'Rebe' is the title of a Hasidic Rabbi]. This is the way they address all Jewish men in Horodets. He thought that he had eliminate the distance between him and his pupils and not frighten them. Second, there was no "*palke*" [whip, lash] in his *kheyder* customarily used by *melamdim*. Third, there was no fear of Thursday like by other *melamdim* who taught one thing the whole week and Thursday every pupil had to know the lesson or else – alack! At Asher's *kheyder* it was possible to start studying a new matter each day provided they mastered the previous one. The pupils had to master their learning material forwards and backwards. And how can they master the material so well? Very simple. They repeat it so long until they know it. Repetition is considered by Asher to be the foundation of acquiring knowledge. Asher does not mean repetition in pairs or by the whole class together. Asher hardly had a class. Each pupil was a distinct class.

When a child was early in arriving at the *kheyder* Asher would tell him: "Sit down and memorize". The boy would sit down, Asher besides him, and they would repeat the text. Another boy arrived – Asher would tell him to sit down and memorize.

When a boy knows his lesson as he should, he may go out to the courtyard and play. It does no harm. A child learns better after such an invigoration and his love for learning is even stronger. Asher knew this from practice. One should not overburden a child. A child remains a child. He needs to play. And not only playing helps learning but also singing and dancing.

It should not be forgotten that Asher was a Stoliner Hasid, with zeal and zest. A Stoliner Hasid serves God with joy. Teaching children God's Torah is serving God. And how does a Stoliner Hasid serve the Almighty above? –with dance and song. When Asher sees that the day of teaching is about to end and the children's learning has been blessed, he joins hands with his pupils and starts dancing with them. Asher believes that in this way he plants in his pupils his own Jewishness. It is not a trifle: a Stoliner melody and a Hasidic dance.

Asher planted love of God and his Torah by an additional means –teaching Proverbs. Proverbs is the book that Asher loves best. It is full of wisdom and moral code. If a child knows Proverbs by heart Asher is sure that he would be a good person and devoted to his mother and father.

Besides Proverbs, Asher taught Job as well. True, Job is quite difficult, but through studying the book of Job one becomes an educated Jew by drawing the

moral of the story of Job and his suffering. Quite often he used to study with the children *Trey-Asar* [the 12 Prophets besides Jesaia, Jeremiah and Ezekiel]. True, the "*sfarbe*" (twenty four)] *nigun*- did not fit the translation of the words [of *Trey-Asar*] but they still remained engraved in their hearts, as is written in Proverbs.

[The last sentence merits some clarification.

1. "sfarbe"=twenty four relates to the 24 books of the bible: <u>Torah</u>: Genesis, Exodus, Leviticus, Numbers, Deuteronomy, <u>First Prophets</u>: Joshua, Judges, Samuel (2 parts), Kings (2 parts), <u>Last prophets</u>: Jesaia, Jeremiah and Ezekiel and Trey-Asar (12 prophet), then: Psalms, Proverbs, Job, Song of songs, Ruth, Lamentations, Ecclesiastes, Esther, Daniel, Ezra & Nehemiah, Chronicles (two parts)]
2. *nigun*=[usually Hasidic melody/song, with or without words. Here it is the melodious-intonation that accompanies reading in the Bible]
3. Is written in Proberbs: Proverbs ch.3;3 "Write them upon the table of thine heart"]

Asher was not satisfied with the commentaries of Rashi or "*metzudat*". Before teaching a new chapter, he used to consult the "מלבי״ם" [well known commentator] as well, and here and there offered his own interpretation, according to the understanding of the pupil.

Asher did the same before he went to teach Gemara. He studied the issue on his own with all the commentators and afterwards taught it to his pupils. He used to teach certain tractates. His favorite tractate was *Kidushin*. He would not proceed to the next page before the pupils mastered the previous page. He taught the same page over and over so many times until the page became worn out. One page was mastered!

The pupils learned at Asher's but did not learn to write. Writing was learnt from a teacher. That involved an extra expenditure and not every father in Horodets had the means to pay separately for a *melamed* and a teacher. This is one of the reasons why Asher's *kheyder* became smaller and smaller. In the end he was forced to leave for America.

In America, too, in the land of opportunities, he became a *melamed*. His pupils include many sons of Rabbis, with whom he studies the Bible and Gemara.

We wish Asher, not a youngster anymore, many healthy years to produce many good pupils and serve God in the real Stoliner way.

[Page 124]

Yudl the Melamed

by Ami

[Ami is one of the pen-names of Akiva Ben-Ezra]

Translated by Hannah Kadmon

[Translator's notes – in square brackets]

Melamed = teacher in *kheyder*. *Besmedresh* = house of study and prayer

Yudl the Melamed

Just looking at Yudl, one would say that "*melamed*" was not an appropriate title for him. Here comes a dignified and tidy Jew, walking slowly, deep in thought - like a philosopher. Who would guess he was a *melamed*?

Still, this is Yudl the *melamed* of Gemara: a slim man of medium-height with a small blond beard, wearing a short overcoat on his shoulders. He is on his way to eat lunch. He has finished teaching the boys a page of Gemara with *tosfos* [collective summation of Rabbis elucidation of issues in the Talmud], is tired and somewhat hungry, and he is walking from his *"kheyder"* located in "The Street", to his house in the market place, to his Sure Bayle and his children.

Yudl the *melamed* was known as an interpreter who used logic and reason. He could tackle a difficult Ibn-Ezra [scholar in the Middle Ages excelling in philosophy, astronomy/astrology, mathematics, poetry, linguistics, and exegesis] and explain a geometric or algebraic problem. When one was burdened with an entangled business, one would approach Yudl for an advice. Yudl was also invited to serve as an arbitrator. In the *besmedresh* he had the last word. In the *shtetl* nothing was carried out without Yudl.

As a *melamed*, Yudl was a discipliner through and through. He established a strict discipline in his *kheyder*. The children were scared to death by him.

After lunch, Yudl returned to the *kheyder*. The children had already been sitting around a long table and he used to lie down for a while. The children would sit and write. A complete silence reigned in the *kheyder* - the Rabbi is asleep.

Those who attended Yudl's *kheyder* had a head for Gemara. He would not accept just any child. He was picky and his *kheyder* contained 8-10 pupils. The tuition fee that he charged was higher than was charged by other teachers. It was not a trifle teaching Gemara.

Yudl was not only a teacher of small children but also of grown-ups. On the wintery Friday nights he used to teach *mishnayes* [collection of post biblical laws; part of the Talmud] in the *besmedresh* to quite a large audience. Over there, sitting around a table, were *balebatim* [house-owners] who could learn a chapter of *mishnayes*. Craftsmen who could understand what was being taught, used to sit at the table as well, especially when Yudl eloquently expounded, using analogies from present and past. He started with the portion of the week, incorporating in it events of the week, and gradually approached the *mishna* that he finished teaching the previous week, and then the one he was preparing to teach. The listeners devoured every word that came out of Yudl's mouth. Sometimes Yudl would tell a story from the big city of New York, where he lived for about a year, and the listeners kept their mouth and ears open with full attention to all the details.

Once, Yudl let himself be persuaded by his family in New York, and traveled to America. He left his Sure Bayle to her dressmaking for women, left his children and went to the far America. However, he could not live there. That country was foreign to him and so was the way of living there, especially the boorish Jewish customs and the way they taught *Kadish* [prayer over the dead] and *Kiddesh* [benediction over the wine]. Little by little he peddled with wine and whisky and once in a while with a *"tzetl"* [lottery ticket] but he did not make a good living. He longed for Horodets, for his wife, children, pupils and Horodets community matters. So, Yudl returned to Horodets. True, he was only a short time in America, but he had much to tell about that "golden" country where even the stones were *"treif"* [non-kosher] and a genuine Jew should stay away from it. On every occasion, Yudl used to tell about America and its peculiar Jews.

Such was Yudl's life until WW1 broke out. That is when his pride and dignity were shattered. His house was burnt down and Yudl and his family went into exile. After the war he could not set up a *kheyder* and in his old age he turned up in a village as a *melamed*. His children grew up, some of them died, some departed for Argentina and Yudl with Sure Bayle were left poor and wretched. Who knows how they ended their life. May they rest in peace.

[Pages 125-127]

R' Asher David

by Ami

[Ami is one of the pen-names of Akiva Ben-Ezra]

Translated by Hannah Kadmon

[Translator's notes – in square brackets]

R' Asher David was a lively man. He was a ritual slaughterer [*shoykhet*], a circumciser [*moyel*], a teacher in *kheyder* [*melamed*] and a cantor (the first two jobs – to make a living and the two others – because he loved them and considered them a mitzvah). Despite his two honorable jobs he was "almost" a poor man and lived sparingly. It is said: "almost a poor man" because the Jews in Horodets, especially the "*sheyne*" Jews, [the word means beautiful but it relates to their personality, distinction], used to smooth and cover up their poverty.

In addition, R' Asher David was a Stoliner Hasid, and with the small amount of money that he saved he used to travel to get to the Rabbi in Stolin on the second day of Succoth.

He was small in stature but he compensated for that with his energy. He did not walk. He ran with petite steps, fast, fast, as if he was afraid of being late for something… He would thus ran to the butcher shop to slaughter and from the butcher shop back to his *kheyder* and again start the overly chewed studying with the kids. With the same fast trotting he used to run to the *shtiebl* to pray, and Sabbath at dawn – to and from the cold ritual pool where he immersed himself before praying.

His *kheyder* consisted of Gemara boys who, as such, were more independent. It happened, not once, that he was called by a butcher to slaughter something. On such occasions the children studied by themselves or conducted a "reading".

The number of pupils was small, about eighteen children, usually sons of Hasidic parents. They used to study the same page the whole week, and by Thursday they were supposed to know their lesson. And if not – Don't ask… That is why children who could not take a beating did not attend R' Asher David's *kheyder*.

Besides Gemara they studied also the portions of the week [section assigned for a week's reading in the bible], with Rashi's commentary. That was already easier as they were more familiar with the subject and also with the traditional elementary reading of Hebrew. When they studied the portions dealing with the building the Tabernacle, they actually caught their breath. R' Asher David exhibited his mastery of architecture and the pupils drew a great deal of pleasure. First, the Rabbi was not so strict and second, he was occupied with making the doorsteps and curtains of the Tabernacle. He used to take a few kerchiefs, spread them like the curtains mentioned in the Bible, and let the children hold them. He made the doorsteps from potatoes that were cut and fitted with all the details.

R' Asher David the *Shoykhet*
[the ritual slaughterer]
Drawn by the deceased well-known
painter Eliyes M. Grossman

When they learned how the camps were moved in the desert, he exhibited his knowledge once more. The children forgot that they were sitting in R' Asher David's *kheyder* and were carried by their imagination far away in the desert with the banners, and only the pillar of fire was missing or a cloud above their heads. R' Asher David did not devote himself to teaching hand-writing. In the beginning of the year he wrote a *fir-ksav* [practice sheet with written text] and the pupils had to write over it again and again until the sheet was torn. I still remember the first rows of that *fir-ksav* as follows:

"To my master, father, the Rabbinical nobleman, I hope, with God's help, that my studying will not be a parched rock". It is doubtful that each father was a Rabbi or a nobleman, or that every pupil realized this hope. Generally, Asher David's pupils kept on studying, some - more than others.

As was mentioned, R' Asher David was a ritual slaughterer. When he was offered to perform the ritual, he became jolly and studied with the kids with great enthusiasm. However, when, God forbid, after working for some hours on the lungs, the Rabbi found some flaw in the ritual to declare the meat *treyf* [non-kosher], he was sad. Then he taught with no zest and was mournful as if he lost something… He mourned the butcher's loss and felt that he was to blame for it, even though the flaw was Heaven's will.

Although he was very busy, he found time to study a page of Gemara every day, and also a chapter of *mishnayes* [collection of post biblical laws; part of the Talmud] in between the afternoon and evening prayers. He liked to pray next to the cantor's desk as a leader in prayer - mainly the extensions of the morning prayers on Rosh-Hashanah and Yom-Kippur – and it was a cause for the outbreak of disputes in the Karliner *shtiebl*. He poured so much heart and soul into his prayer that it was a mystery how such an overwhelming enthusiasm and energy emerged from such a small body. He pronounced each word sharp and clear, so that even the ignorant could understand. During the prayer of '*shimenesre*' [18 –main prayer on weekdays during the 3 daily prayers, said quietly, standing up with legs fastened together] he stood on his feet longer than others. He moved heaven and earth especially during the circular procession with the Torah on *Simkhes To'yre* [joy of finishing the year's reading cycle of the Torah]. When he danced, the floor under his feet was blazing, and he swept others with his enthusiasm. It seemed as if Asher David wished, through his transcendence, to be carried to Stolin for the circular procession, close to the "*Yenuka*" [from Aramaic: "baby". It was the nickname given to their chief Hasids when they earned their status before 13 years of age, such as Rabbi Shlomo from Kalin].

R' Asher David was a real "Stoliner" Hasid. He was a "Stoliner" to the core. Even his family name was Stolinsky because this is what he wished for: "A Stoliner Hasid should call himself Stolinsky".

He was a strict and meticulous Jew. He was fastidious about not touching what belonged to others as well as about others not touching what belonged to him. He was really fastidious…

Every thing he did was with fire and devoutness. It happened quite often that out of his great devoutness he said the blessing "*Al Hash'khita*" [ritual slaughtering] at a circumcision ceremony.

They used to say in the *shtetl* that R' Asher David could sometimes make a mistake, and say the blessing over circumcision at a ritual slaughtering instead of "*Al Hash'khita*"…

In his old age, R' Asher David dream was to spend the rest of his life in Eretz-Israel, and he fulfilled his dream. He saved all the coins he could spare and stuck them in the beams of the ceiling. When he was asked several times if he was not afraid of fire or thieves – he used to answer that such coins people did not steal, and a fire could not harm them…

Around 1930 he traveled with his wife to Eretz-Israel and stayed in an old-age home in Jerusalem, where he and his wife had a room for themselves. He passed away before the second world war, when he was about 100 years old. He lived and died the way he wished and earned. May he rest in peace in the earth of Eretz-Israel.

[Page 127]

An Improved *Kheyder*

[kheyder = a room; traditional Jewish religious school in a one room setting]

by Ami

[Ami is one of the pen-names of Akiva Ben-Ezra]

Translated by Hannah Kadmon

[Translator's notes – in square brackets]

In Horodets they knew little of an "improved *kheyder*" where Hebrew is taught in the modern method. Admittedly, Horodets is not far from Pinsk - the leader for "improved *kheyders*" - but from the beginning Horodets did not believe in having "schools". They taught in the *kheyders* around a long table from early morning till late in the evening, the way it was the custom of our fathers and grandfathers. When a child grew up he started having a glimpse of Hebrew and a taste of a grammar book. Only Shimon Izik included learning of Hebrew in his curriculum. However, nobody dreamt of having the learning of Hebrew as the main subject of learning.

The *melamdim* [teachers in the *kheyders*] taught their pupils the way they had been taught. To pronounce the letter with the vowel, the prayer book, psalms, *Khumesh* [first part of the Bible] in accordance with the week's portion or chapter after chapter, *Gemore*, various parts from the Bible, Rashi, a bit of writing and that was all.

Suddenly, in 1907 there is a rumor that in Horodets they are going to have an "improved *kheyder*" like in other towns. And who will the teacher be? - Eliya Zavil's son.

Who is this Eliya? People start recalling that he is the son of Zavil, the ritual-slaughterer. He is still very young. He became a *melamed* in a village and got his training in the villages where he was a *melamed*. In other words: Eliya is an autodidact - what he knows he has accumulated on his own. They say that he has a great deal of knowledge, and he teaches the children using a modern method, indeed from books.

And who says so? - Those few landlords who share an interest that Eliya should establish a *kheyder*.

Here a piece of information should be presented: two or three landlords who are blessed with two or three children each, the fate of a *melamed* lies in their hands: At their will they can raise him or ruin him. They just take their children away from him and he is no more a *melamed*.

So, a few such landlords could afford hiring Eliya and he became the *melamed* of their children. Thus a "improved *kheyder*" came into existence in Horodets.

What does a "improved *kheyder*" mean in Horodets? First of all, Eliya rented a separate apartment for the *kheyder*. It was in the "*shtibl*" of Khayim Hirsh. We say "*shtibl*" when in effect it was a narrow half dark room. There were "*skamykes*" in the room - plain long wooden desks and next to them - long benches. Eliya sat on a platform, and near the wall there was a chamber pot, exactly like in a "school"- to make a distinction…

From what book did Eliya teach? That was a "school" [name of a book] by Sneider, where before the pupil starts studying the few abridged verses from the *khumesh* [first 5 books of the bible] he has to translate the new words to Yiddish, drill them, and so on. This "school" was the main topic of the curriculum in Eliya's *kheyder*. However, Eliya did not divert entirely from the old *kheyder*. He taught *Khumesh, Rishonim*, and before Passover he taught the "*Hagadah*" - like in all *kheyders*.

Then, also, Eliya's *kheyder* differed from the other *kheyders* in that the children did not learn in the winter evening and during the day on Sabbath.

All those merits attracted the boys of Horodets to Eliya's *kheyder*, but the parents had reservations about Eliya's *kheyder* and preferred the old *kheyder*. Also, those fathers who established Eliya's *kheyder* realized that their sons were not doing much in there. So they took their sons away from Eliya and gave them to the other *melamdim*. Eliya's *kheyder* was abolished. All in all, it existed a few years.

Nevertheless, it must be pointed out that Horodets had an "improved *kheyder*" after its own fashion.

[Page 128]

Hershel, the Teacher

by Ami

[Ami is one of the pen-names of Akiva Ben-Ezra]

Translated by Hannah Kadmon

[Translator's notes – in square brackets]

Hershel the teacher

For many years boys of Horodets were taught by *melamdim* [teachers in *kheyder*] and girls were taught by teachers/tutors. The boys studied *Khumesh* [Pentateuch, Torah] some of the other parts of the 24 books of the Bible and *Gemore* [the part of Talmud that comments on the *Mishna*]. Girls learned how to pray as well as to read and write Yiddish. When the inspector came to Horodets, the *kheyders* were "abolished" for the moment and boys and girls were seen learning together, pretending that this was the usual custom…

Hershel, the teacher, introduced into Horodets other innovations.

Who was Hershel the teacher? Where did he come from? Who were his parents? Where did he acquire his education?

When Hershel was asked all these questions, he found it complicated to answer because *"the whole earth is full of his glory"*. He had been everywhere, every *shtetl* and village had had a share in him, or he had a share in them, because he "nibbled" [learned something] from every place he spent time in, and brought the collected "nibble" [acquired knowledge] to Horodets in 1909.

Hershel was a good-looking young man. He had a wonderful memory and a sharp tongue and he clearly put the words into his pupils' mouth. In addition, he could sing nicely (he was once a singer besides the cantors), could actually read notes and in addition he played the violin. He was tall, dark skinned, with a black mustache. He wore a cloak and held a black stick with a silvery handle in his hand, as if saying: "Look at me, this is I, Hershel the teacher?!"

Everybody indeed looked, and looked again and each used to pose another question:

Fathers used to ask: "Where is he going?"

Mothers used to ask: "To whom is he going?"

Girls used to ask: "With whom is he going?"

Really, how did he come to Horodets? This is separate story as he himself once reported in the "daily newspaper" under the title: "The Swapped Brides" [such a title was included in a published collection in Warsaw in 1901-2 and Hershel probably used such a title for his piece. There is a hint at the biblical story of swapping Lea for Rachel].

Hershel was lucky to marry the youngest daughter of Khayim-son-of-Itzik. [her name was Miriam-Maryem and she was the sister of my grandfather Moshe-Elkana. HK]

Horodets was lucky to have Hershel so that the boys and girls would learn Hebrew, Russian and arithmetic as was the case in the big towns.

Hershel got a house from Khayim [full name: Abraham-Khayim. HK] as a dowry. He turned it into a classroom. Indeed, it was a real classroom, and Khayim had to rent another place for a *"kheyder"*. In the classroom there were pupils' chairs and desks with books both in Hebrew and Russian, and several notebooks for calculations. On the wall there was a certificate/permit. There was also a blackboard with chalk in the room.

Hershel's handwriting was beautiful. All Jewish children should be blessed with such handwriting. The children indeed started moving to Hershel's class. It evoked turmoil in *shtetl:* Hershel robs the livelihood of the *melamdim*! If parents did not take a child from a *melamed* to move him to Hershel's class, they at least hired Hershel as a private tutor in their house. Poor parents used to gather 2 or three children to be tutored together by Hershel.

What did Hershel teach? First, he used to start teaching from a small book in which every word had a meaning. This in itself was something new. Second, he taught a higher class Hebrew from a selection. Hershel was not content with the story alone. He also taught grammar from a booklet. When the children understood what they were reading, he ordered "The Friend" or "The flowers" from Lugansk. Third, he taught real Russian. When they finished the first part, he taught the second and even the third part from the same Russian book. In addition to all these, he taught grammar, arithmetic and geography.

Hershel taught an abridged *Khumesh* [first five books of the Bible]. However, he taught the Bible with "Mikra Meforash" [commentary] by Trivaush and Natek and here Hershel found the opportunity to display his knowledge of the Bible and grammar in which he excelled. He knew almost the whole Bible by heart.

When Hershel noticed a talented boy or girl, he was not content with the time that he spent teaching in the classroom, and he became a frequent visitor in their house, carrying a conversation with them, thereby sneaking in either a translation of the Bible or a grammatical rule. The parents were very satisfied. Hershel had turned their children into accomplished scholars.

Hershel was not content with dull teaching. He brought into his teaching his knowledge of music, sang songs with his pupils and organized recitals, etc.

Hershel took pains to prepare a real Hanukah production. The children rehearsed for quite some time. The parents wished to draw pleasure and pride and the *shtetl* as a whole was thirsty for something new. Everything was ready, even Shakhno, the police constable… Hershel rented a big house for this purpose, from Khayim-Nissel. He built a stage with a curtain, a real theatre. The house was full of pupils, parents and guests from other *shtetles*. Everybody was waiting impatiently for the curtain to rise, and all of a sudden a policeman came in and asked for a formal permit. Hershel almost fainted, he assumed that cooperating with Shakhno, the constable, was enough, but not by a far shot. He tried bargaining but the policeman did not let words of persuasion get to him nor did he let the pupils say anything. The people had to leave the hall with deep sorrow, and Hershel had to drop the idea of organizing any production as long as the Tsar Nicholas I II was still alive.

[The editor of this book commented that the incidence was recorded in the newspaper "Heint" (=today) of 1911.]

* *
*

Hershel was the teacher (underline "the") of Horodets until WW1. People ran away, the Russians burned down a large part of the *shtetl*, the Germans invaded with their organization, and Hershel remained without a class. What can a Jew do when he has to provide for a wife and 4 daughters who need food, dresses and shoes? He had to work in the field even though he was a teacher. He toiled in the field: plowing, sowing, reaping, etc., and when the Germans opened a public school, he became a teacher there, teaching German and other subjects.

However, Hershel did not derive satisfaction from the public school. He longed for the Hebrew school. The Germans left Horodets and the Poles invaded and brought in their sadistic hatred for the Jews – tearing beards from Jews in the middle of the street, executing Jews without any reason. Hershel and Tevye the hump-backed were caught by the Poles to be shot. Polish riders, racing a horse, goaded the two to Kobryn to be executed. Pleas and weeping do not help. The Poles screamed: "Communist Jews", and Hershel and Tevye were marked as "communists" and they had to be shot.

[Martha, Hershel's daughter, told me that in her father's room/classroom hung some maps that bore a trace of the Russian revolution. She also told me that the two were accused of treason and on the way to Kobryn they were ordered to run ahead of the horses and call out: "Left-right, left right". Hershel was imprisoned in a food-closet. HK].

Hardly alive and breathless, Hershel and Tevye reached Kobryn. The community of Kobryn was scared. Every person was afraid that he would be the next innocent victim. However some courageous Jews approached the Poles with a plea saying that these two accused persons were absolutely innocent, that they were honest, quiet people. The Polish priest of Kobryn interceded too for the two accused persons. After a lot of effort the two half-dead people were freed. [Martha told me that one of the intercessors was my grandfather Moshe Elkana, probably using some bribes, and that the priest probably knew Hershel from Horodets as the translator for any of the invading armies. HK]

After the sorrowful incidence, Hershel concluded that Horodets was not for him anymore, and that he had to flee from the blood-thirsty Poles to the free America. Just before Passover, 1921, Hershel arrived in America.

Hershel, even though he does not know English well, nor the customs of America, immediately gets himself a position of a teacher in the "Talmud Torah" of Springfield, and Pomerantz (that is his family name by which he is addressed) is treated with love by his pupils and their parents, and is also respected by the board of directors of that "Talmud Torah".

Pomerantz's name becomes well-known in the neighborhood thanks to his method of teaching and to his arranging of performances. He also becomes active in communal affairs. When the Hebrew association "Ben-Yehuda" is established in Springfield in 1923, Pomerantz is one of its active members and one of the founders of the Hebrew library over there. Although he derives satisfaction from living in Springfield, in a sense, he is drawn to the big New-York. He moves to New York and settles in Flatbush where he becomes a teacher in a private school, American style. He joins a synagogue, holds his teaching position and wants to take on some activity but it seems impossible. It is not Horodets and not even Springfield! Sometimes he attempts to organize a concert but it does not turn out well. The former Hershel-the- teacher and now the American "Rabbi" Pomerantz is broken physically and spiritually, walking like a shadow. He talks about his past accomplishments, recalls his past success and activity and like an impoverished man speaks of his past riches. This is how Hershel keeps talking of his good and splendid years when he was respected by old and young. He keeps talking like that until the 9th of April 1943, when he swoons and on the way to the hospital he departs this life. May his memory be blessed.

[Pages 130-131]

Moshe son of Khaya-Dvorah

by Ami

[Ami is one of the pen-names of Akiva Ben-Ezra]

Translated by Hannah Kadmon

[Translator's notes – in square brackets]

Moshe son of Khaya-Dvorah

Years ago, Khaya-Dvorah's house was a kind of domestic club in Horodets. Khaya-Dvorah was the daughter of Shalom Kostrinsky. She was a modern and enlightened woman. She was the first woman in Horodets to take off her wig. In this spirit she raised her three daughters: Ester, Makhle, Tzivia and her youngest, only son, Moshe. Khaya-Dvorah's house was open for the young and old. When one wanted to hear a wise word - one went to Khaya-Dvorah, because she was a very wise woman. Also when one felt the desire to sing or dance - one went to her house, because in there youth used to get together; boys and girls. They used to spend time and have fun. They also talked about the land of Israel and sang Hebrew songs.

Observant parents did not permit their children to go to Khaya-Dvorah's house, because the boys sat there without a cap and allowed themselves all kinds of small liberties.

Moshe was raised in that house, and received, as was the custom, traditional education as well. He was taught by *melamdim*, went to pray, and the like. However, when he grew up, Khaya-Dvorah looked for a different occupation for Moshe than the ones chosen by the youth of the *shtetl*. She decided that her Moshe with his brains was not meant to be a craftsman, a shopkeeper and not even a *melamed*. So what then? - Moshe must learn Russian and get a general education. He was meant to be an educated person so that the world would be open for him.

So, what can be done about it? Moshe went away to Warsaw and studied there in the gymnasium, excelling with distinction. He returned to Horodets for Holidays and vacations, and all saw that he was a Gymnasium student as he was wearing his formal apparel. However, Moshe was very quiet, modest and unassuming.

After having studied some time in Warsaw, Moshe went away to Vilna, studied there in an institute and was one of the best students. When he returned to Horodets, the whole *shtetl* was in turmoil; and people would ask one another: "Have you already seen Moshe, son of Khaya-Dvorah? How do you like his uniform?"

The last question worried Khaya-Dvorah mostly. What is going to happen next? What is there in being idle? True, Moshe had already evaded being conscripted [to the Tsar's army]. But will he end up like all the other youth - get married?

All those questions bore into Dvorah's mind. In the meanwhile, to make a long story short, Moshe became a teacher in *shtetl*, giving lessons by the hour. Whoever wished his son or daughter to have general education - had Moshe teach them. Moshe taught them Russian, mathematics, geography and also German.

More than all, Moshe loved teaching mathematics. In teaching this subject he came alive. The other subjects that he taught were just secondary, to get rid of quickly. When he got to algebra or geometry he was revived. Otherwise, Moshe spoke very little and was dreamy.

What did Moshe dream about? - About a different garment/uniform without brass buttons and without worn sleeves? Maybe he was dreaming about a girl? Or maybe he was pondering about a better occupation than just giving lessons?

No, these were not the issues that occupied his small world. Moshe contented himself with little: he had a cigarette - he was already satisfied. Actually, he did not have a match because he had forgotten it in his pupil's home - but he was not worried. He would eventually get a match for his half-cigarette. What else did Moshe need? - In winter to go sliding on the river. He did not have any "*kankes*" [ice-skates]? - He would somehow get them. He would borrow them. People were not bad. How about summer? - He bathed in the river. One did not have to pay for that, for sure, and one did not have to ask for favors. The river was good for all, if only they could swim. Moshe son of Khaya-Dvorah, a Horodetser young man, could indeed swim, like all Horodetser young men.

Still, what was Moshe thinking about? Why did he speak so very little? Why did he keep so quiet? What was he dreaming about?

We knew that Moshe was full of thoughts to judge by his handwriting. When he took the pen in his hand - one letter was warped with the other, and mainly blotted, as if his thoughts aimed to pour all at once. Moshe went on writing. What was he writing about? Was he writing poems or stories or actually articles in Russian?

That was a secret. Only those who were very close to him knew what he was writing about. He was writing a book about mathematics. He wrote a whole book, and had negotiated with a publishing house to print it.

Suddenly, the First World War broke out. Businesses were ruined, printing shops were burnt down and people were running away where their eyes directed them. Among the drifting people were also Moshe and his closest family, who settled in Russia. Moshe started teaching again - new pupils in a new state. Were Moshe's thoughts new? Did his dreams get new wings? Was he influenced by the spirits of revolution in Russia? How did they affect Moshe's ideals? Did he think of the problems of the world?

Who Knows? Moshe stayed the same man of few words, a dreamer. He again delved in complicated mathematical problems and in the ways to solve them. When he had only a bit of free time, it did not matter that he had or did not have what to eat - he was sitting and thinking out his reckonings. One day, this dreamy Moshe disappeared like a dream. Until this very day nobody knows what had become of him.

Did he die a natural death? Did he die of hunger? Or, was he killed. Nobody knows.

May his name be inscribed in our book, and his memory stay with all Horodetsers.

[Page 132]

Kheyders for Girls

by Ami

[Ami is one of the pen-names of Akiva Ben-Ezra]

Translated by Hannah Kadmon

[Translator's notes – in square brackets]

This question was raised many times: "Where did our learned mothers and grandmothers learn to pray, to read the *tietch khumesh* [a Yiddish version of the Torah mostly for women], to write a letter in Yiddish, and (some of them) even to write down an address in Russian? Who were their teachers who enabled some of them to understand more or less the contents of their prayer?"

Actually, in Horodets they did not teach the girls *khumesh*, [Torah] *but* they did read every Sabbath the "*tsena ure'ena*" [a Yiddish translation of the Torah enriched with illustrative stories intended traditionally for women], and if grandmother did not finish the week's portion on Sabbath, she finished it during the week. And, which mother did not go to the *Besmedresh* [the study house, where people used to pray as well] to pray on Sabbath? And if she could not pray so well or was confused as to where they were reading in the prayer book, she would stay close to another woman who knew, who told her what part they were reading. Who infused the religious feeling in the hearts of these Jewish women?

Where did our grandmothers get that religious spark that made them pray even *Minkhe* [Jewish afternoon prayer] and *Mayrev* [evening prayer]? And where from did many of the elderly women draw the holy respect that made them stand up during the entire prayer on Rosh Hashanah and Yom Kippur and never sit down?

We must admit that the spiritual religious atmosphere created the circumstances that raised such grandmothers and mothers, but the *re'betzns* [Rabbis' wives] contributed quite a lot by teaching them. Those female teachers were very pious and observant Jewish women and they indeed molded future Jewish mothers.

The *re'betzn* differed from the *melamed*. Most of the *melamdim* taught all year long for many years until they died. On the other hand, the *re'betzn* taught on a temporary basis. Teaching was for them a sideline, for a short while, and often it was as a "helper" to their husband.

A hundred years ago, Miriam the *re'betzn* lived in Horodets. She was Yirmiyahu Zerakh's wife. Yirmiyahu Zerakh was a *shoykhet* [ritual slaughterer] and a melamed and his wife taught the girls. The girls used to come to her house to learn.

She was considered a very educated woman. What did she teach her girls? She taught them prayers, to read the *teitch-Khumesh* and how to write a letter to their future bridegroom. Their mothers taught them all the rest: How to make the meat kosher, and other rules that girls should know.

When Vishke, Izik's wife became a widow, she opened a "*kheyder*" in her own house and started teaching the girls of Horodets the same things that Miriam, the *re'betzn* taught her.

It seems that the above mentioned education did not satisfy the new generation; "new birds - new songs", and people started demanding that girls, too, should be expected to write down a Russian address. Here a man was needed - a man who knew a little Russian and who was more modern. Vishke could not fulfill these functions.

Then Avraham Moshe showed up, the son of Itshe Silke's, a young man who had already tasted the secular and was half-intellectual. He came to the girls to their homes, and taught them there. He brought with him a letter writing exercise booklet and taught the girls how to write a letter to a bridegroom, a father-in-law etc.

Almost every girl in Horodes got such an education. The daughters were satisfied and the parents were pleased too. They spent their money well, and the girls grew up to be Jewish daughters.

However, progress does not halt in one place. New winds started blowing and settled in Horodets. People were not content with the letter exercise booklet and a Russian address. They already wanted the girls to know how to read Russian books and other girls had the desire to learn Hebrew. Those requests were fulfilled through a young man of Horodets called Shanshen, son of Alter Visotzki. Shanshen came from the very aristocratic descent - the Mazurski family. He himself was aristocratic: good looking, knew Hebrew and Russian and was skilled in calculations.

Shamshen established a *kheyder* for girls. He taught them to write Yiddish and Russian and also calculus. That was an achievement. However Shamshen's *kheyder* did not last too long. As we said before, the girls' *kheyder* was a temporary way of making a living until something better came along. Shamshen went away to Vilna and became an accountant.

What is to be done now for the girls of Horodets who are "thirsty" for education?

The opportunity was seized by Yudel, Khaya-Miriam's son. He was a young man who earned it by right of his ancestry but also by his own right. He stemmed from the second aristocratic family - the Kostrinsky family. He was a very well educated young man. Yudel followed Shamshen's example and continued his way of teaching. This, too, did not last for long because Yudel died at an early age.

God did not forsake Horodets. A girls' *kheyder* was opened in the main street and the teacher was a *melamed's* son - Khana, son of Tzadok. Khana taught the girls the beginning of *Khumesh* [Torah], writing of letters, the right Russian pronunciation, and when they did not understand the German words that sneaked into the Yiddish in the guide to letter-writing, it did not matter. The girls came out quite "knowledgeable".

Khana's *kheyder*, too, did not last for long. A stranger appeared all of a sudden and with him a new epoch started in the Horodetser education. The stranger was Hershel Pomerantz. As a result Khana's *kheyder* declined until Khana himself left Horodets and settled in America.

* *
*

A lot of water has flowed under the bridge since then and we look back and say: Thank you pious honest *Re'betzns* and *melamdim* who taught our mothers and grandmothers. May accumulated merits be credited to you.

[Page 134]

Doctors

[Pages 134-135]

Naphtali the Doctor

by Rabbi Mordechai Greenberg

Translated by Hannah Kadmon

[Translator's notes – in square brackets]

Naphtali (Veissman) the Doctor

The truth of the matter is that Naphtali the doctor was not born in Horodets. However, he was so acclimated in Horodets that all were sure he and his ancestors were from Horodets. Naphtali came from Drohitzin, not far from Horodets. His father was R' Shimon, the famous doctor in Drohitzin and surroundings. He probably got his first knowledge in medicine from his father.

Naphtali cam to Horodets after the death of his grandfather, Binyamin the doctor, whose place he took over. He had already practiced a bit and won a name as a good doctor. This gave him the right to get the salary of one hundred rubles a year from the *shtetl*. By agreement he could charge a fixed price for a visit - besides medications that he prepared himself. The price was one for all - rich and poor. However, Naphtali did not want to receive money from the needy patients. He used to cure them free of charge. He even used to help them, quite often, by giving them money off his own small earnings.

Naphtali was a very friendly person. He respected everybody and showed his friendliness to all. Most of all, his attitude toward the poor was outstandingly friendly. He expressed his sympathy and strove to make them feel good. When he encountered a poor person in the street, he was first to greet him. After the prayers in the synagogue on Sabbath, he said "*goot Shabes*" [Good Saturday] to each and every plain and poor person. When he made a home visit to a sick person, he brought with him joy and encouragement. His motto was the verse from Job [4;4]: "Thy words have upholden him that was falling, and thou hast strengthened the feeble knees" which means that your words would raise to their feet the one who stumbles. Therefore, he gave the sick person the spiritual medication that he needed - strengthening him with words and sympathy. He gave the patient spiritual vitamins, infusing him with the hope that he would soon be healthy. All this won him the recognition of all the residents of Horodets. Everybody trusted him. Non-Jews as well as Jews respected and valued him. He was also famous for the generous charity that he gave to the needy.

The first years Naphtali could not make a living in Horodets. Various circumstances were the cause. Those circumstances had to do, understandably, with the sort of life that he led. The main factor was competition. There were two other doctors in Horodets, Non-Jews. They were knowledgeable about sicknesses but they were satisfied with little money for their service. The price they charged was small. Most or their patients were farmers from the surrounding villages. They were of low culture and went only to non-Jewish doctors and Naphtali was left with no patients.

Having no income, Naphtali travelled to Warsaw and became a student. His father enabled him, financially, to do so.

Naphtali stayed some time in Warsaw, attended courses and returned to Horodets as a dentist. He brought with him all the necessary instruments and started practicing dentistry. From then on peopled addressed him as "Vaissman". From all neighboring *shtetls* and villages people came to him to fix their teeth. He also continued to treat people as a doctor. However, the problem of making a living was not entirely solved. Dentistry was a small help. So, he travelled a second time to Warsaw and became a student once again. This time he stayed in Warsaw a longer while attending courses and returned as an eye-doctor. Thus Naphtali became an expert in three fields of medicine, but with no diploma. The restrictions that the Russian government imposed on Jewish students made it impossible for him to get the official title "Doctor".

The problem of making a living remained the same as before. His wife, Dina, died and left him with a number of small children. Naphtali was desperate but led his life the same way as before, as if nothing happened in his personal life. He started looking for ways to better his material status. He started thinking of leaving Horodets and settling in a bigger city. It was difficult to depart from Horodets. He did not want to, but he had to take the step because of his great hardship.

After a difficult inner struggle Naphtali decided to leave Horodets and he settled in the nearest bigger city - Kobryn. He immediately became friendly with the local doctors. He became their colleague and in Kobryn, like in Horodets, he was daily visitor with the local Rabbis, and cured the poor free of charge.

After WW1 Naphtali left Kobryn and settled in Brisk. There he practiced exclusively as an eye-doctor and became friendly with all the local doctors. However, Naphtali went on with his routine life like in Horodets. He studied Torah, treated patients free of charge, and enjoyed the company of Rabbis discussing Torah. Naphtali stayed the same "rich man" as he was before, because it was impossible to make a living leading this kind of life. He possessed only spiritual wealth but not material wealth. He had "Torah without the flour". [In *Pirkey Avot* R' Azaria says: "If there is no flour - there is no Torah" which means that material existence is a condition to the study of Torah.]

Naphtali was a bookworm. He was drawn to books. In a letter he wrote to me at the eve of WW2 he wrote with enthusiasm that he had finally composed a book - a sort of encyclopedia - with the sermons of our sages that are scattered in the interpretations of the Talmud and Zohar. He wrote also that the Rabbis in Brisk gave their written recommendations to his book and acclaimed it as beneficial to all. The war broke out and I received no more letters from him. I don't know what became of his book.

A very unique person was Naphtali the doctor. He combined Torah with wisdom, good qualities and good deeds. He was a sample of spiritual strength and refined morality. He mingled with the crowd and treated all as his equals.

[Page 136]

Vitkin

by Makhla Timoner

Translated by Hannah Kadmon

[Translator's notes – in square brackets]

When Naphtali the doctor left Horodets, the shtetl remained in mourning: How can they live without a doctor? It is clearly written in the Gemore (*Yerushalmi*, end of *Kidushin*): "It is forbidden to live in a city that does not have both a doctor and a bathhouse". So they started looking for a doctor. However, not every doctor could take Naphtali's place. Finally a doctor appeared from another town and the landlords of Horodets concluded that he deserved to serve as a doctor in Horodets: First of all, he is a skilled doctor; Second, he has a fine big family and this means that he will not leave the *shtetl* so quickly; Third, he has a son who is a barber. This last fact was included in the "dowry" because there was no barber in Horodets. When a Jew needed a haircut, he travelled to Antipolye or to Kobryn to get it. Otherwise, his wife or someone else of the family did the job of a barber. Very seldom, a barber from Antipolye came to Horodets to offer a haircut to the overgrown hair. That would occur on *Lag Ba'omer* or sometimes on the eve of a Holiday.

Horodets did not make any mistake with regard to the doctor. However, he had two flaws: He loved to "canker", meaning: make the illness worse so that people would need his treatment for long (so they said in *shtetl*). The second flaw was that he loved the "bitter drop" [intoxicating drinks]…

The landlords of Horodets saw that it was bad, and started thinking of ways to get rid of that doctor. After a few years in Horodets, he left with his family. Horodets was left once again depressed and again had committees discussing in what way to save the *shtetl* and get a good honest doctor. They printed advertisements in the newspapers, and doctors from all over Russia and Poland, old and young, landed in Horodets. Not a day passed without some doctor coming for interviews. One of the doctors, old with a beard, was an expert in healing with cupping-glasses, offering to apply them even to handicapped rheumatic feet…

This is how they suffered and toiled until doctor David Vitkin came to Horodets.

Vitkin was also a certified dentist and patients came to fix their teeth from the whole neighborhood. In addition to his being a doctor and a dentist, his wife was a certified experienced midwife - greatly in need in Horodets. Both of them - the doctor and his wife contributed a great deal to Horodets. It lasted from 1908 until 1915, when we started fleeing from the Germans. The doctor and his family also fled to Russia where he became a military doctor.

They did not call Vitkin "doctor" like they called the previous doctors. They bestowed on him the Russian title: *Feldsher*. This is because he and his whole household were very Russian-oriented. Yiddish was not heard in his house. At first he and his wife spoke a very poor Yiddish. His was the first house in Horodets where they spoke only Russian. There it was possible to get Russian daily newspapers from Petersburg or from Moscow. If someone wished to take a look at a liberal Russian journal, they found it in Vitkin's house. In general, his house became the center of the Russian-oriented intellectuals of Horodets. The post-officials and other state officials came to his house to meet each other over a glass of tea.

Even though Vitkin was very Russian-oriented, and was not involved with the Jewish congregation he had a host of admirers among the Jews of Horodets and the neighborhood, because of his honesty and his generosity for both Jews and Christians. He was respected by both. His waiting room was always full with patients. In his free time he always busy with preparing prescriptions.

Until this very day, Horodetsers remember Vikin the *feldsher* with respect and esteem.

[Pages 139-142]

A Quarter Century (1914-1939)

In the First World War

by Binyomin Shloymeh Zusman
(Benjamin Solomon Sussman)

Translated by Moishe Dolman

Donated by Jane Cooper

"The Redeemer"

The savage war had been raging over the world for a good few months. It had been said, and the newspapers had written, that the German was moving closer and closer to Brisk [Brest-Litovsk]. Now fighting had broken out in Brisk. All of a sudden (I think it was on a Thursday morning) we detected the sound of the first German airplane. Everybody ran out into the street, fixed their gaze upon the sky and – yes! – we saw that something small, perhaps like a big bird, was flying in the air and making a frightful noise. We beheld this bird-of-prey for no more than about five minutes. Then it disappeared somewhere in the sky. This served as a signal for everyone that we had to do something fast – run away, hide – because a fear had come over us all that at any moment the war would be at our doorstep, at the Horodetz Dnieper-Bug River. But where should we run? And how? All at once the whole of Horodetz began to run to the railway station. Here is why: The Russian regime had issued an arrangement, according to which it would transport for free on the train those who wished to escape deep into Russia and thus avoid the oncoming Germans. So practically all the gentiles who lived in our little town of Horodetz packed everything they could and made their way to the train station. And because they could not take along their horses and wagons they sold them dirt-cheap. Therefore everyone ran to the train station to buy these horses and wagons. I got wind of this situation, and I also ran right away to the train station. I purchased a small white horse that was a bit lame, together with a nice wagon which even had four functioning wheels. And I came home. At that time my father was in Moscow, where he had gone to undergo treatment on his ailing legs. My sister Babel and my brother Yudl had already been in America for a few years. My brother Yisroel [Israel] was a soldier in the Russian army. All of Horodetz packed up its belongings, and so did my mother and I. We gathered together a little bedding, clothes, a chair and a small table, tethered the cow to the wagon with a cord and set off down the road. No sooner did we get out onto the highway that leads to Antopol than we were halted by the Russian police. No civilian wagons were allowed to use the highway, because the road had to be kept free for the army, which ran like locusts to the front and from the front (mostly the latter). So we got down off the highway and started to ramble through fields and various unfamiliar roads. Because of this situation there formed a long line of hundreds of wagons from Horodetz and vicinity, moving, speeding with no destination, hurrying to find a hiding place out of the line of fire.

After eight hours of trudging through the strange fields and roads, we arrived in Antopol. Following a brief discussion we decided to go no further. A lot of people continued on, but we stopped here. We got to work right away: I dug a pit and buried the few worldly possessions we brought with us. We then set out by ourselves with the horse and wagon for a spot a few versts away from the city, where we would wait until after the Germans entered. It had become impossible to remain in the city. Everyone had run away. On the field there were literally thousands of people with their horses and wagons and cows. Thus we "sat" there for three days and three nights. The terror and grief we went through at that time are not easy to describe. We would lie at night in the fields, and the artillery fire would pass right over our very heads. The Czar's soldiers would always come to us and take away young men and their horses and wagons for the army. However, because our little horse was a bit lame, they didn't take it. On the last night, I think it was a Wednesday, we could see how all of Horodetz was aflame. Then we saw that the area where the train station stood was burning, and we could hear terrible explosions. As such, we understood that help was truly imminent. In other words, we would soon be rid of the whole Czarist order, and the redeemer, the German, would come in. In the last hours of the final night it became very quiet. A deathly calm ruled over the whole horizon, and when day broke we caught sight of the first German soldier, riding wildly upon a horse. He rode amidst us, the hundreds of people standing with outstretched hands and open eyes. We followed every gallop and every leap of the horse which bore this proud German. "Russky no here? Russky no here?" he shouted continuously. Then the German rode quickly off, galloping away. A little later more and more Germans arrived on horseback. We all truly rejoiced and congratulated each other. Everyone felt that finally, thank God, we had been liberated from the Czar and that we now had with us the good, fine friend of the Jews: the German.

Under the German

Upon our return home, we witnessed the great catastrophe which had befallen Horodetz. The town had practically been consumed by fire. Nevertheless, a few Jewish houses, and even more Christian houses, had remained standing. Our own house was also still there. The greatest wonder concerned R' Arn-Yoysef [Reb Aaron Joseph] and his wife Shifra, two old-timers and a dear couple, who had not left the town. They were the two people who quite literally "sat through" the crisis and survived. They had hid in the end of the pipe which was situated at the post office.

There now began very difficult and frightening times. We were a community without life: no stores in which to buy something, no doctor, no tailor, no shoemaker, no House of Study and – *let there a separation between the sacred and the profane* – no bathhouse. Moreover, the houses that did remain standing had been damaged. But what could we do? We still needed bread to eat! So it was truly a miracle that now was the end of the summer, the time to gather the produce of the field; and whereas the Christians of the town had all left for the farther reaches of Russia, all of *our brethren, the children of Israel* became farmers. We went out into the fields, cut grain, dug potatoes and even cut hay for the cattle and horses to eat. And in this manner Horodetz accustomed itself to a new, difficult but honest life. Horodetz Jews from that point on took to the fields: They tilled, sowed and harvested. Horodetz Jews (as did those of other towns) became Jewish peasants, toilers. They tilled the fields and worked well. The little boys, *yours truly among them,* would go out bright and early (even before there was daylight) to bring the horses from the pasture, harness them to their wagons, set up the ploughshares and… it was off to the fields! True, it was difficult: at the beginning we weren't familiar with the techniques of the job, and therefore Horodetz Jews had to work harder than experienced peasants. But we worked diligently. From this we had subsistence, and there would still remain something to sell so we could make a few roubles. As the saying goes: "*Those who sow in tears shall reap in joy* [Ps. CXXVI: 5]." However: "*Man does not live by bread alone* [Deut. VIII: 3]." We needed clothes, we needed shoes. But there was nothing from which to make them and nowhere to buy them. We went around barefoot and in rags. Still, as the saying goes: "a Jew copes," and when they need to and when they must, Horodetz Jews can do anything. They started to dye, and made dresses, blouses, pants and so on. In this manner, little by little Horodetz clothed itself. But footwear? You obviously can't dye linen and turn it into a pair of boots! But we found a means: The German had developed a desire to unearth all his fallen soldiers from the battlefields around Horodetz and bring them for burial in one place near the church. German gendarmes would (violently) take Jewish youth, would go out with them into the fields, find the dead German soldiers, dig them up and bring them for burial in Horodetz (according to the procedure appropriate for Germans). Naturally, no one was eager to do this lovely job, and as soon as we would see the gendarmes we would go into hiding. This took place nearly every day over a long period of time.

A few weeks later we started to see individuals going around in new boots, in good shoes. What was this? From where? Then we found out that those who would go to dig up the dead Germans would remove their footwear, which they would bring home, clean with kerosene, alter and put on. When we witnessed this, we no longer hid from the gendarmes: on the contrary, we went out to meet them face-to-face. Can you believe it? Good boots, good shoes – and German yet! And from a dead German, to boot! And in a little while I also had a pair of good boots.

I become a policeman

They had begun to take our young people for forced labour. I was in the group that was sent away to the Nuretz Forest, not far from Kamenetz-Litovsk. There we would chop down trees, saw them, carry them out of the woods and load them onto wagons (probably bound for Germany). It was winter; we were quartered in an abandoned village. The houses were empty; there were no windows or doors. We slept on straw. Bright and early, when it was still dark, we were awoken and – it's hard to believe – quite simply chased out to work. Our nourishment consisted of one two-and- three-quarter pound bread every three days, black coffee without sugar in the morning and warm water – they called it soup – for lunch. In the evening, it was once again black coffee. That was all. It doesn't take long to get sick from such a life. Well, I became really ill and developed a high fever. My comrades decided that one person should not go to work so as to take care of me. However a German, *may his name be blotted out*, charged into the house and gave his almighty command: "The young one (that is to say, me) can just die quietly, and you (my caregiver) can just go to work!" But I tricked this German: God took care of me and I got better. Having slaved away in the woods for about two months, some friends agreed upon a plan of escape from this camp. We hired three wagons, driven by local Christians who knew the forests well, and in the middle of one night we made a break for it. It was a frightful and risky undertaking, because had we been caught they would have surely shot us. But we arrived unharmed in Kamenetz, and from there good Jews sent us over to Horodetz.

From the camp they telephoned the Horodetz commandant about this incident. At that time Yirmieh [Jeremiah] Shub was living in our house together with his family. He was at that time the burgomaster and was friendly with the secretary of the *kommandantur*. So he advised me to act sick, and when the police came to "take" me, they found me "seriously ill" in bed. Okay, but then what? Once again Yirmieh Shub came to my aid and arranged that I should become a translator and a policeman. The next day I was already wearing a stamp taped to my arm, indicating that I had been appointed a policeman by the commandant. So when the German regime needed to take someone for a job, or a horse and wagon for a day's work, or some eggs or butter, we, the Jewish policemen, had to tell this one or that one to go, travel or bring – according to the order. This was not pleasant work, but we did it honestly.

Once, on a Sabbath morning, when I checked in to the kommandantur, the secretary ordered me to shine his shoes. I told him that this day was our Sabbath and so I could not do it, whereupon he lifted up his right hand and let it fall across my face. That was too much for me to swallow. What was the meaning of this? Wasn't I supposed to be some kind of a policeman? An interpreter? I tore the tape from my sleeve and threw it in the secretary's face and – finished! He cursed me and I left and went home.

Lodging and Justice Society

It was harder for the Germans to subdue our tiny town of Horodetz than the big fortress-city of Brisk (Brest-Litovsk). For several days stiff and bloody combat was waged around Horodetz, and when the Germans at last entered the town, Horodetz was already three-quarters burned and laid-to-waste. Many inhabitants had escaped deep into Russia. The life of those who remained was terrible. There was not enough food to eat or clothes to put on. When winter came, the situation became even more frightful, because there was nowhere to buy anything and even had there been, there was nothing for which to shop. The houses were cold, because there was no heat with which to heat them.

Living in such circumstances, many people in Horodetz became ill with typhus. The situation became even more horrible because there was neither doctor nor dispensary.

As is well-known, this illness is contagious, and hence not everyone wanted to be around a sick person. But the ill needed day-and-night care! People died before their time, and we were powerless to help. Then, in those difficult and frightful times, the youth of Horodetz heeded the call. We convened the boys and girls of the town and discussed the horrible situation and what we could do to help those who were suffering. After several suggestions and opinions we united around one plan: to found a *[Free] Lodging and Justice Society* [Yid./Heb.: *liness-hatzedek*;]. Our work consisted of the following duties:

Every day we would gather milk, butter and other necessities for the afflicted families. Every night two people from Lodging and Justice would tend to a sick person for the entire night, thereby freeing the family members of that individual to go and rest up and sleep for a few hours, which for them was an urgent necessary.

This noble work was accomplished by fifteen and sixteen year-old boys and girls. Thanks to them many people in Horodetz were rescued; it is to these boys and girls that they owed their lives.

Cultural Work

The years of German occupation were difficult and frightful. People went about worried, working very hard for a piece of bread. But our new rulers gave us none; their motto was: "*sheli – sheli, v'shelkho – sheli*," (i.e., what's mine – is mine, and what's yours – is mine) [*Ethics of the Fathers,* V: 13].

It was winter, the house was cold, and our stomachs were also not totally satisfied. Our hearts were sad and the long and boring evenings dragged on. There were no schools or libraries where one could learn something or read in order to forget a little the difficulties of daily life. So the few older and more learned among us organized evening courses.

The "Shkola" (the Russian school) happened not to have burned down and – because the Christians had all run away to Russia – no one was using it. So we gathered there several times a week. Young people like Shloymeh [Solomon] Podolevsky, Yeshayeh [Isaiah] Elman and others would give lectures and the young people would discuss their talks. In this manner we spent several warm cultural hours in the cold winter evenings.

A short time later, many of the inhabitants of Horodetz returned from their wanderings in Russia and my brother Yisroel [Israel] came back home from the Russian army. It was truly under his leadership that a drama group and a choir were organized. It was then that we staged *Scattered Far and Wide* and *People* by Sholem-Aleykhem [usual English spelling: Sholem-Aleichem], as well as other short plays, and we sang Jewish songs heartily and with gusto. Thanks to this revival life became a lot more interesting, bright and hopeful.

"Silhouette" drawing by Israel Sussman

[Pages 143-144]

The Economic Situation

By S. Podolevsky

Translated by Hannah Kadmon

[Translator notes in square brackets]

On the whole, the inhabitants of Horodets were store-keepers, craftsmen and clergy. The store-keepers did business with the local farmers but also with farmers and *Poretzes* [Poretz = a gentile landowner; lord] in the surroundings. The craftsmen also worked for them.

This was the case until WW1. The war brought about a violent upheaval, destroying the old way of living, not bringing forth a new one. Thus, the *shtetl* remained neither here nor there. Located strategically next to two tall banks of a river, it became a battlefield between the Russians and the Germans. The canal changed hands between the two. The *shtetl* was almost totally demolished. The Jewish houses were burnt down, especially those in the center of town.

While the battle was raging, the Jews ran away to Antipolye, and when they returned, they found a pile of ashes in place of their houses.

The wooden bridge was burnt down and a temporary bridge was placed above the canal. The iron bridge was broken and the rails of the railroad protruded upwards.

The whole region which had always been full of life looked like a valley of devastation, destruction and death. The Jews who had returned and found their homes burnt down, started settling in houses that had belonged to the gentiles. All the gentiles fled with the retreating Czarist-Russian army which was unwilling to take the Jews along with them. So, the Jews found empty gentile houses and barns full of wheat.

When the Jews settled down a bit, they let the surrounding villages thresh the wheat. Many Jewish families who were driven away by the Germans arrived from Brisk [Brest]. The German evacuated Brisk from all civilian population and settled them in the surrounding *shtetls*. The Jews prepared themselves with food for the first winter.

Spring arrived. Since the whole gentile population - including the land-owners for whom the Jews worked - was gone, the Jews started thinking of farming and attending to the neglected gentile property. Something happened worth noting - something that never occurred not only in our *shtetl* but also in the whole surroundings.

Jew became farmers - cultivating the land. Former teachers, store-keepers, shoemakers and tailors held the plow and became farmers not only excelling in their work done on the gentile's farms but even outshining considerably the work of the gentiles. Later, when the gentiles returned, they did not recognize their farms and shrugged their shoulders with astonishment at the Jewish labor and diligence. It was amazing to watch Khayim, Moshe, Yosl and Binyamin behind the plow and also mow the hay as though their fathers and grandfathers were born and bred farmers, and to watch Khana, Rakhel and Sarah dig out potatoes, cut the wheat and bundle it as though they had been doing that since the creation of the world.

Some Jews, during the few years of the German occupation and later until the peace treaty between the new Soviet Russia and Poland, became in fact very rich as farmers. They were able to own a few horses and cows so that they did not only work on the farms belonging to gentiles, but also cultivate waste lands of the *poritz's* court.

Later, when the gentiles returned they did not know how to thank the Jews who attended so well to their farms. On those farms of gentiles not attended to by the Jews, the buildings deteriorated and wild grass covered the ground

The new way of life continued for five years, 1915 to 1921. In 1921, after the peace treaty between Russia and Poland, the gentiles moved back to Horodets and the Jews left the farms and started engaging in post-war occupations. However, things were not like before. A great part of the farmers did not return. The river that nourished the *shtetl* half year round - was inactive. The people on the other bank of the river, who used in previous years to send lumber abroad, belonged now to Russia and the new Soviet Russia was not interested in sending lumber abroad. The Polish government which occupied our area after the war was not friendly to the Jews. Jews started suffering hunger and their situation was worse than at the time of the war.

True, support came from America, but it was slight. The Jewish population of the *shtetl* and the surrounding villages conceived the idea that perhaps they should turn to the *Poritz* of the *shtetl*-previously a Russian and now a Pole, who had come back after the war - hoping that he would let them cultivate the desolate part of his estate. They would pay him either in money or in grain.

I, the writer of these lines, and some other home-owners in the *shtetl* solicited the help of IK"A in Warsaw to send some messengers to talk with the *Poritz* because he did not want to talk to us. He even launched his dogs at us when we went to talk to him. [IK"A = Jewish Colonization Association founded by the Baron Hirsh to re-settle Russian Jews]. The IK"A sent an agronomist, a young man, a graduate of a Polish school, who contacted the *Poritz*. Later, we joined him as well. At the end of an exchange that lasted an hour, we concluded that nothing would come out of the negotiations.

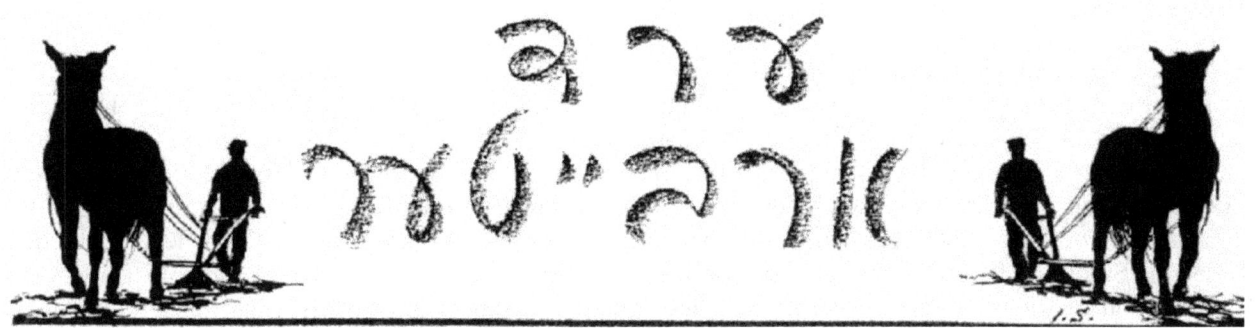

"Earth Workers", drawing by Israel Sussman

I left for America in 1925, met our landsmen there and told them everything. For several years they did all they could and quite often sent over money. However, it was a drop in the bucket. [In Hebrew and Yiddish: "A handful does not satisfy the lion"]. The situation in Horodets grew worse and worse. The letters from there were more and more tearful. However, what could we do? A ladies Auxiliary was founded to raise money and with the help of this association a *gmiles-khesed* [loan without interest] for Horodets was established.

After the disintegration of Poland in 1939, The Red Army occupied the *shtetl* and happier letters started arriving, with a great deal of hope. We thought that this would end all troubles. However, now our poor *shtetl* is dead and desolate and who knows whether it will revive one day.

[Pages 145-146]

The Transition Period

by Binyamin M. Israel

Translated by Hannah Kadmon

[Translator notes in square brackets]

A.

The Germans ruled Horodets for more than 3 years. Those were years of hunger and degradation. However, they were nowhere near the days when the Germans withdrew from our region, when the whole region from Brest to Pinsk was, for several months, in 1919, a totally no-man's-land. Those who could – took control of the region, looted, raped, beat and killed. Our region changed many bloody hands: *Petliortzes* Balakhovtzes*** and other gangs of robbers fell upon those poor neighborhoods and especially upon the poor wretched Jews who survived the war and its painful aftereffects.

* [Petliura was a top Ukrainian commander fighting the Red army, was defeated and his followers, – Petliurites -, carried out pogroms against the Jews.]

** [the volunteer army of General Bulak- Balakhovitch, the leader of the White Guards fought the Red Army and "helped" the Poles.]

Not a day passed without saying prayers for the approaching night, and in the evening they said a prayer for the next day. They did not know where to hide and did not have anything of worth to hide. Their life hung by a thread. That gave rise to the idea of organizing a self-defense unit ("*Sama Obarone*"). The youth got hold of some rusty revolvers, shot-gun and some daggers. A farmer, an acquaintance, promised to get a good German gun for them. Israel Zusselman, who had just returned from the war, was entrusted to organize the youth and teach them how to use weapons. The sons of Aharon Asher, Menashe and Abrem'l Rodetzki, Shlomo Lieber, Yeshaya Alter son of Shefe, Nyomke brother of Israel, Shlomo Burshtein, Naphtali son of Moshe Aharon, David Kaplansky and a few others joined this self-defense unit. Their meeting was, naturally, very secretive and they hardly knew the whereabouts of each other.

Every night 2 members patrolled. One would walk around in the market and the other - in the main street. They knew quite well that if an armed band attacked Horodets they were helpless, because what could they do, Heaven forbid, with a rusty revolver and an old gun? Still, this organization lifted the moral and strengthened us. It also granted us a measure of peace-of-mind. The knowledge that the "young men watch over them" calmed down our Jewish population,

Horrible news arrived from the neighboring *shtetls* and villages, about the "accomplishments" of the murderous-gangs and how they treated the Jews. There was fear of something else: that our "good neighbors", the gentiles, would betray us to the Poles who would then arrest us for holding weapons and would not be content with pinching our cheek…All members of the self-defense unit lived in fear of the two dangers.

In the middle of 1920, many members of the self-defense unit, among them Israel Zusselman, left for America. A few weeks after their departure, *Balakhovtzes* invaded Horodets, entered Itzik'l's house searching for his son, Israel. When he told them that his son had left for America, they did not believe him. They told him they would return the next morning and he must hand his son over to them. That night, Itzik'l burned all the books, manuscripts, drawings, photos and all that had some connection to his son, and went to Hannah-Malka's house where she hid him in bed under a quilt. He lay there until the *Balakhovtzes* were gone. After a couple of days they came again. When Minye, Itzik'l's wife saw them from afar, she immediately let her husband lie on the floor, covered him with a cloth and arranged lit candles around him. When the bandits came in she told them that Itzik'l had just died. The bandits wanted to stick Itzik with the gun to see whether he was really dead. His wife fell on her knees and begged them not to do so, as it would disgrace the dead. After begging for a long time, they left.

That episode illustrates the chaotic situation of the Jews of Horodets in those horrible days.

Soon, some "order" was reinstalled. The Poles took over the region. Alack to that "order"! Wild murderous soldiers from Poznan ("*poanantshikes*") and from general Haliyer's army ("*haliyertshikes*") landed in Horodets and beat and killed whoever was within the reach of their hands, and as a joke – bloody joke – they used to shear, that is: tear, half a beard and the victim had to wear a bandage over half his face until the half beard grew again, as in the case of Shimon Izik and Simkha Yudl.

B.

Things cooled a bit. The Poles started restraining their wild soldiers who were freedom-drunk. However, war broke between the Poles and the Bolsheviks.

The new threat was now the capture of Bolsheviks. The Poles considered every Jew a Bolshevik. Many Jews were killed because of this and many, many, were scared to death.

[Editor's note: see for example the article about "Hershel the Teacher" and "The Town Joker"]

In the summer of 1920, when the war flared and the Poles started fleeing from the Bolsheviks, the Jews were completely abandoned and the Poles looted them endlessly.

When the Bolsheviks conquered our region, the middle-class Jews did not have a ball [in Yiddish: "did not lick honey"]. They confiscated property, they arrested for violating the Bolshevist rules and so forth.

They could stand all that until the real shooting. Bullets flew above their heads and heavy shot from all directions. Horodets was a strategic spot because of the river. The Poles were on the Kobryner side and the Bolsheviks – on the other side.

That was before Rosh Hashanah. About 10-15 Jewish families moved into a cellar in a farm, where they used to make "Swiss"-cheese. They simply filled the whole cellar and could not even stretch their legs. They hid in the dark cellar for 12 whole days, till after Succoth, when the Bolsheviks left. During those terrible 12 days Leibe Roytkopff of the goat-farm was killed by a bullet when he once came out of a trench. Some people became sick out of fear and died.

It should be noted that in this very ghostly time, several Jewish family gathered a *minyan* [at least 10 men] to pray on Yom Kippur with a scroll of Torah and all the features of this holy day.

Thus they suffered until the fighting was over and the Poles, once again, ruled our region and again bullied the poor Jewish survivors of Horodets. However, not many Jews remained. Those who could afford it - immigrated. Some immigrated to The United States, others – to South America or to the land of Israel. Those who remained in Horodets were poor, helpless, Jews who did not have relatives in America or did not possess the courage to run away. They stayed in the *shtetl* where they were murdered by the Hands of the Germans, may their names be erased!

[Pages 146-147]

The Pole

by Yudl Greenberg

Translated by Hannah Kadmon

[Translator notes in square brackets]

The year 1921 marked the beginning of a new epoch in the history of Horodets. After the cruel war between the young Soviet government and the young Polish Republic, a peace treaty was signed in Riga on the 18th of March, 1921. Horodets finally remained under the Polish rule. Horodets, like the whole region, was destroyed during the battles. The fields on the farms were deserted and the cattle were slaughtered. Most houses were in ruins and those that remained were badly damaged by shelling. All pieces of furniture were also victims of the war; they were used as firewood.

The bridge which connected the "market" with the "street" [Main Street] was blocked. Horodets looked like a skeleton of a town without a sign of life.

Very slowly, those who had fled deep into Russia, because of the Germans, started coming back. Those who were lucky to find their homes started repairing them to make them fit to live in.

The returning Jews had it really bad, because they had no fields to sow and they did not bring with them any treasures of gold. They had to adjust to the circumstances and start from scratch.

The population of Horodets consisted of two groups: White-Russians and Jews. The few Polish residents were: the *poretz* [gentile land-owner] for whom the farmers worked, A Polish teacher and 3 policemen. These "dignified" Poles treated the residents of Horodets as their servants. There was an unwritten rule that when someone met the above mentioned Poles, he had to take off his hat to him. If, God forbid, someone forgot to take off his hat – he was in trouble. Hitting and insulting for every trifle was a common matter. The Poles applied their rule especially to the poor Jews.

Even though Poland was officially a republic with equal rights to all citizens, this was not so in reality. There was freedom of religion but no freedom of press, or assembling. They permitted social recreation and cultural assemblies. However, to get a permit it was necessary to send a request to the governor. The permit was not always granted.

Political convening or rallies were absolutely prohibited. Even before elections, assembling was not permitted. A Zionist meeting was also absolutely prohibited even though the Zionist Organization was legal in Poland.

A mere stage-performance without any implied political meaning was also forbidden. Once, when the youth of Horodets wanted to stage a play, some Polish policemen appeared and broke up the gathering.

This autocratic regime was the reason for the rise of dissatisfaction among the non-Polish population, especially among the White-Russian gentiles. They preferred to belong to their motherland Russia. Therefore, there were communists among the White-Russian youth. When the Polish government tracked down a communist – he did not get away alive.

The Jewish youth of Horodets gave vent to their protest against the tyrannical Polish policy by preparing for *Aliya* [emigrating] to the Land of Israel, to live there as Jews.

The goal of the Polish government was to "Polanize" the whole region. [transform the whole region to be completely Polish], at the same time sowing anti-Semitism wherever one turned. To reach their goal, they established a Polish public-school where all the children had to learn Polish as a means to make them absorb the Patriotic spirit of the Poles and also their hatred of Jews.

Here is an illustration: the Polish teacher pointed to her four-year-old son two people walking in the street, remarking: "That one is a noble man and the other is a Jew".

Naturally, the Jewish children could not attend this school for long with this kind of education very soon left the Polish school. Some travelled to Brest to attend the "*Tarbut*" schools and others left to study in *yeshives* [Religious institutions of higher Talmudic learning].

* *

At the end of 1928, when I left Horodets, many Jews had already recovered. Many rebuilt their life from scratch, and lived a productive Jewish life with the hope for a brighter future for the community and for each person. Unfortunately this dream did not materialize. It was shattered and a painful tragedy befell our *shtetl*. Only a single Jew survived - the only living witness to a community that was erased and would never live again.

[Pages 148-152]

My Visit

by Israel Zussman (Israel)

Translated by Hannah Kadmon

[Translator notes in square brackets]

In the summer of 1927 I went with my wife on a belated honeymoon trip to Horodets. Since my father did not have the good fortune to lead even one child to the *khupe* [canopy of marriage ceremony], I wanted to let him meet at least his first daughter-in-law.

When we arrived in Warsaw from Paris, I called my father from the telephone of my wife's relative. The telephone in Horodets was in the post office and it took about six hours to get us connected. When I finally heard my father's voice, his first words were: "...שהחיינו" [Shekheyonu vekiymonu vehigionu lazman haze = benediction over a happy occurrence: "for keeping us alive to reach this occasion"]. He spoke hurriedly and his voice quivered. Since I, too, spoke very fast – we understood each other very well.

In the morning we travelled to Brest where we met in the terminal Avraham-Khayim Kostrinsky (Motye's son) with his daughter, Noakh Polyak with his wife Ester (Vinograd) and Makhle, sister of Tzivia Greenglass. Since we had to wait a few hours for the Polesian* train, I could spend some good time with them. They said that in all terminals we would meet acquaintances because all knew of our arrival. [Polesia = a marshy region lining the Pripyat River in Southern Belarus]

From Brest, the ride was more familiar. Here is Zshabinke and here we are already in Kobryn. Many acquaintances, many kisses, exchange of questions and the few moments pass very quickly – the train moves on the way to Horodets… My face is glued to the window. The train passes quickly along familiar fields and here is the village Kamen; I devour the whole panorama like in a dream. The cemetery can be seen now from afar. My eyes are tired, my heart palpitates louder – the wheels pound also as if they want to compete with each other … and I already see from afar the top of our *galovnik* (pigeon coop). I want to have a good look, but we are already on the bridge. Trakh-trakh, tiyakh-tiyakh – and we are already near the brick-yard. The train slows down and I can see the terminal from afar. Wow, how shrunken it has become. All at once the train stops. I run down hurriedly and I see unexpectedly how the policemen pay their respect to me. (Later I found out that they had read in the papers that I was supposed to draw a picture of their president Pilsudsky). My eyes search swiftly for my father and I see him pressed against the wall with stretched arms. The first words that he uttered were: "לראות את פניך לא פללתי" [Hebrew: "I did not believe I would see your face"]. We let a tear fall, he kissed his first daughter-in-law, and together with our good-hearted aunt Minye (my father's second wife) we sat on Aharon-David's cart which looked very festive with fresh hay spread all over – and forward to the *shtetl*.

Many people and children came to the terminal to welcome us. More than any of the folks, my friend Motl, son of Khayim Nissan (Vinograd), caught my eye. He was riding a big horse. On the way we did not talk much – only eyed each other and kept quiet. Approaching the *shtetl* it seemed to me as if the houses had become smaller. When we arrived at our own house, the street was full of people. The welcoming celebration was beyond description and we did not know what to say or ask first. We sat and talked until dawn.

In the morning the Polish commander arrived to pay his respect and ceremoniously kissed my wife's hand. He was very cordial. It seemed that even the old Poland had a great deal of respect for an American who was assigned to paint their president.

Later on I walked about the *shtetl* which looked different than in 1920 when I left it. The streets were nicely rebuilt, and there was also a new *besmedresh* [study house, where people used to pray as well]. Alter, the blacksmith, built a nice house and new houses on both sides of the *besmedresh*. Even the bridge was new and longer. The market place was also rebuilt and Khayim Nissan's house was the most beautiful of all houses in the *shtetl*. Still, poverty remained the same.

I walked to the cemetery to bow my head at my mother's grave. I did not notice that Alter the blacksmith was standing in a distance saying quietly "אל מלא רחמים" [prayer on a grave]. The cemetery did not shrink in size. On the contrary, it grew in size. Many new graves had been added – with or without tombs. In the middle of the cemetery, was yet to be found the "tent" of the old Rabbi as if watching over the other graves.

In former years there were two places to pray in: the Hassidim prayed At Shepsl, in the "wall" [house built with brick] (Stolin and Kobryn Hassidim) and the *Misnogdim* [*opponents to the Hassidic movement*] and the "*gasser*" [ordinary people] prayed in the new *besmedresh*. On the first Sabbath I prayed with the Hassidim. They honored me with reading the *maftir* [the reading of the lesson from the Prophets] and, poor me; I had to read the whole lesson. This same thing repeated itself the next Sabbath in the *besmedresh*. The first Sabbath, the *shtetl* sent us drinks like for "seven blessings" [said at a wedding] (at my father's it was virtually a wedding). A child would come with a bottle of beer or wine, or a plate covered with a cloth like *shalakh Mones* [the ritual sending of baked and prepared sweets on Purim] and would say: "welcome to your guests"… The next morning, Khayim Nissan told us that people bought all the drinks in his cellar…

Khayim Nissel's house

My good aunt Minye wanted to cater to her guest and to all my requests to cook the plain local Horodetser *krupnik* [barley soup] she answered: "Leave me alone! For such a guest a mere *krupnik* soup? You will eat at my place a roast…" In short, she roasted the roast for such a long time, till I fell sick. Then she cooked the *krupnik*.

During the two weeks of my stay in Horodets, I visited almost every house in the *shtetl*. (In many houses they treated us to tea and *varenye* [jam]. I paid a visit to the good Rabbi R' Ari' Greenman who lived in a modest room in what used to be Simkha-Yudl's house and was now owned by Yankl the mason. I visited Uncle Asher-David the *shoykhet* [ritual slaughterer] who lived in Izik Izrael's house but his heart was in the Land in Israel. He actually emigrated there and died there at the age of about one hundred. I visited my Rabbi and scholar R' Shimon Izik who always longed for big towns and craved for knowledge but remained in Horodets. I had a conversation with Tuvia the shoemaker, the oddball and "town-joker". I talked to Shlomo Burshtein - teacher, idealist and *bundist* [follower of the socialist Jewish labor party] who had become a shop keeper - while he was weighing cereal. He really pondered about the world's hardships and dreamed of world-redemption. I talked to Yaakov Polyak, the eternal fashion- shopkeeper who regarded taking measures as a sacred procedure. I paid a visit to Alter the smith, the pubic leader, active in the community, a member of *Khevre Kedi'she* [voluntary burial society] "second in importance". I did not miss seeing shepsl the *Stoliner* [Hassid] always joyful, a wide smile on his face, who used to help the fathers sing Sabbath songs. I also had an "interview" with Yankl the mason who used to laugh at the world and loved people, mainly the poor. I also visited Khayim Nissan Vinograd, of short stature but with a big heart, a big family and a comfortable house, well-established like an oak, and many good children. The modest Motye, the Rabbi with his wife, who lived in our house, asked many questions about America because he had one foot already there.

I talked to many people in Horodets from all social classes: workers, toilers, shop-keepers, and intellectuals. I talked to all of them, asked about their life and heard from all of them the same response: "Bless America! This *shtetl* exists more than ever thanks to America". There was hardly any family that did not have one of its members in America and only their kin's support kept them alive. The American dollars were to the people of Horodets like the manna to the people of Israel in the desert.

I spent time enjoying our fruit orchard and even the pigeons knew that an American guest was there and they flew about more happily than ever…

Everyone admired the American. An American was a man who knew everything, a man of integrity – and what not? It happened to me, as an American, to be chosen even as a judge and I was approached with a *dintoyre* [lawsuit before a rabbinical court].

Did I satisfy the two parties? – I don't know. There was enough shouting at each other. The shouts could be heard in New-York. However, when it ended late after midnight and I read the verdict, they drank *lekhayim* [to (long) life] and everybody was happy.

I became acquainted with the new Rabbi, R' Arye Greenman. He was a genteel person and a great scholar. He was a man with a good heart and the people of Horodets were lucky to have him in those days, gentle, very dedicated, always ready to help each person with counsel and in deeds. However, he hardly made ends meet. They used to say that he sometimes went hungry, very quietly, never complaining.

The two weeks ended swiftly like a dream. It was a great festival. The house swarmed with people and those who could not get in, at least peeped through the windows to catch a glimpse of the American.

My heart told me that this was my last visit in my birthplace, that I would never again see this *shtetl*. Therefore I wanted to inhale everything, to treasure it for later. I wanted to re-live my childhood and my early youth. I wished to go once again through all the places which reminded me of the near and far past. Therefore, I took a walk with my young friend Motl Vinograd to visit the "*pakoy*" ["hall"] where we held our Zionist concerts and performances after WW1 and now stood bleak and deserted. I strolled with Motl along the "*batshvenikes*" (the two banks of the river) to the sluice and walked through all the trails which awoke many memories of the good, sweet years of my childhood.

I had taken along my led-pencil and sitting on our open balcony I would draw many types that are about to vanish. I also took pictures of our small street and of the main street viewed from the bridge with almost the whole *shtetl* gathering there.

Time has come to depart. On a fixed day, I think it was a Sunday, we woke up quite early and around 6 o'clock we left the house. Israel Moshe's cart was already waiting for us as also many people who woke up early with us to say goodbye. We took leave in silence, kissed the neighbors, Yosl the mason and Motye with Uncle Asher David, Shimon Izik, Khayim Nissan, David Moshe, Aharon Asher and many more. Then we climbed to the cart. Then I stood straight and made motions with my hand as though gathering the whole *shtetl* to me and said: "Be well…" Tears rolled down my cheeks and choked my throat so I could not continue the sentence. I restrained myself from crying and asked Israel-Moshe to get moving fast. Viya! – He pulled the reins. The horse woke as if from a nap, cheerless and not in a hurry to pull himself from the place. Then we were on our way to the train station.

The "Street" (after the First World War)

In the terminal each of us took heart and made an effort to be joyful. However it was useless. So we deliberately talked about trivial matters at this important moment…

The train arrives. We quickly start to take leave of each other, hug each other, eye each other wordlessly and we swallow our tears…Soon I am standing on the steps of the wagon, take a good look at my father wishing to engrave his image in my memory.

Timeless scarce seconds – wish we could stretch them – but we hear a sharp honking and the train pulls in a sudden start from its place.

It tears my heart. I hear my father's "צאתך לשלום" ["leave in peace"] and "יברכך ד' וישמרך" [may god bless you and watch over you"]. My eyes are tired. I bite my lips in order not to cry. Now I see my father as if through a mist, leaning on his stick whispering a prayer.

He becomes smaller and smaller, shrunken, until he vanishes in space. ..

The train starts moving faster, wheels pounding noisily as if willing to drive away my thoughts.

I have the feeling that this is the last time I see my father.

[Pages 152-154]

The Pioneer Movement

By Bella Feinshtein (Israel)

Translated by Hannah Kadmon

[Translator notes in square brackets]

[Bella Feinshtein lived first in Kibbutz Shfayim with her husband Ben-Zion. When the members of the Kibbutz split because of ideological conflicts, they moved to Kibbutz Ramat-Yokhanan and raised 3 sons. They both lived there until their death. I knew both of them very well and loved them very much. Both were very active in the Kibbutz communal life. This translation is dedicated to their memory. HK]

[Akiva Ben-Ezra's commented as editor:
In addition to the article that covers in general the nationalistic revival in Horodets in between the two World Wars by Shmuel Hoyzman, we received this article by Bilhah [Bella] Feinshtein (Beyle daughter of Moshe the blacksmith) from the Land of Israel. She is the only one left of her whole family. We offer this article because there are certain details and notes not mentioned in Hoyzman's article.]

* * *

I cannot remember the exact date when "*Hekhalutz*" [the Pioneer] was established in Horodets. However, in 1926 the members of "*Hekhlutz Haboger*" [the adults] decided that "*Hekhalutz*" must have continuity. For this goal they founded "*Hekhalutz Hatza'ir*" [the young pioneer] which included a few dozen members whose age was 13-15. In the shtetl, at that time, there were no Yiddish schools at all. All the children had to attend the Polish schools. However, their parents were imbued with the spirit of nationalism and therefore they saved every coin from their meager income to enable their children to learn Hebrew in the free hours from the Polish school. Lieber and Yaakov Adrezinsky helped them in this matter. Those two were also the teachers. Thus almost all the members of "*Hekhalutz Hatza'ir*" got the same education, knew Hebrew more or less, and were imbued with the spirit of Patriotism that enabled fertile and systematic work.

The work in the Chapter, and even later, when we were already in "*Hekhalutz Haboger*", was always illegal because we did not have the sufficient means to rent a place and carry the work formally. All the meetings were held under cover. For each meeting we had to look for a new place. In summer – on the bank of the river, a few kilometers away from the shtetl, or in the forest or in the field. In winter –in one of the members' house, each time in a different home. Naturally, it made our work more difficult. The people on duty had to look for a place to gather the members.

Occasionally, when all was ready, the meeting could not take place for unforeseen reasons. For some time we used the name of the library which was legal, and which was founded by the same members of "*hekhalutz*" and sympathized with us. This was also not always possible because we had to get permission for each assembly.

Lieber Polyak

I recall two illegal gatherings. The first gathering was held one summery Sabbath on the river bank. A police commander suddenly appeared from nowhere. He was a tall, broad shouldered gentile with a pair of red cheeks. He confiscated our "*Bamesila*" [=on the road] (a book about the land of Israel written by workers in the land of Israel) and other brochures and newspaper such as the "*He'atid*" =[the future] (a Hebrew newspaper that was published in Warsaw).

The second gathering was held in the "Tzigelnyer" forest led by Khayim Biletzky from Kobryn and the commander got wind of it and took us to the Police station. They beat some of us and warned the others they would be beaten too. The commander wanted to know who the leader was. From us he could not retrieve his name. Finally he found out his name and he succeeded to detain the man in Kobryn. The "*Mored Bemalkhut*" [Hebrew: rebel against royalty/authority] was caught. Only thanks to the League-leader in the Federation, Biletzky came out of it frightened but unharmed.

[Editor's comment: Khayim Biletzky was later a fellow worker in "*Al Hamishmar*" [a socialistic newspaper in Israel] and the author of a book of poems.]

The main activity was educational and cultural. Three times a week the members were gathered under the leadership of the two men mentioned above.

They taught us the following subjects: Jewish news - political and economical- and Zionist news. We also discussed various Zionist and Socialistic issues.

A group of pioneers

First row, sitting, from right to left: Abraham Vinograd, Chaya Kuprianski, Abraham Garber
Second row: Chashke Veisman, Yaakov Adrezinsky, Pelte Glatzer, Lieber Polyak, Yehudit Rubinshtein.
Third row, standing: David Rodetzki, the daughter of Hershel the chimney sweeper, Yaakov Goldberg, Feigel Greblovsky, Michal Helershtein, Genendil Vinograd

Horodetser pioneers in front of Moshe Ber Kuprianski's house

In time, some members joined us from rather poor families. They could not attend the Hebrew courses. We made efforts to make them feel part of us and we taught them Hebrew. Our means were scant. We had only the membership monthly fees contributed by a small number of members. So, we cultivated a garden and from the income we set up a small library at "*Hekhalutz Hatza'ir*". The work in the garden was voluntary, but almost all members took part.

In winter we set up courses for poor small children who could not take private lessons and had to attend the Polish school. Some of us – Khaya Olchik, Yossef Mantak, Yehuda Greenberg and I – volunteered a few times a week for this purpose. The children acquired quite a lot during the winter.

Naturally, we also took part in the work of collecting money with the "*Keren Kayemet*" boxes. [the fund for buying land in the land of Israel], which was for us a holy ctivity. I went with Yaakov Adrezinsky to distribute the first "*Keren Kayemet*" boxes. I still remember very well with what joy some very poor women welcomed us. They gave away the last coins left from the scant savings that they put aside after hard toiling. Horodets became quite poor after the wars. Most of the families existed thanks to the support of their American relatives.

We also got together with friends from Antipolye and Kobryn. When we visited these members from the Center, we heard each time, how satisfied they were with our Chapter, saying that it was one of the best in the neighborhood. That was because of the two following reasons: First, the nationalistic education and second, the leadership of the two leaders mentioned above. Our aspiration, naturally, was "*Aliya*" [immigration to Israel] and " *Hagshama*" [implementation/actualization]. However, actualization was entangled with many external obstacles and not everybody was able to persist in coping with them. Only a part of the members are now in the Land of Israel. I am the only one from our shtetl on a Kibbutz. The others are outstanding and productive members in this land. Lieber Polyak's yield is plentiful- our being here.

[Pages 155-162]

Under the Polish Regime

By Rabbi Shalom Podolevsky

Translated by Hannah Kadmon

[Translator notes in square brackets]

Between 1918 and 1939, until WW2, our tiny shtetl Horodets was under the Polish rule. The population included 50 Jewish families (about 200 souls), around 100 Belarussian families and 15 Polish families. All the Russians were farmers. The Poles were civil officers such as police officers, community officers, teachers, postal clerks, railroad officials, etc.

Rabbi Shalom Podolevsky

The Jewish population was composed of workers, shop-keepers, and small dealers. Our shtetl became even smaller and poorer as the result of WW1, and many wished to immigrate, or had already immigrated, to other lands because the Polish government did everything to embitter the life of the Jews, to oust them from their occupations in order to hand them over to the Polish farmers.

Thus the authorities very often issued distressing decrees against Jews. For example: The Jews had to pay very heavy taxes for their houses. They had to pay the Polish *Poritz* [the gentile land-owner] money for the piece of land on which the house, store or workshop was built. When someone was sick and could not be conscripted to the army, he had to pay special taxes all continuously. The Jewish worker had to pay taxes to get a permit to work. He also had to pay a high income tax to the government. The Jewish shop-keepers and the small dealers alike had to pay risk-taxes.

The Poles also introduced the cooperatives which could belong only to Poles. The worst decree was called "*karte zshimitznitze*", without which one could not work. To get such a card, a Jew had to finish a trade-school or pass an examination and prove that he, his father and his grandfather and great-grandfather were born in the same shtetl.

The Jews in bigger towns found ways of getting such a card. Public schools were established and advisors and middlemen helped get such a card. However, in the smaller shtetles Jews had a lower level of education and it was almost impossible to get such a card. Thus work was gradually slipping off Jewish hands. Bitter was the fate of a Jew who managed to get the card or the permission to open a grocery store, but could not pay all the taxes. That is when the bailiff would come to execute confiscation - selling his quilt, his bed, his workshop and his sewing machine. When the bailiff arrived in Horodetz, the Jewish town-elder (Asher Mendel, the mason's son) would hasten to tell these individuals to hide everything. The poor people, pitifully, locked their houses, chased the cows, horse, calves and hens out to the fields, put out of sight their sewing machines and their beddings and hid somewhere until the bailiff left the shtetl.

When Hitler, may his name be erased forever, forbade the ritual of slaughtering in his evil regime, Germany, the Poles, wishing to imitate the Germans, also decided to forbid slaughtering, under the pretext that slaughtering is not humane enough and is a barbaric act. Their goal was to stop Jewish trade in meat, and in general to snatch the piece of meat from Jewish mouth. When a Jew slaughtered a cow with a slaughtering knife as the religious custom requires, not wanting to eat from a killed or dead cow, he could get 5 years in jail or he could lose his life.

In the bigger town one could get a piece of meat for a high price, because over there, the authorities allowed the slaughtering of a very small amount of cows. However, a Jew in a small shtetl, and especially a poor Jew, did not have any meat. Thus in our shtetl Horodets there was no meat and the small children did not even know what meat meant.

Itzik's *shtiebl* [a small Hasidic prayer house] was well known in the whole neighborhood because besides its being used for prayer, Itzik built a nice *Hakhnoses-O'rkhim* [Shelter/inn for poor wanderers]. He kept improving this inn from day to day. In summer, in Itzik's yard behind the house, grew some good fruit trees and the poor enjoyed them and blessed the landlord who had built the inn, not aware that this landlord was present and living among them.

Since the smaller and bigger shtetles around Horodets did not have any *Hakhnoses-O'rkhim*, poor wanderers planned to arrive in Horodetz for Sabbath. Every evening, poor wanderers and vagabonds, would come to Horodets. This changed completely the appearance of our shtetl. *Hakhnoses-O'rkhim* made our dear shtetl famous in the towns and shtetles of Poland, especially during the last years prior to WW2, when Hitler, his name be erased for ever, was already in power. Thousands of sick and desperate people, who fled the concentration camps, started coming to Horodets. Here, Itzik's *Hakhnoses-O'rkhim* was very helpful. When the displaced Jews rode the highway or on the train through Horodets, they would stop and rest in the *Hakhnoses-O'rkhim*.

A character from among Itikl's "guests"
(Drawn by Israel Zussman)

The *shames* [attendant] in *Hakhnoses-O'rkhim* was Itzik himself. He was a sick man, and actually without legs, since during the last years his artificial legs wore out. Thanks to my father who mended these artificial legs and adjusted them for Itzik, he could still use them. Itzik himself used to say: "I walk to perform *mitzves* [good deeds] with Lieber's legs". Itzik would be standing like Abraham our Father and performing *Hakhnoses-O'rkhim* [attending to his guests] from early morning till night. Itzik felt greatly honored when the guests used to call him "*shames*" even as they were angry and were yelling that the "*shames*" was not so good and that there should have been a better "*shames*"…

Thus the Jews of Horodets, despite their poverty, had to share their very little money and piece of bread with the poor folks of the *Hakhnoses-O'rkhim*. Every day, Horodetser Jews and volunteers used to go and collect money for an important guest and for the sick and wounded from other lands.

In 1938, I happened to collect money for a refugee from Germany. I had just come home for a Holiday from the Yeshiva of Mear and the Rabbi and a few Jews approached me and asked me to go on this errand. That was a short time before I departed for America. I did not feel like going because I knew how poor our shtetl was. I did not have the heart to ask them to donate from their meager money. My father was irritated and explained that I ought to perform the greatest *mitzve* - *Hakhnoses-O'rkhim* - and that everybody would welcome me with respect. So, I went along, having no other choice. My partner was my friend and cousin Rabbi Kalman Kuprianski, Moshe Ber's son and Alter the blacksmith's grandson. I was touched by the fact that the folks greeted us with respect, handing out their alms and food and while doing so they blessed us for bothering to go from door to door.

In Itzik's shtiebl the prayer was conducted in the Sephardic version. Still, all the market people, Ashkenazi and Sephardic, prayed together, and even the Rabbi prayed at Itzik's because he lived in the market place. The older people from the market place also used to pray in this *shtiebl* every morning and evening, and even studied there a bit. Others used to sit there a whole day and study. On Sabbath and Holiday, all the people - young, old and even small children - went to pray in the *shtiebl*. While being there, the young ones used to snatch some rumors about politics and stealthily glanced at a newspaper. The young children used to play, yell and carry on and while this was going on the fathers and grandfathers watched with glee and joy the young "fruit trees" that were growing in our shtetl and would go on drawing their spiritual nourishment from the Horodetser tradition. They said: "with such good children that we are blessed with, our shtetl will never go under, a generation goes and a new generation comes. It is true we are old but our children will fill our place and our shtetl will continue to exist".

In summer, Sabbath evening, people used to go into the *shtiebl* or *besmedresh* [the study house, where people used to pray as well] to read a chapter, and in winter – "*Borkhi Nafshi*" [prayer from psalms; "My soul blesses God", etc.]

Others used to browse through a page of the Gemara [part of the Talmud] or read psalms. There was also in our *shtiebl* a group for *mishnayes* [collection of post biblical laws; part of the Talmud]. Rabbi R' Arye Greenman used to teach *mishnayes* every Sabbath evening to the folks and those who had a taste for *mishnayes* would sit at the table to listen. Even the young used to listen from a distance while the lecture was on and posed a query to the Rabbi, to which he would answer with a great deal of affection.

Before my departure, before the war broke out, they were learning "*Sanhedrin*" [=one of the *mishnayes* dealing with capital offence laws and procedures of trial; also the name of the high court in the land of Israel of 70-71 wise men]. The Rabbi spoke about how they led a murderer to be executed, and even while leading him to the place of execution, if they saw from afar a rider coming towards them, they stopped and turned back and they didn't kill the man. Shlomo Burshtein, the shopkeeper, posed a query: "if the Sanhedrin has already found him guilty, why should they revise the verdict"? and the Rabbi explained that even for a murderer it is necessary to look for some virtue or credit. Even if a person killed but some virtue or good deed can be found to his credit, he should not be killed. It is possible that the approaching rider has something good to say about the condemned man. That is why he is led back.

Now, remembering this Talmudic story the Rabbi told, we should cry out with the question: "Truly, this Rabbi and such dear Jews did not have anything to their credit?"

After the afternoon prayer, they arranged the traditional "three meals". Actually, there was only a piece of hallah with some water on the table. However, this did not prevent Avraham-Ezra, the mason, together with Shepsl the carpenter, to sing in ecstasy Hassidic songs and start dancing with rapture, pulling the rest of the folks to a circle dance. Even the small children, the *Moshe'lekh* and the *Shloyme'lekh*, were drawn in, pulling at their fathers' and grandparents' hems to dance with them, all the while laughing and having fun in their childish naïve way. After *havdole* [ceremony when Sabbath is over], they danced to the hymn "*Hamavdil*" [the hymn after *havdole:*" He who makes a distinction between the holy and the every-day"], with the accompaniment of a violin and a drum like in happy times, unaware that the angel of death was standing among them, and in a short while there would be no memory of Jews ever existing there.

An exception was *Shmini Atzeret* [eighth day of Sukkot] at the *hakofes* [circular procession with the Torah scrolls around the reading platform]. That is when all the folks would gather - men, women and youngsters –in the market place and in the main street and proceed to Itzik's *shtiebl* to rejoice around the Torah. Issar the tailor, serving as a *gabe* [manager of affairs] used to stand on a chair to be able to see who was present in the *shtiebl* so as not to embarrass anyone by not giving him the scroll for a *hakofe*. He called out in a loud voice: "the bridegroom Yossef, son of R' Khayim Nissl is honored with a *hakofe*. The bridegroom Berl, son of R' Aharon David is honored with a *hakofe*". Or, our yeshiva students were honored with the first *hakofe*. Even the small children were not excluded from calling them by the name of their grandfather; Yaakov, Shimon-Itzick's grandson, and Pessakh, Lieber's grandson and Avraham, Ezra's grandson adding the words: "because they knock over the *shtiebl* and break the window panes – they earn a *hakofe*." All the while, Young and old, all together clapped their hands and united in a circle. The fathers and grandfathers rejoiced watching the young children, with flaming cheeks, carrying the scroll. The mothers and grandmothers were muttering "knock on wood" watching how their children were moving so gracefully and looking so handsome.

In the *Besmedresh* they prayed according to the Ashkenazi version and they already followed the customs of the *Misnogdim* [opponents of the Hassidim]. All the folks "from the street" Hassidim and *Misnogdim* came together to pray in the *Besmedresh*. And there, sitting by a long table, Alter, the blacksmith, used to teach the congregation *Pirke-o'ves* ["ethics of the Fathers"] in summer, and *Ein Yaakov* [a compilation of the legendary material in the Talmud with commentaries] in winter, talking about the good qualities a Jew should have and how a Jew should conduct himself. He explained that thanks to these qualities the Jews would never go under. As an example he brought Horodets: "Surrounded by so many gentiles, we have been living in Horodets hundreds of years and we will continue to exist until the coming of the Messiah, when all Jews will go to the Land of Israel." He adorned his lesson with beautiful proverbs and phraseology, and the congregation was enchanted and the folks sat and watched Alter's permanent smile, white beard and clever eyes, expressing their great respect and reverence for Alter and believing in the wise words that he spoke.

At another table sat Alter the Levi, a Jew above 100 years old, still healthy and strong, teaching *mishnaye* in the *Misnogdim*'s straightforward manner, and discussing in a scholarly way the dispute between the *Tano'im* [rabbis whose teachings in the first two centuries A.D. that are included in the *Mishnah*] and why did Rabbi held this one opinion while R' Natan held a different opinion, and this is how they spent their Sabbath and Holiday.

The *Besmedresh* was also the place to hold meetings. At the meetings all were equal, without a chairman. Everybody talked, made noise and all were equally interested in the issues discussed. The meetings were always about economic issues and the needs of the shtetl such as: fixing the fence around the cemetery that was getting worn-out to the point of breaking down, having enough water in the bathhouse, where to get enough wood to heat the bathhouse and the *Besmedresh*, or a fair distribution of the relief money that arrives before Passover from the American countrymen, not wronging anybody, etc.,

The *shoykhet* [ritual slaughterer] of the shtetl, Yoel, was still a young man. He was Zlatke's son-in-law. He was also a music player and served as a cantor during the High Holidays, or at a special festive event that took place in the *Besmedresh*. He was a quiet and nice young man, and when the old *shoykhet* Asher-David, 10 years before ww2 broke out, departed for the Land of Israel, he sold his right to Yoel. However, Yoel did not hold his job too long in Horodets because a short while after that, the Poles forbade ritual slaughtering. So he engaged a little bit in teaching and taught a few children. His *kheyder* was in the market place, in Brakha Kostrinsky's house. He did not have luck with being a *melamed*. The chief *melamed* in shtetl was Sender, son of Khayim-Sender's and the son-in-law of Mendel the mason. He called himself a "teacher". Almost all the children in the shtetl were Sender's pupils. He considered himself a modern man and his conduct was modern. He wore modern clothes; always carried a cane in his hand, like a dandy, and in his other and he held a book. He boasted of being the teacher of the shtetl. Actually he was a very good *melamed* and the children loved him dearly, but they did not learn from him too much. The children had to learn in the Polish public school from nine in the morning to three in the afternoon.

There was a bathhouse attendant in our shtetl. In addition to being a bathhouse attendant he was also the undertaker and the caretaker of the cemetery. His job was to keep away the cows or swine that were grazing in the pasture next to the cemetery and were threatening to break in through the torn fence and, God forbid, damage the tombs and headstones. This attendant was Israel Moshe, the gravedigger's son-in-law who got the concession to be a bathhouse attendant and caretaker of the cemetery as a dowry. When Israel Moshe became old and later passed away, his son-in-law got the concession. His house was near the bathhouse close to the cemetery in the rear end of the shtetl.

Sender's *kheyder,* or as he called it: "school", was in the *besmedresh* and consisted of 30 boys and girls. When a boy was talented and his father wanted him to study further, he would send him to Antepolye, because they had a big *Talmetoyre* [traditionally, a tuition free elementary school maintained by the community for the poorest children]. Over there, the children attended the *Talmetoyre* from early morning till evening, learning also Polish, Yiddish, *khumesh* [first 5 books of the Bible] and *Gemore* [Gemara, the part of Talmud that comments on the *Mishna*]. The *melamdim* in Antipolye were scholars and taught the children until they could study a page of *Gemore* independently. Many of the Horodetserchildren studied in Antepolye a whole week and would go home on foot for Sabbath. Sometimes they could get a ride with a Horodetser who would drive them to their homes, or with a coachman from Antepolye who would let them off at the station.

There were in the shtetl some modern and rich Jews who sent their children to Brest (Brisk) or to other towns to a "Tarbut" school. That was a Hebrew public school or high school. Great scholars did not emerge in Horodets under the Polish regime. However, all were good, honest, proud and conscientious youth. Still 4 yeshiva youth, the pride of Horodets, came out of Horodets who were quite big scholars. One of them, Kalman, Moshe Ber's son, Alter the blacksmith's grandson, was really a genius. Someone with such a scholarly mind can be found only once in several generations. In addition, he was very clever and handsome – indeed a prince. One year before the war, he married a wife who stemmed from the family of the Gaon R' Pessakh Rruskin, the head of the yeshiva of Kobryn. That was a sensation for us. His wife, Dina, was also a great scholar and a beauty.

The second yeshiva youth was my friend Barukh, son of Shimon Yaakov. He was a great diligent student. He labored and toiled a lot to be able to study and in the midst of night when all around was quiet and the shtetl and the yeshiva were all asleep, his voice could be heard in the yeshiva, studying the holy Torah. I remember that when we were quite young, studying in Antipolye or in Kobryn, it never happened that Barukh raised his eyes from the *Gemore* out of fear lest he would lose a word, and would not be able to interpret it on his own. He never had the time to eat and studied the text again and again with the purpose of not lagging behind.

Barukh Greblovsky
Yehoshua Ozornitzki

Kalman Kuprianski

In addition he was very God fearing and pious young man and very virtuous. Barukh had a great talent for commerce. He was a great contractor and very industrious. Three years before WW2 broke out, he established a bakery in Pruzshane that prepared matzos not only for Pruzshane but also for Kobryn, Brest and Horodets and the whole surroundings. His matzos were famous all over Poland. A year later he got married in Visokey near Brest. His wife was the daughter of a big corn merchant and he opened there a matzo bakery doing great business. The third yeshiva youth was my cousin Yehoshua, Khayim Ozornitzki's son and Aharon-Itshe Leizer's grandson. He was a few years younger than me. He was also a great and diligent scholar and a good young man. He had a great talent for painting. In his free time when he stayed in Horodets, he painted and carved. When the war broke out he fled to Vilna – being then under the Lithuanian rule - with the purpose of immigrating to Shanghai with other yeshiva students.

When the Nazis, may their name be erased, set-up concentration camps, the Poles imitated them and set up concentration camps as well. Near Horodets, in Kartozbreze, they set up the most horrible concentration camp to which they sent, without any reason, Jewish and Russian youth who never returned alive. They did not even send back their corpses except for a small box with ashes for which they charged quite a lot.

The Russian population near us was in a very bad situation because the Russian farmer had to pay a third of his yield to the Polish land-owner. It was not permitted to have Russian schools. The Russian-Provoslav cloister that stood in the center of the market place of Horodets, was turned into a Polish Catholic cloister and this the Russian farmers could not forgive.

[Ben-Ezra, the editor, remarks as follows:

"For historic accuracy it must be admitted that the big white cloister in the market place belonged at one time to the Polish church and the small wooden cloister in the Pritzisher alley near the uriadnik [police constable], belonged to the Provoslavs. After the *"miatezsh"* in 1863 [Polish uprising], the Russian regime confiscated the big cloister for the Provoslavs and gave the small cloister to the Poles who lived then in Horodets and the surroundings].

The Russian youth, in their despair, became more left-winged and formed an organization aiming to bring about the secession of our region from Poland, to return it to Russia and thus be united again with their motherland. This activity entailed a death penalty. Many young farmers, from the shtetles and villages, were hanged. From our shtetl Horodets they also hanged in 1936 the leader of the Horodetser gentile youth, near the Kobryner jail. Another youth, Nikolai Tshinik, the *feldsher's* [old-time surgeon-barber] nephew, was shot [and not hanged], as a favor, because he had served in the Polish army. That was the type of Polish clemency… and as for the very young, they put them in jail. Through all this, the Horodetser Jews lived and hoped – the youth were striving to go to the Land of Israel, brave and proud. They often gathered to have good time together, and even sang and danced. They loved their shtetl, their houses and land. They married among themselves; children were born, increased and procreated. The children were raised on the street, walked always barefoot but were always happy. Every day they ran to the autobus that would stop on the highway near the market, and with clever-curiosity and naïveté scanned the faces of the arriving and departing people. They ran to the Tzigelner forest and even sometimes stealthily entered the Land-owner's forest near a big orchard, where they were caught red-handed... Among themselves the Jews were like a big family: invited each other to a wedding, or just to a small celebration. All participated in a funeral or a calamity. They named each other by their occupation: David the blacksmith, Shepsl the carpenter, Shami the quilt-maker, Naphtali the cobbler/shoemaker, Shlomo the shopkeeper, and Yoel the *shoykhet*, etc,. The youth and children were called in connection to their elders: Khashke Zlatke's, Motl Khana-Lea's, Yankl Khayim-Nisl's, David Shami's, etc. They did not call each other by their family-names.

The spiritual nourishment of the Horodetser Jews was the *shtiebl* and the *besmedresh*. The *shtiebl* was in the "market" [market place] and the *besmedresh* was in the "gas" [main street]. The *shtiebl* in the market place was built by Itzik the mason, in his own house, and paid for with his own money – sent to him by his children in America. Being alone, without legs, but wishing not to be isolated in his house, and also being a scholar and understanding what the *shtiebl* meant to him and for all the folks in the market place, he kept building, renovating, enlarging, improving and embellishing the *shtiebl*. Itzik alone decided how the work should be done, and as his regular carpenter he kept Shlomo Berger (in the shtetl they named him: Shlomo Lieber's – after his father-in-law).

The *besmedresh* was on the main street on the same grounds where the old *besmedresh* stood and was burnt down during WW1. It was rebuilt with the money donated by American countrymen.

I see you always, my Horodetser brothers, coming out to accompany me as I departed for America. I always remember your last words of goodbye hoping we would meet each other again. These words stab my heart. Now I write with blood and I say *"Kadish"* [mourner's prayer] over all of you.

"Yis-gadal v'yis-kadash sh'mai-rabo"!

"The Community"

Standing from right to left: Berl Lakhovitski (Aharon-David's son) Motl Orlovski (Moshe-Eliyahu's son) Yaakov Nadritzni (Acraham Ezra's son), Gershon Lakhovitski (Aharon-David's son), Hershel Volinietz (Shmuel the carpenter's son), Shlomo Yarmetski (Yaakov-Meir the cobber's son)
Sitting from right to left: Berl Rikhter (Liakhover), Shniska Blatzky (the eldest of the community) and Yaakov Bergman (Yaakov the mason)

[The two words on the roof of the house are in Polish: "community office"]

[Pages 162-163]

Once there was

[A Lament]

By A. Varsha

Translated by Hannah Kadmon

[Translator's notes – in square brackets]

In my early youth, part of our big garden was supposed to become an orchard. A certain *porets* [gentile landowner] gave my father, the painter, a gift – 30 "stshepes" [a coin] rewarding him for my father's good and fine work in the porets' *pokoy* [estate]…

It was after the Holiday of Succoth. The garden beds lay faint, bare. Here and there some wild plants strove stubbornly to survive. The "titchkes" of the wrinkled string–beans shuddered in the cold and the yellow dry leaves, as if glued to the rod, were telling stories about a nice and blossoming day.

– "Tomorrow we will dig pits", announced our father in the house, "the agronomist will come for measurements. Therefore, gather all the trash that is strewn in the garden"…

Something new was going on in the street. Neighbors were gathering, watching the agronomist's every step and marveling at the tricks of measuring. Two gentiles in blue garments dug pits and threw in, one after the other, spades full of yellow gravel.

"Hey, people!", one of the diggers shouted: "galava!" (a head!). Everybody rushed to the pit with bewilderment. I started shivering from the cold despite the warmth of the noon–time sun.

"Throw out the head over here and continue to dig", the agronomist told the sweating digger. A skull with three holes fell on the yellow sand. The agronomist shook the sand with a cane and started speculating how old the skull could be.

The news about the human skull spread around the *shtetl*. People came to see the wonder. I felt quite exalted. Men pondered over it, shook their head sorrowfully – "God forbid!". Women stood and watched from afar.

Simkha Yudl, my father's friend, heard about the skull and that Shlomo the painter is planting an orchard. He then made a short visit to Mitzrayim [Egypt] alley to watch with his own eyes, so that he had news to carry from Antipolye to Horodets. Shmuel, son of Leibe Hersh, the chronicler of our city, told the amazed folks about the great wars hundreds of years ago. "Here is the proof: Look at the skeleton!" and he went on: "Here was once a very big city spread over 10 versts [1 Russian verst = 0.66 of a mile]. Horodets and Antipolye were one city which was called "Small Danzig".

Since then, I imagined in my childish fantasy a city which stretches 10 versts and the main street proceeds through the forest, cutting through Kodlin – all is one city. Then, Friday towards evening, Sabbath candles are lit and the lights flutter solemnly for 10 versts and the sound of the melody of "*Lekhu Neranena*" [words from Psalms] is carried from one *besmedresh* [the study house, where people used to pray as well] to another. That was pure imagination but it left me with a longing to see Horodets. Perhaps some sings of "Small Danzig" were to be found in the remains from the times that we were one city.

In the *kheyder* years, I met a boy from Horodets who came to study in Antipolye. His name was Menashe. Menashe told me about the river of Horodets, about two bridges, about ships and steamers. On "Tisha Be–av" [9th of Av= day of fast and mourning commemorating the destruction of the first and second Temple in Jerusalem] when we, children, were free from learning, three of us started on the way to see Horodets, the continuation of Antipolye. That was before they thought of constructing a highway. We, the three brave boys, walked with beating hearts, armed with sticks and stones, either to defend us from the gentile Pastukher ill–bred boys or from Strazshnik's hounds. We arrived safely in Horodets – tired and hungry. We saw the two bridges, the river and the "shloyze" [sluice–gate] and we were lucky to see a small streamer approaching from Kobryn side and the opening of the sluice–gate. Tubs were lazily moving from the west, telling of far away routs. We devoured these wonders. However, our stomachs demanded food. We, three 8–9 years old boys, looked at each other as if seeking each other's permission to eat something.

We returned to the marketplace. On the way back home from the marketplace to Antipolye, we came upon Efrayim Itzel. "Who are you, children? Where do you come from?"

"From Antipolye"

"Who are your parents? Have you eaten? You seem very tired"

We kept quiet. Eat on Tisha Be–Av?

"Come with me, you "rostatels" [a local endearment word?]. Do your mothers know that you are in Horodets?"

We became a little scared of the cross–examination, of the unfamiliar Jew with the black beard, and we kept quiet.

"Come, you should eat something and have the strength to go back home." He led us, three bare–footed guests, to his home and told his wife to offer us something to eat. She welcomed us with motherly warmth, got us a pitcher of milk, cut a slice of bread and poured the milk into mugs. We were delighted and satisfied our hunger.

Seven or eight years passed since my first visit in the quiet hospitable Horodets. When I became a workman, to me Horodets became a part of Antipolye. I worked in the yards of Rodets, Lipove, Balat, and I acquired a large group of acquaintances in Horodets. The 7 km between Antipolye and Horodets had shrinked. I saw, for a fact, that Shmuel Leibe, son of Hersh, was right. For me it was one city. It was just that some Jewish houses were missing along a certain stretch of land. On Sabbath we met in the wood, having fun and a fling as well as discussing political problems. Later, when WW1 broke out, I had a great deal of work in Kobryn, and I used to sneak into Horodets on quiet nights and during turbulent days. I knew almost all the construction–workers in Horodets. A Horodetser workman was a Jew who could study and be a first class expert, which calls to mind the Jews of old who probed over the written letters. Many of the workmen carried with them, to their places of work, a *Tales*–case in which they inserted *mishnayes* [collection of post–biblical laws; part of the Talmud]and *Ein Yaakov*[a compilation of all the legendary material in the Talmud together with commentaries] to leaf through after work. The younger generation set their heart on world affairs and revolutionary activities.

It was under the German occupation, in 1915, before Passover. They set up a forced labor unit in Antopolye including some farmers. The unit was out to repair the ragged highway. We came to Horodets and gathered the bricks from the burned down ruins. We loaded the bricks on a carriage and drove it to the highway to fill the gaping holes.

In one of the houses, not far from the bridge, in a corner of the marketplace, we removed the remnants of a baking–oven. Suddenly one of us, Noakh Rishes, uttered a cry: "A burnt Torah scroll!"

We all shuddered. A burnt Torah scroll, "My goodness, wow is to us" cried Noakh. The Germans guard looked strangely at Noach. Did he break a hand? What kind of commotion do they raise here?

Noakh did not let anybody move any more bricks from the basement or the heap where the Torah scroll was hidden. He went to look for Jews.

As soon as the news spread, grown–ups and children surrounded the place. *Khevre Kedi'she* [voluntary burial society] started working. Tenderly they pulled out pieces of scroll and lay them in an old *Tales* [striped tasseled shawl worn during prayer]. Women and men were weeping over the ill fate that had befallen Horodets.

Rabbi Hershel, an Antipoler, the blacksmith's son, very near–sighted, arrived wearing a long coat and shook with fever.

"We would carry the loss to the place where the synagogue once stood. We will carry the stretcher to that place and perform a *hesped* [a funeral oration]". From his near–sighted eyes and blond eyelashes tears were trickling down. However, they did not let us walk to the other side of the bridge. The German, curse him, disrupted the impressive funeral…

Now, when we commemorate Horodets and other thousands of communities – they did not even have the privilege to find even burnt scrolls.

Antipolye, Horodets, kindled stars in the Jewish sky – you have been extinguished forever…

With deep feelings of awe and a bent head I offer my broken lines, a brick to the spiritual monument to the Horodets of the past.

[Page 164]

My Shtetl

By Tzivia Greenglass

[Tzivia was my mother's first cousin. She was an ardent Zionist and lover of Hebrew. She spent the last years of her life In Israel.]

Translated by Hannah Kadmon

[Translator's notes – in square brackets]

Here, not so long ago – very far from here,
Beyond mountains and sea,
Beyond the land of the Hitlerites
Beyond rivers of Jewish tears
Not long ago, very far from here
Existed a small Jewish *shtetl*

The *shtetl*'s name was Horodets
And Jews were proud of her
Because it was so beautiful
In spite of its being small,
Fermenting with Jewish life
Seeking the Torah

God blessed my *shtetl*
People lived in it like a family
One's wedding was a celebration for all

The whole *shtetl* was dancing with pleasure
And when someone died – he was everybody's relative
The whole *shtetl* accompanied him to his burial

There was a river over there – a wonder
It provided livelihood
The river divided the *shtetl*
Into "marketplace" and "main street" – two equal parts.
A tall strong stone bridge connected the "street" with the "market".

The banks of that river
Were straight like strings
And the two *batchvenikes* [stretches of land along the banks*]
Who can forget them?
Built high, lined with abundance of trees
Stretching parallel to the river.

And green trees of all kinds,
Offered shade to the passers by
On one side, the *batchvenik*
Led to an iron bridge.
And if one strolled to the second side,
The *bathvenik* led him to the *shloiz* [sluice].

Rich and poor Jews
Poured to the river
On Sabbath after nap, this sweet
Bit of worldly pleasure to taste.
Ah, the two *batchvenikes*
Who can forget you?

My *shtetl* is now in mourning
Nobody walks in its direction
It has been erased
Its Jewish life wiped off
It will never arise again.
Say *Kadish*!, brothers-Jews.

*stems from a Russian word for the cable for towing rafts or boats. The two stretches of land on the river banks were used for towing and therefore were called *batchvenikes*.

[Pages 167-168]

Folklore

Folklore

by R' Akiva

Translated by Hannah Kadmon

[Since Akiva Ben-Ezra wrote many of the articles in the book of Horodetz, he sometimes signed using different names…It is him, all right…HK]

Folklore contains the research of legends, superstitions, customs and the practices of all kinds of talismans and cures.

In the folklore of a people we find the expression of their view of life, their attitude to life and death, their views of mobile and immobile property. The inspirations and enthusiasm of simple people are expressed in folklore. Poets, composers and painters draw from the well of folklore to create meaningful works of art for their people.

Every nation has it own folklore. Every nation adds from its flesh and blood to the legends and traditions. The Greek mythology about the creation of the world cannot be compared to the Jewish comprehension of the creation of the world. There is a huge difference in the folkloristic customs, for example, between the Arabs and German and in the way they are reflected in their two literatures.

True, many of the traditions and beliefs of all peoples are alike. Still, every nation paints them with its own colors and imprints its unique stamp upon them. In each ethnic group we find something that was learned from a foreign ethnic group with whom it came into contact.

Our Jewish nation, one of the oldest nations in the world, because of its political situation, had come in contact with many nations and ethnic groups and willingly or unwillingly had to be somewhat infected by the surrounding nations. However, the Jewish people digested what "stuck" to them and it came out almost as its own. They discarded many of the pagan superstitions and with the passing of time the belief crystallized, in one God, the creator of the world.

Still, foreign elements stole their way into the folkloristic treasure of the people of Israel. It is impossible for a people wandering from land to land, for close to two thousand years, to remain pure, free of foreign influence.

As it is with the gentiles, so it is with us Jews- we became interested in our own folklore. Also, various organizations were founded for this end. They undertook the task of researching the ancient Jewish folklore.

Before WW1 an organization was founded in Petersburg for this particular purpose. S. Ansky took an active part in this field of knowledge. After the war the movement spread and grew and Jewish intellectuals were more meticulous about compiling and preserving Jewish folklore, as the Jewish image started changing and its social structure started to crumble. Noach Prilutzki, blessed is his memory, did a lot to advance this endeavour during the years between WW1 and WW2; also Yehuda Elzet (Rabbi Y.L Zlatnik), may he live long, who collected and adapted that Jewish treasure. In those years the Yivo (Jewish scientific institute) also started publishing many important works dedicated to Jewish folklore.

Hebrew literature, too, began to be interested in Jewish folklore, and personalities such as Byalik, Druyanov, and others, published special books "Reshumot" (records) dedicated to this subject. Nowadays, special journals are published in Israel that deal with issues concerning Jewish folklore and its creations.

The research in Jewish folklore has become an integral part of Judaic Studies that exercises Jewish intellects all over the world.

Our Jewish shtetl Horodetz, which existed for many hundred of years, preserved in it many traditions and customs that exist no more. It also absorbed from the surroundings beliefs and superstitions, which evaporated. To do them justice, these specific Horodetzer customs, idioms, sayings, proverbs, witticisms, etc., should be listed so that the historian and the researcher will have more material for their work.

It is quite probable that in the material [from Horodets] placed before them, they will find items appearing in other shtetles and shtetlech. This is also worthwhile because it may shed light as to whether a saying, a witticism or a custom was widespread or mainly a local phenomenon.

May the following section be an additional brick in the structure called Jewish Folklore.

Here, I have thrown here together some words and expressions that are worth pondering and whose origins are worth researching. I hope that the researcher of the Yiddish language will find in my short article added material for his work.

[Page 168-169] [redensarten]

Sayings – Manners of Speech*

by R' Akiva

Translated by Hannah Kadmon

* These, in a certain sense, are based on local events. Since people wander, and especially Jews, sayings from one region were carried to another region, according to where Jews went or stayed. We often encounter these manners of speech, transferred into a modified version.
The same happens with witticisms and proverbs. Therefore, it is possible that some of the following sayings, used in another shtetl or region, infiltrated into our collection. We hope that the reader will surely forgive us.

[Translator's note: In square brackets - Ben-Ezra's own comments that appear, in the original, in footnotes. When it is my comment - I sign HK.]

1. About a very old thing you say: "*s'gedenkt shoyn melekh Savyesky's yorn*" - "One already reminds the years of King Savyesky" or : "*s'gedenkt shoyn Shveden*" – "One already recalls Sweden."
2. When one does not want to answer the question "*foon vanen kumstu*" - where are you from?" one answers: "*foon hatzenplatz*" – "from hatzenplatz" [a city in the Check Republic. Since it was very far, it acquired the meaning of a very far place.]

3. When one does not want to answer the question "*Voohin geystu*" - where are you going? one says: "*to Kandrikeve*" (an unknown place) or: "*Ikh gay in t..t groypen klyben*" - I am going in 'rear end' to sort barley
4. When a child wants something and his mother wants to shake free of him, she says: "*Vos zol ikh dir geben kalbebe mit Lakritz?*" – "what should I give you Kalbebe with Lakritz?" [names of medications] or: "*Martzipanes zol ikh dir geben?*" – "Marzipans should I give you?"
5. When the child wants "sak" (syrup) and his mother does not want to give him, she says: "*Ikh vell dir geben sak foon alten bok*" – "I will give you syrup from the old goat."
6. If the child asks something and the mother does not want to answer, she says "*kindrzoymen*" [zoymen= hem. probably meaning: holding on to the hem of her dress to detain her. HK]
7. When the mother-in-law supplies a good room-and-board to her son-in-law, she says: "I have "*gekekhelt oon gepregelt*" " I have 'cookied" and 'fried' him." (Bestowed on him baked and fried dishes)
8. "*Zi hot im getakhelt foon forent oon foon hinten*" "she fattened him in the front and in the back" (I guesses that the word *getakhelt* comes from the word "תאכל" = "eat!" in Hebrew)
9. When someone wants a small piece and one does not want to give him, the saying goes: "*Vilst a Shtikel ? – in shul*" meaning: Want a foreskin? – in the synagogue… [Based on a Horodets custom. Look up no.53 in "Customs")
10. When someone asks for a portion, the answer is, jokingly: "*Unter'n bod*" – "Under the bathhouse"
11. When someone puts too much pressure on the landlords, he gets this response: "*landlords! – to the bathhouse!*" [look up "Customs" no. 19.]
12. When someone did not make the grade in his studies people used to say about him: "*He will be a Rabbi in Kodlin*" [Kodlin was a village without any Jews]
13. When someone comes with his unwanted family they say about him: "*Er kumt mit zyn kadle*" - He comes with his *Kadle* [a slang Russian word for young delinquents. HK]
14. When someone asks; "*Tomer?*" (=What if, maybe?) he gets the answer: "*Tamar was a Yiddene* [=Jewish woman; also: talkative. HK]. *Zi iz shoin lang geshtorben*" =Tamar was a Jewess. She passed away a long time ago." [in the first book of the Bible - Breishit 38;6 HK]
15. When someone did not have luck it was said of him: "*punkt dritzen*" Exactly 13"!
16. When someone was not successful it was said of him: "*Es shikhevet im nit*" [the word "*shikhevet*" comes from the word "*shukh*" =shoe, meaning: He does not wear the right shoes. According to the Gemara, Masekhet Kidushin 49, when the husband is 'above' his wife, she says: Msana drav mikra'ai la ba'eina [I don't want a shoe that is bigger than my foot, and Rashi says: The shoe is too big for my foot. In English, when someone wants to be in a better situation, they say: "I want to be in his boots.]
17. [actually, in the book, no. 17 is missing. HK]
18. When someone is in a hurry to go home, he says: "*Tzu vos vel ikh hinien*" [the word "*hinien*" is a combination of "*ahin*" and "*aher*" =back and forth] = "What for do I go back and forth"
19. When someone feels bad he says: "*Vach iz meer, vind und vey iz tsumeer*" meaning: "Woe is me, alas and alack"
20. They said about a dishonest person: "He is a "*kisler*" (this is taken from the Hebrew word "Kis" =a pocket, meaning: he is a pickpocket.)
21. They called a gentile's father "*pakala*" and the mother: "*mamela*" [I wonder if the word should be *papala* and that there was some printing mistake…HK]
22. When someone said: "*Noo!*! (=an impatient word of urging; "come on") they would answer: "*make Hamotzi*" (say the blessing over the bread)
23. About a very clean dress: "*Es fakhelt*" = "It vibrates" .

[Pages 170-172]

The Yiddish Language

by A. Ben-Ezra

Translated by Hannah Kadmon

[In the first section, Ben-Ezra elaborates on the Polish and Russian influence over the diction, pronunciation and accent of the Horodetser Yiddish. My comments in square brackets. HK]

The Vocabulary

Yiddish was the mother-tongue of the Horodets Jews from the crib to the gave. True, when a child was three-four years old they wrapped him in a Talit [the striped tasseled shawl worn by Jews during prayer. HK] and took him to the Kheder, where he was taught another language, the holy tongue [Hebrew], but the Rabbi translated it into Yiddish. The same was true for the girls, who studied the Yiddish version of the first five books of the bible with [Teitsh Khumash] or the letter-writing manual.

Naturally, the studies of the holy tongue had its big effect on the Yiddish language and it absorbed many Hebrew words. Therefore, the Jewish child who started attending the Kheder, acquired a rich vocabulary of Hebrew. The element of *lshon Kodesh* [=holy tongue] was felt all around: in the house, in the street and in the market. When the grocer made notes, it was half Yiddish and half Hebrew. When someone who did not know Hebrew so well, wrote a letter to another, his letter was strewn with a good amount of Hebrew words and expressions.

The Gentile neighborhood also left an impact on the day to day language of the Jews of Horodetz. The Neighborhood was inhabited by Belorussians who spoke White Russian (khakhlatske). We cannot deny that Yiddish absorbed Polish elements. Horodetz belonged at one time to Poland and Poles settled in Horodetz and around it. That was before the *pavstanye* (Polish revolt) and after WW1.

Through Polish language, Latin, French and English elements stole in. Researcher of the Yiddish language pointed out a long time ago that certain expressions or words stemmed from English or Latin; for example "*davnen*" [=praying] stems from the word "divine". It came out odd when we used the expression "*kind oon keit* [=child and links"] for the English "Kith and kin", or "fix oon fartig [=done and ready]" from the English word "fix".

I want to dwell upon a number of words that were used in Horodetz unaware that they were either English or Latin.

While still in the Kheder, the kids heard already from the Rabbi: *"Vayashkef = oon er hot gelookt"* [he looked]. If the Rabbi was good he would take the children on **Stirdes** (=oxen) (from the word "Sturdy"). However, he did not like "a **vysen** (white) khevrenik" [= a mischievous child] and would tell him: "*Sik shoyn sik*! [=hiss]" (from the word "sik") The Rabbi would sometimes feel that "*taren di kishkes*" [his intestines were torn], (from the word "tear"), seeing that such an urchin was busy only with "*teibelekh oon verbliyes*" [= chicks and vertebra] ("warble"). At home you would hear such talk as: "*vos farsvaverste*" [=why force the issue] (from "force")?

The same happened to Israel-Moshe the cemetery-man. He was also the Shamash of the burial society. Once the society had celebrated the completion of *mishnayot* [=collection of postbiblical laws] and asked Israel-Moshe to invite people for the *hadran* [reading at end of the study of a tractate Talmud] ; but instead of *hadran* he called to invite the people to the *khandran*. From that day on they called him *khandran* or *khandranik*. This nickname was not reserved only for him but stuck to every ignorant person…

Forgive me Israel-Moshe. It should be credited to him that he was a quiet and honest Jew.

It also happened that they called someone according to his occupation. There was in Horodetz a Jew with the nickname **dvike**. Why? Because he was a milkman. It is well known that a milkman has to do with **dvinitzes** (=pails of milk) so they called him **dvike**…Why should they call that particular milkman by this name and not any other milkman? This remains a question…

There are persons with nicknames that cannot be explained. For example: Why was Yosl nicknamed *Bak*. Why? Elijah will solve the question… Therefore, other persons with a nickname were "lucky" to knew why and what for.

[Below is an interesting facsimile of an invoice for Khaya Feige [probably paid as there are two diagonal lines over it] and the written words are in Hebrew and Yiddish . On the right side are the K (kopek) and each line starts with the name of the day and then the names of the items bought and sometimes the name of another day in between. The numbers above the items may denote the price (?) or any other notation of the shopkeeper. HK]

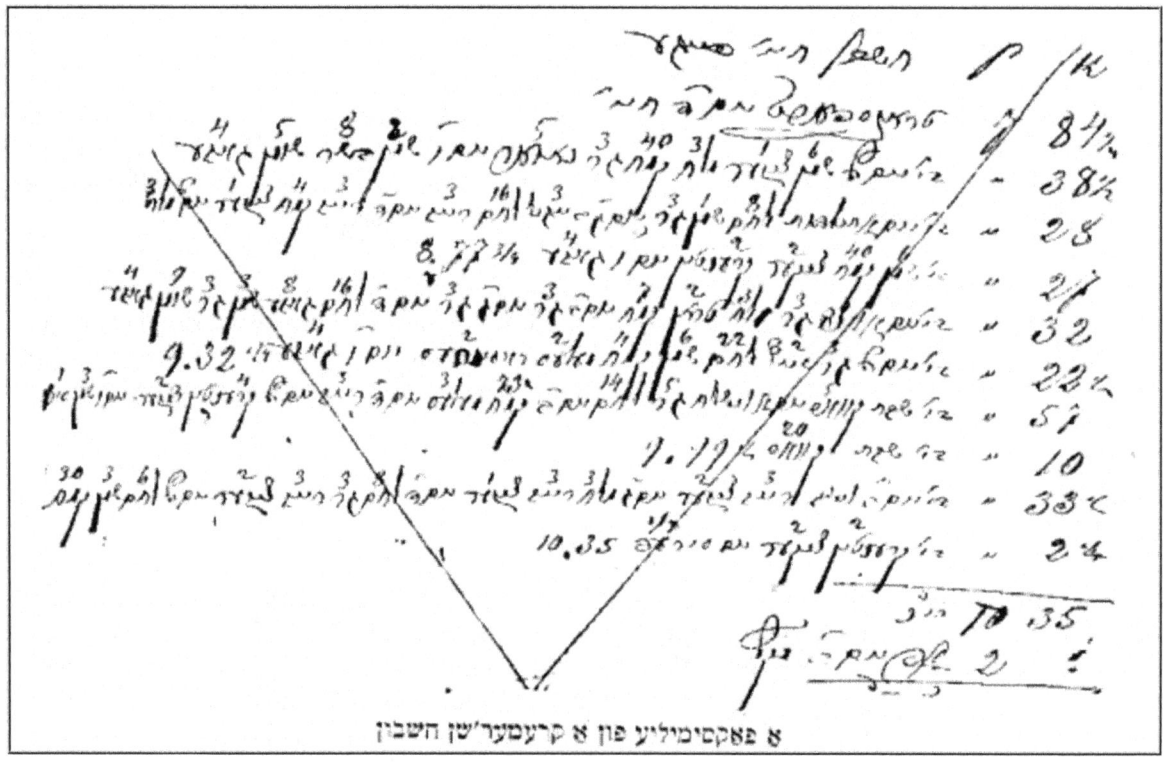

A facsimile of a shopkeeper's account statement

[Pages 172-176]

Customs*

by A. Ben-Ezra

Translated by Hannah Kadmon

* I have dwelt upon only those customs that as far as I know were more or less specific to Horodetz. I have also left out some Horodetz customs that were already mentioned occasionally in various articles in this book. **Translator's note:** My comments are in square brackets. The author's footnotes are in italics.

A. Eating and Drinking

Our Sages said that you can get to know a person by his drinking. (ערובין ס"ה). We can add that we can get to know an ethnic group by their drinking and eating. In the two tractates of the Talmud – דרך ארץ זוטא [small good manners] and דרך ארץ רבא [big good manners] there is a discussion of how a Jew should eat and drink, and in "שולחן ערוך" [the Jewish code of laws] there are a considerable amount of laws about foods – what is allowed and not allowed to eat. Besides the written laws there are those that are not written, those that the people had adopted, and through which we can learn about the way of life of this or that community. Horodetz was not different from Jewish people as a whole.

1. For Shavuot they baked hallahs in the form of the two Tables, to commemorate the ten commandments, that were handed down on Shavuot.
2. For Rosh Hashana they used to make the hallahs in the form of a bird, alluding to the verse: "As birds flying, so will the Lord of hosts defend Jerusalem" (Isaiah 31;5). God should protect us on the Day of Judgment like the birds protect their young chicks.
3. On Yom Kippur [Day of Atonement] they used to bake *hallah* in the form of a ladder, signifying that our prayers should rise up to the Heavens
4. For Sukkoth they used to bake a twisted hallah , alluding to the Lulav [palm branch], Hadas [myrtle branch] and Arava [Willow twigs] - twisted together.
5. For Hoshana Raba [the 7th day of the Sukkoth Holiday when every man's fate for the coming year is irrevocably sealed in Heaven.] they baked a "hand", alluding to "drawing" the good "lottery" ticket [God's good verdict]. Besides the various hallahs, marking the Holiday, there were also distinct dishes for each Holiday.
6. On the first day of Sukkoth they used to eat cabbage borsht [soup].
7. On the first day of Pessakh [Passover] they ate beets borsht, the beets having been preserved right after Purim. "As you prepare on the eve of Sabbath – so will you have food for Sabbath", says a Yiddish proverb. The Jew of Horodetz used to prepare his dishes, for every Holiday - a few months earlier.
8. Right after Sukkoth they used to make hard cheese to eat on Hannukah.
9. On Hannukah they fried goose fat for Pessakh. Naturally, while frying the fat they did not "lose the Bobe's inheritance" [a Yiddish proverb] because at the same time they enjoyed greatly the *gribenes* [well browned roasted bits of goose skin] and made potato pancakes fried in goose fat.
10. In summer they cooked raspberries to prepare for winter, in case you get a cold, hoping you won't need them…
11. They also used to cook or pickle berries - considered good for the stomach. The berries - either bought or picked - had their special week, the week of the Parshe of Korakh [section of the bible read on that week]. They had a reason: when Korakh sank into the earth, berries sprang up in that

place... [Bamidbar 26;10] [Korakh strove against Moshe and Aharon and against God and was punished]

12. Many Jews in Horodetz were careful not to eat tench [a fresh water fish] in the month of Tamuz, because in that particular month the mice disguise themselves as tench. Some admitted to have seen a tench with their own eyes in the granary... *Such a superstition circled around in Brest, the nearby city.*

13. On the eve of Rosh Khodesh Av [first of the month of Ab on which the Temple was destroyed], in the old days, they used to eat the last meaty meal before the "nine days" - in the synagogue yard. [The first nine days in the month of Ab, in which no meat or wine is consumed, an abstention expressing mourning for the last battles of Jerusalem prior to its destruction] *In other towns the "meaty supper" had another expression.*

14. After Shakhrit prayer [morning prayer] on the eve of Yom-Kippur, people used to walk to the cemetery, and on the way back they used to stop at a tent where they would share a lekakh [spongecake].

15. Lekakh was a distinguished refreshment in Jewish weddings. To that they added a herring.

16. For the *Vakhnakht* (=vigil night)(night preceding the circumcision), when they started studying the Zohar [the holiest mystical book of the Kabbalah], they would offer peas / chickpeas, candy. Other people would cook a krupnik made of buckwheat barley. *To judge by the looks of it - that poor meal was a result of the ban that entirely prohibited a meal at the vigil night. (Sate of Lita Rigstry, p.145)*

B. The whole year

19. Every second Friday, during the day, the bathhouse attendant, or his son, used to walk in the "Street" and in the "Market" and summon people to the bathhouse. This is what they called out: "House owners, house owners, come into the bathhouse"

20. Friday at dusk the Shamash [beadle] of the town would go with a box under his arm and everyone would throw in a candle so that there would be enough candles to light up the Beit-Hamidrash. When an out of town Khazan [cantor] with choirboys would come for a Sabbath, the choirboys would go around, before Friday evening, to collect alms.

22. In winter, at dawn, on Sabbath, they would knock on the windows for Tehilim: "Tehilim, Tehilim!" [*Psalms*]. (this was the job of Aharon Leib the house painter)

23. Every Rosh Khodesh [*beginning of the month*] the members of the voluntary burial society would fast and would assemble in the Beit-Hamidrash and would say Slikhot [=forgiveness. Prayer said during the days preceding the High Holidays and on fast days]. (such a custom was also common in other towns).

24. Very religious Men and Women would not sit down during prayers on Rosh Hashana and on Yom Kippur.

25. The morning after Yom Kippur, they used to pray very early so that the devil would not have a pretext, that for the Jews who had already prayed for a good year, the time of praying didn't matter anymore.

26. At Hoshana Raba [*the seventh day of Sukkot, when every man's fate for the coming year is irrevocable sealed in heaven*] the respectable house owners used to go out anad walk around the shtetle to collect alms for the needy.

27. Hanukkah night, the cantor walked from house to house with a lantern in hand, to get Hanukkah money. The Shamash of the town did the same.

28. Purim, the cantor used to send "Shalakh-Manes" [assortment of cakes, cookies, sweets on a tray or dish sent as a gift from one to the other] to the house owners, a hint that they should return Shalakh-Manes to him, bigger than what he sent them...

29. Purim, young and old used to collect alms for the poor, for getting a daughter married, and for other community matters. It seems that this custom is old and was common across countries. In the Netherlands they used to sing:

Purim means eating cookies,
And the poor people should not be forgotten
[it rhymes in Yiddish]

And in Poland they used to sing:

Purim means - giving to the poor
[*also rhymes in Yiddish*]

30. Shushan Purim, when the women were already free from sending and receiving Shalakh-Manes, they used to pay a visit to their family and good friends.
[the day following Purim – celebrated in commemoration of the day when the Jews of Shushan, the Persian capital, finally rested after defeating their enemies.]
31. The men used to go on Shushan Purim to dressmaking-stores to buy material for a *granitor* (garment) for Pessakh.
32. On the eve of Pessakh, whole families used to carry the cutlery and pots to the bathhouse to make them Kosher in the boiler.
33. They would carry the new dishes to the river to immerse them in the water.
34. At dusk, the eve of Pessakh, the shamash of the town would go from house to house to collect eggs for his own needs.
35. After that he would suspend the *big matze* in the anteroom of the synagogue.
36. *Khol-Hamoed* Pessakh [the intermediary weekdays between the first two and last days of the holiday] as well as *Khol-Hamoed* Sukkot, the teachers in Kheider were very busy with preparing the new "term". Therefore, the pupils were free from "Kheider" and would go to the railroad.
37. The grownups used to travel for visits.
38. Between Pessakh and Lag Baomer [spring holiday celebrated in outings 33rd day after Pessakh] certain Jews would stand with bare headed under the rain, believing that this was good for their health. Look up: אי״ש שו״ב, טעמי המנהגים, חלק שני דף מ״ד
39. Sfira time, [counting the 49 days between Pessakh and Shavuot], children would eat supper earlier and in the evening they were not permitted to go out to the street.
40. The eve of Shavuot [Holiday commemorating the giving of the Torah] the children were very busy cutting *Plisniak* and *Tsherat* (tall and thick grass grown in canals), or twigs of trees, to decorate the house with greenery.
41. The grown up girls would be absorbed in cutting from colored paper various forms, flowers and the Ten Commandments - to decorate the windows.
42. During the "three weeks" *["Between the Straits" cf "In Dire Straits" - a period of mourning commemorating the destruction of the first and second Jewish Temples. The Three Weeks start on the seventeenth day of the Jewish month of Tammuz]* the elderly used to go to the Beit-Hamidrash every half night to observe midnight. [*The custom of rising at midnight for study and prayer, in commemoration of the destruction of Jerusalem as practiced by the most pious*]

43. During those weeks – the elderly would sing in Beit-Hamidrash "Shomer Israel" [guardian of Israel] with the melody of "Elei Tzion" [towards Zion] (that was Moshe Mordekhai's assignment)
44. Also during those weeks they used to tie a red ribbon to the arm of a child.

45. During the "nine days" [nine days in the month of Av in which no meat or wine is consumed, an abstention expressing mourning for the last battles of Jerusalem prior to its destruction] they used to tie a piece of garlic to the child's shirt.
46. During the "nine days" they used to shampoo the kids' hair.
47. On the eve of first of the month Av, the slaughterers used to hide away their tools, because there was no more slaughtering until after Tisha Be-av [the ninth of Av the mouning day over the destruction of the Temples].
48. If the ninth of Av fell on Sabbath, the shamash would read out in Beit-Hamidrash on Friday night: "*Dvarim Shebetzina Noheg*" [– Sabbath and Weddings postpone the mourning]
49. On Tisha Be-av after Shakharit [morning prayer], people would walk over to the cemetery and on the way they would toss garlic.
50. Shabat Nakhamu [The **Sabbath** following the Ninth of Av is known as "Comfort ye" **Sabbath**] was a real Holiday. Some days before that Sabbath, they would already whitewash the ovens, scrub the candlesticks and prepare a new dress in honor of Sabbath.

C. General Customs

51. They would place the Khupa [canopy in the marriage ritual ceremony] in the synagogue-yard and mischievous boys would create firecrackers. One boy would fill his mouth with gasoline (oil) and a second boy would hold a lit candle. When the first boy sprayed the gasoline, a ball of fire sparked.
52. When a Bris [circumcision ceremony] was held in town, the Mohel [Circumciser] would come to the Beit-Hamidrash, stand by the synagogue lectern, and chant "*Ookhrot*" up to "*Yishtabakh*" [a specific prayer for this occasion], alternating with the audience. He would chant a part and the audience would respond. Even Asher, the circumciser, a Staliner Khassid, used to go every morning to the Beit-Hamidrash and chant by the lectern the above prayer. (Actually, it was a custom in other communities to sing "*Ookhrot*" in Beit-Hamidrash or in synagogue, only when a Bris was performed there. (see "אוצר התפילות" סידור or "דרך החיים")
53. They used to throw the foreskin into one of the boxes of sand placed in the synagogue to stick in the candles of Yom-Kippur. (a hint to this custom we find in (ילקוט שמעוני, יהושע, רמז ט"ו)
54. They used to send the town-Shamash to deliver the invitation to a Bris whoever they wanted to attend the Bris. They used to do the same with an invitation to a *Pidyon Haben* [Redemption of the Son - a ritual whereby a firstborn son is redeemed from priestly obligations from a Kohen]
55. For a wedding they used to send tickets through the Shamash.

D. Auspicious and Inauspicious Omens, Remedies, Mascots and Charms

56. A pregnant woman used to wear a shooting-star on her neck until the ninth month so that she would not abort…
57. They used to put a red band on a newborn's neck against *Ein Hore* [=the Evil Eye].
58. They used to tie a red band to the right arm of a woman in labor against the Evil Eye.
59. On all these events they would perform the rude gesture "*faigen*" [thumb enclosed by forefinger and third finger] as the guests were taking their leave.
60. For the *Vakhnakht* [vigil night preceding the circumcision] the circumciser used to put away his cutting knife under the pillow of the child until the Bris.
61. They would put on the infant's head, for the Bris, a red cap to which they sewed "Shir Hama'a lot" [Psalms 125] Others sewed it to the pillow on which the child's head rested.
    [A song of ascents:. When Adonai brought the exiles back to Zion it was like a dream. Then our mouths were filled with laughter and our tongues with song. Then was it said among the nations: "Adonai has done great things for them." Truly Adonai has done great things for us, and we rejoiced. Bring us from exile, Adonai, as the streams return to the Negev; those who sow in

tears shall reap in joy. Those who go weeping, bearing sacks of seeds, shall return with joy, bearing their sheaves]
62. Besides the "faigen" [the rude gesture] to counter the Evil Eye, another charm was: to take a bit of water with salt and wash the face.
63. Or, to put some salt in the shirt.
64. Or, to put some salt in the pocket.
65. When a child wore a new garment, they made him hold two "faigens" in the two pockets, so he would not hurt by the Evil Eye.
66. When a child came to visit for the first time, they would give him a piece of sugar. Others would give two eggs to a boy and one egg to a girl.
67. They used to dress an apprehensive child in cotton and a cotton garment until he was eighteen years old. They used to say that it was a mascot for long life: "*M'zol nit darfen onton leivent (shrouds) yunderheint*" [=Let him not need to wear the shrouds at a young age] (the Old Rabbi cites in his book "Misknot Yaakov" p.30, that cotton clothes are a mascot against a spell.)
68. Others would not let such a child wear new things until he was eight years old, but let him wear only used ones [donated by others]
69. Before moving into a new apartment, one should bring bread with salt, candle and sugar.
70. When they slaughtered a calf they used to immerse a string in its blood and tie it around the mother's neck so that she won't long for him.
71. They used to let the cow eat the heart of the calf with a piece of bread so that she would forget about the calf.
72. When buying a cow, you pour over it a bucket of water – a mascot to have the cow produce a great deal of milk like water.
73. Others say that it is a mascot against longing for the former home.
74. A cat – you invalidate/blemish it, (by cutting a piece of tail). In Virbaln,[90 Km from Kovno] They used to say that it was forbidden to keep a cat if it was not with some blemish, because your hair turn gray.(look up: Yiddishe Folklore Yivvo, Vilna 1938;p. 291)
75. A Kheider-child is forbidden to play with a cat, because it harms his learning.
76. Children are not permitted to eat a heart because it causes damage to their memory.
77. They are also not permitted to eat kidneys for the same reason.
78. When you sew up a garment while someone is wearing it, he should chew a thread a mascot against forgetting, mainly with regard to Kheider-children.
(see: 44. אי"ש שו"ב טעמי המנהגים חלק ב, ז)
79. A charm for children to have a good memory was for them to rub the forehead with the first snow.
80. Washing the face with the first snow is also good for causing the face to be whiter.
81. On the first evening of Khol Hamoed Pessakh they used to cook supper earlier – a mascot to be rapid the whole year.
82. A child is not permitted to go out through a window or through a grownup's legs. If he forgets he must go in through the window and, and go back through the person's legs .
83. A Keider-child is forbidden to shake his legs as when he does so it is as if he wants to rebuke his mother and father.
84. It is forbidden to whistle. A gentile whistles.
85. When one sees a bat flying, one must fan with something white and the bat will fall. (the same was said in Pinsk. (See: Yiddisher Folklore Yivvo, Vilna 1938;288)
86. In the evening it is dangerous to walk bare-headed, because of the risk that the bat will get entangled in the hair.(see also the former source)
87. The Bushan (stork) appears between the week of "Shmini" and the week of "Re'e" [Torah portions of the week]. The first person to see her flying - it is a sign for him that the coming summer he will be light on his feet. And if he sees her standing, he will be heavy on his feet…
88. When the sheep used to return from the pasture, the children would run through them so that they would be able to sleep well.

89. If the stork stands on one leg and taps with its beak, it is a sign that the barn will burn.
90. If the goose stands on one leg – there will be frost.
91. If the chicken drags herself in sand – there will be frost.
92. If the chicken dawdles – there will be thawing (the frost becomes soft and is very slippery)
93. In the month of Elul the cow carries grass in its mouth implying: "Now I have got grass and what will be to morrow – who knows?" It wishes that they will throw her a bit of hay…
94. If a person sneezes in the middle of telling something – it is a sign that the story is true.
95. When somebody sneezed, pious Jews used to say:" lishuatkha kiviti" [Genesis 49;18 "I have waited for thy salvation, O Lord"]
96. When someone yawns it is a sign of the Evil Eye. It is necessary to spit.
97. When someone has the hiccups – it means that someone is talking about the one who hiccups.
98. When the right ear rings – an enemy is talking. Others say that a letter would arrive.
99. When the left ear rings – a good friend is talking, or money is about to arrive.
100. When your buttocks get a bite – you will be counting money
101. When you have the chills it is forbidden to eat eggs, fish and herring. However, when the shivering subsides you should eat fish and herring.
102. A remedy for the chills is wearing a bathing cap.
103. For jaundice – to infuse lice [in the original: the "third plague"] into the omelet and eat up the omelet.
104. For scarlet fever – wear red bands.
105. For acne circle turn a ring around the acne wound three times. Then spit through the ring at the third pole in the street.
106. If you have lichen (skin disease)[some kind of fungi around the mouth] – get up very early, go to the window that is covered with dew, wipe out a bit of dew and put it on the lichen and then say the following:
    (In goyish) : Lishai, Lishai Ya tebe nie znayu skol prishla, Eedee sebia
    (In Yiddish translation: Hoit oisshlag, Hoit oisshlag, Ikh ken dir nit, funvanen du bist gekumen gai zikh. (translated by Chaya Pomerantz)
    (In English: Lichen, Lichen, I don't know you, go away to where you came from.]
107. If someone has a wart, it is good to make a small "rolling-pin", cut the wart and roll-smear the wart on it. Afterwards, throw out the rolling pin in the back of the street. He who will find the rolling pin will get the wart and the wart will disappear from the person who had it. If one does not have a rolling pin, one can use a pencil.
108. One can also get rid of a wart with the urine of a dog.
109. Smearing with the urine of the one who suffers is good to put an end to a cut, a stab, swelling, or to a piercing earache.
110. For a blister or abscess it is good to apply the feces of a cow.
111. It is good to apply saliva to a sore spot.
112. When they gave beddings to a bride, they put in coins in the pillow-cases or in the quilts – a charm for her to have good luck.
113. When celebrating a birthday, the mother pulls the ears of the child as many times as the years of his age – a charm for long life, so that his years will stretch.

[Page 177]

Nicknaming

by AB"A [=Akiva Ben-Ezra]

Translated by Hannah Kadmon

If there is a disagreement as to whether a name has a meaning, I think there is no dispute as to a nickname. Everybody agrees that a nickname says something, and often, more than something.

Already in the old days we find people with nicknames, like *Yerubaal* in the Bible [God gave Gideon this name *Judges 6;32*] , *Kalba Savua* in the Talmud and *Richard Lion-Heart* in the Middle Ages.

A nickname not only characterizes the person who bears this designation but also provides insight on the period or the surroundings, in which this person lived. A nickname reflects the spirit of the time and the level of culture in a specific epoch. From a nickname we can learn about the social structure of a specific generation. We can also become aware of the sharpness of mind and the outlook of the individual, or the public in general, that nicknamed him.

Almost every town or shtetl contained jokers who used to "crown" everyone with a nickname, when the person was still a child. If a stranger settled in the shtetl he was immediately given a nickname. If one of the strangers got married in the shtetl he received a nickname immediately under the canopy. Under this nickname the person then lived his life. Often, people did not even know the person's first name.

Some were so "fortunate" that their children and children's children were called by their father's or grandfather's nickname. Their nickname was so naturalized that they were not offended by it at all when they were called by their nickname. Others even felt "wronged" when they were not addressed by their nickname, as though they were not from the same shtetl…

Horodets was not an exception. In it, too, almost everyone had a nickname. You should understand that not all the nicknames seemed to make sense. Some were based on a deformity or character, such as *kolhaver* [talks to please] *horbater* [humpbacked] *stsherbate* jagged] *parkh* [canker/ "rat"]*kaliker* [cripple] *royter* [ruddy/red-head] *morza* [slob] *noz* [nose] etc, or based on their craft such as: shoemaker, tailor, peddler.

Besides, they called others by a father's or by a mother's name such as: *Berl Zavel's, Hashke Frume Hinde's*, or also by a wife's name such as *Khayim Rasel's*

Others had quite a special privilege. They were nicknamed to suit their spiritual status, as for example: *Yankl Chassid* – because he was a great Chassid, or *Itshe Malakh* [=angel] because when he was praying he was entirely stripped off his earthiness. Is, then, the nickname *"hoptshik"* Leib – ugly? Well, that Jew was a great Staliner Chassid and was fulfilling the mitzvah of being joyous.

Or take nicknames such as: *Moishe der groyser* and Moishe *der kleiner*. There were two shopkeepers, one opposite the other. They were both called Moishe. And how do you know which Moishe you mean? The people seized upon an idea: since one Moishe was tall and the other was short, they would name one- *Moishe der groyser* and the other – Moishe *der kleiner*.

The stature of a person had a weight in deciding on a nickname. How does this nickname come to be: *kohen gadol*? [gadol in Hebrew is: "big" and Kohen Gadol is the chief Kohen to preside over the Temple] Very simple: this Jew was a Kohen [of the family of Kohanim] and because of his high stature why shouldn't he be named *Kohen Gadol*? And by his name they also called his wife: *di kohen gadol'she*.

A similar situation was with someone of a small stature who was very agile and could ride a horse like a real "Kozak". They nicknamed him Moishe *Kozak* or in endearment: *Kozakl*.

The endearing suffix had often an additional taste. Adding a suffix "ke" or "le" to a name denoted more, such as fondness, affection.

It happened also that a nickname was given because of a specific situation or circumstance. There was in the shtetl a woman with the nickname of *Bashe di Yoven'te*.

Since her husband, right after their wedding was drafted as a Yoven (Russian soldier) – she was a *Yoven'te*. And thus she remained a *Yoven'te* even when her husband was not a soldier anymore.

Often, a nickname was given because of a quirk of pronunciation. For example: Aharon Leib'n, the house-painter, was nicknamed "*Shleye*" because his speech was very fast, and when he called his wife: "Sheine Leye!" it sounded as if he called out: "Shleye"…

[Pages 179-181]

Folk Medicine

by Dr. Y. Farber

Comments [*onmerkundgen*] by Akiva Ben Ezra

Translated by Hannah Kadmon

Translator's note: Akiva Ben-Ezra's comments appear in the Yiddish original book
under a separate heading on page 181: *Onmerkungen* = Comments.
I have inserted these comments in the text, in *italics,* in square brackets.
My comments appear in square brackets, not in italics.
Dr. Farber is the son of Shaye, mentioned in the article.

Russia is and was a big country. It owned many towns, big and small, Shtetlech and villages - quite countless. Russia did not have a sufficient amount of schools of medicine and doctors to cover the needs of such a huge country. Even in the bigger towns there were not enough doctors for the population. In the small Shtetlech and in the villages there were no doctors at all.

People were born, became sick, recovered, and in the end died, without the help of a doctor. However, it is not entirely correct to say that a shtetl such as Horodets managed entirely without medical care. No, on the contrary, it can be said that Horodets had an adequate amount, and even too many, doctors. Every Jewish community, no matter how small it was, had to have a doctor. This is a Jewish "law" and Jews observed that law. When God helped and the doctor was a specialist, it was fine and most welcome indeed.

It will perhaps not hurt to explain in some words what a *"doctor"* is. Here, in America, there is no such creature. A *"doctor"* had never studied medicine. He was merely infected with medicine. Usually he was a former soldier who happened to serve in a hospital and thus was acquainted with how the doctors conducted themselves. Later, the practice in the Shtetl made him wholly knowledgeable.

Horodets, naturally, always had a doctor. I remember two of them: Binyomin the doctor and his follower – Naphtali. That Naphtali was a character who rightly earned and deserved a separate write-up about him. (See the article "Naphtali the Doctor")

Besides the *doctor*, Horodets had it local specialists who devotedly served the population. We will list them in order.

Horodets had two midwives, or as they were called *"Bobbes"* [="grandmothers" but also "midwives"] – the bobbe Mindl and the bobbe Chaya Zlate. It is also interesting to know that the bobbe Chaya Zlate was the great grandmother of today's great opera singer – Jan Peers. However, then, fifty years back, the second midwife – bobbe Mindl- was, I think, of a higher standing. That, if you understand me, was due to the fact that bobbe Mindl came from the influencial Kostrinsky family. A child is born. Then he gets chicken-pox, measles and other childhood diseases. For that you needed a doctor. As for swollen *zavalkes* (tonsils) it was like this: in ordinary cases they used to put around the child's neck a woolen sock. However, in serious cases, it seemed to me that the *bobbe* Mindl used to press the tonsils with a spoon. [*The "bobbe" mindl used also to lead the sick patient to the chimney, put her finger in his mouth telling him to scream "oy", or to cough.*]

When something falls into your eye here in New York, you go into a pharmacy and you come out well. In Horodets, something could indeed fall into your eye. What? - A little sand was there, in Horodets. There were no paved streets and no tall walls to stop the wind. So, there was enough sand and the wind blew it directly into one's eye. What can, then, be done? Here is where Yitzkhak Aharon's was very useful. He was an expert in licking an eye. You can believe me. Yitzchak Aharon really licked the affected eye with his tongue.

There was no dentist in Horodets. However, a tooth may, and did, hurt in Horodets as well. A cheek may, and did, swell in Horodets, too. What does one do, then? Here the services of Asher Dovid were used. Asher Dovid was the ritual slaughterer and a *melamed* [=teacher in Kheider]. He talked-away a toothache. Yes, you can believe me. He talked away a toothache [=expelled/convinced it to go away]. [*In addition to the incantation he used to take a bit of salt, immerse it in whiskey and put it on the tooth. People also used to put garlic on the hurting tooth or wear the left shoe on the right foot against Jewish customs.*]

You would think that we have already taken care of everything - from cradle to the grave. No, this is not the whole story. A certain health condition was in the middle – neither healthy nor sick. Someone was not sick enough to call the doctor, but was not well enough either. Let us consider such a case: a child yawns and stretches himself. Ah, you start guessing. The mother knows immediately that the child has caught a "good eye". She means: "bad eye", but she counters it with calling it: "good eye", because of: *al tiphtakh pe lasatan* [=don't utter words-of-mouth to allow the devil in]. You see, here neither a <u>doctor</u> nor a <u>doctor</u> can help. Here you have to go to Shaye to have him spell a "good eye". [*In a previous generation, before that of Shaye, Miriam Visotzky daughter of Alter Yosil, used a spell to expel a "Bad eye", or a "roiz" [skin disease], etc. Also Rachel, daughter of Zavil, used to talk away a "bad eye". She used to take grains of barley, turn each grain nine times around the eye of the suffering victim. Also Yosef Leib the mason, Aharon Yosl and his brother Chayim Itzik's, used to practice incantation to expel "bad eye."*]

So, you go to Shaye, he recites a spell - a "good eye" - and the child recovers. He stops yawning and stretching himself, and *shalom al yisrael* [=there is peace over Israel.] It should be clarified that all the experts, enumerated above, such as Yitzchak Aharon, Asher Dovid and Shaye, did not get paid for their effort. They used to do it for the general good. The farmers from the surrounding villages did present Shaye with a bit of grains or potatoes, but he did not charge the locals.

It seems to me that now, when all the Jewish towns and shtetles with their peculiar life and traditions are destroyed forever, we can allow ourselves to dwell upon the striking phenomena such as pretence, exorcism, etc., It is interesting to find out how a Jew, Shaye, born in Horodets, whose parents and forefathers were born and died in Horodets, had become an exorcise and a complete *doctor* with great many followers. Well, since Shaye was my father, and he used to tell us, children, very often, how he had reached that status, I can relate it to you. So this is how the story goes: He had a *"parnose shtub"* [=was making a living at his home] – baking bread and beigel and later on also *holnikes*. His house was also a home-grocery-store. Nobody was standing ready to serve in the store. Only when someone came to buy barley, gauze, raisins, etc., they used to enter the store to sell. This is what happened one day: In a village not far from Horodets, a farmer's child got seriously sick. There was some swelling on his head. The farmer was what you called a *baal goof,* meaning a rich farmer. [=The original meaning of *baal goof* is a corpulent man] with a rich, vast great household. This farmer harnessed a couple of horses, took his wife and child and rode to Kobryn to seek a doctor. The Kobryner doctor gave up on the chance that the child would recover, and told the farmer to return straight home. On the way, they passed a court where the Pritz'te [=the landlady of the court] used also to practice a little medicine. She was pessimistic as well. They continued to travel home and when they drove through Horodets, they halted by Shaye's house to buy bread. The farmer left the wagon, in which his wife was sitting and crying aloud. Shaye, an inquisitive Jew, started questioning the farmer about the reason for her crying. The farmer told Shaye everything and Shaye comforted him: *"Bog Pomozshe"*, the meaning of which is "God will help", and accompanied the famrer to the wagon. He saw the child with the swelling. He noticed that in one place the swelling was softer and whiter than the rest of it. He comforted them further and out of his good heart he showed them the soft place in the swelling and said: "drive home in good health and you will see that by tonight this spot will have become loosened and the child will get well. He had some ointment in the house and he gave it to the farmer telling him to smear it on the soft place and wished them *"Bog Pomozshe"*. They drove away. Very soon Shaye forgot all about it. What was there to remember? Some weeks later, a wagon stopped at Shaye's house, full of bountiful things such as potatoes and grain. The same farmer carried it all, by himself, into the house, with thanks and praise. All had happened the way Shaye foretold them. It shows that he knew better than the doctors. Very swiftly the story spread in the neighborhood and farmers from the surrounding villages started coming with all kinds of diseases. What should be done now? The little grain, or the potatoes that they used to bring, could be put to good use as part of making a living. So, he started chanting a "good eye", and with an encouraging word such as *"Bog Pomozshe"* [=God will help] and the like, he accomplished for his patients more than the great professors. He did not become rich as a result, but considering the poverty of Horodets, with ten mouths to feed, that was a great help. Later he also sold quinine for malaria and scorched a *"roiz")*Erysipelas) [=a serious and infectious skin disease involving fever and pain] and the like. [*Rachel, daughter of Zavil, used to scorch a "roiz" with flax. A great expert in scorching a "roiz" was the Poritz Snishke of Rodetz (a village near Horodets). Yosef Leib, the mason, also used a spell on "roiz" and Lichen skin diseases.*] It also fell to Shaya's lot to have a newspaper write-up about him. This is how it happened:

There was a *"shkole"* (folk-school) Opposite Shaye's house. The teacher was then a tall gentile – Stiapa – the son of Maksim Sverdyuk. One day when Stiapa was standing by the school, he saw a wagon make its way to Shaye's house, with a sick woman lying helpless in it. Stiapa stopped the farmer and talked to him alone. Where from? Where to? The farmer answered that he was from Mekhvedevitch and because his wife was very sick he had driven to Shaye's. Stiapa asked further: If your wife is sick why don't you drive to Kobryn to see a doctor? The farmer answered thus: *"Shtsho doctori znayut? Doktori nitche nie znayot, Shaye znaye"* which means: "what do the doctors know? The doctors know nothing. Shaye knows." Stiapa wrote down all that and mailed it to Petersburgh, to a newspaper called "Birzshevye Vedomosti". The newspaper printed it as a human-interest story. One day the janitor comes in and calls my father to the administration office. The people who gathered there were: the *ispravnik* [=chief of Russian police] of Kobryn, the *pristav* [=assessor] from Antipole and the intellectuals of Horodets, such as the post-master, etc. The prominent men wanted to see the Horodetser Jew about whom they wrote in the newspaper. Maybe a year later my father happened to be in Prujine to visit his mother-in-law. In Beit Hamidrash he became acquainted with a Jew who told him that he was not a Prujiner and that he had already been dragging on, from far, for a long time. He had a sick child and he had already been everywhere with the child and could nowhere get help. Now he was going with the child to Horodets, because he read in the newspaper that a Jew by the name of Shaye was living in Horodets, and was helping everybody. It did not help my father when he told the man that he was actually from Horodets, knew the Jew Shaye and that Shaye not only could not do anything but also never claimed that he could. It didn't help. This man had already travelled so far and he would travel further. In short, father had to admit that he himself was Shaye and as long as he stayed in Prujine he would go to see the child. Did he help that child? – I don't know.

To conclude – a few words should be said about medicine in Horodets. As mentioned above, there were no pharmacies in Horodets. They used folk medicine. For Malaria they took quinine and for belly-ache they took castor oil. I seem to remember that children used to get *"verim-kroit"* [a certain vegetable considered efficient against worms in the digestive system], every first of the month. A sick person would eat a piece of chicken and a little chicken broth. When one cut one's finger, they used to cover the cut with spider-webs. If the cut was deep, they treated it with a cactus which they got from a Gentile. You would not expect that a Horodetser Jews would grow a cactus, would you?

Preserves also served as medications. What preserves? It depended on the sickness. For a light transitional sickness, a "good eye" [=meaning, actually, an evil eye], raspberry syrup would suffice. For a more serious sickness, such as measles, it was necessary to take cherry syrup. Berries-syrup was most seriously regarded. This does not mean that every Horodetser Jew was obliged to have, or actually had, all kinds of preserves and jams. Tut, pooh, nonsense! They managed. They already knew who had what. About the preserves one should understand it more in depth. You would not say or even think that Horodetser housewives all of a sudden would recruit themselves to cook various kinds of preserves. What's the matter? What is there to celebrate? Didn't they have any other things to take care of? Had they already taken care of everything? For the gown-up girls had they already prepared a nice dowry, for the smaller children had they already provide dresses, shoes, outfits and coats for winter? so why then? Had they already paid tuition fee, and stacked hatched wood in the stable? Is a filet of duck and potatoes all prepared? Is nothing missing but cooking all kinds of jams to have something to go with the Sabbath tea after the midday sleep? I am telling you that if in Horodets one could find such a Jew who had all the above mentioned things and his straw roof was not leaking, even such a Jew would be ashamed to deal with these worldly pleasures. You see, when it is, however, a question of medicine, the matter is entirely different. There is no shame, and every housewife cooks whatever she can and indeed in public. The neighbors come in for a visit, taste and relish themselves: "oh, what a pleasure, Freyde Rive, may we never need it. May we live to see next year and cook again preserves". Chayim Itzik's supervised over the cooking of preserves to see that each of the housewives fulfilled her duty according to her ability. Now, so that they *m'zol nit badarfen* [=would hopefully not need it], he proceeded to take care of the needy. [*In the nearest town Prujani there was an old regulation that the Gabai of "Bikur Kholim"* [=Jewish house-call service for the sick] *should always have reviving preserves at hand. (See registry of the town Prujani)*

This is how Jews lived, became sick, recovered and died in Horodets.

[Page 181]

Remedies and Medications

by Yudl Kaplansky

Translated by Hannah Kadmon

Translator's note: My comments are in square brackets. When there is a comment by Ben-Ezra, it is in *italics*.

My father, Aharon Itche, son of Leizer, rest in peace, was a peddler around the villages. He used to pack his bag with merchandise and set out on the road. He would reach quite far. His clients did not include only farmers. Poritzes [=big Gentile landowners] would also buy from him. Thanks to these dignified buyers, my father brought all kinds of medications that circulated in Horodetz and they were indeed referred to as "Malinke" [=a small child in Russian] [*this name is suitable because the dried raspberries would be hidden and used only when catching a cold.*). [The Yiddish word for raspberries is *malinyes*[

My father used to bring home certain herbs (*Korenyes*) that Moshke Lea used to actually snatch and soak then in whiskey as medication for toothache. (I don't know how long its impact lasted, but it is a fact that it was used as a remedy).

Rumianik [=camomile] and dried *yagedes* [=dried berries] were used to cause one to sweat when he had a cold. It took some months for some women to get hold of the medications mentioned above, because not always was my father able to get them. And I forgot the highlight: the year-old wax. Moshke Lea, my aunt Chaya and also aunt Feigl and old Henye used to say that the year-old wax heals all disease, God forbid, only it was necessary to know how to prepare. This sort of wax was taken from young bees. A skilled hand was needed for this type of work. The young bees had to be separated from the old ones and to prepare for them their food for winter. Professionalism was needed, which only the Poritz's gardener could exhibit. My father used to bring home this wonder-wax from Viloysk, from the Poritz Shement. Chaya Zlate and Mindl, The two bobbes of the shtetl, would come to get this wax. So did my aunt Feigl. This *mitzvah* was divided into equal parts. My mother insisted that she should get an equal part in this *mitzvah* and she indeed got it, because she helped in separating the wax from the honey.

My father used to bring home, from his travels, dried raspberries. This was a medication for a juvenile pneumonia. I remember quite well the special bag where my dear mother used to keep the medications.

[Pages 182-184]

Two Bobbes

by A. Kostrinsky [=Akiva Ben-Ezra]

Translated by Hannah Kadmon

Translator's notes: *Bobbe in Yiddish has two meanings: a grandmother and a midwife.*

When a Horodetser child was studying the *Khumash* about the two "bobbes", Shifra and Pua, who saved the Jewish children in Egypt – he did not have to use his fantasy to imagine them. He had seen them with his own eyes. In Horodetz there were two "bobbes" from years back, who delivered children from their Jewish mothers, or from a gentile woman in confinement when she had a difficult labor.

This profession of being a "bobbe" was inherited; from mother to daughter or to a sister. The bobbe was, in a way, also a lady-in-waiting for the mothers until after the *bris*. From the old "bobbes" I remember Sirke, Chayim-Leib's mother. Sirke taught her profession to her sister Chaya-Zlate, and after Sirke's death, Chaya-Zlate practiced the same profession.

The Bobbe Mindl

The Bobbe Chaya Zlate

About Chaya Zlate, we will talk a bit later. Now we will come back to the second "bobbe" - the "bobbe" Felte Machle – or it would be more correct to say – to the first, because she was wife of Itzik Chayim's, a prominent land-lord in addition to his being an important *mohel* [=circumciser] for free. He used to carry his humanitarian-religious mission without pay, just for the doing of *Mitzvah*.

The "bobbe" Felte Machle passed her profession to her eldest daughter Mindl, and for decades delivered children of Jewish mothers, and almost the whole shtetl were her "Children". When a child became sick, they called for the "bobbe" Mindl. She already had her own medications and remedies and did what was necessary and with God's help the child recovered.

The "bobbe" Mindl did not wait for a child to become sick. She preferred to prevent rather than cure. When hearing that, God forbid, Scarlet Fever was spreading in the gentile street, she would bring a red band, put it around the child's neck or sew garlic in a small sack and hang it around his neck. When the old Rabbi passed away, she brought her "children" pieces from the Rabbi's shrouds as a charm for long life (as you know the Rabbi passed away at the age of almost 100 years.)

The "bobbe" Mindl, a short old Jewish woman, was always occupied, always. Even when she did not attend a woman at birth she would run around quickly, never having any free time. Don't forget that she had quite a number of children and grandchildren spread in Russia and America. She had to write letters to her daughter in Yekaterinoslav, send a receipt for money that her daughter and grandchildren had sent her from Amerika (monthly), and she could not write by herself. So she would ask someone to write a letter for her, and another day she would ask somebody else. And when the "bobbe" Mindl asked - one had to fulfill her request. After all, you are one of her "children". And she did not let off. She walked, or rather ran, several times to a person until her letter was written. Then, she would ask another person to help her change the beddings. She was an old woman and did not have the strength to peal off the covers of all the quilts and pillows that lay on her bed like a pile of hay. Her cubicle was tidy and clean. On the table, on the walls, hang photos of her children and grandchildren in America, and on their weddings - with their brides. The "bobbe" Mindl had a good memory. She remembered all of them by their names, how old they were, what they were doing, and the amounts of money each of them sent her. "May they be healthy and strong and God, praise his name, will give me long years" – that is how she concluded telling about each child separately. "Blessed be God's name" was a phrase that she always used, and with God's help she delivered children. In truth, she used other means: She ordered the woman who was in labor to hit the pan with a grinder, and say: "there, there, get out, baby" or she would tell the woman to hit with her hand on the wall and she would in the meantime say: "hit, daughter, with the hand against the wall – you will be helped".

When the "bobbe" Mindl says: "give strength" [=push] – that is when the delivery is starting. Very rarely is it necessary to call for the Polish doctor Tshekhatshinski from Antipole. The "bobbe" Mindl used to say that Tshekhatshinski had said: "If the "bobbe" Mindl is there, they don't need me"…

And when God, blessed be his name, helped and a son was born, there was a double joy in the house: the parents were overjoyed, and also the "bobbe" was pleased. In addition to the weekly Rubel to ten Gulden that she usually got, it was possible also to put a dish at the *bris*, into which the participants would throw two or three Kopeiks – which added another Rubel or Ten Gulden. The sign that the "bobbe" Mindl was pleased was that she opened up her box of tobacco – whiffed the tobacco and everything was fine, and thanks to God, blessed be his name.

In addition to her sideline income, the "bobbe" Mindl had a yearly income. The housewives used to send her *shalakh Mones* [=the ritual sending of baked and prepared sweets on Purim] and besides the sponge-cake, candies and other good things, they would put in the dish some Guldens for the "bobbes". However, after all the good fortunes, the "bobbe" was quite poor - especially the "bobbe" Mindl who was a widow. Thanks to her children in America she managed in her very old age, and after Yom Kippur 1915 she died, her memory be blessed.

The "bobbe" Chaya-Zlate was Sender the *melamed* [=teacher in Kheider]'s wife. In her case, her profession was a sideline income, while her chief income was drawn from teaching. Chaya-Zlate used to say that Kindler, the Kobryner gynecologist said of her that she was a great expert and people could rely on her. However, she was not as popular as the "bobbe" Mindl. Possibly, because the "bobbe" Mindl's family had many branches in Horodetz and her clientele was bigger.

Chaya-Zlate possessed a natural humor. Many wives preferred her because when they were in labor, she used to tell jokes and humoristic episodes, and though the wife was in great pain, she would still laugh through her pains.

In addition to these psychological means, Chaya-Zlate used to give the woman in labor a bottle and tell her to blow into it. And, when it was a difficult labor, they tied a long rope from the woman- in-labor's to *aron-kodesh* [= the ark of the synagogue] so that she herself would open the ark and God, master of the world, would open the gate of mercy and help her.

When God up high had already helped and a son was born, the "bobbes" were very busy. Every evening the children from the *kheider* would come to read *kreeat Shma* [= the words of the prayer that is also said upon going to bed are: "Hear of Israel, our God is the only God". This prayer is said on the eve of a male baby's circumcision, involving also school children]. The Bobbes had to cook chickpeas and give the children handfuls of the peas. On that week's night they also had to give candies in the form of goatees, and for Friday night they had to cook chickpeas with beans for a male child. Why beans? - Because the acronyms of the word beans [in Yiddish *b*ab] spelled: *"Baruch Ata Bvoakha"* [Blessed are you in your coming]. And soon came time for the *bris*. The "bobbes" didn't know what to do: who would they recommend to be the *mohel* [=circumciser]. True, they would like to get a nice coin from the *mohel* when they mediate between him and the *bris*, but for a *Mitzva*h you do not charge money.

When a girl was born there was also a lot of work. On the Sabbath day, women would come to congratulate *"mazel tov"*. That meant that they had to prepare sponge cakes. So, there was never a dull moment – there was always work to be done. However, thanks to the master of the world that things were back to normal, we can say *"mazel tov,* may you live to ring up them the new-born to *torah,* [=learning], *khupa* [=wedding] and *maasim tovim* [=good deeds]".

And son and daughter grew up to become God fearing Jews.

[Page 185]

Legends

On a stick

by M. Timoner

Translated by Hannah Kadmon

[Translator's notes - in square brackets]

The Russian mythology is full of "*skazes*" (tales) about the "*baba yaga*" who arrives on a stick by a short cut. It seems that those legends left an imprint on the Jewish fantasy and little by little they infiltrated Jewish life and many Jewish folk-legends adopted the magic stick in tales of legendary persons who were travelling.

This "riding on a stick" found its way into the treasure of Jewish proverbs. When one Jew asks another Jew: "How will you arrive?" the second Jew answers: "On a stick".

The tale that I am about to tell has in it, too, the "stick" element but the stick has been given a Jewish character, almost unnoticeable but intelligible.

And how does a stick-legend reach Horodets? Who was the happy or unhappy person who arrived on a stick? And who was the miracle-worker who performed the magic? And who benefitted from that?

I see her in front of my eyes: a big fat woman with a small kerchief on her head and a big shawl on her shoulders. She had several under-skirts, each showing from under the other, which made her look like a barrel. Her eyes were full of grief and her mouth did not stop cursing.

She scared us, children, to death. Once we teased her, which made her curse us for several minutes and therefore we called her all kind of names. In *shtetl* they called her "Fat Hannah". When children cried, refusing to go to bed, they were threatened with "Fat Hannah".

When I grew up I asked my grandmother out of curiosity: "Who is Hannah and why is she wicked". She told me this legend:

Hannah was a member of the very aristocratic family Mazursky. She was a very fine girl and was married very young to a young man from Pinsk. She gave birth to a son and lived happy like most of the families in Horodets. Her husband left for some business and disappeared into the wild blue yonder. They looked for him in all the surrounding towns, turned to the Rabbis of the neighboring communities to look for this person - but all in vain.

Several years passed and Hannah remained an abandoned wife [cannot re-marry without getting a divorce]. It so happened that the Karliner Rabbi R' Aharon (the grandfather) came to Horodets to visit his Hassidim for the High Holidays. Hannah's Hassidic relatives convinced Hannah to appeal to the Rabbi. Hannah dropped by the Rabbi to ask him to help her. The Rabbi listened to her, thought it over and said: "He will soon come and you must divorce him without questioning him or complaining to him".

A few months later, on a wintery Friday, Hannah's husband appeared all of a sudden in *shtetl*. The news of the miracle circulated around and everybody came to see Hannah's husband who arrived "on a stick". Some said that they saw with their own eyes how he went into Moshe's shop to buy a package of tobacco and others said that they even saw his shrouds under his coat.

Meanwhile, Hannah's relatives gathered and decided that it was better to reach domestic peace and get together for that purpose. In the house there was much noise and clamor, arguments and quarrels. Suddenly, they looked around and the bird had flown. The person vanished into thin air. The young men and also the police officer rode on horseback in all directions to trace the runaway and detain him. However they did not succeed. He disappeared and sank from view…

Hannah and her relatives travelled to the Karliner Rabbi for advice and for mercy. The Rabbi felt compassion for Hannah but could not do a thing and said: "A miracle occurs only once".

So Hannah remained abandoned all her life, mournful, depressed and angry and the whole world, and for many years people kept telling how Fat Hannah's husband arrived on a stick"

[Page 186]

Motl the Jew

by Itshke

Translated by Hannah Kadmon

[Translator's notes - in square brackets]

When I say Motl the Jew you may think, probably, that there was also a gentile Motl in Horodets. Otherwise, why do I have to call Motl "The Jew"? Nonsense, there was no gentile by the name of Motl in Horodets. The name "The Jew" simply stuck to Motl and it really suited him. He was a tall handsome man with a long white beard, two sad and clever eyes and a sad smile. Actually, motl was not really a Horodetser. I don't know where he came from. This is how it happened: when Shmuel *Kaliker* [the crippled], the sage of Horodets died, his widow, Gutl, was left with a fine house, a nice sum of money and a flour-store. The community brought this Motl "the Jew" from somewhere to marry the widow. This is how Motl became a Horodetser *balebos*. [*pl: balebatim*; proprietor, house-owner, landlord. It has the connotation of a man of means].

I don't know whether Motl could study. Probably not, because if one can study - one studies. I never saw Motl sit down with a book.

To balance, Motl was a talkative man. He talked and talked with no end and with no stop. Not only we, children, but even older *balebatim* could not comprehend where Motle got so many things to talk about. Here, consider this: Let us take a winter day. Evening falls quite early. People finish praying *Mayrev* [evening prayer] and eat dinner. What do they do then? There was no theatre in Horodets, or a movie house. Motl the Jew would not sit down to play cards. There is no sense in sitting idly and wasting kerosene. So, one goes to sleep early. How long can a person such as Motl sleep? Six hours. All right, seven hours or full eight hours. So you reach two or three o'clock a.m. And indeed, Motl arrived in the *besmedresh* [the study house, where people used to pray as well] around 3 a.m. He did not put on the light. What does he need light for if he knows everything by heart? He walks back and forth by the eastern wall, waving his fists and praying on and on without stopping. It is already morning. *Balebatim* are arriving in the *besmedresh* and pray with the first *minyen* [ten men for the prayer] and go back home. Motl, however, is still moving back and forth next to the eastern wall and keeps reciting and waving his fists. This goes on until the horrible "incident" about which I am going to tell you.

Yudl the *melamed* [teacher in Kheyder] had at that time a *kheyder* [traditional Jewish religious school] full of boys: crème de la crème. Each pupil - studious, quiet and fine. They used to say in the *shtetl* that those kids wish to cut above the local population. It cannot be claimed that they did not fulfill this wish. One of those kids is now the highly respected Rabbi of Brooklyn – Dr. Y Bosniak…

The greatest ambition of the boys was to grow up and catch up with the Yeshiva students. Someone told them that Yeshiva students sit *meshamrim* so they started to sit *meshamrim* as well. If you do not know what a *meshamer* is, I will explain what it means. A *meshamer* means that once a week you sit and study the whole night. Don't ask me: "why young children should sit and study the whole night? Is the whole day and evening not enough?" Don't ask me such difficult questions. Different times, different songs and different ideas. In short, Thursday night they used to study the whole night. As a matter of fact, that was not so terrible. The schedule at night was as follows: until 8 or 9 they went home to eat something, got bags full of potatoes and returned to the *besmedresh*. The oven was lit, it was warm and they used to sit around the oven. They studied a bit and afterwards they used do tell each other all kinds of tales. Then they baked the potatoes in the oven, ate the roast potatoes, study a bit, then lay on the bench to nap for a while. That nap was important in itself. Lying on the hard bench and propping up the head with a fist was behaving almost like a real Yeshiva student. They could not sleep like that for long. It was hard and cold. One boy would then wake up the others and they would study a bit more till after the praying of the first *minyen.* Then they would go home and arrive usually around the time when their mother was baking the *khale* [twisted white bread]. Also usually the *toygakhtz=teygekhtz* [in my family it was ground potatoes browned in oil in a pan] was also ready by the early Friday morning. The *meshamer* boy naturally got the largest part of the *toygakhtz* and the other children did not even dare protest. It is not a trifle – he has just arrived from the *mishmer* [literally: night of non sleep]! Altogether, not a bad deal.

And now to the bitter event.

I remember the event as though it occurred yesterday. It was between Purim and Passover. People had already baked the matzo in the tailor's shops [probably because of the tool that perforates…]. The snow had melted in part and the wind was already a pre-spring wind. That particular Thursday night we sat for the *mishmer* and as usual at 2 or 3 o'clock we were already sound asleep on the bench.

Motl the Jew, as usual, arrived in the *besmedresh* without lighting the lamp and started "reciting". As usual he marched back and forth near the eastern wall. However, something was not as usual in the *besmedresh*. There was a feeling of unrest around him. Was it a creak of a bench or did a stand fall down. He kept on looking around but did not notice anything. He continued his reciting. Then he saw suddenly a figure advancing towards him. If he were a Horodetser he would have recognized the boy in the dark. Being a stranger and in the dark, he was convinced that it must be a ghost. Motl had the right cure again a ghost. He started immediately reciting *"shma Israel"*. ["Hear o' Israel, our God is the only God".] The small "ghost" did not disappear. On the contrary, from all corners of the *besmedresh* figures of "ghosts" moved forward. Motl could not stand it and started running out of the *besmedresh* along the street shouting *"shma Israel,* help! People, save me!" People crowded immediately and when Motl saw people, he fainted. A few strong people lifted him on their shoulders and carried him home. They attempted to revive him but he fainted again and again. What can I tell you? Motl was never again the same as before. He shriveled, did not come any more at dawn to the *besmedresh*, his smile became sad and his beard whiter. He believed till his death that he had a terrible encounter with real ghosts.

[Page 187]

Ghosts

by A. Elman

Translated by Hannah Kadmon

[Translator's notes - in square brackets]

a. The river

[This is a legend]

The river of Horodets could not be dug [in order to divert it]. The folks promised the river that every year they would offer it [offer a "sacrifice"] a man. It was really so. It is said that every year a gentile drowned in the "nine days". [This is a name given to the days in between the first of the month of Av and 9th of Av]

When the gentiles noticed it, they stopped bathing [in the river] during the nine days.

b. The dead read the Torah.

Once a Jew passed by the synagogue, after midnight. He heard people reading the Torah, and they called him to read too. He went in, said the blessings for reading the Torah. After he finished reading he walked home but he did not look back. If he did, he would not have come out alive…

[Page 188]

Folk Songs

Dark, Slippery, Late at Night

Translated by Hannah Kadmon

[Translator's notes - in square brackets]

(Editor Ben-Ezra comments: We print this song because of the specific version that circulated in Horodets. The song appears in various versions. Look up "Yiddisher Folk songs in Russia" by Ginsburg Marek No.234 p. 189 Peterburgh 1901; Rosental "Folk Songs" in *rashumot b,* page 369; "Yiddisher Folklore" p.39 Vilna 1938 where the notes are also presented p. 335.)

[It is difficult to translate poems/songs and when a line is not clear to me I make a suggestion.]

Dark, slippery late at night
Walks a girl deep in thought
There is no person to be seen in the street
And her heart is broken from crying.

She walks so that no one will disrupt her
And sings a song about herself:
If you, people, hear my song
You will know what has happened to me.

I press my child to my heart,
My tears drench your body
May God send an angel to you, my child,
To rescue you from the depth of the forest

May good people find you
They will show mercy for you
And you, my child, will behave towards them earnestly
Because my lot is not better than yours.

You will not know your real father
And you will not see your mother anymore
I wish I did not know him as well
And behaved like all the other girls.

I promised myself to your father
And he gave me his right hand
I wish, too, I did not know him
And would not have ended up with this disgrace.

[Page 188]

The Song of the Workman

Translated by Hannah Kadmon

(Editor Ben-Ezra's comments: I found this particular song on the last page of Sheike's store-notebook. It seems that it was written there by his daughter Sarah…)

[to me there are vague parts in this poem/song but I tried my best]

Who suffers more than the workman for his bread
He must work until his last day.
Who suffers chill and hardship as much as the workman.
Oh, who lacks the piece of dry bread,
Who will be arrested
And who will be shipped to Siberia?

And now I am forced to part from my wife
Men with the right mind, watch how they have arrested me,
And I still have no idea what my sin is.
And now I must part from my wife and child.

My child asks me: "Where are you going now, father"?
I have soaked him with tears,
My heart is grieving;

My child, you probably wonder why I sit so sad?
This thought is not without reason. [there is a reason for my sadness]
Your mother is crying:
They have brought her a letter
That your father wrote
From a place far away from us, [the "her" and "us" are in the original]
He has been lying sick in a hospital already for months.

Sick, lies our provider,
Struggling with his death.
October is approaching,
We are hoping in vain
In the house there is no wood, no bread
[For which] he should be sending money home.
He had broken a hand [cannot therefore work]
Standing near the wheelbarrow…[maybe a stretcher? Expressing the fear
of his nearing death?]

[Page 189]

From Asia to Europe

Translated by Hannah Kadmon

(Editor Ben-Ezra's notes: This particular song was sent to us by Dvora Elman, one of the most educated women in Horodets in the old generation.

We print this because of the version that circulated in Horodets. Actually it is the Elyakim Tzunzer's song "The 19th century". Look up: "The collected writings of Elyakim Tzunzer" pp.205-208 NY 1920 with various changes.

Apparently, the version circulating in Horodets was the original version, before it got its printed form; the version which was circulating among the Jewish folks the way it was heard from Tzunzer's mouth)

[This poem is a metaphor – describing the spiritual changes Jews went through with the "Enlightment" movement - from the middle of the 18th century to the second half of the 19th century. I hope that my efforts to understand it are successful at least in part. Some background will be helpful to the reader and some names/words will be explained:

There were two main trends in the "Enlightment" movement: – one, mainly in Germany and Western Europe, called to get out of the closed walls of religious life into the freedom to seek general knowledge, acquire skills of productive work and mingle with the surroundings, shed the outward appearance that differentiated between Jews and gentiles and introduce reforms in the observance of Jewish rules.

The other trend – mostly in Eastern Europe, called to stress the uniqueness of the Jewish people and put more stress on learning Hebrew besides the language of the country. From the middle of the 19th century scholars in Eastern Europe became critical of religion even to the point of being hostile to it, and there was scorn of the Jewish rules.

The philosophers of the general "Enlightment" movement believed in combining thought, education and action towards a better future and stressed the freedom of the individual, etc.

All this finds expression in this metaphorical poem, as well as the author's feelings]

Moshe Mendelssohn is considered "the father" of the Jewish "Enlightment movement and his group of Jewish scholars and literary men printed their essays about literature and science in the yearly periodical *"Bikurey Ha'itim* – at first mostly in German and some in Hebrew and then mostly in Hebrew and some in German.

Hekhalutz **pioneer,** was an organization aiming to acquire skills of productive work towards *aliya* to the Land of Israel

Te'uda 1. Certificate 2. Purpose 3. Testimony 4. Destination.

Riva"l R' Yitzkhak Ber Levinson preached to combine Torah, science, general knowledge, productive manual work and agriculture. He wrote a book, 1823, called *Te'uda Be'Israel* which calls Jews to accept his principles. The Orthodox community treated him and other "Enlighted" people as heretic; any young man who joined the "Enlightenment" camp was nicknamed *Te'ud'ke* after Riva"l's book.]

From Asia to Europe
I have crawled to find an inn
I have made my bed to sleep
In a narrow corridor.

Under my head - faith
On my side confidence [in God]
And thus I have drifted
Eighteen hundred years.

Hard and cold
Combined,
I have not, in sleep,
Felt that I was part of the community

Sleep makes me forget
That I am lying in a prison.
Soon I hear the call:
It is shortly daylight!

Friends from all corners
One, two, three
Are starting to wake up.

"*Bikurey Ha'itim*", "*Hekhalutz*", Mendelssohn's followers
bloom [See underlined above]
The *teuda* with the hammer, [see underlined above]
One, two, three,
Stand up and hit the chamber,

One, two, three,
How does it occur to a philosopher
To despise faith
To be betrothed to freedom,

For freedom to sacrifice
Spirit and body.
And many newspapers
Make us confused.

It is soon daylight, Israel
Wake up!

[Page 189]

Children's songs

Handed over by Khaike Pomerantz

Translated by Hannah Kadmon

[Translator's notes - in square brackets]

In memory of Khaike

a. Hak messer	Chopping knife
Brok messer	Shredding knife
Dir iz goot	You have it good
Mir iz nokh besser	I have it even better
b. A regen, a regen	Rain, Rain
Di ka'le iz gelegen	the "bride"* gave birth
A voo hot zi gelegen	Where did she give birth?
Unter di vegen	On the way/roads
Vos hot zi gehat?	What did she beget?
A yingele	A small boy
Vi hot men gerufen?	What did they name him?
Moyshe'le	Moyshe'le

*[It seems to me that *Ka'le*=bride/bride-to-be/newly married, is a "clean" word for an unmarried girl. HK]

[Page 192]

The End

The End

Translated by Hannah Kadmon

[Translator's notes - in square brackets]

With bent heads we stand up to honor the memory of all our martyrs whose lives were taken away; for the martyrs who struggled with bare hands against machineguns and cannons. We stand up in grief, lacking the words to express our agony about the great disaster that had befallen us.

We bite our lips with rage and fury at the destruction of hundreds of Jewish communities, among them our Horodets – a destruction leaving no trace of those communities. Our hearts are full of feelings of the wish to revenge those murderers, their names be erased, who massacred whole settlements and communities, including the Jews of our *shtetl,* young and old, men and women. The annihilation was absolute, and not a single witness survived who had experienced this indescribable tragedy. Only pieces of stones and wood remain as mute witnesses of the terrible destruction. Bits and pieces of news from passersby were collected, but exactly "how and what" the holy martyrs went through remains sealed from the world.

From a whole community only one Jew stayed alive, fortunate not to have experienced the disaster. His name is David Voliniets. He did not stay in Horodets.

Thanks to this "only son", we received news of the destruction of Horodets. We will present them here together with other letters that we received.

Let the letters be regarded as documents recording the destruction of Horodets and will live in the memory and hearts of the sons and daughters of Horodets spread all over the world. Let them pass it on to their children and grandchildren. Let the embitterment in their hearts burst into a big flame, and make them take revenge on our enemies, wherever they are, and the resulting storm will bring about a better and finer world, where every people will be able to live in their own fashion.

* *
*

We hereby present the letters that was received and in which the destruction of Horodets is conveyed with no literary effects. Here and there we will offer certain comments in order to clarify a place or a name.

[Page 193]

The Letter

Translated by Hannah Kadmon

[Names of people and places were spelled in Yiddish in different ways by the writers and even in by the same writer in his own letter. I left these variations as they are. HK.]

A. From David Volinietz

"On י"ב מנחם-אב , July 26, 1942, they drove all Jews of Horodets 35 km by train to Kartoz-Bereza to Breinsky-Garli (where there were big lime-mines) and there they annihilated all of them.

I must list a small percent of Jews who were killed in Horodets and the vicinity: Moshe-Dov Kuprianski, my uncle, rest in peace. He and his family lived 10 km from Horodets in a village Tzelishtzevitch. They had a store over there. A short while after the Germans' invasion, the Germans ordered them to turn over their only son who was then in the field. When they found him, they killed Moshe-Dov and his son.

Eliyahu Lakhovitski, Ahron-David's son, was murdered immediately in Horodets. Once they ordered R' Khayim-Nissan Vinograd to look immediately for his son Avraham. When he was found, they acted the same way. The same was the fate of Mosh-Dov the miller and Guttmann the motorist (from Vladov). They were both killed in the orchard behind Khayim Vinograd's house.

The Ghetto stretched from Shamai Rakhensky's house to the *besmedresh*. At one time, my father went to the farm to get something to eat and they beat him cruelly. When the fatal date arrived [י"ב מנחם-אב July 26th], everybody was at work. Fetching them without delay, they arranged them in rows and drove them to be slaughtered. My father, rest in peace, was very weak, so they let my two brothers, Avraham and Barukh, carry him. It was a 200 meters walk to the train. Whoever could not walk, was harshly beaten. Then they picked up the craftsmen and left them to work. Among them were my uncle Shamai Ravinski, Sender London, Khyaim Volinietz (grandson of Alter the Levite) Khayim Koval and others; around 15 men. Some worked in Horodets and some in Kobryn. In a short while, the ones who worked in Horodets were picked in Shamai's barn and they were killed there.

Yitzkhak Zussman had a *besmedresh* in his house for many years. They dragged R' Zussman outside, took out all the books, set fire to them and made fun of R' Zussman, the great charitable person.

I got all these news from the Horodetser Christians which I saw this summer, staying 2 days in Horodets, from the 5th to the 8th of July 1946. I could not stay there any longer…

B. by Binyamin Volf

(He is from Lekhevich, son-in-law of Zavel Pomerantz from Antepolye)

"In the month of Iyar [April-May] 1942, the ghetto was established in Horodets. The ghetto was on the Kobryner side of the river. In the ghetto, the Jews were divided into two categories: a) those who were suitable for work. b) old and unable to work. The latter were taken on the 11th of Av [25th of July] and were driven to Brana-Gora, near Kartoz-Bereza, where large lime- mines- pits were ready. The bandit-murderers brutally murdered our Jewish brothers and sister, mothers and fathers and also small children, and were killed and thrown to that pit. Jews from Drohychin, Antopol, Kobryn, Zshabinke, Brisk and from other ghettos were brought to be buried in the same pit.

"The remaining Jews, those who were able to work, were deluded by the promise that they would be given food because they needed workers... Those who stayed alive became slaves and worked very hard. After the 11th of Av [25th of July] 1942, all the workers from Horodets were "herded" into our ghetto. I say were "herded" because they were rushed forward on foot, like sheep. They got a place to stay in our ghetto. All of them, together, were taken out to work, at 7 o'clock every morning.

"As to the families from Horodets, I know only of Volinietz. I don't remember any more. I don't know about Vinograd and nobody has any news about him, because after the first slaughter on the 25th of July, he fled to the woods. There was no trace of him since then.

"The last "selection" was in Antopole on the 15th of October 1942. On that fatal day all Jews of Antopole in Horodets were murdered. They are all in a mass grave in Antipolye near Frishikhvast, Zanivye and in the forest...On that fatal day I was in the Kobryn ghetto. I fled and hid in the forests. After wandering for 6 months, I met a Partisan and joined their units and fought with them until the liberation by the Red Army.

C. A letter from a Christian about the ghetto in Horodets.

"... מכח [Mkh?] Shmuel's (He means Shmuel Hoyzman from Mekhvedevich) request concerning his family, they were killed by accursed Germans in July 1942. I don't remember the exact date. That was a horrible sight. They gathered all Horodetser and our Jews (from Mekhvedevich) in one ghetto in Horodets. They stayed there for two months behind wire fences. Our Provoslavs were forbidden to cross the wires. It was forbidden to make even one step past the wires. However, we helped. We used to smuggle in food secretly and stealthily. The Germans killed those who were caught past the wires. This is what happened not only in our village but in every place (that the Germans occupied).

"At the end of July some automobiles arrived. They stripped the unfortunate Jews off their clothes and loaded them on trucks. They ordered them to sing "Katyusha" (the Soviet folksong). The miserable people sang until death. They were driven to a lime-pit, somewhere in the outskirts of Kobryn (the writer means the lime-mines at Brane-Gore near Kartoz-Bereza). Over there, they threw them in, naked and face down. They slaughtered thousands in one lime-pit.

"Only the Jews who were in Russia and those who fled from the Ghetto to join the Partisans survived. The Germans spared no one, wherever they had control..."

D. About the Horodetser accomplices to the slaughtering, David Volinietz writes as follows:

There were many of them. In the time of the German Occupation 1941-1944' there was a mayor in Horodets – a Horodetser Christian by the name of Volodia Kazik. His house was near R' Yitskhak Zusselman's house. Kalia Glavatski (his mother was named Nastsia and she lived next to the cloister) was serving then in the militia.

As for Volodia Kazik, I have heard that he is in Poland near Lodz. He works as a Polish government official. His assistants were the corporal Vania Glavatski and Marian Bramkilises. The latter two got their "ugly death" in 1944 in the hands of the Partisans. (the writer means the lime-mines at Brane-Gore near Kartoz-Bereza).

E. The destruction of Horodets

David Voliniets writes to Israel Zussman about the present sight of Horodets:

"…Today the roofs and walls of the houses are moss-covered. It looks as if the houses have caved in roofs. The road from your former house (Itzikl's) to the highway, is paved with tombstones from the Jewish cemetery"

In front – the tombstone of Mattityahu [Mattes] the "filchik" [furrier/felt craftsman].

The structure over the grave of "the old Rabbi" Z"l and the tombstone of Alte, Itzikl's wife A"h

A tombstone of three brothers: Betzalel Kuprianski, Aharon Itche son of Leizer, and Israel-Tsadok Kuprianski

[Page 196]

Abraham Winograd

Translated by Moishe Dolman

Donated by Jane Cooper

Precisely which of our Horodets brothers were partisans is not certain. From the above-mentioned notice regarding the death of the two despicable people and Benjamin Wolf's observation regarding Winograd's son (Abraham), that he "escaped into the forest," we see that our brothers defended their human and Jewish honour.

In a second letter, Benjamin Wolf writes: "Abraham Winograd, a son of Haim-Nisl, had escaped into the woods. But ultimately he perished in the forest."

Abraham Winograd was born in 1908 to his parents Haim-Nisl and Leah. Like the other Horodets boys, he received a traditional Jewish education. When he became older, and Horodets was by then under the yoke of the Poles, he moreover learned Polish. In addition, he gradually became versed in Polish literature. Abraham Winograd practically became a "real Pole," but on the inside he was a proud Jew, always ready to defend Jewish honour. While he served in the Polish army, it so happened that on more than one occasion he gave a Polish soldier a thrashing for insulting him or some other Jew.

Abraham Winograd distinguished himself in the Polish army, attaining the rank of corporal. He was, in fact, on the point of being sent to officers' school, but his Jewishness got in the way.

His father was in the lumber business. He became involved, too, and would leave home for weeks at a time, roaming the forests and bringing boatloads of timber.

When the Russians were in Horodets during 1940-1941, Abraham Winograd was appointed treasurer of some forests in the area. In this field as well he exhibited considerable expertise.

After the retreat of the Russians no more was heard from him, as was true of the other inhabitants of Horodets.

The character of Abraham Winograd must have led him to join the partisans in order to avenge his people.

Let his name be engraved upon our hearts, together with the names of all our heroes!

Memorialize his name!

[Page 197]

David Volinietz

Translated by Hannah Kadmon

David Volinietz was born in Horodets on the 25th of December 1918, to his parents: Shlomo and Breine. In his childhood, David attended the Horodetser *kheyders* and, later, a *Talmetoyre* [a tuition free Jewish elementary school] in Antopolye. Then, in the years 1933-1938 he studied in the Yeshiva of Kobryn.

Since his childhood he dreamed about the Land of Israel as a home for the Jewish people in general and for himself in particular. However, his dream was not realized. He continued to nurture his dream until the outbreak of WW2 when the Russians occupied Horodets. He did not see any other choice but to join the Russian army and fight on the Krim front.

In 1942 a dictate was issued that all who were Polish citizens until 1939 were released from the army. Together with other Polish citizens he was led deep into Russia to work there, later on - to the Stalingrad front, and then to Saratow where they used to work from 4 in the morning till 10-11 in the evening.

Naturally, many became sick due to the hard labor and among them David. When he recovered, they sent him to work in the wild Arkhangelsk Oblast.

When David heard that the Germans, their names be erased, destroyed all the Jewish communities including his hometown Horodets, he decided to avenge the murderers. So, he enlisted once again in the Russian army and chased the German murderers to Szczecin and farther.

**David Volinietz
(the only living survivor)**

When the war ended, although he knew that there was nobody left in Horodets, he yearned to go there and have a look at his beloved hometown.

The horrible destruction of Horodets shocked him. He once again started wandering to Austria to Germany from one [refugee] camp to another, until he finally came to America. God be with him!

[Page 198]

THE NEW YORK TIMES, THURSDAY, JULY 20, 1944.

RED ARMY AGAIN EXTENDS THE FLAMING EASTERN FRONT

In a new offensive near the northeastern corner of Latvia the Russians advanced on a broad front between Zabolotye, near Ostrov, and Ragoziki (1). In the center of the long battle line Krynki station (2), twenty-five miles from Bialystok, the Bialystok-Brest-Kleshcheli (3), nine-ty-five miles from Warsaw. Near Brest-Litovsk itself the Russians took Imenin and Gorodets (4). The Bug River and 1939 Polish partition line were crossed at Krystynopol (5). Around Lwow Soviet forces pocketed Germans west of Brody and moved forward to Dzibulki and Remenov (6), only eight and a half miles from Lwow.

Gain on Other Fronts

There were fresh advances in the Brest-Litovsk direction including the capture of the county center of Kleshcheli and the railway station of Gorodets, as well as fifty other places.

Courtesy "New York Times"

דער פראָנט אַרום האָראָדעץ דעם 20-סטן יולי, 1944.
(איבערגעדרוקט פֿון דער "ניו־יאָרק טײמס")

" The Front near Horodetz on July 20, 1944" (copied from the New York Times)

[Page 199]

[Page 200]

We present here two lists and both are not full. The first list has photos of the martyrs that we got from their family, who gave permission to post them. The second list includes only the names of the martyrs for whom we could not get photos. The names are listed alphabetically according to their surnames. [Alphabetically in accordance with the Hebrew alphabet]

Because of technical reasons some photos are bigger than others.

[Page 201]

Our Martyrs

[Page 202]

Goldman, Yehudit (Zlatke's) with her brother Abraham's child

Goldman, Joel (the last shokhet)

Azarnitski, Bashke (Icishte Leyzer's grand daughter)

Dubin, Tadres

Goldberg, Shimon (Shepsele's)

Berger, Pesakh, Tsvia and Israel Tsadok (Liber's grand children)

Hoizman family from Mekhvedevitsh: Shalom, Henye, Jacob Hersh, Khanna, Mashe, Freidel and an additional child

Dubin, Moshe

Dubin, Liba

[Page 203]

Volinietz, Shmuel
(the miller)

Hellershtein, Michael

Hellershtein, Sarah
(from Slatzia)

Volinietz, Rukhama
(Hershel's wife)

Volinietz, Hershel
(Shmuel's son)

Volinietz, Bavtshe
(his wife)

Volinietz, Shloimele
(Shmuel's son)

Volinietz, Yente
(his wife)

Volinietz, Khayim
(Shmuel's son)

[Page 204]

Vingard family:
Khayim Nissan, Leah, Esther, Ginendel, Abraham and Leibl

Lebovetski, Gershon (Khanna Bashe's)

Zusselman, Yitzkhak (Itzik!)

Vingard, Abraham

Melamed, Sheyne (Mendel's), Brayne Rubinski (Shammai's)

Melamed, Sender

Lakhovitski, Berl

[Page 205]

[Page 206]

Freedman, Menakhem (Shammai's)

Petrushka, Abraham and Itke (the Old Rav's grandchild)

Eppelboim, Yekhezki (from Kamen)

Kastrinski, Khanna (Matye Isaac's grandchild)

[Freedman], Fatye (Esther's son)

Freedman, Esther (Khaya Devorah's)

Kilman, Sorkhe (Liber's)

Kuprinski, Kalman

Kuprinski, Riva

[Page 206]

[Page 208 - 209]

Our Martyrs

| א Alef | ב Bet | ג Gimmel | ד Dalet | ה Hey | ו Vav | ז Zayin | ח Chet | ט Tet | י Yod | כ Kaf |
| ל Lamed | מ Mem | נ Nun | ס Samech | ע Ayin | פ Peh | צ Tzadik | ק Kof | ר Resh | ש Shin | ת Tav |

Family name	First name	Remarks
ALEF		
Azarnitski	Khayim	
Azarnitski	Rakhel Leah	
Azarnitski	Malka	
Azarnitski	Joshua	
Altvarg	Tzvia	
Altzik	Issar	
Altzik	Hashke	
Altzik	Frumeh	
Orlovski	Moshe Eliyahu	
Orlovski	Ginendel	
Orlovski	Joseph	
Orlovski	Zalman	
Orlovski	Aaron	
Orlovski	Bashe Reyzel	
BET		
Bontzik	Khanna Malka	
Bontzik	Shammai	
Bontzik	Esther	
Bontzik	Leah	
Bontzik	Leybl	
Bontzik	M.	
Borshteyn	Samuel	
Borshteyn	his daughter	

Borshteyn	his son	
Birenboim	Guttmann	
Bergman	Malya	
Bergman	Jacob	
Bergman	Samuel	
Berger	Solomon	
Berger	Khanna	
GIMMEL		
Goldberg	Shepsel	
Ganilski	Solomon	
Ganilski	Rebecca	
Ganilski	Libeh	
Ganilski	Sonye	
Ganilski	Sheyke	
Garfinkel	Beyle	
Garfinkel	Asher	
Garfinkel	Itke	
Garfinkel	Israel Tzadok	
Garfinkel	Elke	
Garfinkel	A.	
Groshnievsky	Leybke	
Groshnievsky	Alte	
Groshnievsky	Pessl	
Groshnievsky	Eliyahu	
Groshnievsky	A.	
Grimland	Henye Beyle	
Greenman	Rabbi Aryeh z"l	(the last Rabbi)
DALET		
Dubin	Freydke	
Dubin	daughter	
HEY		

Helershtein	P.	
Helershtein	M.	
VAV		
Volinietz	Alter the Levite	(His picture is in the article ""The Social Structure")
Volinietz	Solomon	
Volinietz	Breyne	
Volinietz	Yente	
Volinietz	Abraham	
Volinietz	Rukhama	
Volinietz	Barukh	
Veysman	P.	
Veysman	Yankl	
Vinograd	Hinde	
Vinograd	daughter	
ZAYIN		
Zusselman	Sarah	
YOD		
Yarmetski	Jacob Meyer	
Yarmetski	Feygl	
Yarmetski	Hershel	
Yarmetski	Eliyahu	
Yarmetski	Ettl	
LAMED		
Lakhovitski	Hashke	
Lakhovitski	her child	
Lakhovitski	Reyzel	
Lakhovitski	her child	
London	Sheyne Libeh	
London	Sendr	
London	Khaya	
London	T.	

London	Khayim	
London	Malka	
Lin	Nakhum	
Lin	his wife	
Lin	Feyvil	
MEM		
Molyar	Jacob Berl	
Molyar	Abraham Jacob	
Molyar	Yussl	
Molyar	Tzvia	
Molyar	child	
Molyar	child	
Melamed	Khayim	
Melamed	Esther	
Melamed	Ben-Tzion	
NUN		
Nadritzni	Freyde	
Nadritzni	Abraham Ezra	
Nadritzni	Khayim	
Nadritzni	Khayke	
Nadritzni	Moshe	
Nadritzni	a child	
Nadritzni	Breyne	
Nadritzni	Rukhama	
Nadritzni	her husband	
AYIN		
Eppelboim	Hillel	
Eppelboim	Miriam	
Eppelboim	their 2 children	
PEH		
Polyak	Jacob	
Polyak	Barukh	

Polyak	Noah	
Polyak	Esther	
Polyak	Rebecca	
Pomerantz	Sheyne	
Pomerantz	Tzvia	
Pomerantz	Sarah	
Fefferberg	Beyle	
Fefferberg	Tuvia	
Fefferberg	Reyne	
Fefferberg	Judith	
Fefferberg	Berl	
Fefferberg	Hertzl (Yitzkhak)	
Fefferberg	Naftaly	
Fefferberg	his wife	
Fefferberg	their son	
Pekovsky	Abraham	
Pekovsky	Brakha	
KOF		
Kagan	Shaya	
Kagan	his daughter	
Kagan	his son	
Kagan	Doveh	
Kagan	Moshe	
Kaminsky	Rakhel	
Kaminsky	Sarah	
Kopriansky	Alter	the blacksmith (his picture is in the article "The Social Structure")
Kopriansky	Miriam	
Kopriansky	Moshe	
Kopriansky	Sarah Leah	
Kopriansky	Joseph	

Kopriansky	Barukh	
RESH		
Ravinski	Shammai	
Ravinski	Henye	
Rubinshtein	Abraham	
Rubinshtein	Aaron	
Rubinshtein	Samuel	
Rubinshtein	a small child	
Roitkop	Henye	
Rikhter	Berl	
Rikhter	his wife	
Rikhter	Blumeh	
Rikhter	Feyge	
Rikhter	M.	
SHIN		
Shukhovitzky	Khanna Leah	
Shukhovitzky	Mottl	

Family Names Unkown

Avigdor, Israel Moshe's
Reyzel, his wife
Their son

Khayim, the blacksmith
Khanna, his wife
Their 4 children

[Pages 211-232]

Horodetzers in the World

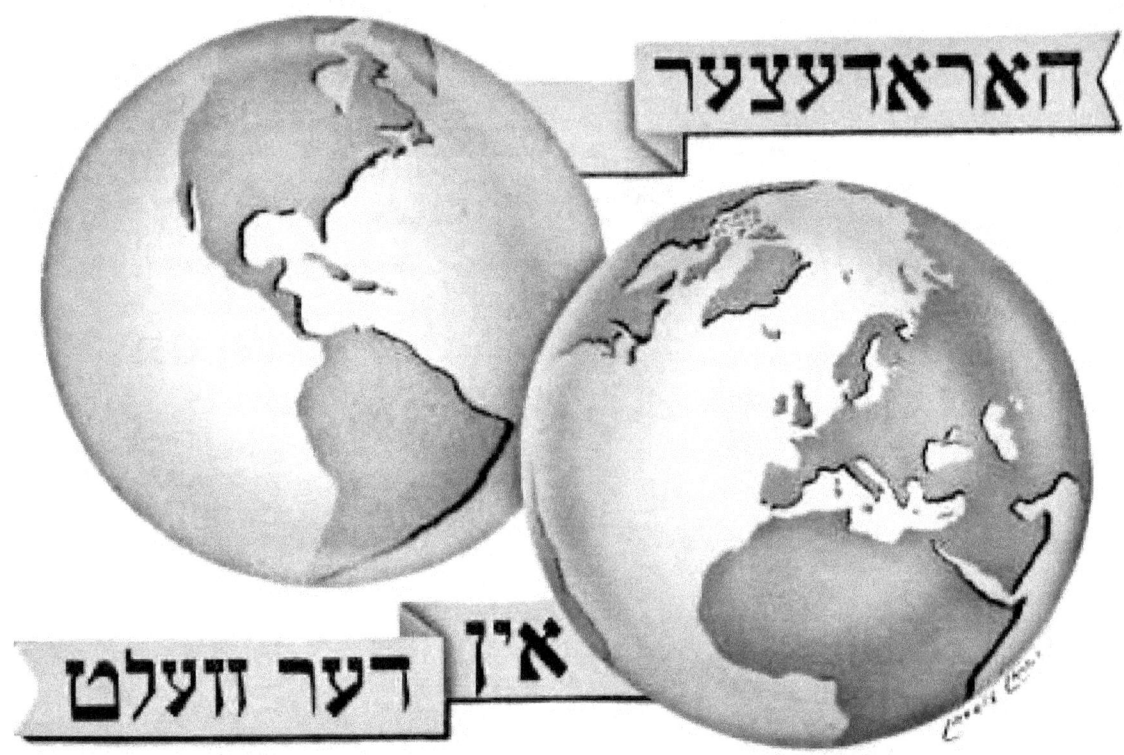

In America

by Bessi Greblovsky

Translated by Hannah Kadmon
and dedicated to Peggy Milstein, descendent of the Greblovsky family

[Translator's notes in brackets]

Until the end of the 19th century, America was a land to which only adventurers and rogues would travel. Virtuous, decent *balebatim* [proprietors, landlords] and those who were not forced to flee because of a frame-up or another affliction – for them America was not "Kosher". Even its stones were not to be touched.

Besides the fact that a Jew could not live as a Jew in America, the mere travel to America was physically quite difficult. First, one had to get a Pass (Passport) - which was not an easy job. One had to go to the authorities to get a *kharashe pavedenye* (character reference) and send it to the governor. All this takes between a month and 6 weeks. Since not everybody wanted or was able to get a pass, some risked their life and crossed the border illegally.

These were the preparation for the travel: it was necessary to prepare *sukhares* [zwiebacks] (dried bread) to take along, various brandies or liquors and whiskey to refresh oneself on the ship, and other things that today one does not need. And, when one succeeded to cross the border illegally, it was necessary to go through a "bath" where one was physically examined. And, if God helped and one got successfully through the "bath", it was necessary to wait for a ship. A ship was not available every Monday and Thursday [an idiomatic expression in Yiddish to say "often"]. Traveling on the ship was not a luxurious cruise. It was more like hell. It lasted between two to three weeks and often even longer when it was necessary to take first a small ship and then transfer to a big ship. And when one lived through the ordeal, and reached the "Castle Garden" [America's first official immigration center before Elis Island] – one did not necessarily lick honey. In short, travelling to America was not a small venture. Not without reason did people say a confession before taking off for such an awful voyage.

The journey from the shtetl was even more difficult. Horodets, for example, did not have a railroad until 1884. Still in the 70th there were several "adventurers" who travelled to America such as Ephrayim the mason - Shmerl's brother, Natan Yitzkhak - Hersh's son, Aba Tankhum - Ber's son, and Moshe-Ber the tailor. The latter, if I am not mistaken, was the first of Horodets who died on American land.

Moshe-Ber, let us say, was the father of those who reached America later on. He used to host the "green" newcomers in his house up to a week, advise them how to start doing things, or what kind of trade to learn. When the whole family was brought to America, Moshe-Ber or his wife, Eidel, helped them look for an apartment in the neighborhood, of course, so they could feel at home.

Moshe-Ber Portnoy

The Horodetsers, like all other Jews, settled on the "east side" such as Monroe Street, Madison Street and other close by streets. The first Horodetser families felt like a big Horodetser family.

Those who were not tradesmen from home, learned to be tailors, pressers, etc. Others started peddling or became distributers of blocks-of-ice to the houses in summer and coal in winter. That job was very hard but it was satisfying: they could observe the Sabbath and Holidays. The same was true of peddling that did not demand desecration of the Sabbath.

Many of the former peddlers and workers did well in this land of opportunity and today they occupy a distinguished place in American industrial and business-life, such as Akiva Sirota - ("The Superior Clothing Company"), Aharon Milner's children – in big liquor industry and Velvel, Sheikin's son – in the production of various machines that were intensively used in war-time.

Not only in war industry are our Horodetser folks involved, nor only in articles of daily use. Proudly we can list the Daitch Brothers who have a chain of milk products grocery shops in the Bronx and in Manhattan (the Daitch Dairies).

In the silk industry, A. Liman holds a high position. He is son of Binyamin Palaener and great-grandchild of Berl Rodetzer. His firm "Belvedere Fabric" is one of the most famous in the trade of silk. It produces Rayon that is very much in demand and has a good market.

The well known firm "Smith's Overalls" holds a high position. It is popular all over America. The owners are the two brothers Sam and Izzi Bosnyak, sons of Zelig. The founder of that firm was their father Zelig, who started very small on a side street in Brooklyn and his sons brought it to the present level.

Another Horodetser, a great businessman (real estate) who is very modest in his social work, is Hillel Apelman (son of Leizer Varatinitsher). He is very outstanding in his contributions to the building of Israel. His house in Borrow Park is a real meeting place for scholars. Of a similar type we can add Julius (Yudl) Greenberg, the son of Rabbi Mordechai Greenberg. He came here as a young child and worked his way very well. His firm "Perfect Shoulder Company" has won a good name in the dress industry. Besides his big business he stands out in his contributions to various organizations, also in a very modest way.

In the realm of inventions the Horodetsers have nothing to be ashamed of. For example, the Eagle Electric Company" has its own important invention and is owned by Ludvig (Lewis Grushevsky), son of David Grushevsky the long-time treasurer of the Horodetser Society. Lewis Ludvig is also well known among those who helped the "Haganah" in the historical years of 1947-1948.

Some Horodetsers, former workers, have reached administrative positions in the workers union. Such is Yehoshua Reznik (Matityahu, son of Filshtshik) who has been for many years one of the leading powers in the "Furrier Union". He helps a lot in organizing the workers of that trade to improve their economic conditions.

It is worthwhile to note a project that was very much developed through Shepsel (Shabtai Greblovsky), one of the learned men of Horodetz. That project was trading in lottery cards. In his house they distributed not only lottery cards all over America but also spread Jewish culture and knowledge. It should be noted for history that in Shepsel's house, in the year 1912, the famous "Young Israel" organization was founded, having its branches not only in America but also in Israel. Thanks to Shepsel's children: Shimon, Max and Bessy who were among the first founders of that organization, new approaches were opened to Jewish American life.

Shepsil Greblovsky

A branch of the Greblovsky family, Naphtali Goldberg, is in Charleston and leads the family tradition. Naphtali Goldberg plays a very active role in the Zionist movement and is very active in religious and cultural work in the state.

Naphtali Goldberg

In Chicago, Alter Divinsky is very active in the local social work.

One of the distinguished Horodetsers who were active on the American social arena, was R' Aharon-Yosl Zusselman, one of the first Jewish residents of Hartford Connecticut. He came to the States the end of the 19th century and there he dedicated himself to religious and educational institutions. Thanks to him, *Talmetoyre* [tuition free religious elementary school] were established, and also the society for the Study of the six books of Mishnah [part of the Talmud] and society for the study of *mishnayes* [collection of post biblical laws; part of the Talmud]. He was one of the first founders of the State-wide Jewish Institutions such as a Committee on *Kashrus, Hakhnoses-O'rkhim* [Shelter for poor wanderers] etc. He spent the last years of his life studying *Ein Yaakov* [a compilation of all the legendary material in the Talmud, with commentaries] with the congregation, in between the afternoon and evening prayers.

R'Aharon Yosef Zusselman

Besides being active in Jewish matters, his hand was open for all, regardless of religious affiliation. Everybody was acquainted with the beloved Jew with the nickname "Yibane Hamiksash" [Hebrew: "the temple will be rebuilt"]. He died in the summer of 1948 at the age of 87.

In the field of culture in America, Rabbi Dr. Yitzkhak Yaakov Bosniak is much esteemed. He was one of the closest pupils of Prof. Solomon Z. Schechter. [Solomon Schechter, founder and President of the United Synagogue of America, President of the Jewish Theological Seminary of America, and leader of the American Conservative Jewish movement].

Rabbi Dr. Yaakov Bosnyak has been serving as the Rabbi of a center in Brooklyn for already more than 25 years. He is active also outside of his center, writing articles and lecturing about Jewish culture problems. [A. Ben Ezra comments: look up his book "Intercepting Jewish Life, 1944].

Rabbi Dr. Yitzkhak Yaakov Bosnyak

Akiva Ben-Ezra holds a quite distinct position in the Yiddish and Hebraic literature, especially concerning Jewish education [look up his books "Days of Atonement" "Passover" "Shavuot" and articles in various Hebrew pedagogic Journals.], research of grammar and the Hebrew language [He wrote a lot about these subjects in "Bitzaron", "Khorev", "Talpiot" and "Ha'doar" Hebrew Journals], and Jewish Holidays folklore [read the article "Sender the *Melamed*" and "The two Bobbes" in this book]. He is also the editor of this memorial book of Horodets.

Akiva Ben-Ezra

As for the realm of culture and education, Tzvia Greenglass hold an honorable position. She publishes quite often, in Yiddish and Hebrew, plays (dramas) and songs for children. Her songs are heard often over the radio with the music composed by the well known composer S. Golob.

Tzvia Greenglass

Horodets plays a part in English literature as well. Sidney Schuman, son of Beile-Machle (great-grandchild of Berl Rodetzer) used to write stories in various English journals. He also has in print a book of short stories. Sidney Schuman exhibited fine fictional abilities, but he died very young (end of 1949) and did not live to full bloom.

In the realm of music Horodets has good reason to be proud. Jean Pearce, the famous tenor singer in the "Metropolitan Opera" in New-York who gives concerts not only all over America but also abroad, is the son of Horodetser parents.

Jean Pearce, who was called once Pinki (Pinye Perlmuter) is the son of Levi and Henye Perlmuter, quite well known among the folks of Horodets. Henye was the granddaughter of Sender the *Melamed* and Chaya Zlate the Bobbe in Horodets. [see the articles: "Sender the *Melamed*" and "Two Bobbes" in this book.]

Jean Pearce

He received his first lesson in singing from Shalom Melnik, the cantor of the Horodetser synagogue. Pinye used to help him during the High Holidays. Even today he is drawn to the cantor's desk/column. He inherited his talent in the art of cantillation, for sure, from his father, who even today recites a whole *musef* [extension of the morning prayer on Sabbath and Holidays] every year on High Holidays, in the Horodetser synagogue.

Jean Pearce, though born in America, regards himself as a Horodetser, as if he was born in Horodets. He is a member of the Horodetser Society "Yeshu'ot Ya'akov". When he is needed – he is there with his heart and pocket.

There is a descent of Horodets, Walter Schuman (Sindney's brother), who writes music for the stage.

Horodets has no reason to be ashamed in the realm of art of painting. We have a really gifted Jewish painter. He is Israel Zussman (son of Itzik), the chairman of the Horodets book-committee and the artistic editor of "Horodets".

Israel Zussman

I. Zussman graduated from the Tzar's school of art in Odessa. Since his coming to America in 1920 he has joined English newspapers and journals as a painter and illustrator. In 1930 he became artistic editor of the big English newspaper "The Graphic" and has worked for it along the years of its existence. At present he contributes his drawings to one of the biggest English journals in America.

Israel Zusman's painting of president Franklin D. Roosevelt can be viewed in the Roosevelt museum in Hyde Park, and a painting of Albert Einstein is in the Einstein Institute next to the Hebrew University in Jerusalem. He also drew Senator Wagner and the painting is exhibited in the Senate in Washington. The drawings of Governor Herbert Lehman, Walter Damrash, General Douglas McArthur, General Eisenhower and other famous personalities that Zussman had painted can be viewed in the distinguished American journals.

Besides his outstanding place in the realm of art, he plays an important role in the building of Israel.

Prof. Herman A. Gray

Prof. Herman A. Gray plays a prominent role in the American cultural and social life. Prof. Gray is considered one of the greatest specialists in the field of real estate. He is also one of the authors of the unemployment insurance law. He is often called to Washington and other states as a mediator in labor disputes.

In addition to his activity in the general American society, he was very outstanding in the Jewish society, serving it with his expertise and mastery. He heads the committee for foreign affairs of the "American Jewish Committee". In the winter of 1946 he was sent to Europe by that organization, to offer legal help to the Jewish survivors to retrieve their property. In the summer of 1948 he was sent to Europe

once again, by the same organization, to help the displaced Jews in the camps not to fall under German custody.

Prof. Grey was born in America, the son of Israel Ephrayim and Henye Greblovsky, a grandson of R' Shalom Kostrinsky. His grandfather's name is very dear to him and with great respect he holds his grandfather's six books of the Mishnah among his various countless law-books.

Abraham Asler

Horodets has some quite young but esteemed scholars. One of them is Abraham Asler, son of Mendl Hersh and Feige-Chaya Asafsky. He specializes in Bacteriology, and is at present the director of Serum Laboratory in Johns Hopkins Hospital in Baltimore, Md. He writes scientific articles that are highly esteemed in the scientific world.

In the field of medicine, Dr. Saul (Shlomo) Gratzer is acclaimed. He is the son of Yitkhak and Chava Glatzer. He is a diagnostic specialist of internal diseases. Dr. Glatzer also applied his great expertise to the American army, which he joined in time for the Second World War In the army he achieved the rank of lieutenant-colonel.

Dr. Saul Glatzer

Another scholar is Dr. Sidney Schmukler, son of Beyle Itzil's. Dr. Shmukler graduated with distinction the University of Wisconsin. He specializes in economic problems. In this field he has contributed articles to various journals. At present he serves as assistant Professor of Economy in Drake University, Iowa, where he is much liked.

Dr. Sidney Schmukler

Another gifted young man from Horodets is Shlomo Gar'in (Gara'in), son of R' Mordechai Greenberg. He came to America as a young boy and here he received his academic degree in Law and also graduated from the Seminary for Teachers of Hebrew – "Hertzeliya". He became one of the "missionaries" of Hebrew in America and one of the organizers of the Hebrew theatre "Pargod" in America. Wishing to refine his Hebrew, Shlomo Gar'in traveled to Jerusalem and studied there at the Hebrew University. In Israel he spoke on the Israeli radio: "Kol Yerushalyim".

Upon returning to America, Shlomo Gar'in dedicates himself to practicing as a lawyer. He also helped the "Horodets book committee" with legal advice, free of charge of course.

Shlomo Gar'in

Horodetsers make headways in South America as well. Also in hot Argentina they participate very diligently in Jewish social life, such as Moshe Vinograd (son of Nisl) and Abraham Tshernik (son of Arye and Shifra) in Buenos Aires.

We should mention that Moshe Vinograd is one of those who initiated the publishing of the book of "Horodets". When he visited New York in the summer of 1946 it was decided to publish this book – a dream shared by a few Horodetsers for some years to eternalize Horodets in the Jewish history.

Moshe Vinograd

There are also Horodetsers in Uruguay Paraguay, Brazil and other South-American countries where they play an admirable role in Jewish social life.

[Pages 219-221]

"Society Yeshu'ot Ya'akov Support Union of the people of Horodetz"
[Yeshu'ot Ya'akov = salvation of Yaakov]

by Chayim Greblovsky

Translated by Hannah Kadmon

[Translator's notes in brackets]

The big tide of Jewish immigration from Russia to America in the last years of the 19th century, did not skip our shtetl Horodets. Many poor inhabitants of Horodets and the villages around it, envisioning no economic future, started their exodus to America. Naturally the first stop was New York. Many came here hoping to earn some money and return to Horodets to try their luck with that money back home. However, most of these people were disappointed when they returned home to Horodets. It did not take long before they went back to America with the scant money left.

Other people came to America with the direct goal of saving some money and sending it to their families. In 1902, about 50-60 families from Horodets and the surroundings were already here. Many of the Horodets folks were already affiliated with various societies of other nearby shtetles such as Kobryn, Antipolye, Drohytchin etc., but most of the folks were not affiliated with any society. So, naturally, when the folks met each other in the street or at someone's house, they hit on the idea that they had to have a Horodetser society. In the beginning the folks met together at R' Yehuda Leib Greblovsky's home. He was living then with his family at 36 Essex Street. Almost every Saturday afternoon, after having discussed the events of the week, or talked about who the new arrivals were that week and who were thinking of going back "home", they immediately turned to discuss the founding of a society. So one such Saturday, in Yehuda Leib Greblovsky's house, quite a number of folks from Horodets gathered and decided to call a general big meeting for the following Saturday evening in the synagogue of the "European Painters Union". R' Yehuda was a member of that union since he held his *kheyder* there. The synagogue was on Norfolk Street. That took place in the Fall of 1902. At that meeting, it was decided to found a Horodetser Society. 36 people signed in on the spot and each paid $1. Right after that, they discussed names for the society and its goals. Most of the middle aged and elderly folks, whose leader was Shimon Portnoy, were of the opinion that the main goal was to have a synagogue and cemetery and all other benefits were not necessary. Therefore, the name of the society should be "Society Yeshuot Yaakov people of Horodets". However, the younger folks, whose leader was the writer of these lines, Chayim Greblovsky, son of R' Yehuda Leib, argued that they were not against having a synagogue but it should not be the only goal. A more important goal was to have sick-benefits and various other benefits and therefore the name should be "Union of Horodets". If not – they threatened to leave the meeting and found a separate union. Then, R' Shabtai Greblovsky suggested that if such a thing happened there would be no society and no union, as there would not be enough members for two societies. Therefore, to avoid it, and appease both sides, the society would adopt the goal that with time it would arrange for various benefits like in all other unions, and the name would be "Society Yeshuot Yaakov

Support Union of the people of Horodets". True, it is quite a long name, but as a compromise all agreed to adopt it.

R' Yehuda Leib Greblovsky

They immediately voted for the functionaries and Shimon Portnoy was elected as president, Simcha Rubin as vice president, Michael Kooper treasurer and Chayim Greblovsky as secretary in charge of the protocol. As soon as the Horodetsers heard of the founding of the society, they were present as members in each meeting.

Soon, the society rented a synagogue on Orchard Street and also bought a cemetery on "Mount Zion Cemetery". After a while, they set up a committee to work out a constitution.

The constitution took care of many benefits for the members. There was a fund for sick-care, $1 fee for every member of the family - for the dead, and various other big or small benefits.

It is regretful that the log books of the first 14 years were lost probably in the transfer from one synagogue to the other. Therefore it is impossible to list in detail the course the society took and its growth, as the writer of these lines would have liked. He must only rely on his memory. However, 45 years have passed since the foundation of the society and it is impossible to remember everything. So, many first events will thus be lost.

In short we can say, though, that the Horodetser society was a success from its first day, thanks to the dedication of its members. In no time there were more than 100 members and the number grew steadily. Every newly arrived immigrant felt proud when a bit after settling down he was accepted as a member of the family of Horodets. Years afterwards, when the immigration stopped, the members started bringing into the society sons, sons-in-law and brothers-in-law, many of whom were already born in America. Prior to the Second World War the number of the members was around three hundred. With the growth of the society, there were new and bigger benefits for the members. The system of per capita tax had long been cancelled. Instead there was an endowment fund that paid to families of the dead $200 for a deceased man, $100 for a deceased wife and a yearly payment of $84 for sick benefits.

We also have a sick-care fund to help the needy and sick members who have exhausted their benefit payments and an "emergency dues loan fund" for the occasion that a member sometimes cannot pay his dues on time and can borrow from the fund until he is able to pay his dues. It was understood right from the beginning that the member who took the loan would not be prompted to return the money if he did not repay it.

We also had an "old people's fund" the purpose of which was to help members who reached 70 years of age, had been dues-paying members of the society for thirty years and reported that it was difficult for them to pay the dues. They would not have to pay dues anymore, except the contribution to the endowment fund.

We are also affiliated with "Deborah Sanitarium" for the consumptive patients, situated in Browns Mills, New-Jersey, to which we pay yearly dues and where we have obtained a bed for a large sum of money, in the name of our society. We sent consumptive members who returned cured from there. We are also affiliated with "Hospital and home for the incurable" in Brooklyn, for a yearly fee.

After the First World War we sent to Horodets thousands of dollars to help our wretched brothers.

As for offering support to various social organizations, we do what we can. We support "Hayas" yearly as also dozens of other smaller and bigger organizations engaged in social and Jewish relief work.

In 1947 we donated $1000 to the "United Jewish Appeal". In 1948 our society donated close to $1000 to the UJA and an ambulance for the "Haganah". This year, 1949, the society has undertaken to raise enough money to buy two homes in Israel for the holocaust survivors. It is getting off to a good start.

It is worthwhile to note that for many years the society had a "Saving and Loan Fund" ("shares") that was of great help to the folks of Horodets. The bookkeeper of this fund was Yaakov Hersh Kaplansky, son of Aharon Itche Leizer.

Thanks to his knowledge of bookkeeping and his integrity and dedication to the society, he was its secretary for 25 years, until he died in June 1938.

Here are the names of the present functionaries: President: B. Goldberg. Vice president: Moshe Eppelboim, secretary of finance: M. Kaplan, protocol-secretary: M. Rubinshtein, treasurer: Benny Palevsky. First trustee: Yona Shmuel Bosnyak, Second trustee: H. Erlich, third trustee: Abraham Bantshok, fourth trustee: Ezra Birenboim, inner-controller; Yosef Korin, *hospiteler* : Max Bosnyak. *Gabai* [manager]: Aharon Reznik and Moshe Erlich.

The following are the presidents who were the leaders of the society from the day it was founded until now: Shimon Portnoy, Shmuel Dubin, Eliyahu Grushevsky, Abraham Bogus, Chayim Shimon Portnoy, Dov Dubin, Moshe Erlich, Yosef Rozenbaum, Arye Leib Tshernavsky, Chayim Gerblovsky, Benny Goldberg.

An ambulance which the Horodetz society, "Salvation of Jacob", donated to the Haganah in 1948.

From right to left: David Goldfarb; Moshe Eppelboim; Aryeh Leib Tsherniavsky; Mottel Kastrinski; Zalman Cohen; Jonah Hoyzman; Rabbi Mordekhai Greenberg; Moshe Erlich.

[Pages 222-223]

"Young Horodets"

by Binyamin S. Zussman

Translated by Hannah Kadmon

[Translator's notes in brackets]

When WW1 broke out, the immigration to America actually stopped altogether. As a result, the help that we received from friends and relatives in America stopped as well. The war period was difficult and harsh. So, as soon as the war ended, all wished to get away – to escape from the difficult life of poverty, from the horrible days and nights in which they were attacked by the gangs such as those of the bandits Petlurov* and Makhno.** People lived in daily fear and did not know what the next day had in store for them. The only hope was America. All did whatever they could to leave for America. Upon arriving here, in America, they naturally encountered difficulty in adjusting - An unfamiliar land, a new language, a completely new way of life, people are running, working hard, travel underground and above houses.

[Petliura was a top Ukrainian commander fighting the Red army, was defeated and his followers, – Petliurites –, carried out pogroms against the Jews.]

** [the volunteer army of General Bulak-Balakhovitch, the leader of the White Guards fought the Red Army and "helped" the Poles.]

They got to meet other new arrivals – friends from Horodets. They talked about the old beloved home which they were forced to desert and about the new home with the new sort of life which they lovingly embraced. They often went to the Horodets Association to get together with the old countrymen they had known or had remembered. Only few young people joined in. They did not find there the warm and friendly atmosphere needed for the newcomers.

A place was needed to enable the "green" immigrants to get together and spend time in a more home-like way, and would not draw apart too fast.

The new immigrants saw how other new arrivals from various towns organized auxiliaries, societies and clubs and envied their acquaintances from other *shtetls* who were as "green" as they were. So, the "green" newcomers decided together to establish a club. Two American "*landsleit*": Yudl Zussman and Dr. Y Farber lent a helping hand.

The constituent assembly took place in Dr. Farber's house on the 14th of January 1923. It was decided to establish a club by the name of "Young Horodets". The assembly elected a board of nine members: Tzivia Greenglass, Rivka Dyness, Yudl Zussman, Yisrael Zussman, Binyamin S. Zussman, Yeshayahu Elman, Dr. Y. Farber, Sarah Rodin and Menashe Shvarts. They got down to the task with a great deal of enthusiasm and did their utmost to make "Young Horodets" a place for whoever wanted to join in. They worked out a constitution with a charter and "Young Horodets" became an authorized organization. The main principles of the club where as follows: 1. The club would not assume a political character. 2. It would offer a place where all immigrants from Horodets and their friends could get together and feel at home. 3. It would collect money through various ventures and send it to Horodets for those who need help. In order to realize the above mentioned principles, they organized cultural evenings and discussions of various issues.

At the start, when they did not have enough money, the gatherings took place in Dr. Farber's house. When they already had several dollars, they rented club-rooms on Denlancey Street and it was not worse than anywhere else.

It should be noted that once they organized a ball in a hall, downtown, and so many people attended that some people simply could not get in. The net income from that evening was 200 dollars out of which they sent 150 dollars to Horodets. They organized a Hanukkah and Purim evenings with humorous magazines. They also had lectures. Akiva Ben-Ezra, the editor of this book, gave once a lecture about the Jewish scholar Dr. Israel Mikhl Rabinovitz, whose home town was Horodets. Our fellow countryman, Mr. V. Shuman played his violin quite often to the delight of the audience.

The club became popular among the *landsleit* [compatriots] of other towns and *shtetls* such as Kobryn, Antipolye and Pruzshine. "Young Horodets" became a center of attraction for all the young boys and girls of those towns and *shtetls*. They arranged summer journeys, rented club-rooms in Coney Island, thus offering the new young immigrants the opportunity to enjoy a cool place in the hot summer, while sharing a group atmosphere.

The following members were, at times, in the executive board: Yudl M. Zussman, Dr. Y. Farber, Binyamin S. Zussman, Tzivia Greenglass, Sarah Rodin, Rivka Dyness, Menashe Shvarts, Yisrael Zussman, Yehayahu Elman, David Kaplan, Yosef Farber, Menashe Rodin, T. Valiniets and Yehoshua Reznik (and if we omitted any other names, we should be forgiven because we cannot remember all names).

We can justly say that almost all the work and responsibility for "Young Horodets" was carried by only a few members: Dr. Y Farber, David Kaplan, Yehoshua Reznik, Menashe Shvarts and Binyamin S. Zussman. The club owes its existence to their dedicated work.

After a several years of existence, the club became weaker. Some members got married and did not have the time to dedicate to the club. Others left New York, etc. The fund-money was exhausted, there were fewer members and after several years of activity "Young Horodets" had to shut down, regretfully.

The charter for "Young Horodets" still exists. Maybe there is a chance that "Young Horodets" will be revived? It is worthwhile to look into this matter.

[Page 223]

Horodetser "Ladies Auxiliary"

by Feigl Greenberg

Translated by Hannah Kadmon

[Translator's notes in brackets]

The Vocabulary

This particular organization was founded February 1937. The purpose was to extend help to Horodets. The idea that this was necessary hovered on the air for many years. Letters from Horodets reached America, in which they described the great misery and poverty and asked for help. This call for help stroke a cord with many members of the "Society Yeshuot Yaakov" and a plan emerged to found a "ladies auxiliary".

The first founding-assembly was called by Mr. Moshe Erlich. Twenty women participated. The following functionaries were elected: Mrs. Ester Eidelman -chairlady, Mrs. Sarah Erlich - vice chairlady, Mrs. Bertah Volinietz - treasurer, Miss Bessye Grablovsky - secretary, Mrs. Aide Hoyzman- trustee. Within a short time they raised enough money to fulfill their mission. They immediately sent to Horodets $500 to establish there a *Gmiles-khe'sed* [charitable loan-without-interest], then sent every year for Passover *mose-khi'tim* [alms for providing the poor with their Passover needs], alms to individuals and to conspicuous New-Yorker institutes and individuals.

In 1946 the "Ladies Auxiliary" donated to the "United Jewish Appeal" $300 to support orphans in Europe.

Taking into account the small number of members, "Ladies Auxiliary" has done a great deal during the last ten years of its existence.

The present functionaries are: Moshe Erlich –President, Mrs. Blume Goldberg – vice president, Mrs. Bertah Volinietz – treasurer (lately Mrs. Aida Eppelboim took over), Mrs. Aida Hoyzman – trustee, Mrs. Feigl Greenberg – secretary.

The functionaries together with the members, now 50 of them, are dedicated to their assignments; they hold frequent campaigns and recruit new members. They know that they are doing a superior job of which they are proud, and the "Ladies Auxiliary" is growing and making progress.

At this moment, sorrowfully, Horodets does not exist anymore for Jews. The activity of "Ladies Auxiliary" is applied to help the Jews of Europe, orphans, Israel, New-Yorker institutes and individuals. All these are in need and the sister-members are determined to carry on their holy service.

[Pages 224-225]

Horodetser in Russia

by A. Horodetser

Translated by Hannah Kadmon

[Translator's notes in brackets]

Seventy-eighty years ago [1875 approximately] Russian cities such as Kiev, Yekaterinoslav, Odessa or Baku were not only just geographically far from the Jews of Horodets, but also far in concept. To travel to one of those cities meant for a Jew in Horodets to part from his wife and children, from the tradition of the *shtetl*, leave behind his talith and tephillin, change his name to sound Russian, wear clothes like a gentile, God forbid, and behave like a Russian.

Still, there were a few Jews from Horodets who accepted those complications and stayed Jews like all the other former settlers from Horodets, without losing any hair because of that. However, they could not forsake Horodets. They longed for Horodets and at least once a year went to see their wife and children and took a deep breath of Horodets with them to suffice for a whole year.

One of those Jews was Hillel, the subsequent *gabe* [manager of affairs] of *Khevre Kedi'she* [voluntary burial society]. He used to travel to Kiev for a whole year and come home only for Passover. He did that for several years until he returned to his "roots" and became once again a Horodetser. One trace of Kiev remained with him – the Russian hat that he wore to shuffle snow in winter and to sweep the "*padvar*" (yard) in summer.

What did Hillel do in Kiev? People say that he was there a *frikazshtzik* (an employee) in a store.

How did Hillel come to be in Kiev? It is probably because he had relatives on his wife's side, who was of the Mazursky family, and that was the reason for his leaving for Kiev.

It looks as though the Mazursky family possessed an adventurous nature which did not let them stay in one place and spend the rest of their life in Horodets.

Another branch of the family, Aharon Shmuel, husband of Hannah, daughter of Pelte, did business all year round in Paltava and came to Horodets once a year. When Aharon Shmuel came for a Holiday, he was the same Karliner Hassid, wearing a long traditional overcoat with the special belt, as if the big city did not affect him at all.

Aharon Shmuel and his family were drawn to the big city and at the end they left for Baku to join Aharon Shmuel's brother, Khayim Cohen who was well known as an oil-magnate. Aharon Shmuel probably helped his brother to develop his brother's oil-well.

Years later, their relatives Motye's - son of Hillel - children and their families left for Baku as well.

The second eminent family, Kostrinsky, also had a stormy blood and left Horodets. Motye Itzik's sisters settled in Yekaterinoslav and little by little other parts of the family followed suit. Still, the emigration to Russia was not big. People married, had children – lived and died in Horodets.

In 1915, when the Germans invaded Horodets, the folks of Horodets started looking for a distant relative to whom they could escape. Only then did the emigration deep into Russia start and the farther from Horodets, the better. Almost half the population of Horodets escaped deep into Russia and many of them did not return from there. Among those who did not return: Motye, Hillel's son, Izikl (Izrael) with his family, Itzel son of Shimon'ke (Vinik) with his family, Shmuel Khayim's (Sirota) family, and others. From then on, Horodets had representatives in all the big cities of Russia such as Leningrad, Moscow, Perm, etc., where they helped build and shape the Soviet state. Many sacrificed their life to free Russia from the Nazi occupation. One of them was Hershel, the Rabbi's son. He was the second of R' Yaakov Khayim's sons. Already in his childhood he stood out as wise and talented in general knowledge and was studying to become a dentist.

Dr. Hershl Greenberg

Hershel was not happy with his profession and studied further to become a doctor of medicine, practicing in Moscow. In WW2 he was a military doctor in the Russian army and fell on duty - hit by a German bullet. It should be noted that Hershel was also interested in Law, and especially in Jewish law. On the occasions that he visited Horodets, either from the Yeshiva or from the big city, he studied with his father Jewish laws. May he rest in peace.

**

Unfortunately, the connection with Russia is weak [this was written in 1949]. We have no exact knowledge of the fate of our folks from Horodets. From time to time a sign of life reaches us but it is very weak so we cannot really know the extent of their participation in social, industrial and cultural life of Russia.

I have got word that Yirmiyahu, son of Zlatke (Rubinshtein), has become a professor of Mathematics in one of the Russian universities in Odessa. Is he the only scholar from Horodets in Russia? – Possibly not. The people of Horodets were bright enough to show their talents also in other fields of science. Let us hope that it will be possible to approach our brothers in Russia and get more information about our Horodetsers in that land which is now behind an iron curtain. We hope to hear good news from them, as Jews and as humans.

[Pages 226-227]

In Eretz Israel

Former Years

by A. Kostrinsky

Translated by Hannah Kadmon

[Translator's notes in brackets]

Eretz Israel [land of Israel] was always the past and future of the Jews. The Jew always dreamed of *Eretz* Israel and aspired to see or hear about it. Whenever an emissary from *Eretz* Israel came to the *shtetl* the folks surrounded him wishing to hear more and more about that land of our fathers, prophets, kings, saintly men and cabalists. If a Jew did not have the privilege of dying there, he would at least obtain a small bag with the earth of the land of Israel to pour into his grave when he died.

If a Jew was privileged to travel to the land of Israel, it was not just his personal great experience but it was a general event for the whole town and the topic of conversations for a long time. That is how it was in the Jewish communities all over the world, and that is how it was also in Horodets.

One must not forget that 60 years ago [approximately 1889] there was no train connection in all places, people were only talking about airplanes and the ships of those times were far from being luxurious. When a Jew traveled to the land of Israel in those days, he suffered quite a bit before arriving in the land of his life-long dreams.

Horodets was not an exception. At that time there was no train. When a Jew wanted to travel to the land of Israel, he had to travel first with the "ax" (wagon) to Pinsk, from there continue tediously upon the "parakhad" (steam-ship) and then take a train until he made it to Odessa. Afterwards he had to travel for two weeks on the sea. When he finally arrived in the land of Israel, he had to be included in the "*khaluka*" [money donated by Jews in the Diaspora to support the new comers to the land of Israel]. The money was divided in the "*kolel*" [institute for full-time, advanced study of the Talmud and rabbinic literature also for married men]. Not every "*kolel*" was rich enough to offer its members a decent support.

* *
*

In those days there were two men with the same name – Yankel. They nicknamed one of them Eliya Yankel and the other – Yankel Hassid. Both were devoted Karliner Hassids and great scholars. Eliya Yankel was very proficient in Talmud and Yankel Hassid was an "*uprooter of mountains*" [erudite scholar] and very sharp minded. As a devout Hassid he used to go every day to the ritual bath and used to travel often to the Rabbi [of the Karlin Hassidim]

Eliya Yankel was the Hassidic *shoykhet* [ritual slaughterer] in the *shtetl*. When he was old, he and his wife Rukhama, decided to live the rest of their life in the land of Israel. They already had a son with wife and children in the land of Israel.

The lucky day arrived. Eliya Yankel with Rukhama were about to leave for the land of Israel. As luck would have it, the wedding of Gitl, Motye Hill's daughter was planned for the same day. The *klezmers* [musicians] came out to the street, playing and singing to see off the old couple. They walked from the bridge to the road to Antipolye. Men and women followed them, dancing. Each person dropped a coin into Rukhama's apron, thus appointing the couple to be "missionaries of good deeds" because, as such, they would be protected if they, God forbid, encountered any misfortune on their way.

The celebration was not private, it was everybody's celebration. Each of the folks felt as if he himself was also joining the old couple to the land of Israel for the rest of his life.

A short while later, Yankel Hassid also left for the land of Israel and again this event aroused a great interest in the *shtetl*. The folks in Horodets were envious of those fine house-owners who were lucky to travel to the land of Israel.

Settling in the land of Israel did not weaken the ties with the *shtetl*. They often wrote letters. This strengthened the love for the land of Israel that was kept alive in the heart of every Jew.

The letters varied: Yankel Hassid loved the land of Israel very much. It is a holy land and everything is very good. It is possible to study and observe Hassidism. However, for Eliya Yankel life in the land of Israel was not so much to his taste. Still, his letters did not scare the folks in Horodets who still yearned to spend the rest of their days in the land of Israel. Few others tried to fulfill their dream, such as R' Yitzkhak Aharon and others, but, regrettably they did not succeed.

[Pages 227-228]

Present Times

by Yossef Montag

Translated by Hannah Kadmon

[Translator's notes in brackets]

The "*Hekhalutz*" [the pioneer] movement in Horodets spurred on greatly the process of emigration to the land of Israel. Many members of the "*Hekhalutz Haboger*" [adult pioneer] and the "*Hekhalutz Hatza'ir*" [young pioneer] started immigrating to the Land of Israel in 1925. They participated in all sorts of work that the land needed such as agricultural work, building of houses, activities in the *Hagana* [underground Jewish militia during the British Mandate], etc., Part of these members were among the first to convert uncultivated land into prosperous *kibbutzim* [communal settlements sharing everything] or *moshavim* [agricultural settlements sharing tools and selling of products]. Among them: Khaya Kuprianski, Shlomo Yarmetski (Benhari), David Grimland, Fruma Kaminsky, Sheintshe (Yafa) Arlavsky, Beiltshe Kuprianski, and others.

One of the first to settle in Kiryat Khayim, near Haifa, was Pelte daughter of Shimon Izik (Ben-Dov) whose husband was very active in the *Histadrut* [General Federation of Laborers in the Land of Israel] and headed the "*shikun*" section that dealt with building houses for the workers.

Among those who had an honorable part in the construction work in the Land of Israel is Binyamin Olchik (son of Issar), a talented contractor. He is credited with a great percentage of the construction done in Tel-Aviv.

In addition to the above mentioned, the emigrants from Horodets have played an active part in the defense and strengthening of the State of Israel. They are: Yossef Vinograd (Khayim Nissl's son), Yossef

Montag – until 1947 very active in the labor organization, fulfilling many tasks and missions such as "conquest of labor" and "protection" [keeping these tasks in Jewish hands]. During WW2 he was appointed a policeman to prepare for a possible invasion of the Nazis.

There is in Israel also a different element of people from Horodets who came to the Land of Israel out of their own initiative, to have a hand in the rebuilding of the Land.

I must mention that one of the first establishers of the American colony, Ra'anana, was Rukhama, daughter of Izyikl (Rozenberg). After living for many years in America, she, her husband and daughters settled in Ra'anana, built there a house and planted orchards.

Yaakov Kostrinsky

One of the few, who help scientifically the economy of Israel, is Yaakov Kostrinsky (son of Motye, grandson of Izik.) He travels all over the land as an agronomist to instruct the work done in the fields. He is employed by the Experimental Service Station in Rekhovot. Many *kibbutzim* and *moshavim* improved their crops thanks to his great expertise in agriculture. Very often he writes scientific articles for the farmers in professional journals. In 1948 he published his book "Growing Wheat" that tackles various problems of growing wheat.

* *
*

Horodets was destroyed but its sons and daughters carry on the sacred tradition passed from generation to generation to settle in the Land of Israel. There, also, the ideals of those who were murdered are finally realized –freedom of the Jewish people in their own State of Israel.

[Pages 228-229]

R' Khayim Mendl Z"l

by A. Kast

Translated by Hannah Kadmon

[Translator's notes in brackets]

R'Khyaim-Mendel (Kostrometzki)

R' Khayim Mendl (son of Aharon Yossel) played a distinguished part in the old city of Jerusalem. He was killed by Arab shrapnel on the fifteenth of the month of Iyar, 1948, when he was 87 years old. He was a very rare type of person and deserves some further mention.

When he was only 6 years old he started studying Gomorrah and when he was 8 years old, Shmuel Kalike let him read from the commentary of *Maharsha* [acronym of Rabbi Shmuel Idelsh, Talmud commentator in 16-17th century]. This small statured boy found a mistake in the commentary. Shmuel Kalike could not believe it and went to the *besmedresh* [the study house, where people used to pray as well] to have a look in the book of Talmud that belonged to the old Rabbi, R' Moshe-Tzvi. And indeed, the old Rabbi had also noticed the same mistake in *Maharsha* and scribbled a note on the margins of the page about that same mistake.

When he was 9 years old, R' Khayim Mendl studied with the Kobryner religious judge, R' Zalman Tishes, and later on with R' Pinkhas Mikhael in Antipolye.

After his marriage he settled in Brest and was one of the closest to R' Khayim Brisker. When R' Khayim Brisker was asked to recommend someone to head the Yeshiva of Ludmir, only R' Khayim Mendl was his only choice.

R' Khyaim Mendl headed the Yeshiva of Ludmir until WW1 broke out. Afterwards he moved to Stolin to be R' Israel' right hand. After the Rabbi's death, when the Yeshiva "Or LeIsrael" [light to Israel], named after the deceased, was founded in Sarne (Vohlin), R' Khayim Mendl became the head of the new Yeshiva. Later on, when that Yeshiva was moved to Luninyetz, R' Khayim Mendl moved there as well.

R' Khayim Mendl did not favor hair-splitting argumentation. He preferred profundity and the logic of *Maharsha* and *Maharam* Shif [acronym for R' Meir son of Yaakov Shif, Gomorrah commentator in Germany, 17th century]. R' Khayim Mendl was famous for his commonsense and great scholarship not only among the Hassidim of Stolin who worshipped him but also among Talmudic *Misnogdim* [opponents to the Hasidic movement]. It is said that once, before WW1, there was in Vilna [Vilnius] a convention of Rabbis and heads of Yeshivas about education in Russia. The "Khafetz Khayim" [R' Israel Meir HaCohen known by the name of his first book "Khafetz Khayim"= love of life] was the chairman of that convention and the Talmudic scholars honored him greatly. The "Khafetz Khayim" pointed at R' Khayim Mendl and said: "If you want to honor the Torah – honor this Jew".

Many towns wanted R' Khayim Mendl to be their Rabbi. However, because of his great Hassidism he abstained from accepting the offers. Only once, when the town of Sarne was in great need of a Rabbi, he agreed to accept the offer as the temporary local Rabbi of Sarne.

R' Khayim Mendl settled in the old city of Jerusalem and lived there for 15 years, near the Karliner *Shtibl* [a small Hassidic praying house] until his death. He refused to evacuate the old city even in the turbulent time of 1936-9. When the War of Independence broke out in 1947 he refused to leave the old city where he had an immense influence over the world of Hassidim in and outside Jerusalem.

R' Khayim Mendl left behind writings which contain innovations in commentary on the Talmud - its legislative part and its *Aggadah* [legend] part. The Stolin* Hassidim of Israel prepare to publish those documents.

R' Khayim Mendl's name is holy and dear to many people of Horodets and to people outside Horodets. May his memory be blessed.

*[Aharon Ben Ya'akov [Hagadol] (1736–1772), founded the Karlin-Stolin Hassidic dynasty in Karlin. His son settled in Stolin. Therefore the two names Karlin and Stolin are used for this dynasty of Hassidim]

Translator's additional comment:

R' Menakhem Mendl Kostrometzki was of the Kostrinsky family. At the Tzar's time, to avoid military conscription as "only sons", members of the family changed their family name into Kast, and Kostrometzki.

R' Yokhanan, grandson of the *Admor* of Stolin-Karlin Hassidism has in his possession 2 letters that his Grandfather got, concerning the death of R' Khyaim-Mendl and kindly offered to show them to me.

The letters were written by R' Leibke Gloyberman of the Beit-Israel synagogue of Karlin-Stolin Hassidim, in the Beit-Israel quarter of Jerusalem.

In a letter from January 1948 he tells of the hardships in the Old City of Jerusalem. "There are news of Arab gangs rushing to the Old City and it grieves us that the Old City should be evacuated. There were very hot arguments in our Beit-Midrash about getting old Khyaim-Mendl by force out of the Old City and there were people for and against it. Moshe Hlatovski said that he did not want to help force R' Khyim Mendle evacuate the Old City. Zalman Grossman shouted at him "If he were somebody's father or mother, his children would have made vigorous efforts to get him out of the Old City… However, when it comes to Khyaim Mendl you think only of abandoning the Old City? Ask our Rabbi what he thinks about it!" Moshe Yosef Hlatovsky answered: "I am paying for the telephone call, and whatever our Rabbi decides – that is what we will do". Yehoshua Shimon Samet said : "It is possible to get R' Khayim Mendl out by a British armored vehicle for 8 pounds". Heshil responded scornfully: "I give you 10 pounds and you go ahead…"

In the second letter dated 30th of May 1948 Leibke Gloyberman writes: "For over two weeks we have been shelled ceaselessly by heavy mortars, causing many casualties, among them our dear Hassidim. In the Old City, last week on Sunday, old Khayim Mendl son of Shifra Kostrometzki was wounded in his leg by a shrapnel while staying in the shelter of R' Zeev Mintzberg's house [Rabbi and religious judge of the Old City]. He was carried to "Misgav Ladakh" hospital (his leg was amputated up to his knee) and he lived 24 more hours before he passed away on May 23rd 1948. He was buried together with 60 other people who were killed, inside the walls of the Old City."

[Page 230]

Conclusion

The Horodets Book Committee

Machla Timoner
(Cor. Secretary)

Julius Greenberg
(finance secretary)

Israel Zussman
(chairman and art editor)

Akiva Ben-Ezra
(literary editor)

Tzivia Greenglass

David Kaplan

Moshe Rubinshtein

Dr. Yitkhak Farber

Israel Grablovsky

Binyamin Shlomo Zussman

Shlomo Podolevsky

Naphtali Goldberg
(Representing the southern states)

Rabbi Shalom Podolevsky

Yeshayahu Kostrinsky
(representing Israel)

Moshe Vinograd
(representing Argentina)

[Page 231]

Thanks to the contributors

The book-committee "Horodets" expresses hearty thanks to the following men and women who with their very decent financial support made it possible to publish this book "Horodets"

Asafsky, David
Apelman, Hillel
Bosniak, Sem and Izi (brothers)
Bloy, Hannah
Goldberg Naphtali (Charlstone S.C.)
Goldberg-Dalinski (vinesborough Ga)
Grablovsky, Israel
Greenberg, Yudl
Greenglass, Tzivia
Dubin, Binyamin
Divinsky, alter (Chicago)
Daitch, L
Horodetser Ladies Auxilary
Horvits, Yerukham Itzkhak Halevi
Vinograd, Moshe (Buenos Iyres, Argentina)
Zussman, Binyamin Shlomo
Zussman, Yudl and Dvora (Baltimor, Md.)
Association "Yeshuot Yaakov" support union people of Horodets
Timoner, Machla
Ludvig, l.
Liman, Y
Neiten, Moris
Sophein, a
Sirota, Akiva
Farber, Yosef
Farber Yitzkhak Dr.
Pears, Jan
Fioris-Zussman Bobil and Yosef
Kaplan, Bessi
Daplan, David
Rubinshtein, Moshe
Shulman, l.

Name Index

A

Adrezinsky, 137, 224, 226, 227
Allman, 27, 79, 82
Altvarg, 284, 291
Altzik, 291
Ami, 167, 169, 171, 175, 178, 181, 184, 187, 189, 192, 194, 198, 200
Andronovsky, 159
Apelman, 301, 330
Arenshtein, 115
Arlinski, 284
Arlavsky, 284. 323
Asafsky, 309, 330
Asher, 7, 19, 68, 106, 113, 114, 115, 128, 157, 173, 184, 185, 186, 189, 190, 216, 221, 222, 229, 233, 250, 255, 256, 292
Ashkenazi, 48, 54, 115, 231, 232
Asler, 309
Atlas, 39
August Poniatavski, 12
Azarnitski, 284, 285, 291

B

Babrovski, 9, 10, 16
Bakhrakh, 80
Balat, 238
Bantshok, 31, 314
Bar Yokhai, 100
Bartenboim, 132, 284
Beilis, 111
Ben-Ezra, 1, 3, 9, 17, 58, 75, 80, 82, 83, 89, 100, 113, 116, 134, 137, 141, 153, 160, 161, 167, 169, 171, 173, 175, 178, 181, 184, 187, 189, 192, 194, 198, 200, 224, 235, 242, 243, 245, 247, 253, 254, 258, 259, 268, 269, 270, 304, 316, 329
Ben-Haviv, 161
Berditshever, 116
Berenholtz, 7

Berger, 235, 285, 292
Bergman, 236, 292
Biletzky, 225
Birenboim, 292, 314
Blatzky, 236
Bloy, 330
Bogus, 314
Bontzik, 291
Borshteyn, 284, 291, 292
Bosniak, 21, 265, 303, 330
Bosnyak, 53, 58, 59, 62, 301, 303, 304, 314
Bramkilises, 276
Bregman, 157
Brisker, 326
Buber, 75
Burshtein, 77, 128, 129, 137, 157, 164, 216, 221, 231

C

Cohen, 68, 96, 315, 319

D

Daitch, 300, 330
Daplan, 330
Dines, 157
Divinsky, 302, 330
Dubin, 31, 157, 285, 292, 314, 330
Dubner, 42
Dyness, 316

E

Eaminski, 139
Eidelman, 317
Ein Hakoray, 41
Elkhanan, 45, 105, 107
Elman, 7, 39, 179, 212, 266, 270, 316, 317
Elzet, 242
Eppelboim, 289, 294, 314, 315, 317
Erlich, 314, 315, 317

Erter, 143

F

Farber, 7, 126, 129, 254, 316, 317, 329, 330
Fefferberg, 295
Feinshtein, 224
Fioris, 330
Fioris-Zussman, 330
Freedman, 289

G

Ganilski, 139, 292
Gar'in, 100, 310, 311
Garber, 226
Garfinkel, 292
General Bulak- Balakhovitch, 216, 316
Gerblovsky, 314
Ginsburg, 59, 143, 268
Gitelman, 102
Glantzer, 128
Glatzer, 226, 309
Glavatski, 276
Gloyberman, 326, 327
Goldberg, 7, 134, 226, 285, 292, 302, 314, 317, 329, 330
Goldberg-Dalinski, 330
Goldfarb, 315
Goldman, 285
Golob, 305
Gootmakher, 113
Gordon, 44, 127, 128, 132
Grablovsky, 317, 329, 330
Gratzer, 309
Gray, 308
Grazovski, 183
Greblovsky, 7, 226, 234, 299, 301, 302, 308, 312, 313
Greenberg, 3, 6, 7, 34, 36, 37, 39, 45, 49, 79, 148, 204, 217, 227, 301, 310, 315, 317, 319, 329, 330
Greenglass, 7, 92, 93, 94, 95, 97, 102, 219, 239, 305, 316, 329, 330
Greenman, 50, 51, 221, 222, 231, 292

Grey, 308
Grimland, 292, 323
Groshnievsky, 292
Grossman, 190, 327
Grushevsky, 301, 314
Guttmann, 275, 292

H

Hakohen, 113, 114, 115, 143
Haller, 102
Haranovitz, 11
Harris, 17
Hellershteyn, 133, 226, 286, 293
Hertzel, 14, 131, 132
Hill, 322
Hirshenzon, 119
Hitler, 15, 229
Hlatovski, 327
Hoizman, 137, 285
Horodetser, 58, 59, 60, 79, 80, 87, 89, 100, 109, 112, 113, 158, 161, 167, 168, 306, 312, 313, 317, 318, 330
Horvits, 330
Hoyzman, 139, 224, 276, 315, 317

I

Idelsh, 72, 325
Israel, 215
Itzil, 157, 174, 310
Izik, 72, 75, 115, 181, 182, 183, 192, 201, 216, 221, 222, 323, 324

K

Kadliner, 68, 71
Kadmon, 1
Kagan, 295
Kalike, 107, 325
Kaliker, 58, 107, 108, 109, 264
Kamenetski, 17, 82
Kaminsky, 295, 323
Kaplan, 6, 99, 121, 146, 163, 314, 317, 329, 330
Kaplansky, 216, 258, 314

Karliner, 37, 53, 68, 72, 75, 82, 87, 98, 105, 106, 122, 159, 180, 191, 263, 264, 318, 322, 326
Karlinski, 19, 27, 74, 98, 108, 127, 128, 132, 133, 146, 147, 148, 164, 182
Kast, 325, 326
Kastrinski, 7, 289, 315
Katrosy, 153
Kazik, 276
Khabad, 163
Khwolson, 144
Kilman, 289, 290
King Savyesky, 243
Kobrin, 7, 9, 10, 12, 13, 14, 16, 17, 24, 28, 31, 39, 50, 51, 75, 111
Kobriner, 7, 74, 75, 76, 77, 95, 98, 105, 106, 110, 172
Kodliner, 93, 94, 157, 175, 176, 177, 178
Kooper, 313
Kopriansky, 295, 296
Korin, 314
Kostrinsky, 79, 82, 87, 92, 93, 134, 135, 150, 152, 153, 154, 198, 201, 219, 233, 255, 259, 308, 319, 322, 324, 326, 329
Kostrometzki, 105, 325, 326, 327
Koval, 275
Krinski, 132, 183
Kuprianski, 139, 226, 227, 230, 234, 275, 278, 289, 323

L

Lebovetski, 287
Lekhevitsher, 75
Levinson, 122, 143, 270
Lakhovitski, 236, 275, 287, 293
Libers, 87
Lifshitz, 37, 157, 290
Liliental, 143
Liman, 300, 330
Lin, 294
Lipove, 238
London, 139, 275, 293, 294
Ludvig, 301, 330

M

Makhvedevitsh, 24
Maller, 17
Mantak, 139, 227
Matyes, 32
Mazursky, 79, 82, 146, 148, 263, 318
Melamed, 166, 167, 178, 187, 287, 294, 304, 305
Melnik, 306
Mendelssohn, 143, 183, 270, 271
Milner, 300
Milstein, 299
Mintzberg, 327
Mishkin, 116
Mokhavetz, 9
Molyar, 294
Montag, 323, 324
Moyer, 25

N

Nadritchni, 126, 127
Nadritzni, 236, 294
Natanzon, 7, 76
Neiten, 330
Nisenboim, 120
Nissan, 10, 11, 19, 219, 220, 222, 275
Nissel, 28, 196, 221
Novoselker, 157

O

Olchik, 227, 323
Orlovski, 139, 236, 291
Oshmener, 116
Ozornitzki, 234

P

Padva, 115
Palaener, 300
Palevsky, 314
Pekovsky, 295
Perlmuter, 305
Petrushka, 289
Pearce, 255, 305, 306, 330

Pininke, 39
Podolevsky, 6, 7, 50, 74, 135, 139, 155, 160, 212, 213, 228, 288, 329
Polyak, 30, 135, 137, 164, 219, 221, 225, 226, 228, 288, 294, 295
Pomerantz, 197, 202, 252, 272, 275, 295
Portnoy, 300, 312, 313, 314
Pugatchov, 132

R

Rabinovitz, 14, 17, 36, 38, 41, 44, 82, 106, 115, 141, 142, 144, 145, 146, 316
Ravinski, 17, 31, 275, 296
Rakhensky, 275
Ravitsh, 157
Reznik, 301, 314, 317
Rikhter, 139, 236, 296
Rishes, 238
Rodets, 155, 156, 238
Rodetski, 157
Rodetzer, 39, 55, 155, 157, 300, 305
Rodetzki, 216, 226
Rodin, 316
Roitkop, 290, 296
Romanov, 9, 11, 25, 168
Rosenbaum, 125
Rovinski, 290
Roytkopf, 157, 217
Rozenbaum, 314
Rozenberg, 324
Rozenblatts, 184
Rruskin, 233
Rubin, 313
Rubinshtein, 7, 60, 226, 290, 296, 314, 320, 329, 330
Rubinski, 287
Rushevsky, 112

S

Samet, 327
Savitski, 288
Schechter, 303
Schmukler, 310
Schuman, 305, 306
Schwartz, 39
Shaf, 83, 158
Shakhnow, 25, 112, 196
Shefes, 59
Shement, 258
Shick, 39
Shif, 326
Shloper, 118
Shmulevitsh, 17
Shor, 144
Shter, 12, 25, 158, 159
Shtern, 156
Shtshopak, 157
Shub, 157, 211
Shukhovitzky, 296
Shulman, 330
Shuman, 316
Shvarts, 316, 317
Sirota, 11, 77, 300, 319, 330
Skavolev, 7
Slonimer, 116
Soloveitchik, 115
Sophein, 330
Stanislav, 12
Stavski, 115, 157, 288
Sussman, 3, 6, 7, 17, 209, 213, 215
Sverdyuk, 127, 156, 257

T

Telekhaner, 71
Timoner, 6, 206, 263, 329, 330
Tsadok, 285
Tsar Alexander Ii, 144
Tsar Nicholas I, 87, 158, 196
Tshernavsky, 314
Tshernetski, 109, 110, 111, 112
Tshemavsky, 314, 315
Tshernik, 311
Tshinik, 235
Tsunzer, 28
Tzeitlezon, 146
Tzemerinski, 123
Tzioni, 131

Tzunzer, 270

V

Valdimir Vasilevitsh, 9
Valiniets, 317
Valkin, 162
Varatinitsher, 301
Varmesser, 112
Varsha, 236
Veissman, 119, 204
Veitzel-Rozenblat, 116
Veysman, 293
Vinograd, 6, 135, 219, 222, 226, 275, 276, 287, 293, 311, 323, 329, 330
Visotzky, 255
Vitkin, 206, 207
Volf, 275
Volinietz, 15, 17, 139, 157, 236, 275, 276, 280, 281, 286, 293, 317

W

Weinberg, 128
Winograd, 279, 280
Wolf, 279

Y

Yarmetski, 139, 236, 293, 323
Yarmok, 82
Yitskhaki, 72, 83

Z

Zerakh, 58, 105, 201
Zlantke, 290
Zlate, 139, 255, 258, 259, 260, 261, 305
Zlatnik, 242
Zusselman, 84, 216, 276, 287, 293, 302, 303
Zussman, 16, 41, 53, 67, 73, 117, 137, 209, 219, 230, 275, 277, 306, 307, 315, 316, 317, 329, 330

www.ingramcontent.com/pod-product-compliance
Lightning Source LLC
Chambersburg PA
CBHW082004150426
42814CB00005BA/227